Confidence in Public Speaking

Confidence in Public Speaking

Paul E. Nelson
Ohio University, Athens

Judy C. Pearson
*Virginia Polytechnic Institute
and State University*

Sixth Edition

Boston, Massachusetts   Burr Ridge, Illinios . Dubuque, Iowa
Madison, Wisconsin   New York, New York   San Francisco, California   St. Louis, Missouri

McGraw·Hill

*A Division of The **McGraw·Hill** Companies*

Book Team

Executive Publisher *Edgar J. Laube*
Acquisitions Editor *Eric Ziegler*
Developmental Editor *Mary Rossa*
Production Editor *Kristine Queck*
Proofreading Coordinator *Carrie Barker*
Designer *LuAnn Schrandt*
Art Editor *Brenda Ernzen*
Photo Editor *Laura Fuller*
Permissions Coordinator *Pat Barth*
Production Manager *Beth Kundert*
Production/Costing Manager *Sherry Padden*
Marketing Manager *Katie Rose*
Copywriter *M. J. Kelly*

Basal Text *10/12 Times Roman*
Display Type *Willow*
Typesetting System *Macintosh*™ QuarkXPress™
Paper Stock *50# Mirror Matte*

President and Chief Executive Officer *Thomas E. Doran*
Vice President of Production and Business Development *Vickie Putman*
Vice President of Sales and Marketing *Bob McLaughlin*
Director of Marketing *John Finn*

The credits section for this book begins on page CR-1 and is considered an extension of the copyright page.

For the two of our
six children who
have not yet left
the nest:
Benjamin Joseph
Pearson-Nelson

&

Rebekah Kristina

Pearson-Nelson

Brief Contents

Contents

LISTENING

THE AUDIENCE

THE SPEAKER

SELECTING A TOPIC AND PURPOSE

FINDING INFORMATION

SPEECH ORGANIZATION AND OUTLINING

THE ETHICAL AND EFFECTIVE USE
OF EVIDENCE, PROOF, AND ARGUMENT

INTRODUCING AND CONCLUDING YOUR SPEECH

LANGUAGE IN PUBLIC SPEAKING

DELIVERING YOUR SPEECH

PRESENTATIONAL AIDS

INFORMATIVE SPEAKING

THE PRINCIPLES AND TYPES OF PERSUASIVE SPEECHES

Preface

This sixth edition of *Confidence in Public Speaking* is our first "menu driven" edition, and includes twenty-five chapters from which to choose. Some chapters offer different presentations of similar topics. For example, this text features two approaches to persuasive speaking: one chapter focuses on the principles of persuasion, and the other focuses on the types of proofs. We have also included some summary chapters that combine the highlights of two or more highly detailed chapters. For example, one chapter combines the main points of the in-depth chapters on speech organization and speech outlining in a more succinct form. These different options allow instructors to formulate a mix of information to meet their specific needs.

This edition was written by multiple authors and was reviewed by specialized critics. The chapters were written by Paul Nelson and Judy Pearson, along with five contributing authors: John A. Hess, University of Minnesota, wrote Chapter D, "Ethics in Public Speaking"; Candice Thomas, Ohio University, wrote Chapter E, "Conquering Speech Anxiety; Wendy H. Papa and Michael J. Papa, Ohio University, wrote Chapter U, "Speeches for Special Occasions"; and Gloria J. Galanes, Southwest Missouri State University, wrote Chapter V, "Dynamics of Small Group Discussion," Chapter W, "Group Leadership and Problem Solving," and Chapter X, "Small Group Communication and Leadership." The manuscript was carefully reviewed by Jeanne Porter, De Paul University, and Mark Orbe, Indiana University, Southeast, for cultural sensitivity and diversity.

Cultural diversity permeates this edition. Example speeches by numerous members of different co-cultures, including, but not limited to, visually impaired individuals, Native Americans, African Americans, Asian Americans, older Americans, and women from many different cultures, have been used throughout the text. Ethical considerations are included in nearly every chapter to underline the importance of this concept in public speech making.

Chapter A is a more inviting opening than in older editions. A new Chapter B quickly prepares students for the first brief speech that is assigned by many public speaking teachers. Chapter C instructs students on how to listen effectively to public speeches. Chapter D is a new chapter on ethics in public speaking. Chapter E is a new chapter on conquering speech anxiety. Chapter F reveals the concept of source credibility and how to achieve it as a speaker. Chapter G provides methods of audience analysis and means of adapting to audiences. Chapter H covers speech purpose and topic selection. Chapter I, on finding information, has been heavily revised to include consideration of electronic information sources.

Chapter J, on speech organization, discusses macro-organizational features such as the main parts of a speech, as well as micro-organizational features like transitions, signposts, previews, and reviews, while Chapter K addresses speech outlining. Chapter L is a

What Is New in the Sixth Edition?

What Information Is Included in Each Chapter?

concise summary combining the highlights of speech organization and outlining covered in Chapters J and K. There are, then, three possible chapters on organization.

Chapter M tells how to introduce and to conclude a speech. Chapter N, "Language in Public Speaking," retains traditional topics on language while rendering the information relevant to students with sections on the politically correct movement, college "hate speech" codes, and sexist and racist language. Chapter O covers methods of delivery, and also discusses the use of voice, body movements and gestures. Chapter P reviews a variety of presentational aids, including computer-generated aids.

Chapter Q is an extensive chapter on informative speaking, and Chapter R is a new chapter titled "The Ethical and Effective Use of Evidence, Proof, and Argument." Chapters S and T offer two different approaches to persuasive speaking. Chapter S covers the principles of persuasion, while Chapter T discusses the types of proofs. Chapter U s a new chapter on special occasions speeches.

Three new chapters examine small group communication. Chapter V, "Dynamics of Small Group Discussion," introduces small group communication, the types of small groups, and concepts such as group culture, norms, roles, and climate. Chapter W, "Group Leadership and Problem Solving," covers theoretical approaches to leadership, and discusses how to maintain organization, encourage creativity, and manage conflict in group problem solving. Chapter X, "Small Group Communication and Leadership," combines the main points of Chapters V and W.

Who Wrote This Book?

The primary authors of this book are Paul Nelson and Judy Pearson. Paul is the Dean of the College of Communication at Ohio University, and has co-authored six editions of *Confidence in Public Speaking* and six editions of *Understanding and Sharing: An Introduction to Human Communication*. Judy Pearson is the Director of the Northern Virginia Graduate Center in Falls Church, Virginia, and a professor at Virginia Polytechnic Institute and State University. She co-authored the two books above, authored or co-authored six other text books, and authored two trade books.

We have been writing basic course texts for almost twenty years because the beginning courses are our first love. Both of us began as basic course directors in large programs, and we even met at a basic course conference.

We seek feedback from you about this book. You can let us know what you like or dislike by calling Paul Nelson at 614–593–4884 or Judy Pearson at 703–698–6006. Paul can be reached by writing to him at this address:

483 R-TV Building
College of Communication
Ohio University
Athens, Ohio 45701

His Internet address is NELSONP@ouvaxa.cats.ohiou.edu.

Judy can be reached by writing to her at this address:

Northern Virginia Graduate Center
2990 Telestar Court
Falls Church, VA 22042

Her Internet address is JCP@vt.edu.

We would like to extend our appreciation to our many colleagues who have reviewed all six editions. We especially want to thank these reviewers for their keen insights and suggestions:

Reviewers

David Bashore, College of San Mateo; Doug Brenner, University of South Dakota; Jackie Buckrup, Ball State University; Larry Caillouet, Western Kentucky University; Robert Greenstreet, East Central University; Jon A. Hess, University of Minnesota; Diana K. Ivy, Texas A&M; Clark Olson, Arizona State University; Mark P. Orbe, Indiana University, Southeast; Jeanne Porter, De Paul University, Athens; Deanna Sellnow, North Dakota State University; Deborah Smith-Howell, University of Nebraska, Omaha.

Questionnaire Respondents

Rusalyn H. Andrews, Troy State University, Dothan; David Bashore, College of San Mateo; Mary R. Burrows, Texas State Technical College; Raymond Collins, San Jose City College; Sandra Cross, Edmonds Community College; Samuel Gant, Nashville State Technical Institute; Arlie V. Daniel, East Central University; Layne Darden, Ricks College; Charlene Handford, Louisiana State University, Shreveport; Marty Hatton, Mississippi University for Women; Lesley King, Northern New Mexico Community College; Thurman Knight, Anoka-Ramsey Community College; Mark Morman, Johnson County Community College; Lynette Mullins, University of Minnesota, Crookston; Paul C. Sabelka, Iowa Wesleyan College; Robert Smith, Deborah Smith-Howell, University of Nebraska, Omaha; Robert Smith, Western Michigan University; JuJuan Carolyn Taylor, School Craft College; Todd Thomas, Indiana University, Bloomington; David Turnbull, Seneca College; Richard W. Ullman, California State, Fresno; Gregory T. White, Dodge City Community College; Beth M. Waggenspack, Virginia Polytechnic Institute and State University; and Arthur E. Williams, University of Maine, Machias.

Chapter A

DEVELOPING CONFIDENCE

*Speech is civilization itself.
The word, even the most
contradictory word,
preserves contact—it is
silence which isolates.*

Thomas Mann

QUESTION OUTLINE

I. What are three reasons public speaking is an important subject for you to learn?

II. What are the similarities and differences between public speaking and interpersonal communication?

III. How can one become more confident in public speaking?

IV. What are the seven components of the public speaking process?

V. In what way is public speaking a process?

VI. In what way is public speaking a transaction?

Marcus Washington had seen it all, and he was not afraid of much of anything. Now he found himself—through no fault of his own—taking a public speaking course. His advisor said he had to take the course because it was required for education majors. He had faced guys almost twice his size in football and he had been beaten up more than once in the school yard, but—he thought to himself—he would rather do that all over again than give a speech in front of class.

As you sit in your first class in public speaking, you might wonder why you should bother to learn how to speak in public. After all, public speaking is frightening to many people and, generally, we try to avoid doing things that frighten us. We will start by looking briefly at some of the reasons you might want to learn from this course.

Personal Advantages

Public speaking holds a number of personal advantages for you. First, you will gain a high degree of self-satisfaction. Second, you will become more confident. Finally, you will become more sensitive. Let us explore each of these personal advantages.

One reason you might want to learn how to speak in public is that this activity can give you a high degree of self-satisfaction. Many of the top public speakers of our time were once timid and afraid of other people. Thousands of people in business take the Dale Carnegie course in public speaking. A teacher in the Carnegie program once said that he decided to teach that course because he had spent so many years being afraid and inadequate in public situations. He found that conquering his fears and developing his skills were so self-satisfying that he ended up devoting his life to teaching other adults how to do the same thing.

You may also want to study public speaking because you will gain confidence. Indeed, the title of this book highlights this reason. Although people often come to a public speaking course with some fear, most people leave the course feeling very confident about public speaking opportunities. They feel higher in self-esteem and generally more secure in their speaking abilities than before they took the course.

Finally, public speaking will teach you to be more sensitive to other people. You will learn that public speaking is not a one-directional activity in which a speaker simply provides a message. Effective public speaking occurs only when the audience has been carefully considered in both the preparation and delivery of the speech. In the preparation phase, the speaker considers the audience's interest in the topic, their knowledge about it, and how they might be best informed or persuaded on the topic. In the delivery of the speech, the competent communicator responds to the audience's nonverbal and verbal feedback. Public speaking instruction also reminds us of the cultural diversity in our world and encourages us to consider the different ways that people come to know and experience that world.

Professional Gains

Professionally, you will benefit from your study of public speaking for three reasons. First, public speaking will help you immediately to achieve your occupational goals by helping you earn higher grades in college. Second, public speaking skills will help you acquire employment. Third, public speaking will help you advance in your career. Let us explore each of these in more detail.

You know that graduating from college will help you attain higher-paying positions than those you would qualify for if you stopped your education at the high school level. You also know that people with higher grades in college are able to compete more favorably for professional occupations than are those with lower grades. Public speaking can help you earn higher grades in college, because a number of skills that are taught in public speaking courses are directly transferable to other academic subjects. For example, you will learn about active and critical listening in your public speaking course. Listening skills are basic to most learning situations. Similarly, you will learn how to organize ideas, which is important for most fields of inquiry.

Public speaking skills can help you acquire part-time positions and full-time employment after college. You will learn how to analyze an audience and respond to them appropriately, which will help you in job interviews. You will learn how to find information that will be useful as you are attempting to learn about employment opportunities. You will learn more about language, which will help you sound educated and aware of the world around you.

Public speaking will also help you advance in your career. Studies indicate that people who say little or nothing rarely, if ever, assume positions of leadership. People who are good at encouraging, explaining, motivating, and articulating goals tend to move up to more responsible positions. One of the authors once taught public speaking to union leaders, none of whom had finished college, and found that they needed no encouragement to learn, because they had already discovered that knowing something and being able to communicate it to others moved them up in the union hierarchy.

Public Benefits

Learning about public speaking also has implications for our culture and society. Civilized people have been using public speaking as a primary mode of communication since people emerged from caves. The Greeks and Romans honored people skilled in public speaking, as we still do today. Public speaking is valued because it is necessary if we are to live in a civilized world.

Our political system is based on the open and free expression of ideas. We probably do not think often enough about the First Amendment right of **freedom of speech.** Unlike some other countries, where everything from individual conversations to phone calls to public speeches and broadcasts is monitored by government officials, the United States

Americans have the right to assemble and the right to speak out on issues that concern them.

3

protects the right of its citizens to speak freely on any ideas. In fact, the laws even protect obnoxious people who say things they shouldn't about others. Most people in this country believe in the free expression of ideas.

To understand this notion of freedom of speech, read the following ideas derived from the "Credo for Free and Responsible Communication in a Democratic Society," a statement created and endorsed by the Speech Communication Association.[1]

Principles of Freedom of Speech

1. The right of peaceful expression by any communicative means is a central constitutional principle.
2. A free society is better off absorbing some speeches that are unfortunate than suppressing speech and expression.
3. Neither powerful majorities nor loud minorities should restrict free expression through intimidation or coercion.
4. Classrooms should serve as models for demonstrating respect for accuracy, reasoning, evidence, and values.
5. Students should act as intelligent, informed citizens who defend the rights of those with whom they disagree.

At the beginning of the 1990s, the freedom of speech issue focused on "politically correct" speech on campuses. With good intentions, campus officials tried to stem the flow of hate, but others worried with equally good reason that prohibiting hateful speech might alter our right to speak at all. The following editorial from *USA Today*[2] catches the flavor of the debate:

Colleges Must Not Muzzle Free Speech*

The mood is getting ugly on some college campuses.

Hate based on race, gender, religion, ethnic origin and sexual preference is taking over where earlier generations of students proclaimed "love, not war."

Blacks, Jews, Hispanics, Asians, women, gays and lesbians are the victims of growing intolerance on campus. So are faculty and students who make unpopular statements.

But too many institutions of higher learning are trying to ease tensions by restricting speech, by censorship. They are adopting codes that ban words and expressions considered racially or sexually offensive, or not "politically correct."

- Stanford University forbids speech intended to stigmatize individuals or small numbers of individuals.
- After a lawsuit, the University of Connecticut rewrote its code that once prohibited even "inappropriately directed laughter" and "inconsiderate jokes."
- The University of Michigan's code was ruled unconstitutional. There's a lawsuit challenging Wisconsin's.

There also have been speech code controversies reported at Brown University, Emory, Penn State and Tufts.

Codes restricting speech are wrongheaded, despite the opinion of the writer across this page. Free speech shouldn't become one more victim of this venom.

Hate incidents have been documented in recent reports by *USA TODAY*, People for the American Way, the National Institute Against Prejudice and Violence and the Justice Department's Community Relations Service.

*Copyright 1991 *USA TODAY*. Reprinted with permission.

Bill of Rights

First Amendment
freedom of religion
freedom of speech, assembly, and association
freedom of press
Second Amendment
right to keep...
Third...

Prejudice and bigotry and the hatred they inspire have no place on college campuses, or anywhere else. Expressions that demean others or their beliefs or that perpetuate stereotypes don't belong on campus, either.

But muzzling students will not change attitudes or behavior. It could harden them. It sure sends a strange message.

Campus speech codes are not necessary. There already are laws and rules against harassment and discriminatory conduct. These laws and rules must be enforced vigorously.

That leaves intact the constitutional protections for even speech that some find offensive, not just popular speech.

University officials who admit they have a problem on campus are to be commended. They have taken the first step. But there are better ways to deal with their problems.

The University of Kansas has cultural-sensitivity workshops. The University of Maine at Farmington encourages students to discuss sexism and homophobia. The University of California at Berkeley trains counselors.

Instead of limiting speech, university officials should teach students to fight back with their own words. They should help students to understand cultural differences.

Offensive speech should be condemned and criticized. But not banned.

College campuses are where minds should be opened and expanded by inquiry and debate. Not where doors are slammed shut by censorship and pressure to conform.

College censors should think twice before closing doors.

Today, campus speech codes might be adopted under the misguided goal of protecting minorities. Tomorrow, similar codes could be used to prevent them from speaking out.

That is an ugly possibility we must never tolerate.

In our society, we have the right of assembly and free speech. The public speaking classroom is a place where you can learn to use your constitutional right of free speech. Your teacher will help you learn to inform and persuade, to make ethical choices, and to speak fairly with reason and evidence.

Students sometimes think that freedom of speech means they can speak on anything they want in any way they want. However, the public speaking classroom is a laboratory where you can gain experience. You will be asked to deliver certain types of speeches (for example, informative, persuasive). You may even be asked to speak on certain subjects or not to speak on others. This latter restriction often comes about because the teacher has already heard dozens of speeches on a particular topic and he or she is weary of hearing about it. Because the teacher is your most important evaluator, you will want to heed any limits (length, topic, type of speech, mode of delivery) that the teacher places on an assignment. Remember, though, that you are practicing to use a freedom that many people in the world do not have.

Similarities and Differences Between Public Speaking and Interpersonal Communication

Most of us spend many hours each day talking to others. Indeed, some sources suggest that the average adult spends roughly one-third of the time talking with others. Because this form of communication is familiar to you, it may be helpful to point out the similarities and differences between casual communication and public speaking. You will see that some of the skills you have already developed in daily conversation will extend to your public speeches. You will also learn that some differences exist between conversations and public speaking.

Similarities Between Public Speaking and Interpersonal Communication

Interpersonal communication is communication between two or more people when relatively mutual opportunities for speaking and listening occur. Interpersonal communication includes the kinds of communication that occur at home, between friends, among work associates, between lovers, and even occasionally with strangers. We communicate with others interpersonally in order to express ourselves, to provide information, or to persuade others. Public speaking may serve all of these **purposes,** too.

You know the purposes of both interpersonal and public communication, and daily you practice the skills that are used in both. For example, you arrange your thoughts, adapt them to your listeners, and respond to their reactions.

1. *You arrange your thoughts.* As you walked around campus today, someone may have asked you the location of a certain building. Your response may have been something like this: "Do you see that red brick building over there? Well, the building you are looking for is a three-story building right across the street from the building you see." The arrangement of your thoughts in casual communication is the same as the **organization** of your ideas in formal communication, such as public speaking. You do it daily.

2. *You adapt your thoughts to your listener.* In interpersonal communication, you might observe that the person who asked you the question appeared to be a campus visitor, not a student, so you avoided using names of buildings and streets that only students and local residents would be likely to know. You did not say, without pointing, that the building the visitor sought was "on the other side of Old Main"—a familiar reference that another student might have understood. Adapting your thoughts to the listener is something you practice all the time. Called "listener adaptation" in casual communication, this concept becomes **audience adaptation** in public speaking.

3. *You respond to your listener's reactions.* If the stranger on campus says, "I'm sorry; I am color-blind and I do not know which building you mean," then you would, with ease, use another referent: "That is the building over there (pointing), with the statue in front." You adjust your message to your listener in both casual and formal communication. Responding to your listener's reactions is another communication skill that you have been practicing for years. Called "responding" in interpersonal communication, it is called **audience feedback** in public speaking.

You are already a person with speaking skills. You have been using them since you were a child, and you have probably improved them with experience. You are not coming into your class in public speaking without any background; instead, you have only to learn how to further develop the skills and abilities you already possess.

Public speaking is more formal than conversation.

Differences Between Public Speaking and Interpersonal Communication

Although you are already a practiced speaker in conversation, you need to learn how to apply those skills and abilities to more public situations. The purposes—self-expression, information, and persuasion—are essentially the same in interpersonal and public communication. The skills of arranging, adapting, and responding are the same as organization, audience adaptation, and feedback in a more formal public speaking situation. What, then, are the differences between communicating interpersonally and communicating publicly?

Some important differences between interpersonal communication and public communication are improved language, more effective organization, increased preparation, and better delivery. All you have to learn is how to be even more successful at what you already do daily in your conversations with other people.

1. *Improved language.* In our everyday communication, we are careless with language. We might drop an occasional profanity among friends, have little concern about what words we use to express ourselves, and show little regard for the niceties of grammar, syntax, or diction. However, the language of the home, the factory, and the street may not be appropriate behind the pulpit, the podium, or the microphone. Public communication calls for care in word choice, concern for audience response to the words, and constant editing of our conversational talk for the more discerning scrutiny of a larger audience.

2. *More effective organization.* Although you may have been fairly careful in the arrangement of your thoughts for the stranger on campus, and you probably tell a story without blowing the punch line, you are going to have to be even more careful in public communication. You might be able to scribble out a plan for a doghouse with a pencil on a tablet, but a building of steel, glass, and concrete takes drafting tools, sharp pencils, and an even sharper mind. One of the chief ways to clarify your thoughts for an audience is to organize them in ways that audience members, not you, understand. **Empathy**—seeing things from another person's perspective—is an essential element in organizing your thoughts so the audience can understand them.

3. *Increased preparation.* You may not prepare for interpersonal communication: your words to friendly fellow employees may be spontaneous. However, in public communication, the speaker often prepares by speaking from knowledge reflecting

research, by practicing what to say to avoid errors, and by exercising care to stay on the topic being addressed. This preparation is an important part of your college education because, through it, you will not only learn more about a variety of topics in which you are interested, but you will also learn how to communicate those ideas to others.

4. *Better delivery.* In interpersonal communication, we are not as careful about how we communicate a message, particularly if it is to someone we know, such as our spouse or classmate. We don't care if we are standing or seated, droppin' our g's, or leaving large gaps of silence in our talk. When we speak publicly, however, we must be aware of how we communicate. How we look and act when we speak may determine whether or not the audience listens. You are already more careful when you talk to someone higher in status, when you are asking a stranger for help, and when you are speaking for others. Generally the more people you are addressing, the more careful you have to be about how you deliver your message.

Confidence in Public Speaking

Although you have been speaking interpersonally all of your life, and perhaps as much as one-third of your waking day, you may still have some apprehension about public speaking. Indeed, many people express some anxiety about public speaking. A survey done over two decades ago identified public speaking as Americans' number one fear.[3] Although 41 percent of those surveyed identified public speaking as their greatest fear, only 18 percent listed death. The contrast between these two numbers led comedian Jerry Seinfeld to conclude that, if people go to a funeral, they would rather be the one in the casket than the one delivering the eulogy.

A later study that focused on social situations identified public speaking as the second most feared activity. The only situation more fearful was a party with strangers.[4] In general, we appear to fear the unknown—the unknown person at a party or the unknown situation of presenting a public speech. Although we cannot help you learn about interacting with strangers at parties, our goal in this book is to help you conquer the unknowns of speaking in front of an audience. We will start by informing you about a commonly felt fear—the fear of public speaking.

Fear of Public Speaking

The fear of speaking in public goes by many different names. Once called "stage fright" because it was a fear most often seen in beginning actors, it is now called **communication apprehension.** The term covers many kinds of communication fears in diverse situations: fear of talking on the telephone, fear of face-to-face conversations, fear of talking to authority figures or high-status individuals, fear of speaking to another individual, fear of speaking in a small group, and fear of speaking to an audience.

Why should you learn about communication apprehension? Even the question is controversial. Some teachers of public speaking feel that discussing communication apprehension—even in a textbook—is questionable because students who read about the fear of public speaking may see themselves as more apprehensive than those who do not know about it. However, as more teachers learn about communication apprehension, they support its discussion in texts.

There are at least two reasons you should know about communication apprehension. The first is that you need to be able to see the difference between the normal fear most people experience before they give a speech and high communication apprehension, which is a more serious problem. The second reason is that people who are highly apprehensive about communication should receive special treatment for their problem, or they will spend a lifetime handicapped by their fear.

Let us look first at the scope, symptoms, and effects of high communication apprehension. Then we will examine some solutions to this problem.[5]

High Communication Apprehension

About one out of every five persons is communication apprehensive, that is, 20 percent of all college students. Fortunately, that statistic means that four out of every five students, or 80 percent, are not apprehensive. Communication apprehensive people may not appear apprehensive unless they are engaging in a particular type of communication. High communication apprehension seems unrelated to general anxiety and intelligence. You may show no overt signs of anxiety in such activities as playing football, studying, eating, watching television, or walking to class. However, the high communication apprehensive (HCA) person has such strong negative feelings about communicating with other people that he or she typically avoids communication, or exhibits considerable fear when communicating. The scope of the communication apprehension problem may not appear large, but millions of people suffer from the fear of communicating.

One symptom of communication apprehension is that the HCA tries to avoid communication situations. Two researchers conducted a study to find out what would happen if HCA students had a choice of an interpersonal communication course or a public speaking course. They found that HCA students overwhelmingly chose the interpersonal communication course. The researchers suspected that students perceived the public speaking course as much more threatening than the interpersonal communication course.[6] Similarly, in small group communication courses, HCA students tend to be nonparticipants or to repeatedly register for, and drop, the class. HCA students try to avoid participating in the kind of communication that arouses their fears.

What are some other behaviors characteristic of HCA people? They choose dorm rooms at the ends of halls away from other people or housing away from busy streets and playgrounds. HCA people sit away from others or in places where leadership is not expected (along the side of the table, far from the end). When HCA people do find themselves in communication situations, they talk less, show less interest in the topic, take fewer risks, and say less about themselves than their classmates do. HCA people may be difficult to get to know. Even when they do find themselves in situations where communication is unavoidable, they discourage talk with signs of disinterest and silence.

The effects of high communication apprehension can be serious. HCA people are rarely perceived as leaders. They are seen as less extroverted, less sociable, less popular, and less competent than their peers.[7] They are not perceived as desirable partners for courtship or marriage. They are viewed as less composed, less attractive socially, and less attractive as work partners. Because they communicate reluctantly and seem so uneasy when they do, HCA people are perceived negatively by others. Therefore, they tend to do poorly in interviews and tend not to get the same quality of jobs as nonapprehensive people do. However, they are not less intellectual, mentally healthy, or physically attractive.[8] The consequences of being HCA seem serious enough to encourage us to look next at solutions.

One way to reduce high communication apprehension is to be aware of the malady and to understand that people with anxiety actually prepare differently, and less effectively, than do people without anxiety. Professor John Daly, of the University of Texas at Austin, and three doctoral students showed that anxious people are overly concerned with self and are negative in their assessments. They choose speech topics with which they are less familiar and have less sensitivity to public speaking situations.[9] A self-fulfilling prophecy is thus created. Anxious individuals are fearful, they prepare less effectively, and consequently they perform worse, reinforcing their fear of the public speaking situation. This cycle may be broken by more effective preparation.

Calming High Communication Apprehension

In order to practice the relaxation techniques, do the following:

1. Sit in a comfortable chair or lie down in a comfortable place. As much as possible, rid the area of distracting noises. If possible, play relaxing music or a tape with the sounds of nature.
2. Tense the muscles of your face and neck. Then relax them. Repeat the tensing and hold the tensed position for 10 seconds. Relax again.
3. Tense your hands by clenching your fists. Relax. Tense again and hold for 10 seconds. Relax.
4. Tense your arms above your hands and to your shoulders. Relax. Tense again and hold for 10 seconds. Relax.
5. Tense your chest and stomach. Relax. Tense again and hold for 10 seconds. Relax.
6. Tense your feet by pulling the toes under. Relax. Tense again and hold for 10 seconds. Relax.
7. Tense your legs above the feet and up to the hips. Relax. Tense again and hold for 10 seconds. Relax.
8. Tense your entire body and hold for 10 seconds. Relax and breathe slowly.
9. Repeat the word *calm* to yourself. This will help you relate the word to the relaxed feeling you are now experiencing. In the future, when you feel anxious the word *calm* should help you arrest the apprehension you experience.

From Teri Gamble and Michael Gamble, *Communication Works,* 2d ed. Copyright © 1987. Reprinted by permission of McGraw-Hill, Inc., New York, NY.

A second way to resolve feelings of high apprehension is through relaxation. Two techniques are possible. First, you can practice muscle relaxation, which will assist you with the physical symptoms you may have. When you deliberately tense a muscle and then relax it, you experience physical relaxation. You can become less physically tense by consciously tensing and relaxing the muscles in the various parts of your body. You may wish to work systematically from head to toe or in another reasonable progression. You may want to sit in a comfortable position or lie down as you relax your muscles.

The other side of relaxation is stopping those thoughts that make you nervous. When you begin to have anxiety-producing thoughts, you may wish to consciously calm yourself. Textbook writers Teri and Michael Gamble describe this technique:

A variation on the "calm technique" is to precede the word calm *with the word* stop. *In other words, when you begin to think upsetting thoughts, say to yourself, "Stop!" Then follow that command with, "Calm." For example:*
"I just can't get up in front of all those people."
"Look at their cold stares and mean smirks."
"Stop!"
"Calm." [10]

These two techniques can calm your physical and mental fears and allow you to be more relaxed in a communication situation.

Another remedy for high communication apprehension is professional help. The negative feelings about communication in the HCA person have often been developing since childhood. They do not disappear easily. Many schools and colleges have psychologists and counselors who have had professional training in reducing students' fears about speaking in public. Treatments that include training in the control of anxiety appear to be particularly helpful.[11] If you think you are among the small percentage of people who have unusually high fear of public speaking situations, then you may want to talk to your public speaking teacher about the services available to you.

A final possibility for treating the fear of public speaking is called systematic desensitization. **Systematic desensitization** is the repeated exposure to small doses of whatever makes you apprehensive. A public speaking student might be asked over a number of weeks to think of what is frightening (e.g., going to the front of the room to speak) and then to immediately follow the frightening thought with thoughts that relax, as in the box on page A-10. This process repeated over time tends to diminish a person's anxiety about communicating.

So far, this section on fear of public speaking has concentrated on the individual with extreme fear. What about the vast majority of persons who have a normal fear of public speaking? What are the signs of normal fear, and what can you do about reducing this normal fear—or even getting it to work *for* you instead of *against* you?

Normal Communication Apprehension

Most human beings feel fear when they speak in public. New teachers march into their classes armed with twelve hours' worth of material—just to be sure they will have plenty to say in their one-hour class. Experienced speakers feel anxiety when they face audiences that are new to them. Nearly all of the students in a public speaking class feel anxiety when they think about giving their speeches and when they deliver them.

What are the classic symptoms of communication apprehension for the public speaker? The authors of this book have given hundreds of speeches but still cannot sleep well the night before an important speech—one sign of anxiety or fear. Another common symptom is worry: you can't seem to get the speech out of your mind. You keep thinking about what giving the speech is going to be like, and you keep feeling inadequate for the task. When you actually give the speech, the common symptoms of fear are shaking—usually the hands, knees, and voice; dryness of the mouth—often called cottonmouth; and sweating—usually on the palms of the hands. One wit noted that public speakers suffer so often from dryness of the mouth and wetness of the palms that they should stick their hands in their mouth. For the public speaker, however, fear is no laughing matter. Let us turn from what the normal speaker *feels* to how the normal speaker *behaves* when afraid.

The speaker who is afraid—even with normal fear—tends to avoid eye contact, speak softly, utter vocalized pauses, ("Well," "You know," "Mmmmm"), speak too slowly or too quickly, not know what to do with hands or feet, stand as far away from the audience as possible, and place as many obstacles as possible between the speaker and the audience (distance, lecterns, notes). The speaker who is overcoming fear looks at the audience; speaks so all can hear easily; avoids vocalized pauses; speaks at a normal rate; moves body, arms, and feet in ways that do not appear awkward; stands at the usual distance from the audience; and uses the lectern to hold notes instead of as a hiding place.

Research on audience responses to public speakers indicates the importance of overcoming fear of public speaking for improved effectiveness. For example, one study shows that speakers who look at their audience are judged as credible and are seen as more persuasive than those who do not.[12] Another study shows that apprehensive speakers who employ more vocalized pauses or hesitations are less persuasive.[13] Finally, speakers who appear unusually slow or powerless are perceived as less knowledgeable about the topic and, therefore, less credible.[14]

Now that you understand the fear of public speaking and the way a speaker acts when afraid, you need to understand how you can replace anxiety with confidence.

Becoming Confident by Becoming Competent

This book is called "Confidence in Public Speaking" because gaining confidence goes hand in hand with gaining competence in public speaking.

At first you have to overcome fear, learn how to organize thoughts, learn how to best communicate those thoughts to an audience, and learn how to evaluate your effectiveness. Ordinarily, one course in public speaking will not be enough to make you a professional, but it is a necessary first step. This course will be your starting place, enough to give you the tools for future growth. The activities outlined in this book, with careful coaching by your teacher and the encouragement of your classmates, can launch you into a lifetime of increasing satisfaction and effectiveness as a public speaker.

People can learn to be more confident public speakers.

You should be careful not to have unrealistic expectations. Not everyone starts from the same place. Colleges today are populated by people of all ages, cultures, nationalities, and experiences. Some students have been active in the work world for years. Some have come to college with half a lifetime or more of experience; others have very little experience and may even be uncertain about their command of the English language.

This book works on building your confidence, so you can spend a lifetime working on your competence and your effectiveness with audiences in public speaking situations. With education and experience, you will learn more so that you can speak with authority on more subjects. During your lifetime, you will occasionally find issues at work, at home, in your neighborhood, and in social and professional organizations that make you want to speak out and influence other people.

Becoming Confident in Incremental Steps

Whatever your age, you have been speaking for many years. Your speaking may have been confined to talking to relatives, friends, classmates, or co-workers. You may not have had much experience talking to 20, 50, or 100 people at once. However, you can learn to speak to larger groups just as you have already learned to talk with those who are close to you.

The method of learning advocated in this book is the **incremental method.** An increment is a brief exposure to a larger whole. Taking a step is an increment in learning to walk. Learning to start a computer is a step in learning to use software. Learning to read a stock market report is a step in learning how to invest. In public speaking, the incremental method is based on the idea that a public speech is complex and can best be learned in increments, or small steps, that lead to mastery of a larger whole.

This book encourages the notion of learning public speaking gradually in small, easy-to-master steps that give you encouragement as you learn. For example, learning to say a few words about yourself to an audience is easier than researching and speaking on a complex issue. Preparing a one-minute speech is easier than delivering a ten-minute speech. The idea of learning a complex activity gradually, in small steps, is the key to incremental learning.

Along with gradual learning, the incremental method depends heavily on cooperative support from your teacher and classmates. Teachers and fellow students who reinforce what you have done well are inviting you to do more of the same. Their constructive comments about what you could improve show support that is necessary for your development as a speaker.

The incremental method of gaining confidence in public speaking, then, is based on two ideas: gradual mastery of simple steps toward a complex goal and continued reinforcement and support as you learn the steps toward effective public communication.

Public speaking is best learned gradually in small, easy-to-master steps.

Some basic elements are present in all public speaking circumstances. They include the source of the message, or the speaker. The audience members, or receivers, must be present. A message—both verbal and nonverbal—is essential. A channel, or means of communication, must be available. Feedback, which includes verbal and nonverbal responses from the audience, must be demonstrated. Noise—any form of interference with the message—usually has a negative influence on the process. Finally, public speaking occurs in a context, or situation. These elements are illustrated in figure 1 and are explained in the following paragraphs.

The Seven Basic Elements of the Public Speaking Process

Source

The **source,** or speaker, originates the message. Who the sender is makes a difference in who, if anyone, will listen. Consider a person walking down a street in New York City. Blind people clink their cups for contributions, street corner evangelists shake their Bibles in the air, and vendors push everything from bagels to booties. Would you listen to the messages they are sending? Some of the talented singers, dancers, and instrumentalists might attract your attention, but few of the many contenders for your eye and ear would succeed. Sources send messages, but no communication occurs until the source and receiver are conjoined by the messages between them. Often we serve concurrently both as source and as receiver.

Similarly, in the lecture hall, you hear some professors who capture your attention and leave you wishing for more. Occasionally you hear others whose ideas put you to sleep. There is no such thing as a source without a receiver or a speaker without an audience, because both are necessary components of effective communication.

Message

Verbal and nonverbal messages are an integral part of the communication process. What else links the source and the receiver? The message is sensed by both the source and the receiver: the facial expressions seen, the words heard, the visual aids illustrated, and the ideas or meanings conveyed simultaneously between source and receiver. **Verbal messages** are

Figure 1

Public speaking includes seven basic elements.

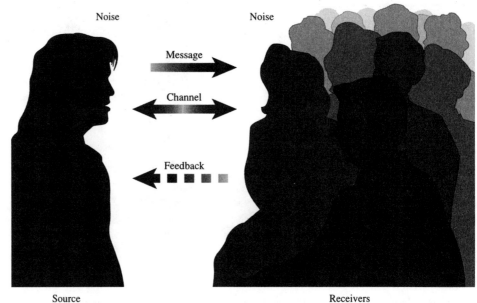

the words chosen for the speech. **Nonverbal messages** are the movements, gestures, facial expressions, and paralinguistic features that reinforce or contradict the words, such as pitch or tone of voice that can alter the meaning of the words.

Receiver

The **receiver,** listener, or audience is the individual or group that hears, and hopefully listens to, the message sent by the source. All individuals are unique. Receivers are individuals who have inherited certain characteristics and developed others as a result of their families, friends, and education.

The best speakers can "read" an audience; they can—through analysis or intuition—tell what an audience wants, needs, or responds to. This sort of group empathy allows some speakers to be seen as charismatic: they seem to exhibit what the audience feels.

Even a beginning speaker can learn to see the world through the audience's eyes. Nothing helps more in the classroom than to listen carefully to your classmates' speeches, because every speech will reveal as much about the speaker as it does about the issue being discussed. Few speakers outside the classroom are able to hear everyone in their audience reveal herself or himself through a speech.

Channel

The **channel** is the means of communication, whether it be coaxial cable, fiber optics, microwave, radio, video, or air. In the public speaking classroom, the channel is the air that carries the sound waves from the mouth of the source to the ear of the receiver. The channel might not seem to make very much difference, but messages have decidedly different impacts depending on whether they are heard as a rumor or observed on network news.

Messages are both seen and heard.

Some public speaking students discover the differences among channels when their teacher videotapes their speeches. Watching oneself electronically reproduced is not the same as watching a live performance, because channels are themselves part of the message. As Marshall McLuhan said, "The medium is the message."

Feedback

Feedback can be verbal or nonverbal. During a public speech, most of the audience feedback is nonverbal: head nodding, smiling, frowning, giving complete attention, fiddling with a watch. All of this nonverbal feedback is data for the speaker to interpret.

The question-and-answer session is a good example of verbal feedback in which the audience has an opportunity to seek clarification, to verify speaker positions on issues, and to challenge the speaker's arguments. In any case, feedback, like the thermostat on a furnace or an air conditioner, is the speaker's monitoring device that continuously tells if the message is working.

Noise

Another component in the communication process is **noise,** the interference with, or obstacles to, communication. Noise is whatever keeps a source from gaining feedback, a receiver from hearing words or seeing facial expressions, and so on. Noise can be internal or external. During a speech, if you are distracted by the presence of another person whom you find attractive, then you are experiencing internal noise that keeps you from receiving the message. If you are unable to hear the speaker because the door is open and you cannot hear over the hall noise, you are experiencing external noise. "Noise" is a broad term used to classify anything that is an obstacle to communication, whether it be the wanderings of the mind or someone's radio music interfering with the speaker's words.

Situation

Communication occurs in a context called the **situation**—the time, place, and occasion in which the message sending and receiving occurs. The situation can determine what kind of message is appropriate. Only certain kinds of messages and speakers are acceptable at funerals, senate debates, bar mitzvahs, court hearings, and dedications.

In the classroom, the situation is a room of a certain size, containing a number of people who fill a specified number of seats. The physical setting can mean that you can talk almost conversationally, or that you must shout to be heard.

The process of communication is the dynamic interrelationship of source, receiver, message, channel, feedback, noise, and situation. None of these components can be isolated, nor do any of them have any meaning without the others. They are what occurs in public speaking.

Public Speaking Is a Process

Public speaking is more than just a dynamic interrelationship of source, receiver, message, channel, feedback, noise, and situation. This relationship is linear; that is, it makes communication look as if the source, or speaker, imposes a message on an audience. Instead, speaker and audience influence each other.

For example, let's say that you are trying to convince fellow workers that they should unionize. You argue first that the union will result in higher pay. The audience appears unimpressed, so you argue that the union will bring such benefits as better working conditions. They doze. Finally you argue that the workers will get better medical and dental plans for their families, reducing their out-of-pocket health expenses. This argument gets attentive looks, some questions, and considerable interest. The audience has influenced what the speaker will say.

The speaker conveys a message through words and action, but the audience gives meaning to that message through its own thought processes. An example is the politician who wants to raise the drinking age. Audience members who are younger may hear the message as anti-youth, as having little to do with alcohol consumption. Mothers and fathers might see it as a way to protect their teenage children. Each audience member gives meaning to the message.

Audiences interpret messages, they construct messages of their own from the words they hear, and they carry with them their own rendition of the message and often others' analyses of the same message. A good example of the latter is the concept of "spin." Political campaigns these days are full of "spin doctors"—that is, media experts who try to tell an audience how to interpret a speaker's message. The experts decide for the audience who won a political debate, for example, by telling the audience what they were supposed to derive from the words. The idea of "spin" recognizes the notion that audiences construct their ideas of the message themselves, together with what others tell them the message meant. The process of communication is a transaction between source and receivers that includes mutual influence, the interpretation and construction of meaning, and the development of an individualized message that includes how others respond.

Public Speaking Is a Transaction

What happens when people communicate? A transaction occurs in which speaker and listener simultaneously send, receive, and interpret messages. In public speaking, the temptation is to see the action as predominantly one-way communication: the speaker sends words and actions to the audience. However, in many public speaking situations, the audience influences the speaker through continuous feedback, sometimes with words and actions and sometimes almost subconsciously.

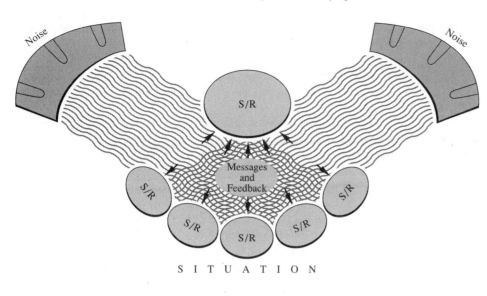

Figure 2

A communication transaction, with S/R indicating that people serve simultaneously as senders and receivers.

To demonstrate the powerful effect of the audience on the speaker, a teacher challenged his class to influence his behavior. One rule was that the moment he knew they were trying to influence him, the game was over. The class had to figure out what they could do to encourage the behavioral change. After ten weeks the teacher had not caught the class trying to influence him. They had documented, however, that, when the experiment began, the teacher stroked his chin once or twice each class period. They decided that the teacher would feel rewarded if they paid more attention, asked questions, and showed interest. Every time the teacher touched his chin, the class subtly rewarded him with their interest, attention, and questions. By the end of the ten-week course, they had the teacher touching his chin over twenty times each class session—and the teacher did not know it.

The point of this anecdote is that audiences influence speakers. In a political rally, they might do so with the words they yell, the movements and noises they make, or even with the signs they hold. In class, it could be the sight of heads nodding or eyes glazing over. The fact is that speakers influence audiences and audiences influence speakers, and they do so continuously in public speaking situations.

Communication is transactional, with speaker and listener simultaneously sending, receiving, and interpreting messages. One way to visually depict this transaction could be seen in figure 1. Figure 1 is accurate in that it incorporates all of the elements of the public speaking process, but it may oversimplify the transactional aspects of public speaking. Figure 2 is more complex, but perhaps more accurate. Neither model completely captures the complexity of the communication process; however, they may help clarify the mutual influence that occurs between speaker and audience.

Summary

The goal of this book is to help you become confident in your public speaking. Learning public speaking is important for you because it has personal advantages, professional gains, and public benefits. Personally, you may gain self-satisfaction, confidence, and sensitivity. Professionally, you may achieve better academic grades, you may have better chances to acquire employment, and you may have more opportunities to advance your career. Finally, you may experience public benefits as you participate as a citizen in a democratic society.

You have already practiced the elements of public speaking even if you have never delivered a speech. Interpersonal conversation, the kind we have with our friends daily, is done for the same purposes as formal speaking: for self-expression, information, and persuasion. Interpersonal communication requires arranging thoughts (organization), adapting to your listener (audience adaptation), and responding to your listener (audience feedback).

There are differences between interpersonal and public communication, too. Among them are the fact that public speaking often requires improved language and organization, increased preparation, and better delivery than does interpersonal communication.

We encourage you to become a more confident public speaker. Most people fear public speaking, but this fear can be overcome. Speakers become increasingly confident as they become more competent in public speaking. Public speaking skills and competence are best learned in incremental steps. The ideas of incremental learning and positive reinforcement are two important aspects of learning confidence. Incremental learning is instruction in small bites that encourage you to feel good about yourself, your message, and your audience. The idea is to move from simple to complex speeches, shorter to longer time limits, and single to multiple ideas—and to do this gradually over the term.

The public speaking process incorporates seven basic elements: the source of a message, the receivers of a message, a message, a channel, feedback, noise, and a situation. Public speaking is a process and a transaction. You are at the beginning of a course that will probably have a positive and lasting effect on the rest of your life. We will be your guide as you navigate these sometimes familiar, and sometimes unfamiliar, waters.

Vocabulary

audience adaptation The preparation of messages with a particular audience in mind

audience feedback The speaker's adjustments in the message based on the audience's responses to the speech

channel The means by which a message is sent: air, paper, microwaves, wire, radio signals, video, and so on

communication apprehension Communication anxiety in diverse situations: fear of talking on the telephone, fear of face-to-face conversations, fear of talking to authority figures or high-status individuals, fear of speaking to another individual, fear of speaking in a small group, and fear of speaking to an audience

empathy Seeing things from another person's perspective

feedback Verbal and nonverbal messages from an audience to a speaker, who must interpret those messages

freedom of speech The right of freedom of expression guaranteed by the Constitution of the United States, with its Bill of Rights

incremental method Learning public speaking in simple steps over time

interpersonal communication Communication between two or more people when relatively mutual opportunities for speaking and listening occur

noise Whatever interferes with the communication process by impeding the transmission or reception of messages

nonverbal messages The gestures, movements, facial expressions, and nonword sounds (pitch and tone) that communicate meaning

organization Called arrangement of thought in interpersonal communication, a careful structure and design of thoughts and arguments characteristic of public speaking

purposes In both casual and formal communication, self-expression, informing, and persuading

receiver The one to whom a message is sent

situation The context in which communication occurs

source The message sender or—in public speaking—the speaker

systematic desensitization The repeated exposure to small doses of whatever makes you apprehensive

verbal messages The words that are chosen for a speech

Applications

1. Write as many reasons as you can why public speaking could be useful to you now or in the future.

2. Examine the three characteristics of interpersonal communication—arranging, adapting, and responding—and reveal which of those you do best.

3. Examine the characteristics of public speaking—improved language, organization, preparation, and delivery—and speculate about which of them you believe will cause you the fewest problems.

4. On paper, mark one column "Conversation with Friend Between Classes" and a second column "Speech in Front of Class." After six of the seven components of the communication process—source, receiver, message, channel, feedback, noise, and situation—write briefly about how the model would work in the two situations.

Application Exercises

1. In order to learn the names of your classmates and some information about them, use the following suggestions.

    1. The instructor could write on the board those items that class members want to know about one another—name, major, year in college, marital status, hobbies, job, children, and so on.

    2. Have students introduce themselves by talking about whatever items on the board they select.

Class members should take notes on the information given because it can be an important part of their audience analysis for later speeches.

2. Write on paper or state in class some of the written rules (for example, ordinances, laws, court decisions) that govern our behavior. Write on a second sheet or state in class some of the unwritten rules that govern our behavior. Finally, what are some written and unwritten rules that govern what we say in public?

3. Write on paper or state in class some of the things that are said in public that militate against our freedom of speech. That is, what are some things that, said in public, make people dislike freedom of speech? Finally, state your opinion about whether or not this freedom is worth preserving.

Application Assignments

1. Paraphrased from the "Credo for Free and Responsible Communication in a Democratic Society," endorsed by the Speech Communication Association, December 1972.
2. Editorial debate, "Colleges Must Not Muzzle Free Speech," *USA Today* (January 9, 1991).
3. "What Are Americans Afraid Of?" *The Bruskin Report,* 53 (July 1973).
4. Daniel Goleman, "Social Anxiety: New Focus Leads to Insights and Therapy," *New York Times* (December 18, 1984), p. C1.
5. Much of the following information concerning communication apprehension comes from James C. McCroskey and Lawrence R. Wheeless, "The Nature and Effects of Communication Apprehension," in *Introduction to Human Communication* (Boston: Allyn & Bacon, 1976), 81–90.
6. Judy C. Pearson and Donald D. Yoder, "Public Speaking or Interpersonal Communication: The Perspective of the High Communication Apprehensive Student," Educational Resources Information Center (ERIC), ED 173870, May 1979.
7. Alan Feingold, "Correlates of Public Speaking Attitude," *The Journal of Social Psychology* 120 (1983): 285–86.
8. Ibid.

Endnotes

9. John A. Daly, Anita L. Vangelisti, Heather L. Neel, and P. Daniel Cavanaugh, "Pre-Performance Concerns Associated with Public Speaking Anxiety," *Communication Quarterly* 37 (1989): 39–53.

10. Teri Kwal Gamble and Michael Gamble, *Communication Works,* 2nd ed. (New York: Random House, 1987), 401.

11. Everett L. Worthington, Jr., Robert M. Tipton, Janet S. Comley, Thomas Richards, and Robert H. Janke, "Speech and Coping Skills Training and Paradox as Treatment for College Students Anxious about Public Speaking," *Perceptual and Motor Skills* 59 (1984): 394.

12. G. D. Hemsley and A. M. Doob, "The Effect of Looking Behavior on Perceptions of a Communicator's Credibility," *Journal of Applied Social Psychology* 8 (1978): 136–44.

13. E. A. Lind and W. M. O'Barr, "The Social Significance of Speech in the Courtroom," in *Language and Social Psychology,* H. Giles and R. St. Clair eds. (Oxford, England: Blackwells, 1979).

14. N. Miller, G. Maruyama, R. J. Beaber, and K. Valone, "Speed of Speech and Persuasion," *Journal of Personality and Social Psychology* 34 (1976): 615–25.

LISTENING

It is the province of knowledge to speak and it is the privilege of wisdom to listen.

Oliver Wendell Holmes

Chapter C

QUESTION OUTLINE

I. What are three false assumptions about listening?

II. What four activities are involved in the process of listening?

III. What are some barriers to effective listening?

IV. What suggestions can improve your informative listening?

V. What suggestions can improve your evaluative listening?

arah Parker saw herself as more of a talker than a listener. After the first two brief presentations in class, she found herself enjoying the attention she received as a speaker. The difficult part for her was sitting through all the speeches by other people. She had to admit, though, that time went faster when she wrote down what the speeches were about and commented on what the speaker did best. Also, she found that her friends noticed that she was better about listening to them instead of always dominating the conversation.

Just as Sarah did, you will develop confidence as a speaker *and* improve your listening skills in this course. Both speaking and listening are essential components of public communication. In the past, communication studies often focused on speakers and the creation and transmission of messages rather than on listeners and their active participation in the process.[1] Recently, the role of listeners in communication has gained more importance.[2]

You learn more by listening than by talking. Every speech you hear and every question asked and answered provides information about the people who will become your audience. Your serving as an audience member during your classmates' speeches provides you with an opportunity to analyze their choice of topics, the way they think, and the approaches they use. In short, being an audience member invites you to analyze your audience throughout the course.

You may not have thought of this fact when you enrolled in a public speaking class, but you will listen to 20 or more speeches (depending on the size of your class) for every speech you deliver. You will hear between 100 and 200 speeches in most public speaking courses. You will learn ways to evaluate speeches, ways to improve your own speaking, and methods of argument that you can employ.

Listening is also important beyond the classroom. Organizations frequently specify listening as a key communication skill for employees. Organizational leaders and personnel directors view good listening skills as a vital part of employee competence.[3] In one recent study, business managers who were asked to rank the skills that were most important for them identified listening as most important.[4]

Three Myths About Listening

Perhaps you think that you are already an effective listener. Most of us do. You might think that listening, unlike speaking, is something that cannot be taught. You might even think that, because nothing is wrong with your hearing, you are good at listening. If you think any of these things, you subscribe to some common myths about listening. Your effort to understand listening begins with disproving some myths that many people believe about listening.

Assuming That You Listen Well

If you ask a classmate if he or she listens well, the likely answer is yes. Virtually everyone from the kindergarten student to the college sophomore to the graduate professor believes that he or she listens effectively to other people. However, this assumption is not supported by research. Ralph Nichols and his associates conducted research at the University of Minnesota on thousands of students and hundreds of business and professional people. They found that people remember only half of what they hear immediately after a message, and only 25 percent of what they heard when tested two months later.[5] You may be comforted by these statistics the next time you do poorly on a final exam. After all, the average person remembers only 25 percent of what he or she heard earlier in the term. Nichols' research and your own experience in recalling information demonstrate that the assumption that you listen well is probably inaccurate.

Listen to learn from other speakers, who become the audience for your speech.

Assuming That You Cannot Be Taught to Listen Better

If you feel you are already an effective listener, you probably do not attempt to identify ways to improve your listening. On the other hand, if you feel you are not an effective listener, you may have resigned yourself to being inadequate in this area. One of the reasons you may fail to improve your listening is that there are few alternatives available. Studies show that most of your communication time is spent listening, followed in order by speaking, reading, and writing.[6] Curiously, you probably spend an inverse proportion of time in required classes studying these subjects. You probably spent much of your time in grade school, junior high, and high school studying the two communication skills that we actually use the least: reading and writing. However, you have probably never taken a course at any grade level on the communication skill you use the most: listening. Because of the lack of course work and study in listening, we incorrectly assume that listening is a communication skill that cannot be learned.

Assuming That Listening and Hearing Are the Same Thing

How many times have you said or has someone said to you, "What do you mean you don't know? I told you!"? People assume that, if they say something to someone, the person is listening. For instance, you know how frequently you daydream while hearing a lecturer, how often you are distracted by the person next to you as you hear a student speaker, and how regularly you spend time planning your afternoon while sitting in morning classes. In each case, you can hear the speaker, but you may not do well on an examination of the material. Passing a hearing test is not a guarantee that you are listening effectively.

Hearing and listening are separate activities. **Hearing** is a physical function you are able to perform unless you suffer from physiological damage or cerebral dysfunction. On the other hand, **listening** is a selective activity that involves the reception, selection, organization, and interpretation of aural stimuli. You can hear if your ears are normal, but listening is far more complex. Indeed, it involves our other senses, as well. Phillip Emmert believes that listening is not complete unless individuals process nonverbal, as well as verbal, stimuli.[7] Charles Roberts adds, "Listeners generally do not 'listen' with just their ears."[8]

Listening requires receiving, selecting, organizing, and interpreting information.

The Process of Listening

Listening involves a number of activities. Most of us are unaware of the different processes involved in listening because they occur quickly and almost simultaneously. The four activities that we will consider here are receiving, selecting, organizing, and interpreting.

Receiving

Before the listening process can begin, we must receive sounds. Hearing is a requisite first step in listening. Sound waves travel through the air from speakers to listeners when we communicate in face-to-face situations. They are transmitted electronically when we are talking on the telephone, watching television, or listening to our favorite music tape or CD.

We may ready ourselves to receive sounds by going through any number of behaviors. You might turn the volume of your radio or television down low, close the door to your room, and even turn off the lights before making an important phone call, so you are not distracted by other sights and sounds. You might put your glasses on, or take your glasses off, in face-to-face interaction in order to receive sounds more efficiently. Some people rely on their other senses in order to adequately "hear" messages, while others tune their other senses out when they are trying to listen.

Selecting

Once we have received sounds, we select those we will attend to and those we will ignore. None of us listens to all of the sounds in the environment. For example, if you walked to class, you were probably bombarded with a variety of sounds. You may have paid attention to the sound of your name being called behind you, but ignored a construction worker who was noisily drilling a hole in the concrete.

Selection may be divided into two categories: selective attention and selective retention. **Selective attention** means we focus on certain cues and ignore others. In class, you may ignore what a man sitting in the front row has to say, but listen carefully to the whispered comments made by your good friend seated next to you. You might not hear what someone is saying to you directly in a public speech, because you are distracted by noisy water pipes.

Selective retention means that we categorize, store, and retrieve certain information, but we discard other information. If you played the car radio on your way to class, try to recall one of the songs, commercials, or public-service announcements you heard. Although your attention may have been drawn to a particular song or message this morning, you may find that you cannot remember anything you heard. Your mind has disposed of the sounds you heard on the radio. You may recall a criticism your date offered last night, but have forgotten that your mother made a similar comment two days ago.

Organizing

Have you ever listened to a radio broadcast in another language? If you listened long enough, you may have begun to "understand" what the speaker was saying. You listened for common sounds and tried to arrange them into some meaningful message. Although the words were generally unknown, you attempted to place them into familiar patterns.

We do the same thing in a variety of ways when we are listening to our own language. For example, we use the principle of **figure and ground,** which means that we identify some words, phrases, or sentences as more important and others as less important. The more important words become the figure, or focus, and the less important words become the ground or background. If a speaker rambles on, we try to identify what his most important points are and discard the rest.

We also use the principle of closure in our communicative experiences. **Closure** is an organizing method in which we fill in information that does not exist. Some people habitually omit the subject of the sentence, particularly when it is the words "I am" or "I was." So, for example, if a speaker says, "Wondering about another approach," we fill in "I am" at the beginning of the sentence. By supplying the missing pieces of the incomplete thought, we have clarified the speaker's message.

Proximity is another way that we organize the messages we hear. If a speaker tells you that a terrible disease looms on the horizon, and then begins to speak about allergic reactions to drugs, you assume that the disease and the drugs are related in some way. **Proximity** means that we group two or more things that happen to be close to each other.

Similarity is a final method we use to organize messages. **Similarity** means that we group words or phrases together because they are similar in sound, beginning letter, or final syllable. Effective speakers will try to use alliteration—two or more words having the same initial sound—for their main points or for their subpoints. The textbook title, *Interpersonal Communication: Concepts, Components, and Contexts,* tells the reader that the book will be grouped in three sections that are alliterated with similarity in beginning sound. Another textbook, *Understanding and Sharing,* uses the common "ing" ending in its title. When listeners hear words that sound the same, they assume they are parallel in importance. They tend to view them as having some relationship to each other and they tend to remember them longer than words that do not have a common sound. Similarity can likewise be useful for the speaker when organizing and outlining a public speech.

Interpreting

Interpreting occurs when you receive, select, and organize a set of sounds and then blend them with your own understanding. For instance, if you are a staunch Democrat and you listen to a message by the Republican governor of your state, you may interpret her meaning differently than your roommate who is a Young Republican. The message was identical, but your personal attitudes, values, and beliefs created a different mix of understanding. A more simple example occurs when someone uses a word out of context, and you have great difficulty understanding what they are attempting to convey to you. For instance, if someone asks you for a "bib," you may interpret the word to mean a bibliography if you are in a classroom setting, but as an item for a baby to wear when she or he eats if you are with a family in a restaurant. If one of your married friends who has children asks if he has left a bib at your apartment, you might have difficulty figuring out what he is specifically asking about.

Barriers to Effective Listening

After reading the previous section, you may no longer believe that you naturally listen well, that you cannot learn listening skills, and that your hearing ability is the same as your listening ability. What are some of the factors that interfere with your ability to listen? Have you ever sat in a lecture and smiled when the lecturer made a joke, nodded when he or she sought affirmation, established eye contact with the lecturer, and still not remembered a single thing the lecturer said?

Our motivation to listen has not been widely studied, but we know that it is critical to our listening ability.[9] Robert Bostrom observed that while researchers have spent a good deal of time trying to understand why people are motivated to talk, they have not shown the same interest in discovering why they are inspired to listen.[10] Brian Spitzberg and Bill Cupach have argued that competence in communication is not possible without motivation.[11] Motivation is equally important for the listener and the speaker.

Motivation is the key to effective listening. When we are not motivated to listen, we allow barriers to interfere. We will discuss four barriers to effective listening: faking attention, prejudging the speaker, prejudging the speech, and yielding to distractions. We begin by discussing a topic familiar to most college students: faking attention.

Faking Attention

As students, it is easy to learn how to fake attention. You may use this strategy in situations in which the most acceptable social behavior is paying attention. It is the strategy you may use in classes, at social gatherings, and in "listening" to fellow students' speeches. You undoubtedly use this strategy when you are bombarded with more messages than you want to hear. Consequently you may practice the appropriate nonverbal behavior—eye contact, attentive appearance, and apparent note taking—when you are actually wondering if the speaker is as tired as you are as you scribble pictures in your notebook. Faking attention is both a result and a cause of poor listening.

Barriers to Effective Listening

1. Faking attention
2. Prejudging the speaker
3. Prejudging the speech
4. Yielding to distractions

Three additional barriers to effective listening are prejudging the speaker, prejudging the speech, and yielding to distractions. Each of these barriers, in turn, has subtypes that concern you if you wish to improve your listening skills.

Prejudging the Speaker

We all make judgments about speakers before they say a word. You might dismiss a speaker because of attire, posture, stance, or unattractiveness.

Researchers have found that the speaker's gender appears to be an important variable in judgment. For instance, when male and female student speakers are given the same grade, the male speakers receive fewer positive comments than do the female speakers.[12] Female evaluators give men higher evaluations than women,[13] and male evaluators tend to grade women higher than men.[14] In addition, one of the authors found that sexist teachers grade speeches differently than nonsexist teachers: they do not write as many comments.[15]

A speaker's status is an additional preconceived judgment that affects our ability to listen to another person. If a speaker has high status, you may tend to accept the message more easily, without listening critically. You may not exercise careful judgment if the speaker is a visiting dignitary, a physician, an attorney, or a distinguished professor, for example. If you perceive the speaker to be low in status—a beginning student, a maintenance worker in the dormitory, or a student who flunked the midterm—you tend not to listen to his or her message at all, and you are unlikely to remember what the speaker said. Perceived status seems to determine whether you are likely to listen critically or at all.

Stereotypes also affect our ability to listen. If a speaker announces that she is a Republican, is opposed to women's rights, and believes a woman's place is in the home, you may prematurely judge her as a reactionary and ignore her speech. When speakers seem to belong to groups for whom you have little regard—rich people, poor people, jocks, brains, or flirts—you may reject their messages.

Do you dismiss seniors as too pretentious or people who slouch as uninteresting? If you draw such conclusions about speakers before they begin a speech, and then ignore the message as a result of this prejudgment, you are handicapped by a factor that interferes with your listening.

Prejudging the Speech

A third factor that may interfere with your ability to listen to a speaker is your tendency to prejudge the speech. The same human tendency that causes you to judge the speaker before a speech causes you to judge the speech before you understand it. The most common conclusions we draw prematurely about a speech are that it is boring, too difficult to understand, irrelevant, or inconsistent with our own beliefs.

You may judge a speech to be boring because you feel you already know the information the speaker is presenting, you have already experienced what the speaker is describing, or the speaker is trying to persuade you to do something you already do. In other words, your feelings of superiority—informational, experiential, or attitudinal—interfere with your ability to listen.

You may decide a speech is too difficult to understand and ignore it because you "wouldn't understand it anyway." You might tend to categorize many topics as too difficult or you may selectively identify topics that deal with certain subjects, such as thermonuclear power, quantum physics, or Keynesian economics, as too complex for your understanding, even though the speaker's purpose is to simplify the concept or to inform you of the basic terminology.

Sometimes we prejudge a message as too difficult to understand.

Occasionally you may decide that a speech is irrelevant. For some people, nearly all topics seem unimportant. Others dismiss some topics as soon as they are announced. For instance, a business major in the audience may feel that Native American literature does not affect him; a college sophomore may conclude that a speech on retirement is immaterial; an African American student may show no interest in a description of life in a European American community. One of the reasons people dismiss another person's topic as irrelevant is because of **egocentrism,** the tendency to view oneself as the center of any exchange or activity. People who are egocentric are concerned only with themselves and pay little or no attention to others. Whether you refuse to consider most speeches or ignore only certain topics, you are blocking your ability to become an effective listener. If you listen attentively to a speech beyond the statement of its topic or purpose, you may find information that clearly shows the speech's relevance for you.

Finally, you may dismiss a speech because you disagree with the topic or purpose. You may feel that a speaker should not inform you about how to smoke crack, provide information on birth control, show examples of pornography, or persuade you to limit salt or sugar consumption. Your opposition to smoking crack, practicing birth control, seeing nudity, or learning about nutritional findings may block your ability to listen to the speaker. You may conclude that the speaker is "on the other side" of the issue and that your seemingly different attitudes prohibit open communication.

Defensiveness commonly occurs when a speaker's topic or position on an issue is different from your own. You may be threatened by the speaker's position and feel that you must defend your own. You may believe you are being attacked because you champion a specific cause—such as women's rights, energy conservation, or the anti-tax movement—that the speaker opposes. You may be standing ready for anyone who dares provoke you on your favorite cause. You may be only too eager to find fault with another person's speech. In the speaking–listening process, try to recognize the blocks to effective listening caused by defensiveness and dismissal of the speech through disagreement.

The Four Most Common Distractions to Listening

1. Factual distractions
2. Semantic distractions
3. Mental distractions
4. Physical distractions

Yielding to Distractions

The listener's four most common distractions are factual, semantic, mental, and physical. Yielding to **factual distractions** means listening only for the facts instead of the main ideas or general purpose of a speech. The formal educational experiences you have had in which you were required to listen to teachers in order to pass objective exams may have contributed to this tendency. Rather than looking at an entire speech, you may focus on isolated facts. You jeopardize your understanding of the speaker's main idea or purpose when you jump from fact to fact, rather than attempting to weave the major points into an integrated pattern and regarding the facts as supporting information.

Semantic distractions are words or phrases that we allow to affect us emotionally. You may react this way if someone uses a word or phrase in an unusual manner, if you find a particular concept distasteful or inappropriate, or if you do not understand the meaning of a term. Regionalisms—words that are used in a way unique to a particular geographical area—provide one example of words used in an unusual manner. If a speaker talks about the harmful qualities of *pop,* and you refer to soft drinks as *soda,* you may react negatively to the word *pop.* If you feel that *girl* should not be used to designate a woman, then you may be distracted in listening to a speaker who does so.

Mental distractions include your engaging in daydreaming, counterarguments, recollections, or future planning while listening to a speaker. These mental distractions may originate from something the speaker has stated or from your own preoccupation with other thoughts. Perhaps mental distractions occur because of the difference between the speed at which we can listen and the speed at which we can speak. The average American talks at a rate of 125 words per minute but can receive about 425 words per minute. This discrepancy allows us to engage in many mental side trips that may be more relevant to us. Unfortunately, we may become lost on a side trip and fail to return to the original path.

Physical distractions include any physical stimuli that interfere with our attention to a speaker. Stimuli that may affect our listening are sounds such as a speaker's lisp, a buzzing neon light, or an air hammer; sights such as a speaker's white socks, a message on the chalkboard, or bright sunlight; smells such as a familiar perfume, baking bread, or freshly popped corn.

In this section, we surveyed four sets of barriers to effective listening: faking attention; prejudging the speaker on the basis of gender, status, or stereotypes; prejudging the subject and dismissing it as boring, too complex, irrelevant, or opposed to our own point of view; and yielding to factual, semantic, mental, or physical distractions. Consider how you can overcome these barriers and become more effective as a listener.

We have considered three false assumptions about listening and some barriers to effective listening. We will now examine the two types of listening that occur most frequently in public speaking situations: informative listening and evaluative listening.

Practices for Effective Informative Listening

1. Suspend judgments about the speaker.
2. Focus on the speaker as a source of information.
3. Concentrate your attention on the speaker.
4. Listen to the entire message.
5. Focus on the values or experiences you share with the speaker.
6. Focus on the main ideas the speaker is presenting.
7. Recall the arbitrary nature of words.
8. Focus on the intent as well as the content of the message.
9. Be aware of your listening intensity.
10. Remove or ignore physical distractions.

Informative Listening

Informative listening refers to the kind of listening you engage in when you attend class and listen to an instructor, attend baseball practice and listen to the coach, or attend a lecture and listen to a visiting speaker. Your purpose in informative listening is to understand the information the speaker is presenting. You may try to understand relevant information about the speaker and factors that led to the speech, as well as the central idea of the speech itself.

Informative listening requires a high level of involvement in the communication process. Authors Wolvin and Coakley refer to informative listening as comprehensive listening, and observe that it is especially important in employment settings. Without adequate information, they note, workers cannot do an effective job.[16] What are some of the factors that contribute to effective informational or comprehensive listening? What can you do to overcome many of the barriers discussed in the previous section?

In order to be successful at informative listening, you can engage in at least ten practices: (1) suspend judgments about the speaker, (2) focus on the speaker as a source of information, (3) concentrate your attention on the speaker, (4) listen to the entire message, (5) focus on the values or experiences you share with the speaker, (6) focus on the main ideas the speaker is presenting, (7) recall the arbitrary nature of words, (8) focus on the intent as well as the content of the message, (9) be aware of your listening intensity, and (10) remove or ignore physical distractions. Let us consider each of these in more detail.

Suspend Judgments About the Speaker

Suspend your premature judgments about the speaker so you can listen for information. Wait until you have heard a speaker before you conclude that he or she is, or is not, worthy of your attention.

If you make decisions about people because of their membership in a particular group, you risk serious error. For example, beer drinkers may be thin, members of fraternities may not be conformists, and artists are often disciplined.

Focus on the Speaker As a Source of Information

It is easy to dismiss people when you categorize them. When you focus on a speaker as a valuable human resource who can share information, ideas, thoughts, and feelings, you are better able to listen with interest and respect. Every speaker you hear is likely to have some information you do not already know. Try to focus on these opportunities to learn something new.

We listen to the coach for information.

Concentrate Your Attention on the Speaker

If you find yourself dismissing many of the speeches you hear as boring, consider whether you are overly egocentric. Perhaps your inclination to find your classmates' speeches boring is due to your inability to focus on other people. Egocentrism is a trait that is difficult to overcome. The wisest suggestion, in this case, is to keep in mind one of the direct benefits of concentrating your attention on the speaker: if you focus on the other person while she is speaking, that person will probably focus on you when you are speaking. Even more important, you will come across better as a speaker if others perceive you to be a careful listener. Nothing else you can do—including dieting, using makeup, wearing new clothing, or making other improvements—will make you as attractive to others as learning to listen to someone else.

Listen to the Entire Message

Do not tune out a speech after you have heard the topic. More than likely, the speaker will add new information, insights, or experiences that will shed additional light on the subject. One professor teaches an upper-division argumentation course to twenty students each quarter. Four speeches are assigned, but every speech is given on the same topic. In a ten-week period, students hear eighty speeches on the same topic, but every speech contains some new information. The class would be dismal if the students dismissed the speeches after hearing they would all cover the same topic. Instead of considering the speeches boring, the students find them interesting, exciting, and highly creative.

Focus on the Values or Experiences You Share with the Speaker

If you find you are responding emotionally to a speaker's position on a topic and you directly oppose what he or she is recommending, try to concentrate your attention on the attitudes, beliefs, or values you have in common. Try to identify with statements the speaker is making. The speaker might seem to be attacking one of your own beliefs or attitudes, but, if you listen carefully, you may find that the speaker is actually defending it from a different perspective. Maximizing our shared ideas and minimizing our differences result in improved listening and better communication.

Focus on the Main Ideas the Speaker Is Presenting

Keep in mind that you do not have to memorize the facts a speaker presents. Rarely will you be given an objective examination on the material in a student speech. If you want to learn more about the information being presented, ask the speaker after class for a copy of the outline, a bibliography, or other pertinent documentation. Asking the speaker for further information is flattering; however, stating in class that you can recall the figures cited but have no idea of the speaker's purpose may seem offensive.

Recall the Arbitrary Nature of Words

If you find that you sometimes react emotionally to four-letter words or to specific usages of some words, you may be forgetting that words are simply arbitrary symbols people have chosen to represent certain things. Words do not have inherent, intrinsic, "real" meanings. When a speaker uses a word in an unusual way, or when you are unfamiliar with a certain word, do not hesitate to ask how the word is being used. Asking for such information makes the speaker feel good because you are showing interest in the speech, and the inquiry will contribute to your own knowledge. If you cannot overcome a negative reaction to the speaker's choice of words, recognize that the emotional reaction is yours and not necessarily a feeling shared by the rest of the class or the speaker. Listeners need to be open-minded; speakers need to show responsibility in word choice.

Focus on the Intent As Well As the Content of the Message

Use the time between your listening to the speech and the speaker's delivery of the words to increase your understanding of the speech. Instead of embarking on mental excursions about other topics, focus on all aspects of the topic the speaker has selected. Consider the speaker's background and his or her motivation for selecting a particular topic. Try to relate the major points the speaker has made to his or her stated intentions. By refusing to consider other, unrelated matters, you will greatly increase your understanding of the speaker and the speech.

Be Aware of Your Listening Intensity

You listen with varying degrees of intensity. Sometimes when a parent or roommate gives you information, you barely listen. However, when your supervisor calls you in for an unexpected conference, your listening is very intense. Occasionally we trick ourselves into listening less intensely than we should. Everyone knows to take notes when the professor says, "This will be on the test," but only an intense listener captures the important content in an apparently boring lecture. You need to become a good judge of how intensely to listen and to learn ways to alter your listening intensity. Sitting on the front of the chair, acting very interested, and nodding affirmatively when you agree are some methods that people use to listen with appropriate intensity.

Remove or Ignore Physical Distractions

Frequently you can deal with physical distractions, such as an unusual odor, bright lights, or a distracting noise, by moving the stimulus or yourself. In other words, do not choose a seat near the doorway that allows you to observe people passing by in the hall, do not sit so that the sunlight is in your eyes, and do not sit so far away from the speaker that maintenance noises in the building drown out her voice. If you cannot remove the distraction by changing your seat or removing the distracting object, try to ignore it. You probably can study with the radio or television on, sleep without having complete darkness, and eat while other people are milling around you. Similarly, you can focus your attention on the speaker when other physical stimuli are in your environment.

Consider whether you would be able to concentrate on the speech if it were, instead, a movie you have been wanting to see, a musical group you enjoy, or a play that has received a rave review. One man said that, when he had difficulty staying up late to study in graduate school, he considered whether he would have the same difficulty if he were on a date. If the answer was no, he could then convince himself that the fatigue he felt was a function of the task, not of his sleepiness. The same principle can work for you. Consider whether the distractions are merely an excuse for your lack of desire to listen to the speaker. Generally you will find you can ignore the other physical stimuli in your environment if you wish to do so.

As we observed earlier, two kinds of listening are most common in public speaking situations. We have concluded our discussion of informative listening and will turn now to evaluative listening.

Evaluative Listening

Evaluative listening is the kind you engage in when you listen to two opposing political speakers; judge the speaking ability of an author, attorney, or instructor; or listen to students in public speaking class. Your purpose in evaluative listening is to judge the speaker's ability to give an effective speech. Evaluative listening is an essential skill in and out of the classroom. What can you do to become a better evaluative listener?

You can be a more effective evaluative listener by following four guidelines. First, establish standards of appraisal. Second, consider the positive as well as the negative aspects of the speech. Third, view the speech as a whole entity, rather than as a composite of isolated parts. Fourth, consider the speaker's **ethical standards,** the moral choices he or she has made in preparing and delivering the speech. Let us consider each of these guidelines in more depth.

Establish Standards of Appraisal

In order to evaluate another person's public speaking ability, you must establish criteria by which you make your judgments. The criteria you establish should reflect your beliefs and attitudes about public speaking. Your instructor may suggest a set of criteria by which to judge your classmates' speeches. Many different sets of standards can be used to provide equally valid evaluations of public speaking; however, most include a consideration of the topic choice, purpose, arguments, organization, vocal and bodily aspects of delivery, audience analysis, and adaptation. The evaluation form shown in figure 1 follows the suggestions offered in this text.

Ways to Be an Effective Evaluative Listener

1. Establish standards of appraisal.
2. Consider the positive as well as the negative aspects of the speech.
3. View the speech as a unit.
4. Consider the speaker's ethical standards.

Figure 1

An evaluation form for a public speech.

Evaluation Form

Speaker _____
Critic _____
Use this scale to evaluate each of the following:

1	2	3	4	5
Excellent	Good	Average	Fair	Weak

Introduction
_____ The introduction gained and maintained attention.
_____ The introduction related the topic to the audience.
_____ The introduction related the speaker to the topic.
_____ The introduction revealed the thesis and organization of the speech.

Topic selection and statement of purpose
_____ The topic selected was appropriate for the speaker.
_____ The topic selected was appropriate for the audience.
_____ The topic selected was appropriate for the occasion.
_____ The statement of purpose was clear and appropriate for the speaker, audience, and occasion.
_____ The stated purpose was achieved.

Content
_____ The speaker consulted available sources, including personal experience, interviews, and printed materials for information.
_____ The speaker supplied a sufficient amount of evidence and supporting materials.
_____ The speech was organized in a manner that did not distract from the speech.
_____ The main points were clearly identified.
_____ Sufficient transitions were provided.

Source
_____ The speaker described his or her competence.
_____ The speaker demonstrated trustworthiness.
_____ The speaker exhibited dynamism.
_____ The speaker established coorientation.

Delivery
_____ The vocal aspects of delivery—pitch, rate, pause, volume, enunciation, fluency, and vocal variety—added to the message and did not distract from it.
_____ The bodily aspects of delivery—gestures, facial expressions, eye contact, and movement—added to the message and did not distract from it.
_____ Visual aids were used appropriately to clarify the message.

Audience analysis
_____ The speaker demonstrated his or her sensitivity to the interests of the audience.
_____ The speaker adapted the message to the knowledge level of the audience on the topic.
_____ The speaker adapted the message to the demographic variables of the audience.
_____ The speaker adapted the message to the attitudes of the audience.

Conclusion
_____ The conclusion forewarned the audience that the speaker was about to stop.
_____ The conclusion reminded the audience of the central idea or the main points of the speech.
_____ The conclusion specified precisely what the audience was to think or do in response to the speech.

Ethical standards
_____ The speaker earned the audience's trust with an honest approach to the topic.
_____ The speaker cited sources of information and ideas.
_____ The speaker avoided distortion, exaggeration, and oversimplification of the issue.
_____ The speaker recognized other points of view on the issues.

Consider the Positive As Well As the Negative Aspects of the Speech

Too often people use the word *evaluation* to mean negative criticism. In other words, if they are to evaluate a speech, a newspaper article, or a television program, they feel they must state every aspect of it that could be improved or did not meet their standards.

Evaluation should include both positive and negative judgments. As a matter of fact, many speech instructors feel you should begin and end your criticism of a speech with positive comments and "sandwich" your negative remarks in between. Research shows that students perceive positive comments to be more helpful than negative comments.[17]

View the Speech As a Unit

It is very easy to focus on delivery aspects of the speech, to look only for a recognizable organizational plan, or to consider only whether the research is current. In viewing small bits of the speech in isolation, you may be able to justify a low evaluation you give to a classmate. However, considering all of the parts that went into the speech may not allow such a judgment.

Speeches are like the people who give them—composites of many complex, and sometimes conflicting, messages. In order to be evaluated completely and fairly, they must be examined within a variety of contexts. Do not be distracted by a topic that represents one of your pet peeves, allow language choices to overshadow the speaker's creativity, or accept the arguments of a speaker who demonstrates a smooth delivery. In short, consider the entire speech in your evaluation.

Consider the Speaker's Ethical Standards

Speakers make moral choices about audiences when they choose a topic, when they decide what to say about the topic, and when they recommend a response to the speech. For example, a speaker can choose a topic that is appropriate or inappropriate for an audience; a speaker can unethically decide to withhold important information about the topic; or a speaker can recommend actions that are illegal or immoral.

Some ethical questions to ask of a speech and speaker are the following: Did the speaker prepare thoroughly by knowing the subject well? Did the speaker select information and arguments appropriate for the particular audience? Did the speaker choose language understandable to the audience? Did the speaker treat the topic with honesty? Did you trust the speaker's information and ideas? Did the speaker recognize the possibility of other points of view? Did the speaker cite sources of information and ideas? Did the speaker select evidence, illustrations, and examples that avoid distortion and adhere to the rules of reasoning?

Summary

We have considered informative and evaluative listening in this chapter. You learned the role of listening in the public speaking classroom. You learned to identify three false assumptions about listening: most people assume that they listen well, that they cannot be taught how to be better listeners, and that hearing and listening are the same phenomenon. After we dispelled these misconceptions, you learned four sets of barriers to effective listening: faking attention; prejudging the speaker on the basis of gender, status, or stereotypes; prejudging the subject and dismissing it as boring, too complex, irrelevant, or opposed to your own point of view; and yielding to factual, semantic, mental, or physical distractions. You then considered fourteen practices in which you should engage when you listen for informative and evaluative purposes. These practices are to (1) suspend judgments about the speaker, (2) focus on the speaker as a source of information, (3) concentrate your attention on the speaker, (4) listen to the entire message, (5) focus on the values or experiences you share with the speaker, (6) focus on the main ideas the speaker is presenting, (7) recall the arbitrary nature of words, (8) focus on the intent as well as the content of the message, (9) be aware of your listening intensity, (10) remove or ignore physical distractions, (11) establish standards of appraisal, (12) consider the positive as well as the negative aspects of the speech, (13) view the speech as a unit, and (14) consider the speaker's ethical standards.

You will spend considerably more time listening than speaking in this course. Use that opportunity to advance yourself as a person who recognizes effective listening as the hard work that it is, who learns from the words and concerns of others, and who learns the responsibilities of being both a speaker and a listener. Effective listening can help you develop confidence as a communicator.

Vocabulary

closure The organizational method of filling in information that does not exist to clarify an incomplete message

defensiveness The tendency to dismiss a speech because the speaker's topic or position on an issue is different from your own; a barrier to listening

egocentrism The tendency to view oneself as the center of any exchange or activity; overconcern with the presentation of one's self to others; a barrier to listening

ethical standards The moral choices made by a speaker in preparing and delivering a speech to an audience

evaluative listening Listening to a speaker for the purpose of evaluating his or her ability to present an effective speech

factual distractions Factual information that detracts from our attention to primary ideas; a barrier to effective listening

figure and ground The organizational method of identifying some words, phrases, or sentences as more important and others as less important

hearing The physiological process by which sound is received by the ear

informative listening Listening to a speaker in order to understand the information that he or she is presenting

interpreting The process of receiving, selecting, and organizing a set of sounds and then blending them with your own understanding

listening The process of receiving, selecting, organizing, and interpreting sounds

mental distractions Communication with ourselves while we are engaged in communication with others; a barrier to effective listening

physical distractions Environmental stimuli that interfere with our focus on another person's message; a barrier to effective listening

proximity The organizational method of grouping two or more things that happen to be close to each other

selective attention The act of focusing on some cues while ignoring others

selective retention The act of categorizing, storing, and retrieving certain information while discarding other information

semantic distractions Words or phrases that affect the listener emotionally; a barrier to effective listening

similarity The organizational method of grouping words or phrases together because they are similar in sound, beginning letter, or final syllable

 # Applications

Application Exercises

1. State which of the barriers to effective listening will be the least, and the greatest, problem for you.

2. Are you an effective, informative listener? After you have listened to a number of speeches in class, select one and complete the following:

Speaker's name _____

Topic _____

Statement of purpose _____

_____

Main points:

1. _____

2. _____

3. _____

4. _____

What are the speaker's qualifications for speaking on this topic?

_____

_____

What response is the speaker seeking from the audience?

_____

_____

3. Establish standards of appraisal for evaluating speeches. In order to make judgments about your classmates' speeches, you need standards by which to evaluate them. Create a criticism form including all of the essential elements of effective public speaking. Note exactly what you would include and how you would weigh each aspect. (Does delivery count more for you than content? Is a great deal of evidence more important to you than adaptation to the audience?)

4. Write a speech criticism. Using the criticism form that you created in exercise 3, evaluate three speeches that other students delivered in class. After you have completed your criticism, give each form to the speaker. Together discuss how accurately you have assessed the speech. Are you satisfied with the form? Do you believe your form would be useful for others? Does the speaker feel that the form included all the relevant factors? Can he or she suggest items that could or should be included? Is he or she satisfied with your use of the form? What differences of opinion exist between the two of you? Why? Can you resolve these differences? What has the experience demonstrated?

Application Assignments

1. Using the evaluation form shown in figure 1, evaluate one or more speeches delivered by classmates. The form asks you to evaluate introduction, topic selection, statement of purpose, content, source, delivery, audience analysis, conclusion, and ethical standards. Which aspects of the speech do you find easiest to evaluate? What can you do to strengthen your ability to evaluate those aspects?

2. Using the evaluation form shown in figure 1, evaluate a formal speech outside the classroom. Did you notice any differences between a classroom speech and a public speech given in a different context or situation?

Endnotes

1. M. Fitch-Hauser and M. A. Hughes, "Defining the Cognitive Process of Listening: A Dream or a Reality?" *Journal of the International Listening Association* 2 (1988): 75–88.
2. Blaine Goss, "Listening as Information Processing," *Communication Quarterly* 30 (1982): 304–7.
3. A. D. Wolvin and G. C. Coakley, *Listening,* 4th ed. (Dubuque, IA: William C. Brown Publishers, 1992).
4. Bruce E. Gronbeck, "Oral Communication Skills in a Technological Age," *Vital Speeches,* 47 (1981): 431.
5. Ralph Nichols and Leonard Stevens, "Listening to People," *Harvard Business Review* 35 (1957): 85–92.

6. See, for example, P. T. Rankin, "The Measurement of the Ability to Understand Spoken Language," *Dissertation Abstracts* 12 (1926): 847; D. Bird, "Teaching Listening Comprehension," *Journal of Communication* 3 (1953): 127–30; Mariam E. Wilt, "A Study of Teacher Awareness of Listening As a Factor in Elementary Education," *Journal of Educational Research* 43 (1950): 626; D. Bird, "Have You Tried Listening?" *Journal of the American Dietetic Association* 30 (1954): 255–30; and B. Markgraf, "An Observational Study Determining the Amount of Time That Students in the Tenth and Twelfth Grades Are Expected to Listen in the Classroom" (Master's thesis, University of Wisconsin, 1957).

7. Phillip Emmert, "The Reification of Listening" (Paper presented at the International Listening Association Preconvention Research Conference, Jacksonville, FL, March 1991).

8. C. V. Roberts, "The Validation of Listening Tests: Cutting of the Gordian Knot," *Journal of the International Listening Association* 2 (1988): 1–19.

9. C. M. Kelly, "Listening: Complex of Activities—and a Unitary Skill?" *Speech Monographs* 34 (1967): 455–66.

10. Robert Bostrom, *Listening Behavior: Measurement and Application* (New York: Guilford Press, 1990).

11. Brian H. Spitzberg and William R. Cupach, *Interpersonal Communication Competence* (Beverly Hills, CA: Sage, 1984).

12. Judy C. Pearson, "The Influence of Sex and Sexism on the Criticism of Classroom Speeches" (Paper presented at the International Communication Association, Philadelphia, PA, May 1979); and Jo A. Sprague, "An Investigation of the Written Critique Behavior of College Communication Instructors" (Ph.D. dissertation, Purdue University, 1971), 44–46.

13. Emil R. Pfister, "A Study of the Influence of Certain Selected Factors on the Ratings of Speech Performances" (Ed.D. dissertation, Michigan State University, 1955), 88.

14. Pfister, 92.

15. Pearson, 14.

16. Wolvin and Coakley, 1992.

17. Stephen Lee Young, "Student Perceptions of Helpfulness in Classroom Speech Criticism," *Speech Teacher* 23 (1974): 222–34.

THE AUDIENCE

Chapter 6

When we show our respect for other living things, they respond with respect for us.

Arapaho Proverb[1]

QUESTION OUTLINE

I. Why should a speaker analyze the audience?

II. What are three levels of analyzing audiences?

III. What are some of the demographic features of the audience that you should consider in your audience analysis?

IV. What are the four methods of audience analysis?

V. What is the importance of the situation or context in which you speak?

VI. What is unique about your classmates as an audience?

VII. How does a speaker adapt to an audience?

VIII. How are moral choices related to audience analysis?

Introduction

Don London loved politics. When Professional Secretaries International (PSI) invited him to talk to their group, he enthusiastically agreed. They did not give him a topic for his speech, so he decided to promote his favorite candidate, conservative Republican Judge Sanford D. Hodson. On the night of the speech, Don was startled to see as many men in the group as women. Nearly all the men were employers who were there for "Boss's Night" as guests of their secretaries; nearly all the women were secretaries.

As Don delivered his speech, he noticed he was getting very little reaction from the members of PSI, but the men were showing unabashed enthusiasm for his message of support for Judge Hodson. After a rather chilly farewell from his hostesses, Don returned home mystified because half of his audience seemed to dislike his speech, whereas the other half loved it.

The next day, a PSI member who had heard the speech told Don what had happened. The predominantly male guests were affluent middle- or upper-management people and owners of companies. They were mostly Republicans and supporters of Judge Hodson. The secretaries who had invited Don to speak were predominantly registered Democrats who strongly rejected Judge Hodson's political position on the issues. Few of them knew Don before the speech, but afterward they disliked him and his message.

Focusing on the Audience

The story of Don London emphasizes the importance of knowing your audience before you speak. As speakers we too often focus on ourselves. We speak on our favorite topics, without considering what the audience might want or need to hear. We use language that we understand without considering that the audience might not understand.[2]

Don London should have known that the audience would consist of both men and women, that the men were predominantly Republican and the women predominantly Democrats. He should have known beforehand that a talk extolling Judge Hodson was inappropriate for the occasion, that it offended the very people who had invited him to speak. Don could have given a speech with an important message for everyone if he had known about audience analysis.

What is audience analysis? **Audience analysis** is discovering as much as possible about an audience for the purpose of improving communication. Why should a speaker analyze an audience? Think of public speaking as another version of the kind of speaking you do every day. Nearly always, when you meet a stranger, you size up that person before you disclose your message. Similarly, public speaking requires that you meet and know the members of your audience so you are able to create a message for them. Public speaking is not talking to oneself in front of a group; instead, it is effective message transmission from one person to many people in a setting in which speaker and audience influence each other.

Let us consider the wide variety of audiences you might face in your lifetime:

Your classmates	Fellow parents	A religious group
Fellow workers	Retired people	A board of directors
Members of a union	A group of friends	A group of children
A civic organization		

Would you talk to all of these audiences about the same topic or in the same way? Of course not. Your choice of topic and your approach to that topic are both strongly influenced by the nature of your audience. We focus on the audience in a speech by learning the nature of that audience.

Know your audience well if you want your speech to succeed.

When we talk to individuals, we are relatively careful about what we say and how we say it. We speak differently to strangers than to intimates, differently to people we respect than to people we do not respect, and differently to children than to adults. Similarly, we need to be aware of audience characteristics when we choose a topic and when we decide how we are going to present that topic to the audience.

Imagine that you are about to speak to a new audience. How would you learn about the people in your audience? First, you could rely on conventional wisdom. Second, you could conduct a demographic analysis. Finally, you could engage in psychographic analysis. Let us examine each of these increasingly specific ways of learning more about an audience.

Conventional Wisdom

Conventional wisdom is the popular opinions of the time about issues, styles, topics, trends and social moves; the customary set of understandings of what is true or right. Conventional wisdom includes what most people are said to think. It cannot be proven and it may not be lasting. *Newsweek* devotes a few column inches each week to conventional wisdom about people and issues. Sometimes the President of the United States gets an arrow up (positive sign) one week and an arrow down (negative sign) the next week— on the same issue. Let us look at how conventional wisdom relates to audience analysis.

The conventional wisdom about college students goes something like this: in the 1960s, students went from well-behaved, high-conforming, somewhat funloving people to flaming antiwar, pro-civil rights activists; in the 1970s, students were seen as drug-crazed, society-changing folks, and were partially credited with driving a President of the United States out of office, stopping an unpopular war, and getting rid of almost all required courses; in the 1980s, the so-called me generation, students were said to care mainly about highly practical courses, highly lucrative majors, the return of military education, and the revival of fraternities and sororities.

What does conventional wisdom say about the 1990s? The decade's first survey of American college students, the twenty-fifth annual survey of first-year college students by UCLA and the American Council on Education, found business majors (the major of choice in the 1980s) down from 25 percent in 1987 to 18 percent in 1990; the need

Analyzing an Audience

Characteristics such as age, ethnicity, and gender can influence what interests an audience and how an audience receives a message.

to be "very well off financially" was down for the second year in a row after seventeen years of increases (it was still at 74 percent in 1990); the largest number of students ever (43 percent) said it was essential or very important to "influence social values"; increasingly large numbers (88 percent) think the government should do more to control pollution (that was 78 percent in 1981); and, finally, 38 percent of the students said it is essential or very important to help promote racial understanding (the low was 27 percent in 1986). That is what nearly 200,000 first-year students from 382 colleges said about their beliefs.[3]

Keeping in mind that conventional wisdom is a gross oversimplification and that it is sometimes based more on the whim of the moment than on deep-seated convictions, we could still say that, at the beginning of the 1990s, first-year college students were less likely to choose a business major, slightly less concerned (but still extremely high overall) about getting rich, more concerned about influencing social values, more interested in government intervention in the environment, and somewhat more interested in promoting racial equality. Keeping track of trends helps the public speaker address concerns from a context that makes sense to the audience. A pro-military speech in 1970 would have been an act of courage; a pro-military speech in the summer of 1990 during Desert Storm was commonplace.

Demographics

What are some characteristics of the audience that can affect how they interpret your message? Some of the more obvious characteristics of an audience are called **demographics,** which literally means "characteristics of the people." They include gender, age, ethnicity, economic status, occupation, education, religion, organizational memberships, and physical characteristics.[4]

Demographic Components of Audience Analysis

Gender	Education
Age	Religion
Ethnicity	Organizational Membership
Economic Status	Physical Characteristics
Occupation	

Gender

What difference does it make to a speaker whether the audience is composed of men, women, or a mixture of the two? With some topics, the gender represented by the audience may make no difference at all. With others, gender representation may make all the difference in the world.

A recent example that highlights the importance of audience gender is the Anita Hill–Clarence Thomas hearings. As you may recall, all of the people on the Senate Judiciary Committee were men. In a speech given shortly after the hearings, Julia Hughes Jones, Auditor for the State of Arkansas, stated,

> Back in April, the National Women's Political Caucus raised an interesting question: What if fourteen women, instead of fourteen men, had sat on the Senate Judiciary Committee during the Clarence Thomas confirmation hearings?
>
> Many would cry, unfair! Yet, it was just as unfair to have fourteen men and no women. Shouldn't at least half of them have been women, considering that women are more than half the population?
>
> Then, maybe, just maybe, women's voices would have been heard. Maybe the experiences and concerns of women would not have been so quickly dismissed or ridiculed. And maybe all of America would have benefitted.[5]

Jones and many others felt that the outcome of the Anita Hill–Clarence Thomas hearings was a result of the gender of the audience that heard the testimony. Their sentiment was that in this instance, the topic was so sex-linked that a fair outcome would have occurred only if the audience was mixed-sex rather than all men. You may need to consider if your topic is sex-linked or sex-neutral, and modify your treatment of it when speaking before generally male, generally female, or mixed-sex audiences.

Given that the gender of the audience affects how you will plan and deliver your speech, you must consider the factors that may cause women and men to react differently to certain topics. You should be aware of the fact that some women (and some men) feel that women have been discriminated against, and will be watchful for signs of discrimination from speakers.

Throughout history, women have been treated as "less than men." For example, one speaker reminded her audience that:

> More than a thousand years ago in Greece, an entire meeting of the Church Synod was devoted to one question: Is a woman a human being or an animal?
>
> It was finally settled by vote, and the consensus was that we do indeed belong to the human race. It passed, however, by just one vote.[6]

Although you probably cannot remember when women did not have the right to vote, grandmothers and great-grandmothers of our era told stories about the passage of the 19th Amendment in 1920, which gave women the right to vote.

While circumstances are better in some instances for women today, you should keep in mind that women and men are still not treated equally in most arenas. One speaker noted the discrimination that occurs in education:

Three-fourths of all high schools still violate the federal law banning sex discrimination in education.

Collegiate women undergraduates still receive only 70 percent of the aid that undergraduate males get in grants and work-study jobs.

Women's college sports programs have never equalled men's in funding and doubtfully ever will.

Only seven states have anti-discrimination regulations that cover all educational levels.[7]

Economically, women fare even worse. Julia Hughes Jones explained,

Economically, women have the right to own property, inherit estates, and have a job; but American women face the worst gender-based pay gap in the developed world. We still earn seventy-one cents for every dollar earned by a man, and the average female college graduate earns less than the average male high school graduate. Even more telling is that the average female high school graduate earns less than the average male high school dropout.[8]

At the same time, an increasing number of women are working outside the home. Some are providing a second income in a family, many are single heads of family, and many are simply single. National figures continue to indicate that women are commonly in pink-collar jobs—secretarial and clerical—and underrepresented in upper management, ownership, and boards of directors. The earning power of women tends to be less than that of men at almost all educational levels. Women, even working women, continue to be responsible for more of the nurturing, child care, cooking and cleaning, and housekeeping chores than men. Men continue to have shorter lives, more heart attacks, and more lung cancer, though the gap is narrowing. Both men and women seem to have problems with gaining weight too easily, stopping smoking and drinking, and gracefully tolerating the inevitable effects of advancing age.

Gender considerations are linked to public speaking. Analyzing an audience on the basis of gender is not quite such an easy matter, however. While the average woman may earn less money than her male counterpart, many women make more money than the average man. A particular woman may be an executive, and a specific man may be a househusband. Similarly, even though women have had the right to vote for only about 75 years, 10 million more women of voting age reside in the United States today than men. Furthermore, women voters have been the deciding factor in many political races. Assumptions about an audience on the basis of biological sex may or may not be true.

Another gender issue is whether individuals in the audience are masculine or feminine. While most women are feminine and most men are masculine, this is not always the case. Some women have internalized masculine characteristics—they are aggressive, ambitious, and task-oriented. Some men have accepted feminine characteristics—they are nurturing, cooperative, and sensitive. Many women and men are **androgynous**—they combine masculine and feminine traits and exhibit them as they deem appropriate.

Finally, you need to consider the sexual orientation of audience members. Gay and lesbian audience members might not respond to issues in the same ways as their heterosexual counterparts. You also need to be careful of the heterosexist assumptions that you make if you are discussing relationships or other salient topics. For example, if you are discussing couples in cohabiting relationships, you should not assume that these couples always include a male and a female. You should also avoid discussions of relational roles in which you identify "the woman's role" and "the man's role." Furthermore, do not assume that all people in relationships will eventually marry, since most states have laws prohibiting same-sex marriages.

You must also remember to be sensitive to language choices that suggest that people are married or are planning to get married. Do not use terms like "family," which conjures up images of traditional relationships or "husband and wife," which implies heterosexuality. Instead, opt for more inclusive choices like "committed relationships" or "relational partners."

In general, you should exercise caution in making sweeping generalizations based on gender about your audience. Gender issues concern not only our biological sex, but also our internalized masculinity and femininity, and our sexual orientation. In your language choices, be inclusive rather than exclusive. Instead of "You and your wife," say "You and your partner." Do not call attention to biological sex as an exclusive descriptor such as "You men . . ." or "You Women . . ."

Choose topics that are interesting to both women and men. Use examples that are free of stereotypes and that are interesting to people, regardless of gender. Do not assume that the women are housewives or that the men work. Do not downgrade any sexual orientation in examples or illustrations of your main or subpoints.

Age

A *Wall Street Journal* news item entitled "CBS Study Shows the Advantage of Marketing to Older Viewers" inspired Howard Kaufman to write this little ditty:

> *It's me the network's paging,*
> *I'm their viewing angel, aging.*
> *It's on me that they're depending*
> *For watching and then spending.*
> *With my age group now they traffic,*
> *I'm their favorite demographic.*[9]

Advancing maturity changes people's preferences. Whereas small children seem to love loud noise, fast action, and a relatively high level of confusion and messiness, older people may be bothered by these same characteristics. Look at these topics and decide which are more appropriate for youths, middle-aged people, or the elderly.

Placing your kids in college	Selecting a career
Choosing a major	Planning your estate
Health care in hostels	Saving dollars from taxes
Changing careers	Investment opportunities
Dating	Social security reform

The age of your audience members will affect the topic you choose and how you treat a particular topic. You might speak about powerful stereo speakers to a younger audience, but reserve the topic of cashing in your annuities for an older audience. On the other hand, you may discuss financial security with younger people or older people. However, your approach will be different if you know that your audience consists of traditional undergraduate sophomores or members of the American Association of Retired Persons.

The age of your audience will also partly determine what the audience knows from its experience. Some people will know about the Depression, World War II, and Civil Defense. Others will remember the Vietnam War, the Beatles, and the Civil Rights struggles. Today's youths will know the names of the latest music groups and the newest trends in clothing.

When you give your speech, consider the ages of the individuals in the audience and what you need to do to account for that demographic characteristic. How do the ages represented in your audience relate to the topic you selected and the approach you used to communicate it? Age is part of audience focus and it is a primary ingredient in audience analysis.

Ethnic groups have communication traditions that affect how members of that group speak and listen.

Ethnicity

Another important factor of audience analysis includes the ethnic makeup and identity of your audience members. Ethnicity is defined "psychologically and historically through shared symbols, meanings, and norms. Ethnicity includes religious beliefs and practices, language, a sense of historical continuity, common ancestry or place of origin."[10] Ethnic groups have communication traditions that affect how members of that group speak and listen. Many ethnic groups have their own communication systems that are only partially shared with other groups.

Cultural rules, conversational patterns, and expectations arise within interethnic communication events based on ethnic identity of the speaker and listener. For instance, African Americans and European Americans, while sharing aspects of American culture, each have unique styles of communicating. Sometimes dialects differ, sometimes conversational rules and expectations differ, and sometimes interactional styles like use of argument and discussion differ between the two groups.[11]

The following story illustrates some of the influences ethnicity can have on a public speaking event.

> *Reverend Dr. Clarence E. Whitlock, a Presbyterian minister of Scottish descent, was asked to exchange pulpits with Reverend Jackson Brown, the pastor of the local African Methodist Episcopal Church. Accustomed to his own flock, kiddingly known around town as "God's frozen people" for their very proper behavior and quiet demeanor in church, Reverend Dr. Whitlock approached the African American congregation with some newly discovered stagefright. He did not know what to expect. After some spirited singing by a woman who sang loudly and lively while playing the piano, Reverend Dr. Whitlock rose to speak. He had no sooner completed his third sentence when the air was punctuated by "Amens" from scattered members of the congregation. A few sentences later, he heard even more "Amens" from the people. He was on a roll! For a man who had rarely heard*

*a hymnal drop during his sermons, the effect of having a congregation respond to nearly
every sentence was almost more than he could handle. Reverend Dr. Whitlock left the
AME Church that day with a satisfied smile on his face.*

Ethnicity and religion converge in this story to demonstrate how different an African
American congregation was to a minister who had previously preached only to a European American congregation. Ethnic identity is a significant part of audience analysis;
understanding and appreciating the ethnic makeup of your audience should be a factor in
topic selection and approach.

As speakers, we also need to be sure that we do not accidently or needlessly injure or
insult audience members with ethnic backgrounds different than our own. Members of
the dominant culture of the United States have had tumultuous relationships with members of smaller **co-cultures.** For example Cuban Americans, Puerto Ricans, Vietnamese,
and Appalachians are just a few of the groups that have been excluded from partaking in
many of the privileges members of the dominant culture enjoy. Members of various ethnic groups are sensitive to the discrimination that has limited their people. In her speech
entitled "King—From Martin to Rodney: Changing White Attitudes," Harriet R. Michel
described the African American perception of historical and contemporary interethnic relations in the United States.

> *. . . that golden age of civil rights had two major shortcomings, both of which impact on
> the attitudes of today.*
>
> *First, it was too short lived, lasting less than twenty years. Nonetheless, society
> assumed that, in the case of blacks, the effects of 350 years of slavery and legal
> discrimination could be overcome by the new laws and new programs. As far as the
> broader society was concerned this period of attention to racial issues would exonerate
> America, allowing its long standing debt to blacks to be stamped "Paid in Full." That is
> why many whites ask today with annoyance, "What do blacks want? We gave them their
> civil rights, the rest they must earn on individual merit." It appears that few white
> Americans feel an obligation to make any further sacrifices on behalf of the nation's black
> minority.*
>
> *The second shortcoming of that era was despite the claim of conservatives that great
> society programs robbed people of initiative and created what they call a victim mentality,
> the monies committed to training the poor, and providing opportunities for jobs and
> businesses, were never sufficient. Somehow we justified the expenditure of billions of
> dollars to develop weapons like fighter planes which were redundant in an age of nuclear
> warheads, but we haggled about the dollars necessary to develop human capital. If social
> programs were over budget or failed to produce expected results in a limited period of time,
> we scrapped them as useless. Such standards were not applied to the massive bailout of the
> savings and loan industry, or the bailout of the Chrysler corporation. We declared those
> situations critical to our national interest and the money kept flowing.*
>
> *In addition to the shortcomings already mentioned, the civil rights movement also
> produced new problems which continue to plague us.*
>
> *A backlash of resentment developed among many whites who became anxious and
> threatened by the challenge to their traditional position of advantage and privilege.
> Unfortunately, those feelings provided fertile ground for recruiters of the new
> conservatism of the 80s.*
>
> *Finally, while the new laws and programs through affirmative action provided
> institutional access, they did nothing to challenge the traditional standards, values and
> definitions that institutions used to judge, promote or reward their members. Most of the
> conventional thinking and behavior of institutions remained in tact. Therefore, the
> majority culture continued to define each minority group based on existing prejudices
> and misconceptions. An example of this problem is illustrated in a* New York Times
> *article on the racial brawl that shut down Olivet College in Michigan last spring. I quote,*
>
> > *The college is a sociological test tube, mixing white students from mostly rural
> > Michigan towns who have little or no contact with blacks and a tiny minority of*

blacks mostly from Detroit, isolated in a remote and alien setting. It has no black professors or administrators and only one black employee out of 132, the minority recruitment officer, who is frequently on the road.

Olivet College like many colleges was desegregated but not integrated. One analyst on race relations says,

The remedial steps society took to deal with racism have been desegregation steps. We've mixed black students in white institutions without doing anything about the attitudes of whites and the culture of the institutions. As a government and a society we put them there and went home.[12]

Michel offered ideas that can be helpful to the public speaker who wishes to be sensitive to the feelings of many African Americans.

We must fight white misperceptions that:

1. *Discrimination is a thing of the past;*
2. *Our nation's civil rights problems were solved twenty years ago;*
3. *The minority poor are wholly responsible for their own plight;*
4. *Past racial discrimination has no effect on the opportunities that blacks have today;*
5. *Poverty and the social pathology that often accompanies it are a black or minority problem;*
6. *Government programs have not worked because many blacks are still in poverty;*
7. *Blacks and whites have the same opportunities in obtaining jobs, housing, and employment;*
8. *Blacks are angry because they haven't been able to succeed like Asians and other minorities;*
9. *Affirmative action gives undeserving blacks opportunities at the expense of whites;*
10. *Blacks blame racism for everything.*[13]

These misperceptions may be held by people you know. They may even be held by people in your audience. If they are misperceptions, as Michel states, how can you as an ethical public speaker deal with such notions? You need to consider your own assumptions, values, and language in your attempt to be sensitive to members of ethnic co-cultures.

Sometimes even well-known public speakers make errors that are outrageous to members of ethnic co-cultures. Well-meaning people can accidentally use metaphors, language, or examples that members of other co-cultures find offensive. You can learn to be more sensitive to other groups by practicing your speech with friends who have different backgrounds than your own, or by interviewing and observing other people to determine the kind of language they avoid and the types of examples, analogies, and metaphors that they employ.

Economic Status

What is the economic status of your audience? Are they primarily wealthy individuals or are they from lower economic groups? People who are wealthier tend to be more conservative, are often older, may have more education, and have probably traveled more than less wealthy people. Wealthy people may be less open to new ideas because they are accustomed to being treated deferentially, with courteous submission to their wishes or judgments. They may be more difficult to persuade because they feel that they have already made good choices. On the other hand, less wealthy people may be more liberal, younger, may be less educated because of their age, and have probably lived in a relatively smaller geographical area. Less wealthy people may be open to new ideas and may be more easily persuaded because they have less to lose.

Some topics are appropriate for more affluent audiences, while other topics are right for less financially successful people. Tax cuts for the rich may be a fitting topic for residents of pricey retirement villages, while learning to survive on next to nothing might be the right topic for a support group of unmarried, teenage mothers. The appropriateness of topics like ideas for vacations, plans for retirement, or suggestions for investments could vary greatly depending upon the overall economic status of your audience. Topics like these can be relevant to a wide spectrum of people, as long as you tailor your approach to fit the audience's needs and experiences.

Occupation

If you are speaking to a group of employed individuals, you will want to know what occupations are represented. Recently, one of the authors spoke to several hundred women in public service in Ohio. The audience included people in the Governor's cabinet, state senators and representatives, mayors of many Ohio cities, and other women in elected office. The audience also included women in clerical, secretarial, and support staffs. The topic of the speech was the role of gender in the workplace. Needless to say, the task was difficult. Examples and illustrations had to be generic rather than specific. If an anecdote about a successful professional woman was used, it had to be balanced with an anecdote about the difficulties of minimal wage jobs in order to include all audience members.

Your topic choice is affected by the occupations of the people in your audience. If your audience is comprised of physicians, you might not want to talk about increased health care costs. If you are speaking to attorneys, you may want to avoid discussions about settling issues out of court. Some teachers and professors like to hear about labor unions, but their supervisors and educational administrators are less fond of the topic.

The language you use in your speech is similarly affected by the audience members' occupations. You should avoid jargon that is unfamiliar to your audience, but you can use a few words that are unique to them in their work. Do your audience members come from professions in which people use concrete, specific language, or are they more likely to appreciate metaphors and poetic language?

Can you think of illustrations that come from the field of work represented by the people in your audience? Can you draw comparisons between your topic and what the audience members spend the majority of their day doing? Do you know some of the individuals that they hold as expert or as trustworthy? Try to incorporate some of these illustrations, comparisons, and individuals in your speech.

Education

Education is related to economic status and occupation. A person's level of education may tell you very little about his or her intelligence, ambition, sophistication, or status. However, people with more education tend to read and write more, are usually better acquainted with the news, are more likely to have traveled, and are more likely to have higher incomes. What are some of the implications of educational level for how the speaker approaches the audience?

1. People who read and write regularly tend to have more advanced vocabularies, so adjust your language choices to the educational level of your audience.
2. People who are receptive to new information need less background and explanation on current issues than those who are not.
3. People who have seen more of the world tend to be more sophisticated about differences between people and cultures.

Take your audience's educational level into account as part of your analysis, because it may be an important determinant of topics and approaches.

Religion

One of the authors gave her final speech in an introductory public speaking class on the hopefulness of Christmas. Since the speech was scheduled at the end of the fall term, just two weeks before the Christian holiday, she thought her timing was perfect. However, the public speaking instructor was a devout atheist who deducted points from the speech for poor audience analysis.

As the globe shrinks and people travel around the world, we need to be increasingly concerned about acknowledging religious differences. We also, as the anecdote suggests, need to avoid making assumptions that all audience members are Christian. Today, an increasing number of Americans are Muslims. Our audiences may include Buddhists, Hindus, Jews, atheists, or agnostics. Even Christians do not share identical religious beliefs. Evangelical Christians do not hold the same beliefs as Roman Catholics, and Baptists have some fundamentally different beliefs from Presbyterians or Unitarians.

Religious beliefs influence behaviors—even in preferences of food and drink. One religion's pleasure is another religion's poison. For example, for many years, Roman Catholics did not eat meat on Friday. Today, some devout Catholics still substitute cheese or fish dishes for meat on Friday. Orthodox Jews eat only kosher food. Mormons do not indulge in alcoholic or caffeine-laden beverages.

Religious beliefs also influence values. Mormons discourage the use of birth control while Protestants have multiple views on the topic. Unitarians value education and tend to be quite liberal. People in fundamentalist religions are more conservative. Episcopalians may value money more than some other religious groups.

Your own religious beliefs may blind you to religious differences. If you are Jewish, you may be highly verbal and love to argue with others. You might not realize that people with different religious backgrounds have less interest in both verbosity and argument. As a public speaker addressing a generally non-Jewish audience, you might be viewed as long-winded or combative, but if the same speech were to be delivered at a meeting at the synagogue, you might be viewed as humorous, intelligent, reflective, or gifted.

Organizational Membership

My neighbor, Louis Gerrig, would hate to be thought predictable, but if I know just a few of the organizations to which he belongs, then I can accurately infer a number of his beliefs. For example, I know that he is an officer in his local union, the member of a small fundamentalist religious group, and a member of the American Legion. I inferred, based on his membership in these three groups, that he would hold these beliefs:

We should have tariffs to protect our economy.

We should commit more tax dollars to defense.

We should permit prayers in public schools.

We should prohibit abortions.

We should spend less on welfare and Aid to Dependent Children.

We should not have jobs reserved for minorities.

We should not pay women the same as men for similar jobs.

To check my inferences, I went to Louis Gerrig to find out if I was correct. The only one that he disagreed with was reserving some jobs for minorities. He thought that idea was all right when it was limited to tax-supported jobs, such as police and firefighters, so Louis was not 100 percent predictable, but six out of seven is not bad.

Your knowledge about group memberships in your audience is valuable information, because group membership signals sets of beliefs that people tend to embrace. For example, not all Rotarians believe with strong conviction in everything the group represents, but they probably endorse much of it or they would not identify themselves as Rotarians. Organizations typically reflect beliefs about issues, causes, and concerns. People belong to organizations reflecting interlocking clusters of beliefs that help us predict their behavior. Few hard-core conservatives read *The New Republic*, and liberals rarely carry a copy of *National Review*. Our memberships in political parties, street gangs, unions, and

Our memberships in political parties, street gangs, unions, and professional organizations signal our beliefs.

professional organizations signal our beliefs. The confident speaker knows about audience memberships and how they influence topic and approach.

Physical Characteristics

Imagine that you were going to speak to an audience of the American Federation of the Blind, to a group of individuals in wheelchairs, or to people who had another specific physical disability. How would you adjust your speech? Most of us do a poor job of adapting to these situations. Indeed, members of such audiences generally ask that they be treated like those without disabilities. Nonetheless, we tend to speak louder, enunciate more clearly, or make other changes. We also may become self-conscious about language usage that disparages specific people, or we may be insensitive to negative stereotypes that we use. Even if your audience does not include people with physical disabilities, it is important to try to rid yourself of negative stereotyping. A great deal of such negative categorizing is done so routinely by people that they do not even realize they are guilty of perpetuating myths about individuals with disabilities. For example, in his speech "Language and the Future of the Blind," Marc Maurer, President of the National Federation of the Blind, at their annual convention in 1989, discussed one of the stereotypes that he found particularly offensive: the idea that people who are not sighted are incompetent.

> Recently an advertisement appeared from the Carrollton Corporation, a manufacturer of mobile homes. Apparently the Carrollton Corporation was facing fierce competition from other mobile home builders, who were selling their products at a lower price. Consequently, the Carrollton Corporation wanted to show that its higher priced units were superior. In an attempt to convey this impression, the company depicted the blind as sloppy and incompetent. Its advertisement said in part: "Some manufacturers put out low-end products. But they are either as ugly as three miles of bad road, or they have so many defects—crumpled metal, dangling moldings, damaged carpet—that they look like they were built at some school for the blind." What a description! There is the ugliness of three miles of bad road, or crumpled metal, dangling moldings, and damaged carpet. The slipshod work is all attributed to the incompetence of the blind. It is not a portrayal calculated to inspire confidence or likely to assist blind people to find employment.[14]

In this section we discussed the demographic characteristics of an audience. We discussed the importance of gender, age, ethnicity, economic status, occupation, education, religion, organizational membership, and physical characteristics. In the next section, we turn to psychographics, which takes us even further down the path of audience analysis.

Psychographics

Psychographics goes beyond demographics to look at the influences of demographics on a person's behavior. Psychographics began as a way to measure people's thinking about products, issues, and ideas. It quickly became an applied science when companies found that they could find customers, their "target audience," through these measures.

One broadcasting consultant told 500 radio and television station owners and managers how they could use psychographics in their business. The consultant conducted hundreds of telephone interviews, discovered people's interests, and found out where they shopped. The resulting information helped the stations target the audience that would be most appealing to their advertisers. This information went well beyond the demographics of race, income, and occupation to reveal what stations people listened to and why, what products they purchased, and how much they spent at the mall and through mail order. The psychographic study concluded with types of audiences in the community.

One category of people might belong to a country club, shop at the most expensive shopping mall, buy high-cost clothing, purchase a new car every other year, and drink costly liquor and wines. Another category might hang out at a corner bar, shop at discount stores, eat at fast-food outlets, use mass transit, and not drink alcohol at all. The people who sell products want to know who uses them, where they live, how much they spend, and where they buy.

What does psychographics have to do with public speaking? In the same way that businesses are interested in their target audience, a public speaker needs to know the audience members in order to inform or influence them. Just as businesses need to know more than demographics, so do speakers. You do not have to do telephone surveys to discover the psychographic characteristics of your audience. Your demographic analysis might reveal that your audience represents a number of ethnic origins, but a psychographic analysis goes beyond that data to reveal more specific and smaller cultures. The culture might be a category of people who crave expensive clothes, houses, and cars, or it could be another group who are struggling with language, status, and jobs.

As an aspect of audience analysis, psychographics is an important feature for you to consider. Psychographics can help you determine what the audience wants to know about in an informative speech and what the audience is willing to do in a persuasive speech. An audience in a $20,000-per-year private school will be markedly different from an audience in an inner-city community college, and, within each kind of educational institution, the audience in every public speaking classroom will be unique. Demographic and psychographic analysis will help you discover that uniqueness in your audience, as it did when the consultant examined community uniqueness for the broadcasters.

Some examples of questions that can be answered by psychographic analysis of the audience include the following:

What position do my audience members take on issues?

What are their attitudes about information that I could present?

How will their culture invite them to respond to my message?

How does my message fit into the audience's aspirations?

What obstacles to my message are posed by the audience's identity?

Methods of Audience Analysis

Observation
Informants
Interviews
Questionnaires

Using demographic analysis together with psychographic analysis can provide you with useful information. It can also increase your confidence as a public speaker when you have a feel for how the audience will respond to you and your ideas.

Some speakers seem to be able to analyze an audience intuitively, but most of us have to resort to formal and informal means of gathering such information. Individuals in advertising, marketing, and public relations have developed complex technological means of collecting information from audiences before, during, and after their messages.[15] However, for most of us, the ways we commonly collect information about audiences are through observation, informants, interviews, and questionnaires.

Methods of Audience Analysis

Observation

Watching and listening reveal the most about your audience during your **observation.** Looking at audience members might reveal their age, ethnic origin, and gender. More careful observation can reveal marital status by the presence or absence of rings; materialism by furs, expensive jewelry, or costly clothing; and even religious affiliation by such symbols as a cross or Star of David. Many people in an audience advertise their membership in a group by exhibiting the symbols of the group to which they belong.

In the classroom, you have the added advantage of listening to everyone in your audience. Your classmates' speeches, their topics, issues, arguments, and evidence, all reveal more about them than you could learn in a complex questionnaire.

Your eyes and ears become the most important tools of audience analysis as you train yourself to become a skilled observer.

Informants

When you are invited to give a speech outside the classroom, your best source of information may be the person who invites you. This person can be your inside **informant,** who can tell you the following:

1. What topics are appropriate
2. What the organization believes or does
3. How many people are likely to attend
4. What the setting or occasion will be
5. How long you should speak
6. What the characteristics of the audience are

A key question to ask is why you were invited to speak, since that information will help establish credibility in your introduction. If they want you because of your expertise on needlepoint, auto mechanics, or macramé, then you will want to stress that in your speech. If they invited you because you are a model citizen, then emphasize that area of your life. In any case, your informant should be able to help analyze your audience so there will be no surprises.

Within the classroom, all of your classmates serve as informants. Listen to their speeches. What do they value or believe? What topics interest them? With what groups or organizations are they affiliated? Your classmates' speeches can provide you with valuable information about the classroom audience that will listen to your own speeches.

Interviews

When you are invited to speak to a group outside the classroom, you can initiate audience analysis by conducting **interviews** with one or more people from the group—either in person or on the phone. An interview for information on the audience should focus on the same questions listed in the preceding section on informants.

When you are conducting an audience analysis for a classroom speech, you can talk to a few people from class. Try to discover their opinion of your topic, how they think the class will respond to it, and any helpful suggestions for best communicating the topic.

The only problem with interviews is that they take time. Nonetheless, if the outcome is important, interviews are a way to discover more about your audience.

Questionnaires

Whereas interviews take more time to execute than to plan, **questionnaires** take more time to plan than to execute. The key to writing a good questionnaire is to be brief. Respondents tend to register their distaste for long questionnaires by not filling them out.

What should you include in your brief questionnaire? It depends, of course, on what you wish to know. Usually you will be trying to discover what an audience knows about a topic and the audience's predisposition toward that topic. You can ask open-ended questions, yes-or-no questions, degree questions, or a mixture of all three—as long as you do not ask too many questions. **Open-ended questions** are like those on an essay test that asks an opinion—for example:

What do you think should be done about teenage pregnancies?

What policy should govern working men and women when their child is born?

What punishments would be appropriate for white-collar crimes?

Yes-or-no questions force a decision—for example:

Should pregnant teenagers be allowed to complete their high school education?

_____ Yes _____ No

Should a man be allowed paternity leave when his child is born?

_____ Yes _____ No

Degree questions ask to what extent a respondent agrees or disagrees with a question:

I believe that pregnant students should finish high school.

Very strongly agree	Strongly agree	Agree	Strongly disagree	Very strongly disagree

or may present a continuum of possible answers from which the respondent can choose:

Embezzlement of $5,000 should be punished by which of the following?

$5,000 fine 1 year jail	$4,000 fine 2 yrs. jail	$3,000 fine 3 yrs. jail	$2,000 fine 4 yrs. jail	$1,000 5 yrs. jail

---

Teenage Pregnancy

1. I think that pregnant teenagers should finish high school.
   _____ Yes _____ No

2. I think that pregnant teenagers should complete high school with their class instead of in special sections or places.
   _____ Yes _____ No

3. At what grade do you think pregnant teenagers should be allowed to continue their education with their class?
   7th   8th   9th   10th   11th   12th

4. To what extent do you agree that our society punishes pregnant teenagers too much?
   | Very strongly agree | Strongly agree | Neutral | Strongly disagree | Very strongly disagree |

5. What, if anything, do you think should be done about the males who are responsible for the pregnancies?

Figure 1

Sample questionnaire.

How much paternity leave do you think men should receive?

None   Three days   One week   Two weeks   One month   Two months

These three kinds of questions can be used in a questionnaire to determine audience attitudes about an issue. A questionnaire such as the one in figure 1, administered before your speech, can provide you with useful information about your audience's feelings and positions on the issue you plan to discuss. All you have to do is keep it brief, pertinent, and clear.

Four factors are important in analyzing the situation you face as a speaker: the size of the audience, the occasion, the time, and the importance.

Situational Analysis

Size of Audience

The **size of the audience** is an important situational factor because it can determine the level of formality, the amount of interaction with the audience, the need for amplification systems, and the need for special visual aids. The larger the audience, the more responsibility the speaker has to carry the message. Larger audiences usually call for formality in tone and language; smaller audiences allow for a more casual approach, a less formal tone, and informal language. Very large audiences reduce the speaker's ability to observe and respond to subtle cues, such as facial expressions, and they invite audience members to be more passive than they might be in a smaller group. Large audiences often require microphones and podiums that can limit the speaker's movement, and they may require slides or large posters for visual aids.

Speakers need to be flexible enough to adapt to audience size. One of the authors was supposed to give a speech on leadership to an audience of over 100 students in an auditorium that held 250 people. Only 25 students appeared at the conference. Instead of a formal speech to a large group, the author faced a relatively small group in one corner of a large auditorium. Two hours later, the author was supposed to speak to a small group of 12 or 15 that turned out to be 50. Do not depend on the planners to be correct about the size of your audience. Instead, be ready to adapt to the size of the audience that actually appears.

You must also be prepared to adapt to other environmental factors. Your presentation may be plagued with an unusual room arrangement, an unfortunate sound system, poor lighting, a room that is too warm or too cool, the absence of a podium or lectern, a microphone that is not movable, or no access to audiovisual equipment. If you have specific audio, visual,

Situational Analysis

Size of audience
Occasion
Time
Importance

or environmental needs, you should make your requests to the individual who has invited you to speak. At the very least, you will want to inquire about the room in which you are to speak. Even so, you may be surprised to find that equipment is not functioning properly or that the room that was assigned to you has been changed.

Occasion

The **occasion** is the second situational factor that makes a difference in how a speaker adapts to an audience. The occasion sets up a number of unstated constraints. The speaker is supposed to be upbeat and even funny at an after-dinner speech, sober and serious at a ribbon cutting, full of energy and enthusiasm at a pep rally, and prudent and factual in a court of law. Even in the classroom, there are a number of unstated assumptions about the occasion that you violate at your own peril: you are expected to follow the assignment, deliver the speech extemporaneously, maintain eye contact, keep to the time limit, dress appropriately, and so on.

Outside the classroom, the confident speaker finds out what the expectations of the occasion are. Consider for a moment the unstated assumptions for these public speaking occasions:

A high school commencement address

A testimonial at a retirement party

A talk with the team before a big game

An awards ceremony for top employees

A pep talk to your salespeople

A keynote address at a conference

A "shape up" talk to employees

An announcement of layoffs at the plant

Each of these occasions calls for quite a different kind of speech, the parameters of which are not clearly stated but seem to be widely understood. Our society seems to dictate that you should not exhibit levity at funerals, nor should you be too intellectual at a ribbon cutting. One of the best ways to discover what is expected is to find out from the individual or the organization inviting you to speak.

Time

The third aspect of any speaking situation that makes a difference to a speaker is when the speech is given—the **time.** Time can include the time of day, the time that you speak during the occasion, and the amount of time you are expected to fill. Early morning speeches find an audience fresh but not quite ready for serious topics. After-lunch or after-dinner speeches invite the audience to sleep unless the speaker is particularly stimulating. The best situation occurs when the audience has come only to hear the speaker and that is all it expects to do.

The time you give the speech during an occasion can make a big difference in how receptive your audience happens to be. A speaker was asked to speak to an Alumni Academy, an audience consisting entirely of people who gave a thousand dollars or more per year to the university. Seven deans were supposed to tell the Academy about their colleges in a series of five-minute speeches—each of which lasted seven minutes or more. By the time the last speaker was scheduled to speak, the audience was tired. Instead of giving a five-to-seven-minute presentation about the university, the speaker told audience members they would think more kindly of the university if they were simply allowed to go have dinner. The audience applauded and left, thinking good thoughts about the speaker who didn't speak because the audience was too exhausted to listen. Even when you are the last speaker in your class, however, you will not be allowed to avoid giving the speech. Instead, when you know you will be one of the last speakers for the day, you should do your best to be stimulating, novel, and empathetic with an audience that has grown tired of hearing speeches.

The amount of time you are expected to fill is still another aspect of time. You will probably find that people are genuinely relieved when a speech is shorter than expected, because so many speeches are much longer than anyone wants. It is easy as a speaker to fall in love with the sound of your own voice and to overestimate how thrilled the audience is to hear you. However, audiences will be insulted if you give a speech that is far short of expectations—five minutes instead of thirty—but they will often appreciate a forty-five minute speech even when they expect an hour.

Time, then, refers to the time of day, the time when you speak during an occasion, and the amount of time you speak. Time is a situational factor that you should carefully consider as you plan your speech.

Importance

The fourth situational factor is the **importance** of the occasion. Some occasions are relatively low in importance, but generally the presence of a speaker signals that an event is not routine. As a speaker, you need to take into account the importance of the occasion. An occasion of lesser importance must not be treated as if it were of great importance, and an occasion of greater importance should not be treated lightly.

Rituals and ceremonial events are usually perceived as high in importance. The speaker at a university commencement exercise, the speaker at the opening of a new plant, and the speaker for a lecture are seen as important players in a major event. Speakers at informal gatherings or local routine events are somewhat farther down the scale. Nonetheless, a speaker must carefully gauge the importance of an event lest the audience be insulted by his or her frivolous treatment of what the audience regards as serious business.

Students sometimes think of the speeches they deliver in public speaking class as a mere classroom exercise, not a real speech. Nothing could be farther from the truth. Classroom speeches are delivered to people who are influenced by what they see and hear. In fact, your classmates as an audience might be even more susceptible to your influence because of their **uniqueness** as an audience.

The Uniqueness of the Classroom Audience

1. The classroom audience, because of the educational setting in which the speech occurs, is exposed to messages it might otherwise avoid: the audience is "captive."
2. The size of the audience tends to be relatively small (usually twenty to twenty-five students) and constant, so that the class begins to take on some of the characteristics of an organization.
3. The classroom audience is more likely to include a wide range of positions on the issues, including opposition.

4. Classroom audiences include one person—the professor—who is responsible for evaluating and grading each speech.

5. Classroom speeches tend to be short but must be informative or persuasive.

6. The classroom speech is nearly always one of a series of speeches in each class period.

7. The speaker has an opportunity to listen to every member of the audience.

8. The classroom speech audience may be invited to provide written and/or oral commentaries on the speech.

9. The classroom speaker has more than one opportunity to influence or inform the audience.

Your classmates, as the audience, do not stay the same during the quarter or semester during which you speak to them: they have their own positions on issues, but they change as they listen and learn; they have information about some subjects, but they are learning more in this class and others; and they are changing themselves as they prepare for speeches and learn more about the topics than they knew before. Next we will look at how you can adapt to this unique audience.

Adapting to Your Audience

This chapter has given you some tools—observation, informants, interviews, and questionnaires—to use in analyzing your audience. This chapter has also reviewed some audience characteristics that tend to make a difference in how an audience responds to a speaker: age, gender, ethnicity, economic status, occupation, education, religion, organizational membership, and physical characteristics, as well as conventional wisdom, and psychographics. However, the tools of analysis and audience demographics will do you no good unless you use them for the purpose of **audience adaptation.**

In the case of an informative speech, adapting to the audience means **translating** ideas. Just as a translator at the United Nations explains an idea expressed in English to the representative from Brazil in Portuguese, a speaker who knows about baud rates, kilobytes, and megabytes must know how to translate those terms for an audience unfamiliar with them. Perhaps you have already met some apparently intelligent professors who know their subject matter well but are unable to translate it for students who do not. An important part of adapting an informative speech to an audience is the skill of translating ideas.

Your instructors—from kindergarten through college—are essentially informative speakers. You have heard people communicate informative material for thirteen years or more. Consider those experiences that were positive and those that were not. Use your better instructors as role models and try to avoid what the poorer instructors did. These experiences are valuable ones as you improve your own public speaking skills.

Consider some of your best instructors. Why are they effective in the classroom? Most likely it is because they "talk your language" and provide examples with which you can identify. They may use examples from current television programs, from sports events, or from local news. They probably avoid the highly specialized vocabulary that oftentimes accompanies a given subject matter. They probably do not use the style of presenting point after point with no examples; instead, they provide ample illustrations of each of the points they make.

Now consider those instructors you would deem as not so capable. What do they do that causes you to rate them lower? They may talk "over your head" and use sentence structure and language that you do not understand. They may use examples from events that occurred years before you were born and provide no context for them. They might use a great deal of jargon that confuses you. They may speak in a way that makes them seem unapproachable to you.

In the case of persuasive speeches, adaptation means adjusting your message both to the knowledge level of the listeners and to their present position on the issue. Use the tools introduced in this chapter and the audience characteristics to help discern where you should

Effective speakers adapt their message to the audience.

place your message for maximum effect. Too often speakers believe that the audience will simply adopt their point of view on an issue if they explain how they feel about it. Actually, the audience's position on the issue makes a greater difference than the speaker's position, so the speaker has to start by recognizing the audience's position on the issue.

Two students in a public speaking class provided an excellent example of what happens when the speaker does and does not adapt to the audience. Both speakers selected topics that seemed to have little appeal for the audience because both appeared to be expensive hobbies. One of the students spoke about raising an exotic breed of dog that only the rich could afford. The entire speech was difficult for the listeners to identify with, since they could not see themselves in a position of raising dogs for the wealthy. The other student spoke about raising hackney ponies, an equally exclusive business. However, this student started by explaining that he grew up in a poor section of New Haven, Connecticut. His father was an immigrant who never earned much money, even though he spoke six languages. This student came from a large family, and he and his brothers pooled their earnings for many years before they had enough money to buy good breeding stock. They later earned money by selling colts and winning prize money in contests. By first explaining to the audience that he was an unlikely breeder of expensive horses, the speaker improved the chances that the audience could identify with him and his hobby. He adapted his message to the unique audience.

What kinds of messages influence you? Consider the variety of persuasive speakers you have heard—ministers, priests, rabbis, and other clergy people; salespeople; teachers and parents; Presidents of our own and other countries and elected officials; people lobbying for a special interest group; and people trying to convince you to change your long distance telephone service or to make another kind of purchase through a telephone call.

What kinds of appeals work for you—emotional appeals or logical ones? Do you need to believe in the ethical standards of the speaker before you will listen to what he or she has to say? Do you like to hear the most important arguments first or last? Do you believe authorities, statistics, or other kinds of sources? If you use your own experiences and thoughtfully reflect on them, you may be able to understand better how others might respond favorably to you as a persuasive speaker.

Ethics and the Audience

As you prepare to speak to a particular audience, remember ethical considerations, those moral choices you make as a speaker. Remember that audiences expect different levels of truthfulness in different situations. A comedian is expected to exaggerate, distort, and even fabricate stories. A salesperson is expected to highlight the virtues of a product and to think less of the competition. A priest, judge, and professor are expected to tell the truth. In the classroom, the audience expects the speaker to inform with honesty and to persuade with reason.

Most speakers have a position on an issue. The priest tries to articulate the church's position, the judge follows a body of precedents, and the professor tries to reveal what is known from her discipline's point of view. You, too, have reasons for your beliefs, your position on issues, and the values you espouse. The general guideline in your relationship with your audience is that you have that audience's best interests in mind. That is why classroom or community speeches encouraging child abuse, drug addiction, racial unrest, and cheating are viewed with alarm in our society. Making ethical choices begins when you consider your topic and how you will present it to a particular audience.

Summary

The best speakers focus their message and their attention on the audience. They know there is much more to giving a speech than familiarity with the topic. They realize that audience characteristics, demographics, can be important in determining what an audience wants to know and do. Further, they realize that the audience's psychographics, its psychological characteristics, can also indicate what an audience is willing to learn and do.

Your message must be aimed at your target audience. You can conduct your audience analysis through observation, informants, interviews, and questionnaires. Because the speech takes place in a particular situation, you must also be aware of such factors as the size of the audience, the occasion, the time, and the event's importance.

You have discovered that the classroom audience is unique, that it differs in many ways from other audiences. However, the classroom is a laboratory in which you can learn analysis and application through adaptation. It is also a place where you can learn to make moral choices, choices that play to positive development in our society.

Vocabulary

androgynous Combining masculine and feminine traits

audience adaptation Making the message appropriate for the particular audience by using analysis and applying its results to message creation

audience analysis Discovering as much as possible about an audience to improve communication in a public speaking situation

co-cultures Groups of people united by a common element who live in a culture operating within a dominant culture

conventional wisdom The popular opinions of the time about issues, styles, topics, trends, and social mores; the customary set of understandings of what is true or right

degree questions Questions used in interviews and in audience analysis questionnaires that invite an explanation, not just a yes or no response

demographics Such audience characteristics as age, gender, education, and group membership

importance The degree of significance attached to an occasion that dictates the speaker's seriousness, content, and approach

informant The person or group inviting you to speak who informs you about the nature of your audience and its expectations for your speech

interviews Situations in which information is sought by an interviewer from an interviewee in person or on the telephone

observation A method of audience analysis based on what you can see or hear about the audience

occasion A situational factor referring to the event at which a speech is given, and the kinds of speaking behavior appropriate for that event

open-ended questions Like essay questions, questions that invite an explanation and discourage yes or no responses from the person being questioned

psychographics Characteristics of the audience that go beyond demographics to culture, aspirations, style of living, attitudes on issues, and acceptable and unacceptable ideas

questionnaires A method of audience analysis that asks written questions of individuals to discern their knowledge level or attitudes about a topic

size of audience A characteristic that can determine everything from the loudness of voice to the formality of language

time The time of day, the specific time when you are scheduled to speak at an event, and the amount of time you are expected to speak

translating The skill of rendering what you know into language and concepts the audience can understand

uniqueness The particular characteristics of the classroom speaking situation that make it different from other speaking events

yes-or-no questions Questions used in interviews and in audience analysis questionnaires that invite only a yes or no response

 # Applications

1. Given the observations listed here, what do you think would be the audience's probable response to a speech on abortion, inflation, or gun control? Choose one of these topics or another topic suggested by your instructor. For each statement about the audience, state how you believe they would generally feel about the topic. This exercise may be done individually or by the entire class.

The audience responded favorably to an earlier informative speech on race relations.

The audience consists mainly of inner-city people from ethnic neighborhoods.

The audience consists of many married persons with families.

The audience members attend night school on earnings from daytime jobs in factories and retail businesses.

The audience members come from large families.

2. Given the following demographic information, what inferences would you draw about each statement? What inferences would you draw if all five statements described the same audience? This exercise may be done individually or by the entire class.

The audience is predominantly female, aged nineteen to fifty-five.

The audience is predominantly Roman Catholic.

The members of the audience are mainly humanities majors.

The audience members do not have jobs outside the home.

Most audience members belong to all-female organizations.

What topics would be appropriate for an audience described by all five of these statements?

The Assumptions Paper/Speech

1. Write your name at the top of your paper and list five assumptions about your class as an audience. Based on your own observations and the audience's demographics, you should make an assumption or inference and state the basis for it. For example, one item might look like this:

Assumption: A majority of individuals in my audience are interested in the subject of marital happiness.

Application Exercises

Application Assignments

Basis: Nearly everyone is between nineteen and forty-six years of age; most of the persons in class are married or have been; five are divorced and remarried; two women are divorced and still single; the majority of people in the class have children, including the two who are now single.

2. In a two-minute speech, share with your class one of your five assumptions without repeating one that has been explained by someone else. State your assumption and the basis for it to see if the class agrees that it is true of the majority of the class members. In one class hour, you can share between ten and twenty assumptions that will help everyone better understand the audience.

Endnotes

1. In Guy A. Zona, *The Soul Would Have No Rainbow if the Eyes Had No Tears and Other Native American Proverbs* (New York: Simon & Schuster, 1994), 22.
2. The tendency to focus on oneself rather than on the audience may be more pronounced in the United States, the northern and western regions of Europe, and Australia. These countries are generally viewed as individualistic cultures which place priority on personal goals over group goals. People from collectivistic cultures are more likely to place the group before the individual. Collectivistic cultures are generally found in Asia, Africa, South America, and the Pacific Island region. For more reading on individualism and collectivism, please see M. H. Bond and C. K. Venus, "Resistance to Group or Personal Insults in an Ingroup or Outgroup Context," *International Journal of Psychology* 26 (1991): 83–94; H. C. Hui and H. C. Triandis, "Individualism-Collectivism: A Study of Cross-Cultural Researchers," *Journal of Cross-Cultural Psychology* 17 (1986): 225–48; D. Trafimow, H. C. Triandis, and S. G. Goto, "Some Tests of the Distinction Between the Private Self and the Collective Self," *Journal of Personality and Social Psychology* 60 (1991): 649–55; H. C. Triandis, "The Self and Social Behavior in Differing Cultural Contexts," *Psychological Review* 96 (1989): 506–20; and Theodore M. Singelis and William J. Brown, "Collectivist Communication Behavior and Concepts of Self: An Individual Level Analysis," Paper presented to the International Communication Association, Washington, DC, May 27, 1993.
3. Dennis Kelly, "Students' Concern for Society Rises," *USA Today* Life section (January 28, 1991): 1.
4. Many of the demographic variables discussed in this text are similar to the features considered important in defining culture. For instance, in *African American Communication* (Newbury Park, CA: Sage, 1993), M. L. Hecht, M. J. Collier, and S. A. Ribeau define culture as "the common patterns of interactions and perceptions shared by a group of people and can be ethnic, national, professional, organizational or gender-based" (p. 15). Members of a culture use shared beliefs, values, customs, behaviors and artifacts to interact with one another and with their world. Although these cultural elements are important, for ease of use in a beginning public speaking course, key individual elements of culture will be used to guide the speaker in conducting an audience analysis.
5. J. H. Jones, "A Greater Voice in Action: Women and Equality," Delivered at Charlotte, North Carolina, August 26, 1992. Reprinted in *Vital Speeches of the Day,* 59, 109–11. Courtesy of Julia Hughes Jones, former State Auditor of Arkansas.
6. Jones, 1992.
7. Jones, 1992.
8. Jones, 1992.
9. Howard Kaufman, quoted in "Pepper and Salt," *The Wall Street Journal* (December 20, 1990).
10. Hecht, Collier, and Ribeau, 1993.
11. Hecht, Collier, and Ribeau, 1993.
12. Harriet R. Michel, "King—From Martin to Rodney: Changing White Attitudes," *Vital Speeches of the Day,* 59 (10), March 1, 1993. Reprinted with permission.
13. Michel, 1993.
14. Marc Maurer, "Language and the Future of the Blind: Independence and Freedom," Delivered at the Banquet of the Annual Convention, Denver, Colorado, July 8, 1989. Reprinted in *Vital Speeches,* 56 (1) (October 5, 1989): 16–22.
15. See, for example, Ralph R. Behnke, Dan O'Hair, and Audrey Hardman, "Audience Analysis Systems in Advertising and Marketing," *Applied Communication Theory and Research,* eds. Dan O'Hair and Gary L. Kreps (Hillsdale, NJ: Lawrence Erlbaum Associates, 1990), 203–21.

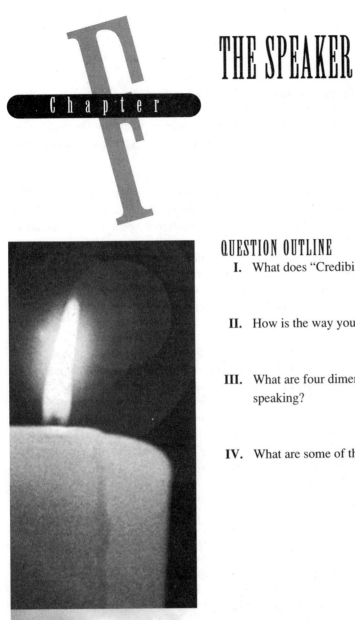

THE SPEAKER

Chapter F

QUESTION OUTLINE

I. What does "Credibility is in the eye of the beholder" mean?

II. How is the way you see yourself related to how audiences perceive you?

III. What are four dimensions of speaker or source credibility in public speaking?

IV. What are some of the ethical choices facing the speaker?

Speech is human, silence is divine, yet also brutish and dead; therefore we must learn both acts.

Thomas Carlyle

Introduction

*S*pring Lee strode up to the podium like a person about to announce a lotto winner. Her hands gripped the sides of the lectern as she leaned toward her audience, her eyes looking directly into theirs. Her words were penetrating, her manner confident, and her voice vigorous. For ten minutes, her audience sat spellbound until she broke it off—leaving them wanting more.

This is the kind of story that many public speaking students would like to experience. The good part about this fantasy is that it is very positive; the speaker is a hero. The bad part is that it is deceptive: this is not the way most communication between speaker and audience really occurs. Instead, we often start public speaking full of uncertainties about ourselves, our message, and our audiences. We need some experience to feel better about ourselves, we need to compose some messages until we get better at organizing our thoughts and ideas, and we need to develop a relationship with listeners until we feel more comfortable communicating with them. We need to grow in confidence by discovering more about ourselves as message sources.

The Speaker-Audience Relationship

The communication process is a transaction; that is, the seven components of the process are interrelated and cannot be isolated. Speaker and audience cannot be separated; they are interdependent. Who the speaker is, what the speaker says, and what the speaker does make a difference, of course. What also makes a difference is how the audience—the receivers—responds to the speaker and the speech. Speaker and audience are connected. This chapter explores the speaker-audience relationship; the idea of ethos, or source credibility; the dimensions of credibility; how credibility can be improved in a speech; and how you can affect a speaker's credibility when you introduce a speaker.

Source Credibility

Twenty-three centuries ago, Aristotle wrote that a speaker's "character may almost be called the most effective means of persuasion he possesses." That idea is as true today as it was then. Your character goes by many names: reputation, honesty, loyalty, sincerity, faithfulness, and responsibility. Aristotle called this idea *ethos;* today it is often called source credibility. Whatever it is called, the idea focuses on the source's, or speaker's, contribution to the speaker-audience relationship. Source credibility is not something that a speaker possesses, like a suit of clothes used to dazzle an audience, nor is it something in you. Instead, credibility is born of the relationship between the speaker and the audience. **Source credibility** is the audience's judgment, or evaluation, of a speaker.

"Credibility is in the eye of the beholder"[1] is a slogan that captures the idea. The audience perceives a speaker at a particular time, place, and occasion, talking about a particular topic. The implications for you as a public speaker are the following:

1. Credibility must be established with every audience you face; it is not readily transferable.

2. You are more credible on some topics than on others: choose topics about which you can establish credibility with an audience.

3. You may be more credible in some situations than in others. You will probably relate well to a classroom audience. You are less likely to be seen as credible at board of directors meetings, at American Medical Association conventions, and on the college lecture circuit.

Acting confident can make you feel confident.

4. You may be more credible with some audiences than with others. Would you be seen as more credible to your classmates, an audience of professors, an organization of quilt makers, or a workshop for automobile mechanics?

5. You may be more credible with one ethnic or cultural group than another. Would you be credible to an audience of African Americans, Latinos, or new immigrants to this country?

Self-Perception

How you see yourself can be how your audience sees you. Since source credibility depends on how your listeners perceive you, you should consider your self-perception, how it is developed, how it can be changed, and why it is important to the public speaker.

Self-perception is how you view yourself, your competencies, your physical self, and your psychological self. The student portrayed in the fantasy at the beginning of the chapter appeared to be high in self-confidence and self-assurance, devoid of anxiety, and determined to communicate.

What is your self-perception? If you were an animal, would you be an eagle or a mouse? Do you see yourself as master of the microphone, princess of the podium, lord of the lectern, or victim of a vicious audience?

A student consulted his teacher because he was shy, and it showed every time he spoke. His voice was meek, his eyes examined the floor, and the audience felt sorry for him. Fellow students tried to be supportive: "Don't be afraid of us; we're your friends," said one. "Look at us," said another, "so we can hear what you say. The little that I heard sounded good to me." The student said that his classmates were seeing him exactly as he felt. To overcome his anxiety, redeem himself in class, and improve his grades, the student decided to try a new approach and act confident. He practiced his speech over and over in the empty classroom. He sometimes pretended the audience did not believe him. At other times, he pretended that they agreed with every word. Acting confident made him feel confident.[2] He behaved more boldly than his self-perception would ordinarily permit. More than ever before, his actions depicted his true feelings about the issue.

Four Dimensions of Source Credibility

Common ground
Dynamism
Trustworthiness
Competence

The way you see yourself is often the way your audience will see you. Maybe you will have to behave confidently before you feel confident, but working on your self-perception is the first step toward being confident. One important way to improve your self-perception is to succeed at every classroom speech.

Audience Perception

An audience will judge you as credible depending on what you show and tell them. Why do you dress up when you go for a job interview? Are you trying to deceive the interviewer into thinking you always look this good? No, but you are trying to make a good impression for the purpose of securing a job. Similarly, audiences judge a speaker even before the speaker talks. Your perceptions of your fellow students are based on everything you sense about them: the way they look, the way they act, the way they sound. When you speak in front of them, you are trying to make a good impression in order to communicate a message.

You can help determine **audience perceptions** with your own choices. The kind of language you use can tell a great deal about your education. Your vocabulary can reveal how much or how little you know about a subject. Your use of arguments and evidence can demonstrate how logical or reasonable you are. How you dress tells the audience what kind of relationship you want with them. A smooth performance can show that you cared enough to prepare and practice a speech for them.

You earn the right to speak about particular topics. As one petite female student said in the beginning of her speech:

> *I am a woman. I am five feet tall. I have spent twenty-five years in a world that seems to be designed for six-foot-tall men. Today I am going to talk about that problem so you can empathize with small people.*

You earn the right to talk about children by raising them, about various jobs by doing them, and about your neighborhood by living there. You can also earn the right to talk by interviewing others, reading about an issue, and studying a topic. Ultimately the audience decides whether you have earned the right to tell them about an issue.

What Do Audiences Seek in a Speaker?

On the premise that good theory breeds good practice, we are going to look at four dimensions of source credibility that seem to affect how audiences perceive speakers. The four components are common ground, dynamism, trustworthiness, and competence.[3]

Common Ground

Before the class began, the speaker, Jack Thomas, "drew" a floor plan on the classroom floor with masking tape. The floor plan filled the room, so most of the classroom chairs were within the tape boundaries. The speaker pointed out that he lived in married student housing. This housing was a joke on campus because it consisted of World War II-vintage

Common ground is what a speaker shares "in common" with the audience.

Quonset huts, tin buildings that looked like half-buried coffee cans. The student walked around his floor plan, telling his audience the square footage in the kitchen, the bedroom, the living room, and the bathroom. Did the people in class have that much space? He pointed out that his housing cost two hundred dollars per month. How much were classmates paying for housing? By the time Jack Thomas finished explaining the facts about married student housing, his audience no longer thought of it as a joke.

Jack Thomas used a dimension of speaker credibility called **common ground,** a term, like communion, communism, and communication, that denotes "sharedness." You can share physical space, ideas, political positions, race, religion, organizational membership, gender, age, or ideology with an audience. Introduced early in a speech, common ground becomes a catalyst for other dimensions of source credibility. Why? Because we like familiarity, because we like to be affirmed ("I agree with you"), and because agreement and affirmation build rapport with an audience.

Common ground is a very relational dimension of source credibility. It says, "Here are the important ways that I, as speaker, am just like you as audience members." Common ground is like a verbal handshake; it tells the audience members that you want to have a relationship with them. You may want to consider features about yourself that you have in common with your audience. What aspects of your past or present experiences may be shared by them? Consider your attitudes, beliefs, and values, too.

Dynamism

Have you ever watched the Sunday morning ministers on television? A few are dressed in Ph.D. gowns, with velvet strips on their arms. They speak with big words and little movement, much like many college lecturers. Others are human dynamos who pace the stage, cry over touching passages from the Bible, bang out songs about Jesus on their piano, yell, sweat, whisper, and shake their fists.

The ministers who stand so stiffly, gesture little, and seem lifeless are lacking in **dynamism;** the preachers who exhibit energy, action, and expression are high in dynamism. You do not have to imitate the Sunday morning orators, but you should learn how to deliver your messages with energy and concern. You should learn how to move, how to gesture, and how to vary your pitch; using these elements of dynamism helps you hold your audience's attention. When you go to the zoo, for example, you spend little time watching the lions sleep in their cage, but everybody likes to watch the monkeys because they swing, groom, and entertain. Effective speakers don't have to be monkeys, but neither do they want to come across as sleepy lions—looking good but boring. Here are some ways that you can add dynamism to your speech delivery.

1. *Purposeful movement.* Animation can be seen as a sign of the speaker's warmth and affection for the audience. The speaker's genuine enthusiasm for the topic can show sincerity. The audience may appreciate some motion and emotion about the topic.

2. *Facial expression.* Use your eyes, eyebrows, and mouth to denote surprise, pleasure, annoyance, disapproval, or skepticism. Your face does not have to be a composite of emotions; instead, a natural, relaxed appearance may be the most appropriate.

3. *Lively language.* Use action verbs and concrete, specific nouns to liven your speech. "He flew through the house like a hornet on fire" is more exciting than "He hurried through the house."

4. *Gestures.* Use your arms, hands, head, and neck to help convey your message. Gestures that reinforce the message result in high-fidelity communication.

All of these are methods of encouraging the audience to see you as dynamic. However, remember that source credibility is an audience perception, so you must be very careful to exhibit dynamism in ways that are appropriate to the audience, the situation, and the topic. Do not act on this section on dynamism, however, by standing up in front of an audience exuding energy without saying anything. Dynamism may or may not be your strength. Do not worry. There are other dimensions of source credibility that may be to your own or the audience's liking.

Trustworthiness

In class one day, David Gold gave what appeared to be an outstanding speech against the censorship of music videos by church groups seeking to limit the raw lyrics and images on late-night television. After David's speech, Drew Everts asked for David's sources. The next week, he gave a speech revealing that David had made up many of the quotes the class heard in his speech. He had paraphrased the words of the church officials to make them sound more extreme than they actually were. Also the position he took on the issue was not supported by some of the groups he cited in his speech. Embarrassed, David decided to drop the course because Drew had shown him to be unethical. Would anyone who heard David's speech and Drew's rejoinder ever trust anything David said? The consequences for violating trust are severe and longlasting.

This dramatic event stunned the class, and was a vivid demonstration of the importance of trustworthiness. **Trustworthiness** is a dimension of source credibility that refers to the speaker's integrity, honesty, fairness, and sincerity.

Trust is difficult to build and easy to destroy. A person who has been faithful in a relationship for years can falter once and find that trust destroyed. A friend who deceives, betrays a confidence, or lies is usually no longer a friend. The worst of family disputes, terrible working relationships, and long-term feuds are based on a loss of trust.

In public speaking, the audience has expectations that, if violated, lead to a speaker's loss of trustworthiness. The audience has the right to expect that you followed the rules in preparing your speech. Their expectations may include the following:

1. The speaker has actually spoken to the people interviewed and is quoting or paraphrasing them accurately.

A speaker's reputation can invite trust.

2. The speaker has actually gathered evidence from the sources claimed and is quoting or paraphrasing it accurately.

3. The speaker reveals which parts of the speech are taken directly or indirectly from other sources.

4. The speaker has the best interests of the audience members in mind and does not encourage them to do things the speaker knows will be psychologically or physically harmful to them.

5. The speaker is expressing personal beliefs and ideas, and is not just putting on a show to impress the audience.

Lest we become too dismal in this discussion of trustworthiness as a dimension of source credibility, we must point out that violations of trust are rare. Nearly all students prepare and deliver their speeches by following the rules. They do not try to trick or deceive their audience, lie, fabricate, exaggerate, or threaten the listeners' welfare. They follow the ten recommendations for public speakers, observe the Golden Rule, and make the moral choices that characterize ethical speakers.

Competence

Twenty-five years ago, an African American professor from an Ivy League school gave a lecture at a midwestern university that had once gone to the Supreme Court to keep an African American student out of its law school. The white listeners were highly skeptical of an African American professor, since they had never seen one before. The professor spoke for fifty minutes without notes. His speech included long quotes from books, which he cited by title, year of publication, and page number. His speech on racism was interesting and novel to the audience, and it overflowed with arguments, evidence, and powerful reasoning. When the speech was completed, the questioning began, and the professor was as adept at debate as he was at public speaking. By the time his lecture was over, the audience was dazzled by his competence.

Your experience can signal competence.

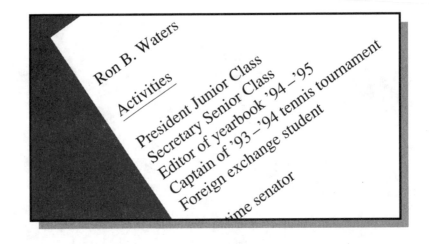

Competence is the audience's perception of the speaker's expertise, knowledge, and experience on the topic or issue at hand. It is the proof that you know what you are talking about.

How do you demonstrate your competence? You might have a résumé that shows your age, education, experience, and goals. A résumé is your statement of competence as it appears on paper. Another way to show your competence is by your ability to do things. A lab technician shows competence by fixing the computers every time they fail. A security person shows competence by achieving a zero property and cash loss in the company served. A financial advisor shows competence by lowering taxes, increasing profit, and decreasing losses.

How do you exhibit competence in a public speech? The professor cited in the preceding true story did it by flashing his photographic mind. You can do it by:

1. Disclosing your relationship to the topic: "Since I am the only Mormon in this class, I would like to explain some of my beliefs so you will understand me and my religion better."

2. Using sources that are not used by everyone else: "According to *Daedalus,* a publication of the National Academy of Arts and Sciences . . ."

3. Wearing clothing or objects to signal your relationship to the topic: "As this lab coat might indicate, I am a biochemistry major. My topic? The safety of sugar substitutes."

4. Using live models to illustrate your point: "To help me with my speech on violence in football, I want you to meet my 280-pound, six-foot-six friend, Rocky Scaradelli."

5. Revealing experiences related to the topic: "I worked at the bottom of city government for over fifteen years, so I have a few stories to tell about inefficiency in government."

6. Demonstrating talent: "These ten watercolors of Wisconsin wildlife are some of the pictures I completed when I was stationed there."

7. Avoiding disorganization: a speech that the audience perceives as sloppily organized reduces the speaker's credibility.

You will think of creative ways to signal your own competence without being blatant. You always tread the fine line between arrogance about your competence and simple openness about your knowledge or ability. More speakers fail to establish their competence than overdo it by boasting about their accomplishments.

Now that you know the four dimensions of source credibility, you might think that a credible speaker has to be equally strong on common ground, dynamism, trustworthiness, and competence. Actually, it may be impossible for a speaker to function positively in all four dimensions at once. For example, the more a speaker emphasizes competence or expertise, the less the listeners may see the speaker as being like them. The more a speaker emphasizes common ground, or similarity, the less the audience may see the speaker as being expert. What you do is emphasize your own strongest dimensions for the audience. If you are not very dynamic, them emphasize your expertise; if you are not very competent, then emphasize your common ground with the audience.

One of the ways you can learn to apply the theory behind common ground, trustworthiness, dynamism, and competence is to introduce another speaker. This is an optional application assignment explained at the end of the chapter, but it is shown here to demonstrate how you can use the ideas presented.

The assignment, in this case, was to interview another student outside class, have both the introducer and the person being introduced stand in front of the room, and have the introducer try to reveal specific details and a general theme about the person. Here is how one student delivered the speech.

> On Thursday, campus voters went to the polls to elect senators for the University Student-Apartment Community. Our duty was to elect the most qualified candidates. I am pleased to report that this duty was fulfilled in at least one instance. I am speaking of Sandra Humphry, the new senator for Zone 13.
>
> Sandra has a genuine interest in our school. Her goal is to develop a more cohesive student community. Sandra has lived in University Village for three years, so she has had firsthand experience with typical problems.
>
> A full-time office assistant in the statistics department for two years, Sandra enjoys time with her husband, Bob, and her five-year-old daughter, Lauri. A hard worker, Sandra has experience selling Avon products, installing wallpaper, and investing in livestock.
>
> Her life has always been busy. In high school, Sandra was an active participant in cheerleading, drama, forensics, ski club, and pep club. She was secretary of the Student Council and was elected to the National Honor Society.
>
> She is also smart. Sandra graduated ninth in a class of 325 students. She earned a State of Michigan Scholarship, attended both the University of Michigan and the University of Kentucky, from which she emerged as an honors student.
>
> Sandra's husband is a varsity basketball player. This gives her opportunities that many of us do not have. She is able to meet many dignitaries, including the governor of Kentucky and the president of this university.
>
> With all of these accomplishments as a political activist and an intelligent human being, you might expect Sandra to be quite egotistical. Instead, she appears shy and reserved, a person who refuses to lose her modest, down-to-earth gracefulness. A gregarious person, Sandra is a human dynamo to her friends, and her dedication to family and community is without parallel.
>
> Fellow classmates, I present to you Sandra Humphry.[4]

In this very brief speech, Gene Turk, the speaker, communicated an immense amount of information about Sandra. His main themes were her political activities and her intelligence, with subthemes about her work and her family.

How would you feel if you were introduced in a classroom speech by someone who knew you well? The introducer mentions that you have been pals for years, that you have gotten drunk together more than a few times, and that you were almost arrested once. Whether you are introducing another speaker or delivering a speech, you are always making **ethical choices** about what to say and how to say it.

Remember that you are trying to help the person you introduce build credibility and that you are trying to support the best interests of the audience when you speak. Thus, saying

Introducing Another Speaker

Ethical Choices and the Speaker

negative things about a speaker or playing to the baser motives of an audience (hate, violence, coercion) are regarded as negative ethical choices. You do not want to exaggerate the speaker's positive qualities, either. Your goal is to present the speaker in a positive light.

As an ethical speaker, you will want to say what you sincerely believe, not just what the audience wishes to hear. While you can strive to make the audience feel good, you should only do so if you are sincere in the message you present. In addition, you do not want to be abrasive or combative. Although your perspective may vary from those of some of your audience members, you must seek to maintain a positive rapport with the audience.

Remember also that the public speaker in a democratic society behaves responsibly by trying to improve or develop that which is good and by trying to eradicate that which is bad. Naturally there will be interesting differences of opinion on what is good or bad, but reasoned debate, valid argument, and uses of evidence are all part of learning to be an effective and ethical speaker.

Finally, you need to heed feedback about your own persona, the way others see you. Do you come across as too dogmatic, too stuck on your own point of view to see alternatives? Are you seen by your audience as too slick to trust, as too naive to believe, or as too uncertain to have a position of your own? What you choose to say and how you choose to say it affect the audience's perceptions of you as a speaker.

Summary

Source credibility is a product of the source-audience transaction. Your view of yourself—whether you are confident or not—can be transmitted to an audience, so an upbeat, positive attitude is vital in a speaker. Most important, though, is how the audience evaluates you and your message, since the listeners determine your effectiveness as a speaker.

Source credibility is also the audience's perception of the speaker's competence, dynamism, trustworthiness, and common ground. Common ground is whatever you have in common with your listeners, trustworthiness is how honest they feel you are, dynamism is determined by how energetic they find you, and competence is how qualified they judge you to be. In all cases, the speaker has to display these characteristics if he or she desires the maximum positive response from listeners. You can apply the theory behind source credibility and its four components when you introduce another speaker.

Your ethical standards as a speaker are reflected in what you talk about (topic), whom you talk to (audience), and how you present your information (full disclosure or partial revelation). The content and delivery of your speech tell the audience what kind of ethical standards you embrace.

Knowing about source credibility can help you grow in confidence as a public speaker, especially if you begin by recognizing that speakers earn credibility through their knowledge, ideas, and relationship to the audience.

Vocabulary

audience perceptions The way the audience assesses the speaker and the message

common ground Similarities between the speaker and the audience; used in introductions of others and early in a speech to help establish source credibility

competence The audience's perception of the speaker's expertise, knowledge, and experience

dynamism The audience's perception of the speaker's boldness, activity, strength, assertiveness, and energy

ethical choices The speaker's choices of topic, argument, evidence, and reasoning that appeal to the audience's higher motives

self-perception How you view your physical and psychological self, an important consideration in how others perceive you

source credibility Called *ethos* by the ancients; the audience's perceptions of a speaker

trustworthiness The extent to which the audience finds a speaker honest, fair, and sincere—high in integrity

Applications

1. The way in which others see you is often influenced by how you see yourself. This exercise should be completed both early and late in the term to see if your public speaking class has altered your self-perception. *Circle* the adjectives that best describe the way you perceive yourself. *Underline* the adjectives that best describe the way you think the audience will perceive you as a speaker. Complete the exercise in pencil the first time so that you can repeat it at the end of the term.

Application Exercises

Assertive	Cautious	Bright	Casual
Friendly	Caring	Fast	Anxious
Talented	Energetic	Effective	Reserved
Attractive	Gracious	Formal	Thorough
Colorful	Experienced	Bold	Scientific
Extreme	Polite	Shy	Conservative
Good looking	Bashful	Daring	Analytical
Exciting	Open-minded	Slow	Poised
Humorous			

2. Write down a topic and list three things you could do to signal your competence on that topic. For example, under the topic "Teenage Pregnancies," you might state (a) I went to a high school where four out of every ten young women were pregnant before graduation, (b) I can tell you what has happened to them in the ten years since they were teenage mothers, and (c) I can tell you what I have read about the issue over the past three years.

3. List all the common ground you share with most people in your audience. Use this list for suggestions when you try to establish common ground with your audience.

1. Write and deliver a brief speech introducing another person by (a) interviewing a classmate for information, (b) composing a speech from that information, revealing at least one theme and one subtheme of their lives, (c) practicing the speech, and (d) delivering it to the class. At the time of the introduction, write the name of the person being introduced and your own on the chalkboard so that the class learns to know both of you. The class should take notes on your introduction, since that information is useful in audience analysis.

Application Assignments

2. Write an introduction of yourself that could be used by a classmate introducing you as a speaker.

Endnotes

1. Ralph L. Rosnow and Edward J. Robinson, eds., *Experiments in Persuasion* (New York: Academic Press, 1967), 18.
2. Daryl Bem argues persuasively that attitudes follow behavior, so acting confident can lead you to be confident. See *Beliefs, Attitudes and Human Affairs* (Belmont, CA: Brooks/Cole, 1970), 3.
3. The dimension called coorientation in earlier editions has been changed to the more commonly used term "common ground." The justification for treating coorientation as a dimension of source credibility is rooted in Christopher J. S. Tuppen, "Dimensions of Communicator Credibility: An Oblique Solution," *Speech Monographs* 41 (1974): 253–60.
4. The name of the student being introduced has been changed in this speech by Gene Turk, a student at Iowa State University who delivered this speech in the honors section of public speaking class. Copyright © Gene A. Turk, Jr. (B.A. Iowa State University 1980; J. D. Yale 1983).

Luck is a matter of preparation meeting opportunity.

Oprah Winfrey

Chapter II

SELECTING A TOPIC AND PURPOSE

QUESTION OUTLINE

I. What are the general purposes of public speaking?

II. What three elements are included in a specific purpose?

III. What is a thesis statement?

IV. How do each of the systematic methods of topic discovery work?

V. What are the six suggestions for selecting a topic?

VI. What criteria can you use to evaluate your topic?

Introduction

ernando Sanchez had sharpened his pencil three times, had changed the background music on his radio twice, and had been thinking for fifteen minutes about topics. His teacher told him to come to public speaking class with three possible speech topics, but in spite of his best efforts he couldn't think of anything to say. Finally, after half an hour of fruitless thinking, he decided to try personal brainstorming, a method suggested in the textbook. He filled a third of a page in five minutes with topics that were in his head. Then he circled three that he cared about and that he could discover more about by searching for information. Fernando had just taken the first step in speech preparation—topic selection.

In this chapter we will consider how to begin the speech preparation process. You will learn how to identify your general purpose, how to develop a specific purpose statement, and how to write a thesis statement. You will also learn how to identify and evaluate topics for a speech. Our discussion begins with a consideration of the general purposes of speeches.

Purposes of Speeches

Speeches have both general purposes and specific purposes. We will consider both of these in this section of the chapter. We will also consider the one-sentence summary of the speech known as the thesis statement.

General Purposes

In the broadest sense, the general purpose of any speech is to inform, to persuade, or to entertain an audience. In a classroom situation, the general purpose of your speech is usually predetermined by your instructor; it may be suggested by your host if you are invited to give a speech to a particular group. If you are not given a general purpose, you should consider the speech occasion, the audience, and your own motivations as you determine the general purpose of your speech.

The three general purposes of speaking can sometimes overlap. You often have to inform your audience before you can persuade them. Sometimes a speech to entertain also serves to inform. Or, you may choose a speech to entertain to persuade an audience to consider alternative attitudes or behaviors. Most speeches, however, can be distinguished as primarily informative, persuasive, or entertaining.

The Speech to Inform

The **speech to inform** seeks to increase the audience's level of understanding or knowledge about a topic. Generally, the speaker provides new information or shows how existing information can be applied in new ways. The speaker does not attempt to persuade or convince the audience to change attitudes or behaviors. The informative speech should be devoid of persuasive tactics. The following topics would lend themselves to a speech to inform.

The causes of disease

Places where auto parts can be found

The origins of language

The African American film industry

The nature of Tourette's syndrome

The history of Native Americans in the last fifty years

The events leading up to the Holocaust

The speech to entertain seeks to amuse or divert the attention of an audience.

The uses of a tool

Types of plants

The dangers of drugs

Sex-segregated education

White-water rafting

The Speech to Persuade

The **speech to persuade** seeks to influence, reinforce, or modify the audience members' feelings, attitudes, beliefs, or behaviors. Persuasive speakers attempt to change what the audience members already know, but go on to alter how the audience feels about what they know, and ultimately how they behave. The following topics would lend themselves to a speech to persuade.

The importance of research on the HIV virus

The value of non-aerobic exercise

The magnitude of the problem of children murdering children

The negative consequences of women in the workforce

The important influence of the UN on world peace

The gravity of increased poverty in the United States

The importance of androgyny

The despair felt by African Americans in the 1990s

The importance of taking steps to reduce heart disease

The urgency of health care reform

The necessity of learning a foreign language

The Speech to Entertain

The **speech to entertain** seeks to amuse or divert the attention of an audience with imaginative and organized humorous, droll, or witty supporting materials. When you listen to a comic's routine on television, when you attend to a storyteller recounting humorous stories, or when you are in the audience of an after dinner speaker, you are provided with a speech to entertain. Speeches to entertain, like speeches to inform or persuade, have a specific purpose and a central idea. The following topics would lend themselves to a speech to entertain.

Love

Marriage

Interest in sports

The differences between women and men

The role of the media in influencing our decisions

Higher education

National government

Politics

Human relationships

Specific Purposes

The general purpose involves nothing more than stating that your goal is to inform, to persuade, or to entertain. The specific purpose goes a step further. Here you identify your purpose more precisely as an outcome or behavioral objective. You also include the audience in your specific purpose. For example, a specific purpose statement might be, "My audience will be able to list the five signs of skin cancer." A **specific purpose statement** thus includes your general purpose, your intended audience, and your precise goal. Some additional examples of specific purpose statements follow.

My audience will be able to explain how hate crimes are legally determined.

My audience will be able to describe the events leading to the Holocaust.

My audience will feel rewarded for exercising.

My audience will be able to list the major symptoms of Tourette's syndrome.

My audience will be able to explain five changes in the Native American co-culture in the past fifty years.

My audience will stop drinking alcohol.

My audience will feel praised for being patriotic.

My audience will give money to Planned Parenthood.

My audience will join a sorority or fraternity.

My audience will donate their organs after their death to another individual.

My audience will avoid refined sugar.

Specific purpose statements are important because they guide the entire speech. When you are developing your specific purpose, you should consider the following characteristics of good purpose statements. First, they are declarative statements rather than imperative (expressing a command, request, or plea) or interrogative (questioning) statements. They make a statement, they do not command behavior nor do they ask a question. Second, strong specific purpose statements are complete statements, they are not phrases, clauses, or fragments of sentences. Third, they are descriptive and specific, rather than figurative and vague or general. Finally, they focus on one idea rather than on a combination of ideas.

Thesis Statement

The general purpose and the specific purpose may be developed early in the speech preparation process. You may decide the general kind of speech you will give and the specific goal you have before you conduct your research. However, until you have become informed on your topic, you will probably not be able to develop the thesis statement.

The **thesis statement** is a one sentence summary of the speech. The thesis statement is similar to the topic sentence or central idea of a written composition. It is a complete sentence that tells exactly what your speech is about. Some examples of thesis statements follow.

Incidents of bigotry are becoming a common occurrence on college campuses.

Elective cosmetic surgery may result in higher self-esteem, improved personal relationships, and better occupational opportunities.

Male bashing has increased in the past two decades.

A college education is no longer a sufficient guarantee of obtaining or maintaining a job.

Friendships with the opposite sex may lead to greater understanding and increased empathy for other people.

Now that we have considered general purposes, specific purposes, and thesis statements, we turn our attention to topic selection. In the next part of the chapter, we will consider how to search for a topic, how to select a topic, and how to evaluate a topic.

Topic Selection

Many people have difficulty getting started with the speech preparation process because they cannot think of topics for their speeches. Like Fernando, they spend time sharpening their pencils, pacing the floor, and doing whatever they can to avoid getting started. After you have read this section of the chapter, you should have an easier time finding a topic for your speech. What are some methods you can use to find a topic that is appropriate for your speech?

Searching for a Topic

Try a systematic method of discovering topics. Among the systematic methods are listing topics, monitoring your behavior, engaging in personal brainstorming, identifying current topics, and clustering topics.

Listing Topics

Listing topics, a systematic method of finding a topic, can be done in two ways. The first is to narrow down a broad category to specifics—for example:

Overpopulation

Overpopulation in developing nations

Overpopulation in India

Religion as a cause of overpopulation in India

The effect of the Hindu religion on overpopulation in India

The second way to use listing is to start with a broad category and then list related ideas under it—for example:

Overpopulation

Historical overpopulation

Sociological effects of overpopulation

Control of overpopulation

A closer look at a category you like can produce a topic for your speech.

Systematic Methods of Topic Discovery

Listing topics
Monitoring your behavior
Engaging in personal brainstorming
Identifying current topics
Clustering topics

Birth control and overpopulation

Overpopulation predictions for the year 2000

The effect of overpopulation on housing

The single term that interests you is used to stimulate thought about a large number of related topics that would make good speech topics.

Monitoring Behavior

Another method of topic selection is **monitoring your behavior.** What do you do each day? How do you spend your time? Monitor your behavior for a week. How much time do you spend reading? Where do you go for entertainment? Do you have any hobbies? What sports do you play? Keeping a diary or log of your behavior may help you identify a topic for your speech.

You may not be fully aware of some of your own interests, so study yourself to discover them. You might not realize you are more interested than most people in biology until you become aware that you have taken more courses in that subject than any other. You might not realize that you are a foreign film afficionado until you note that you go to more of them than most people do. Whether it is taking biology courses or watching films, your behavior often indicates your main interests. Those interests can suggest topics you will enjoy exploring as you prepare for a speech.

Monitor your behavior for a week. How do you spend your time?

After you have monitored your behavior, examine your interests more closely. If you observe that you spend at least thirty minutes each day reading the newspaper, consider what you read. For example, an inventory of your newspaper reading would indicate whether you read front page news; the opinion page; comics; sports; birth and wedding announcements; letters to the editor; or reviews of books, music, TV, or theater. Examine the courses you select, the magazines you read, the hobbies and recreation you most enjoy, and other aspects of your life. Examining your choices helps you pinpoint your areas of interest and expertise and suggests topics that you might already know about.

Engaging in Personal Brainstorming
A third way to discover your own interests is to try **personal brainstorming.** Brainstorming is usually a small-group activity in which the members think of a number of ideas. After gathering a large quantity of ideas, the group reduces the number to a few by assessing their quality. Personal brainstorming is sitting down and giving yourself five minutes to think of as many ideas as you can for speeches. The items do not need to be titles, just ideas. One student who tried this approach came up with the following list:

child abuse	jobs income	IQ	dating
politics	metropolitan	class rank	spouse abuse
education	social status	automobiles	classes
television	love	clothing	critics
violence	health	rape	prejudice
fitness	teachers	HIV	sexism
talk shows	news anchors	Mexican food	elections
salary	music video	marriage	business
cities	inflation	CBS	divorce
white-collar	racism	soaps	networks
GPA	police	recession	radio formats
colors	crime	Cuban Americans	economy
mergers	operation	quotas	classes
hairstyles	fabrics	testing	standard tests
food	taxes	jewelry	cosmetics
production	apartheid	defense	engines

Brainstorming may be easier for you if you identify some categories that can be used to get you started. For example, you may want to think of people, places, or things. Or, you may want to consider events, issues, or concepts.[1] After you have identified some general categories, you can think of items that would fit in each. For example, if we use people, places, or things, we might come up with some of the following ideas:

People	Places	Things
Eleanor Roosevelt	Ireland	rockets
Harry Smith	Moscow	butterflies
Wilma Mankiller	Mille Lacs Ojibway Reservation	salsa
Bill Clinton	Armenia	vegetables
Mohammed Ali	90210	bars
Janet Reno	Alabama	mice
Abraham Lincoln	South Africa	books
Rosa Parks	Wellesley College	red beans and rice
my sister	The Grand Canyon	religion
Michael Jackson	Chicago	celibacy
Bart Simpson	Mayberry, R. F. D.	geography
The Pope	Australia	cocaine

Naturally, the words listed during personal brainstorming need to be evaluated for audience interest and the speaker's ability to gather information. We will consider some general guidelines for selecting topics and how to evaluate topics in a later section of this chapter. We should also note that the chosen topic also needs to be narrowed. However, personal brainstorming is a method of finding topics that yield a large number of ideas, and it may be useful for you.

Identifying Current Topics

Identifying **current topics**—topics of interest today because they are in the news or on the minds of people in your audience—is another method of finding a topic. An encyclopedia, a dictionary, a book of facts, a card catalog—almost any standard resource index can give you ideas. You can also get an idea from a list of topics that have been used recently by other speakers. The following list of topics is from speeches given by students:

The case for nuclear power

The power of poetry

The Neo-Nazi movement

Are professional athletes overpaid?

Junk food and why it is good for you

Problems with insurance companies

Let's increase defense spending

The rise in health care costs

Are college athletics too big?

Women in political office

Avoiding AIDS

What you should know about financial aid

Choosing fabrics for wear

Nursing—a noble calling

Children who have children

The problem with required courses

What does a mechanical engineer do?

Why banks fail

How to get a loan

Should students invest?

Male bashing

Health care reform

Some tips for job interviewing

Our child-support laws

Finding entry-level jobs

The high divorce rate in the U.S.

Why you should consider a communication major

The teacher shortage: an opportunity

The problem with property tax

Women in professional athletics

Overcoming shyness

What can you do about stress?

What is right about our economy?

If you do not find a topic by listing topics, monitoring your behavior, engaging in personal brainstorming, or identifying current topics, then you might want to try an approach to discovering a topic called "clustering."

Clustering Topics

Clustering topics is a method originally devised for helping students with written composition.[2] It can work equally well in helping discover speech topics. The method works like this: think of a concept or an idea you know something about. Write it in the middle of a sheet of paper and circle it. Then, for ten minutes, let your mind free associate as you write down any other subjects related to the first or subsequent ideas. Circle them and attach them to the concept from which they originated. If you wish, use capital letters to indicate a particularly good idea for a speech.

Clustering topics is different from listing topics because in clustering you are relating ideas to each other; when you list topics, they may share no logical connections. Figure 1 shows what a student produced after three minutes of instruction on clustering.[3] He came up with eighteen topics related to genetic engineering in ten minutes. Many could be developed into speech topics by narrowing them, selecting them for appropriateness for the audience, and choosing topics of interest.

Selecting a Topic

Here are some general guidelines for topic selection used successfully by public speaking students:

1. *Speak about topics you already know.* What subjects do you know about—science, cosmetics, mechanics, or child care? Speak about something you already know, and save a lot of research time.

Figure 1

An example of clustering.

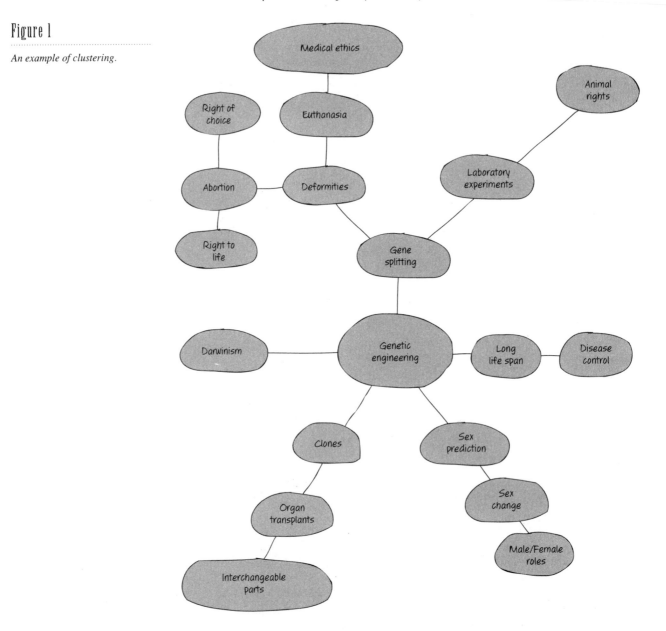

2. *Speak about topics that interest you.* What subjects arouse your interest? What do you like to read about? What elective courses do you choose? Selecting a topic that interests you will make your exploration worth the effort.

3. *Speak about topics that are uniquely your own.* Have you had unusual jobs or travel experiences? Look at your background for ideas to share with your audience.

4. *Speak about current topics.* What are the newspapers, magazines, radio, and TV news covering at the moment? Which of those news items would you like to discuss with a campus expert? Usually people have little background about current news, so items that interest you could be examined more thoroughly in a speech.

5. *Speak about topics your audience finds interesting.* What do people in your class enjoy talking and hearing about? Which of their favorite topics could you discuss with some authority? If people tend to talk with you about certain subjects, then you might want to consider a speech about one of those topics.

6. *Speak about a topic that the audience embraces but you do not.* Are there any ideas that seem to be accepted without question by your audience, but you think could be challenged? Try to convince members of the audience to join your way of thinking on such a topic.

Once you have arrived at a general topic, the next step is evaluation, deciding if the topic meets the standards of **appropriateness** for the speaker, audience, ethical standards, and occasion.

Evaluating Topics

Appropriate for You

Although you must always remember to remain focused on the audience, the first step in evaluating a topic is to consider whether the topic is of interest to you. A speech is appropriate for you as a speaker if you have or can generate interest in and knowledge on the topic. Your ability to deliver an interesting speech depends in part on your own interest in the topic. If you are enthusiastic, then the audience is likely to share your feelings. If you are not, the audience will probably sense your passivity. Avoid audience disinterest by selecting a topic that interests you.

Research is every speaker's obligation. You should either know something about your topic, or you should have a sincere interest in learning more about it. Choose topics about which you know a great deal. A topic is appropriate for you if you know—or can learn—more about it than most of the people in the audience. This criterion is not as difficult as it may first appear. Most of us possess only superficial knowledge on most topics. A speaker can generally learn more about a specific subject than is generally known to an audience. When you have such knowledge, you are said to have subject matter competence.

Appropriate for the Audience

The audience is of central concern to the speaker as she or he considers speech topics. A speech is appropriate for an audience if it is both interesting and worthwhile to the audience.

One of the primary functions of audience analysis is to discern what will interest the audience. The speaker is responsible for generating audience interest. Let us say that you are very interested in coin collecting, but you realize that practically nobody else in the class is. You have both interest and knowledge in the topic. You do not have to give up that topic as long as you can get class members interested. One way to arouse audience interest might be to show how easy and profitable coin collecting can be.

Also consider whether your topic is worthwhile for the audience. If the audience is already familiar with the topic, be careful about the information you are presenting. Try to present new information about familiar topics; do not repeat what the audience is already likely to know. A speech about a topic too familiar to the audience will be highly uninformative. A speech about a topic that is too trivial will not be worth the audience's time. A proper analysis of your audience should reveal both how interesting and how worthwhile your topic will be.

Appropriate Ethical Standards

Your topic should meet ethical standards—that is, the standards of appropriateness in speaking about topics that improve our people and our society. Perhaps the easiest way to illustrate appropriateness is to consider briefly some ideas that are not appropriate: a speech on how to make money through prostitution, drug pushing, and child pornography; a speech encouraging anitSemitism, sexism, and other forms of bigotry; or a speech

Sometimes a speaker is very effective but also unethical.

that fosters negative stereotypes, misogyny, and prejudice. More subtle examples of speeches that are unethical include speeches that provide an audience with information on how to avoid getting a speeding ticket or how to cheat on income taxes. You can avoid violating ethical standards if you remember that, as a public speaker, you strive to improve society, not destroy it. Also remember the difference between effectiveness and ethics—someone who sells unneeded insurance to an elderly person for an unwarranted profit may be effective in sales, but is deficient in ethical standards.

Appropriate for the Occasion

Finally, consider the topic's appropriateness for the occasion: is it significant, timely, and tailored? A speech topic is **significant** if it meets the audience's expectations of what should occur on that occasion. In a classroom speech, for example, a common expectation is that the speech should be on a topic of importance to the class, the campus, the community, or the world. A speech on your breakfast preferences, your date Saturday night, or your most recent fight with your mate may not warrant publicity.

A speech topic is **timely** if it can be linked to the audience's current concerns. A student who gave a speech about a revolution in Liberia did a fine job on the speech, but the revolution had occurred several years before, and the student failed to demonstrate how it related to the present. Ancient history can be timely if the speaker can show how that history speaks to the present.

A speech is **tailored** if the topic is narrowed to fit the time allotted for the speech. It is tough to cover the rise and fall of the Roman Empire in a five-minute speech, but it is quite possible in that amount of time to talk about three ways to avoid osteoporosis through your diet. Most speakers err in selecting too large rather than too small a topic. A narrow topic allows you to use research time more effectively: researching too large a topic will result in cutting much of your material to meet the time requirement of the speech.

Checklist for Topic Appropriateness

_____1. Do you, as the speaker, have *involvement* with the topic?

_____2. Do you, as the speaker, have *competence* in the topic area?

_____3. Based on audience analyses, does this topic hold *interest* for your audience?

_____4. Based on audience analyses, is the topic *worthwhile* to your audience?

_____5. Is the topic *significant* in terms of the speech occasion?

_____6. Is the topic *timely* in terms of the speech occasion?

_____7. Have you appropriately *narrowed and limited* the topic for the occasion?

Speeches have both a general purpose—to inform, to persuade or to entertain—and a specific purpose, which includes your general purpose, your intended audience, and your precise goal. The thesis statement, similar to a central idea in a written composition is a one sentence summary of the speech.

In this chapter, we examined methods of searching for a topic. They included two kinds of listing: using a broad category to suggest a series of more specific, related topics, and using a broad category to suggest a series of other broad but related topics that could be narrowed for public speaking topics. Other methods of searching for a topic include: monitoring your own behavior to see what interests you; engaging in personal brainstorming to generate a large quantity of topics that can be critically analyzed later; consulting a list of current topics; and using clustering, or a free association of ideas related to one main concept, to discover topics.

Once chosen, topics need to be evaluated for their appropriateness for you as speaker (interest and knowledge), their appropriateness for your audience (interest and value), their appropriateness to ethical standards (positive ethical choices), and their appropriateness for the occasion (significant, timely, and tailored). Narrowing the topic appropriately for your time constraints is especially important.

appropriateness The criterion for evaluating a topic; includes its suitability for the speaker, for the audience, for the occasion, and against ethical standards

clustering A method of topic selection in which you start with a broad topic area and then visually free associate by linking and circling your ideas on a sheet of paper

current topics Topics of interest today because they are in the news or on the minds of people in your audience

listing topics A systematic method of discovering a topic by either narrowing down a broad topic or starting with a broad category and listing related ideas

monitoring your behavior Keeping track of how you spend your time to pinpoint areas of interest or expertise that could be potential speech topics

personal brainstorming Writing down as many topics as you can think of without assessing their possibility for a speech

significant A criterion for evaluating if a topic is appropriate for the occasion; meeting the audience's expectations about what should be said by you on this topic and occasion

specific purpose statement A statement that includes your general purpose, your intended audience, and your precise goal

speech to entertain A speech that seeks to amuse or divert the attention of an audience with imaginative and organized humorous, droll, or witty supporting materials

speech to inform A speech that seeks to increase audience understanding or knowledge about a topic

speech to persuade A speech that seeks to influence, reinforce, or modify the audience members' feelings, attitudes, beliefs, or behaviors

tailored A criterion for evaluating if a topic is appropriate for the occasion; narrowed to fit the time allotted for the presentation

thesis statement A one sentence summary of the speech

timely A criterion for evaluating if a topic is appropriate for the occasion; linked to the audience's current concerns

Applications

Application Exercises

Identifying Good Specific Purpose Statements

1. Examine the following specific purpose statements. Identify those which are good examples, and explain why the others are bad examples.

_____ 1. The charms of Venus.

_____ 2. My audience will be able to explain the plans for the United States space program in the year 2000.

_____ 3. What do women want in their personal relationships?

_____ 4. My audience will be able to identify five kinds of love.

_____ 5. To persuade my audience to live and let live.

_____ 6. To entertain my audience about sex.

_____ 7. To identify the primary causes of lung cancer.

_____ 8. To explain early baldness in men.

_____ 9. To inform my audience about having some hoots on a Saturday night.

_____10. My audience will go to graduate school.

2. In order to gain experience in formulating general purposes, specific purpose statements, and thesis statements, complete the following exercise. For each of the topics, specify the missing information.

Topic	General Purpose	Specific Purpose Statement	Thesis Statement
Edible plants	To persuade	_____	_____
Waterbeds	_____	_____	_____
Crack	To persuade	_____	_____
Shoplifting	To inform	_____	_____
Selection of the Pope	_____	My audience will be able to explain the process the Vatican uses to select the Pope	_____
Animal abuse	_____	_____	Incidents of animal abuse are becoming a common occurrence throughout the U.S.

Brainstorming by Topic Areas

3. In order to discover the usefulness of brainstorming and to generate a number of possible topics, try this exercise. Take out a pencil and paper, check the time, and allow yourself exactly five minutes to write down as many topics as come to mind. The topics do not have to be stated as specific speech topics: they can be individual words, phrases, or sentences. The range in number of ideas written in this exercise varies from five or six to as many as thirty possible topics.

After you have written down all the topics you can in five minutes, write three more topics in the next three minutes. Most people find it difficult to write down any more ideas, but some find their best ideas come after they have brainstormed for a period of time.

After you have completed your list of topics, select five that are particularly interesting to you. Finally, from these five, select the one that has the best potential for a public speech. Keep in mind that you should already have or be able to find information about this topic and that you will have to adapt the topic to a specific audience.

4. Take out paper and pencil and divide the paper into four or six sections. Write down one of the following topic areas at the top of each section.

Job experiences you have had

Places you have traveled

City, state, or area you are from

People who make you angry

Happy experiences you have had

Unusual experiences you have had

Personal experiences with crime

Your involvement in marriage, divorce, or other family matters

Experiences with members of other groups—the old, the young, other racial or ethnic groups

The effect of the drug culture on your life

Your relationship to local, state, or federal government

Your background in painting, music, sculpture, theater, dance, or other arts

Your feelings about grades, college education, sororities and fraternities, college requirements, student government, or alternatives to a college education

Your reactions to current radio, television, or film practices, policies, or programming

Recent Supreme Court decisions that affect you

Your personal and career goals

Spend approximately three to five minutes jotting down specific topics for each of the four to six topic areas you chose. Underline one topic in each area that is especially interesting to you. From these four to six underlined topics, select the one for which you have the most information or best access to information and which you can adapt to your specific audience.

5. Individuals' interests are reflected in the magazines they normally read. Complete this exercise to discover your own interests. Consider the magazines you normally purchase or subscribe to and note which ones you read regularly (+), occasionally (0), or rarely or never (–).

_____ News magazines (*Time, Newsweek, U.S. News & World Report*)

_____ Traditional women's magazines (*Ladies' Home Journal, Good Housekeeping, Redbook*)

_____ Feminist publications (*Working Woman, Ms., New Woman*)

_____ Political publications (*Nation, New Republic, National Review*)

_____ Recreational magazines (*Women's Sports and Fitness, Skiing, RV Travel*)

_____ Hobby magazines (*Popular Mechanics, The Workbasket, Travel & Leisure*)

_____ Confession magazines (*True Story, True Confessions, Modern Romances*)

_____ Business magazines (*Fortune, Black Enterprise, Money*)

_____ Culture-specific magazines (*Ebony, Hispanic, Essence*)

_____ Religious magazines (*Commonweal, The Watchtower, The Upper Room*)

_____ Sex emphasis magazines (*Playboy, Playgirl, Penthouse, Cosmopolitan*)

_____ Professional journals (*Elementary English, Journal of Abnormal and Social Psychology, American Educational Research Journal*)

Narrowing Your Topic

6. Narrowing your topic for the time you are allotted to speak is very important, but sometimes forgotten in the process of topic selection. Let us consider three of the topics generated by the student who engaged in personal brainstorming, for example.

rape

date rape

date rape on college campuses

causes of date rape on college campuses

love

lasting love

loving marriages that last fifty years or more

factors that contribute to having a loving marriage that lasts fifty years or more

Cuban Americans

growing numbers of Cuban Americans

showing understanding to Cuban Americans

understanding the Cuban American culture

explaining one aspect of Cuban American culture

To gain practice in narrowing topics, pick three other topics that have been suggested in this chapter and narrow them three or more times until you have a topic appropriate for a relatively short speech.

Application Assignments

Topic and Purpose

1. Select a topic that you found through any of the methods suggested in this chapter. Make sure the topic is appropriate for you, the audience, and the speech occasion. See that it is interesting and worthwhile to the audience as well as significant, timely, and appropriately narrowed and limited. At the top of your paper, write your name and your topic. Then indicate your general purpose, your specific purpose, and your thesis statement.

Appropriate Ethical Standards

2. Consider the following topics in class, individually, or in a group to determine how appropriate or inappropriate they would be in your class:

How to use an automatic pistol   Why you should eat red meat
Using fireworks on July 4th   Beating parking tickets
Legalizing crack cocaine   How to avoid taxes
Choosing a fine wine   The fine art of stripping
Cable without costs   Altering your water meter
Shoplifting for fun   Profits in child porn

Endnotes

1. R. R. Allen and Ray E. McKerrow, *The Pragmatics of Public Communication,* 3rd ed. (Dubuque, Iowa: Kendall/Hunt, 1985), 42–44, suggest a number of categories that can be used to generate topics.
2. The idea of clustering comes from Gabriele Lusser Rico, *Writing the Natural Way* (Los Angeles: J. P. Tarcher, Inc., 1983), 35–36. The authors wish to thank Dr. William Miller, Professor in the School of Telecommunications at Ohio University, for bringing this method to their attention.
3. This cluster was designed by Mr. Brad Peters, a student at Ohio University, Athens, Ohio.

FINDING INFORMATION

QUESTION OUTLINE

   I. What is the role of your personal experience in providing information for your speech?

  II. What should you do before, during, and after an interview?

 III. What are some sources of information in the library, and how do you find them?

 IV. How should you find sources and record information from them?

  V. What is a correct way to cite information from written and interviewed sources?

Knowledge is of two kinds. We know a subject ourselves, or we know where we can find information upon it.

        Dr. Samuel Johnson

Introduction

Dino Caroso had been diagnosed with respiratory allergies, and it created a great deal of discomfort for her. She suffered from a stuffy nose, frequent sneezing, and a cough. Her eyes, nose, and throat were constantly itchy. Her physician told her that the most effective way to control her symptoms was to avoid allergens. However, she learned through allergy tests that she was allergic to molds, dust, and pollen. She had tried non-prescription antihistamines and decongestant tablets, but they didn't seem to work. Nasal sprays and drops worked for awhile, but they seemed to be less helpful after a week or two of regular use.

Dino had heard a newscast about allergies that suggested that an increasing number of people were complaining of allergy symptoms. She thought maybe she could deliver an informative speech about the condition and possible treatments for it.

Dino's problem was finding information. She could have used the newscast if she had remembered the station and date, but she didn't. She could look in the library for magazine articles, but she knew that the topic was fairly specialized, so maybe not much had been written—at least for the layperson. Then she remembered that she had another appointment to see her doctor. Why not ask her? An interview with a doctor would count as a good source of information. Plus, the doctor might have some suggestions about where to learn more about respiratory allergies and their treatment.

Like Dino, you need to find information for your speech. Dino began by drawing upon her own personal experiences, which is a good place to start.

Personal Experience

One of the richest sources of information is you. You have gone to school for a dozen years or more. You have worked at part-time and full-time jobs. You have gone places and met people who taught you lessons in living. You may have married and returned to school after serving in the armed forces or after raising a family. Whatever your story, it is not exactly like anyone else's. In your own personal experience, you can find information that will provide ideas, supporting materials, and arguments for your speeches.

Unfortunately, many students do not see themselves as unique. Sometimes, on the first day of class, instructors ask students to identify themselves by name, major, hometown, year in school, age, and any other demographic characteristics they may wish to share. Then each student is asked to state in what way he or she is unique, different from others in the class. If any characteristic is repeated, then that person has to think of another unique feature. The class decides if the characteristic or experience is unique.

How is this exercise related to discovering information for your speech? Your unique experience with a topic should be part of your speech. Sharing your experience demonstrates your interest and involvement with the topic. A speaker is doing more than simply fulfilling an assignment when he or she talks about alcoholism and its effects on his or her own family. A person who talks about gene transplants is higher in credibility when he reveals his work in the biological sciences.

People are often unaware of their own uniqueness, tending to think that many others have done or experienced what they have. One of the authors spent two years as the chief prelaw advisor for a large university. The biggest difficulty in writing the "Dean's Recommendation" for the prospective law students was getting them to think of how they differed from hundreds of other applicants. Even a twenty-minute interview with each student failed to reveal uniqueness. Often students came back later with second thoughts.

One student came back two days after the interview to ask if it made any difference that she was a concert pianist. "How was that related to law school?" she inquired. A concert

Finding Information

1. Personal experience
2. Interviews
3. Using the library
4. Researching effectively
5. Creating the bibliography
6. Oral footnotes

Your talent can make you unique.

pianist has practiced most of her life. That kind of discipline is exactly what law schools demand. Another student remembered that he had learned the Russian language–in Russia. Still another saw nothing unusual about finishing college in three years with a 4.0 average. Your uniqueness may not be as dramatic as these examples, but the point is that people have difficulty seeing uniqueness in themselves even when it clearly exists.

Although personal experience should be the first consideration in looking for speech material, it should be used critically. Your personal experience should do the following:

1. Enhance your credibility as a speaker on your topic
2. Provide examples or supporting material
3. Demonstrate your relationship to the topic

Some examples of speeches based on personal experiences and interests include a speech on St. Patrick's Day by a woman who was Irish and had celebrated the holiday every year with her family.[1] Another woman talked about body piercing. She herself had several body piercings, had friends who had had body piercings done on everything from "their noses to their foreskins," and she had interviewed a number of professional body piercers.[2] A woman who had collected Walt Disney films all of her life gave a speech on the changes she perceived in Disney's animated films.[3]

Another woman had a long interest in Native Americans. She attended several pow-wows as she grew up in her native state of Ohio. She was also a member of the Native American Center in Columbus, Ohio, and regularly volunteered there. She gave most of her speeches in her public speaking class on Native Americans—one on the warrior, Tecumseh; another on the Native Americans of the Eastern Woodlands; and a third on Native American religious freedom rights.[4]

One effective way of incorporating personal experience into your speech is to use your credentials to establish credibility in the introduction of the speech. One student began his speech like this:

> I have been a sign interpreter for over six years. I have been active in the deaf community and its causes. I taught sign language classes at Youngstown State University for two years, and I also lectured on how to best incorporate a deaf student into a mainstream class for all education majors at YSU. I have enjoyed working in the summers as a counselor at camps designed for deaf children and teens, and I am currently working part-time as an interpreter at East Elementary School here in Athens for a profoundly deaf first-grader. I enjoy my work, and I am glad to be part of this exciting community.[5]

Needless to say, the students were fascinated by this speech on signing. They gave the speaker high marks on credibility.

Consider your own experiences first as you gather information for your speech. Do not assume that any experience you have had will be appropriate, however. Ask yourself if the experience you wish to relate in the speech is typical. Is it so typical that it is boring, or so unusual that it was probably a chance occurrence? Will the audience learn from your experience? Does your experience constitute proof or evidence of anything? If your personal experience meets some of these expectations and does not violate the sensibilities of your audience, then it will probably be an asset in your speech.

Interviews

A second important source of ideas and information for your speech is other people. Your campus is a great resource. It is full of faculty and staff, many of whom are experts on particular subjects. Your community, likewise, is populated with people who have expertise on many issues: government workers on politics; clergy on religion; physicians, psychologists, and nurses on health care; engineers on highways and buildings; and owners and managers on industry and business. The following story illustrates how a speech can be based on an interview.

> Norman Donne went to his speech professor's office in despair. He was supposed to give his speech in two days. He had selected a topic but could find nothing on the subject because someone had cut out all of the information from the magazines, newspapers, and books in the library. Norman was frustrated and angry. His speech professor recommended that he give his speech on a topic that was of highest interest to him at the moment: the destruction of library resources.
>
> Norman made an appointment to see the associate director of the library. He hit a gold mine. The associate director was part of a national study team investigating the destruction of library resources. He was gratified to find a student interested in this issue who would tell other students how serious the problem was.
>
> After two hours with the associate director, the student knew the average number of pages destroyed in the magazines, the cost of repairing or replacing the damaged books, and the amount of damage at his own college. He had more information than he could have found in many days of research. When Norman gave his speech, he supplemented his personal experience with facts and figures that made him more of an authority on library barbarity than anyone in the room.

You may not find all of the information you need in a single interview, but you may discover that interviewing is an efficient way to gather information on your topic. The person you interview can furnish ideas, quotations, and valuable leads to other sources. First, however, learn when and how to conduct an interview, and how to use the results.

Before the Interview

If you can find the information as quickly and easily by looking it up yourself, then do not seek it through an interview. Instead, interview when

1. The information is not readily available. Maybe the issue is so current that it is not covered in the papers. Perhaps the issue affects such a narrow band of people that it has been overlooked. Interviewing can unearth information that is not in books, magazines, newspapers, or on the Internet.

2. The authority on the subject is available. If you have people on your campus or in your community who have expertise on your topic, then their opinions should be sought.

3. Quotations and specific ideas are necessary for your speech. Often you can elicit higher-impact quotes from experts for your speech than the press gets because experts learn to be very prudent around reporters. These quotations and ideas can give your speech the sizzle it needs to gain audience interest.

Before your interview, determine your purpose, write out your questions, select a person to interview, and arrange an appointment.

Your *purpose* for the interview should be related to the immediate response you seek from the audience and your ultimate goal. For example, your immediate response might be "to learn the Heimlich Maneuver," and your ultimate goal might be for your audience "to save lives by using life-saving techniques on victims." What purpose would be served in having an interview about a maneuver to save victims of choking? Persons in medicine or public health can provide you with authoritative quotations, real-life stories, and reasons for your audience to listen. All of this is possible if you ask the right questions.

Your *questions* should be carefully designed to produce the information you need. Make them specific, clear, and necessary. Some can be "yes or no" questions, but most should call for an opinion. All should be questions that cannot be easily answered by simply looking them up. As much as possible, the questions should be stated without bias, without suggesting an answer, and without threat, anger, or hostility.

Following are some sample questions appropriate for a speech on the Heimlich Maneuver.

How many choking victims are there per year in the United States?

What age groups are most likely to be affected?

Where (in the home, restaurants) do such incidents usually occur?

How effective is the maneuver in helping victims?

Are there any dangers in having laypersons use the maneuver?

Before the Interview

1. Determine your purpose.
2. Write out your questions.
3. Select an interviewee.
4. Arrange an appointment.

Find out who can best answer your questions.

Do you think more people should learn the maneuver?

Have you ever used it to help a victim?

Is there anything related to the Heimlich Maneuver that you think I should tell my audience that has not already been mentioned?

Selecting your interviewee is the next important step. Your first consideration is "Who can best answer my questions?" You might want to ask your teacher for an opinion on this issue. Among your criteria for selecting a person for an interview are availability, accessibility, and affability. A person might be on campus or in your community but may not grant interviews, or a person may be available and accessible but unfriendly to interviewers.

The big surprise for many public speaking students is finding out that many important people are willing to submit to an interview for a campus speech. Most people are flattered that others want to know their opinion. If your interview is well planned and well implemented, then other students are likely to be welcomed by this same interviewee.

Making an appointment usually involves talking to a secretary or administrative assistant. This person is correctly called a "gatekeeper" because he or she controls the gate, or door, to the employer's office. The way you treat the secretary can determine whether or not you get an appointment, so be polite, clear about your mission, and reasonable about the amount of time that you want and when you want it.

Some guidelines for securing an interview include the following:

1. Look professional when you ask for the interview. This can help you in gaining an appointment.

2. State your purpose clearly and succinctly. It is best if you can tell the secretary what your mission is, but another alternative is to type a brief note that can be passed to the interviewee.

3. Ask for an appointment early. Some people will be too heavily scheduled to see you on short notice. The earlier you ask for an appointment, the better your chances of securing an interview.

4. Ask for a brief amount of time. Usually a ten-to-twenty-minute appointment is sufficient. It is better to ask for a brief appointment and let the interviewee extend it than to ask for a large amount of time that you do not use.

5. Show up for your appointment at least five or ten minutes early in case your interviewee wants to meet you early. If you are going to be late, call ahead and ask the secretary if you should cancel.

These guidelines will serve you well as you prepare for the interview itself.

During the Interview

One decision you will have to make concerning your interview is whether or not to record it. The advantages of a tape recording are accuracy and completeness. The disadvantages are that some interviewees do not like to be recorded, the presence of a recorder can inhibit disclosures, and sometimes the machine fails, leaving you with a useless tape and no notes. Always ask the person you are interviewing if you can use the tape recorder, and take notes anyway in case technology fails.

Interviews rarely start with the first question. Instead, expect the interviewee to express curiosity about you and your project. Be perfectly frank about your purpose, the assignment, and the audience. The interviewee is doing the verbal equivalent of a handshake with the questioning.

During the interview, be very careful about the *tone* of your questions and comments. You are not in the role of an investigative reporter interrogating a member of a crime syndicate. Instead, you are a speaker seeking information and cooperation from someone who can help you. Your tone should be friendly and your comments constructive.

During the interview, be *flexible*. Even though you have prepared questions, you may find that the responses answer more than one question, and your preplanned order isn't working as well as you thought it would. Relax. Check off questions as you ask them or as they are answered. Take a minute at the conclusion of the interview to see if you have covered all of your questions.

Practice *active listening* during your interview. Show an interest in the person's answers. If you hear something that you want to get verbatim, write it down, or ask the interviewee to repeat it if necessary. Do not try to copy every word but do get an accurate rendition of direct quotations.

Make sure that you have accurate *citation information,* your interviewee's name, title, and the name of the company, agency, or department. You will be citing this person's words and using oral footnotes to credit them, so you need correct source information. If the interviewee has time, you may want to read back your direct quotes for verification.

Finally, remember to *depart*. Give your interviewee an opportunity to stop the interview at the designated time. The interviewee—not you—should extend the interview beyond the designated time. The interviewee will appreciate your gracious good-bye and gratitude for granting the interview. As a parting gesture of good will, thank the secretary as well.

During the Interview

1. Record if permissible.
2. Keep tone positive.
3. Be flexible.
4. Practice active listening.
5. Cite information accurately.
6. Leave as scheduled.

Figure 1

A sample interview notecard.

```
Dr. Carson B. Axelrod (M.D. from Stanford U.)
Chair, Dept. of Internal Medicine
Pomeroy Community Hospital

"Laypersons using the Heimlich Maneuver should be
wary about employing the maneuver on infants. An adult
can take a firm, rapid squeeze without fear of
fracture, but a small child could become a dual victim
of choking and broken ribs."


Interviewed 2/24/95
```

After the Interview

As soon as you can after the interview, *review your notes,* write down items that were discussed without complete notes, and make sure you can read your own direct quotes.

If you taped the interview, *listen to your tape* as soon as possible. If you wait even a few hours, you may have difficulty remembering exactly what was said. Although the words are preserved on the recording, the nonverbal cues are not.

The best way to ensure that your interview can be used in your speech is to write the most important material, especially the direct quotations, on *notecards,* each carefully marked with the name of the source and the sequence of cards (see figure 1). With careful preparation before the interview, attentive listening and accurate note taking during the interview, and quick review and notecard composition after the interview, you will increase your confidence as a speaker.

Phone and Mail Requests

Two additional methods of gaining information for your speeches are making phone calls and sending mail requests.

Phone calls are faster than interviews, but they require the same kind of decorum. Frequently you have to get through a secretary to talk to your interviewee. Phone calls are a good method if the information you need will take very little time to communicate, if it can be communicated entirely by voice, and if it can be done with a minimum of dialogue.

One caution about phone call interviews is to make sure that you are available for a return call if the interviewee is unavailable, or make an appointment to call the interviewee back. A busy person is unlikely to make many return calls to an unanswered phone, but a busy person whose secretary has forewarned the interviewee about an impending phone call will be happy to comply. As with interviews, you need to treat the secretary with respect, take accurate notes during the phone conversation, and write the person's name, title or position, and company or department correctly.

Mail inquiries are a good way to get more information. Your librarian can help you locate the addresses of interest groups for everything from alcoholism to zymologists. You will need to request information well in advance of your speech, but special interest organizations will eagerly respond to speakers who are willing to advance their cause. One possible liability is that your one inquiry may place you on the organization's mailing list for life.

You can also write to government agencies. Again, your librarian may have the information if your college is a federal depository for government documents, or you will learn how to request them from government agencies. In any case, the U.S. mail is a relatively fast way to secure information about your topic.

After the Interview

1. Review your notes.
2. Listen to your tape.
3. Make notecards.

The library is the focal point of most colleges and universities. Your public speaking course gives you an opportunity to use this very useful resource. It will be one of your important sources of information. Unfortunately, most of us do not know how to use the library wisely or well. In addition, we feel foolish asking others for help because we feel that understanding how a library is organized and functions is basic information that we should have learned when we were younger.

Using the Library

One undergraduate woman who had worked in a university library for over two years gave one of her informative speeches on the library. She was wise in selecting this speech topic because many of her classmates had experienced difficulty in using the library. After she established her relationship to the topic, she introduced her topic by saying:

Was doing the research for this speech a hassle? Have you ever gone to the library to do research for a paper and not been able to find anything on your topic? Have you ever had trouble finding a restroom?

Everybody here will have to use the library at some time or another, and I intend to give you a few hints that will make the experience less painful for you and also for those people who work there.

In the next few minutes I would like to discuss the setup of our library, the many resources available to us, and I would like to give you a few helpful hints and shortcuts that will help you with assignments such as speeches and papers.[6]

This speech was highly valued by the student's classmates. Many of them reported that they used the information from it throughout the academic term.

The Library Staff

We have been looking at people who can help with your speeches. One of the most important partners for success in your public speaking class is the library staff. These individuals know the library well, and part of their job is to help you use it to your advantage.

If you have not actively used your library, consider a library tour with a member of the library staff. In addition, many college and university libraries have video programs that describe the various resources they include. Finally, do not be afraid to ask questions when you are frustrated by a problem. Librarians and their assistants are professionals whose jobs are to serve the patrons. Be sure you have specific questions in mind when you approach them, be courteous in your interactions, and show your gratitude for their assistance. The library should not be a mystery to you; instead, it should be a place that can help you succeed. The more you know about the library, the better you can use it.

In the next section of this chapter, you will learn some preliminary information that will help you even before you go to the library. The primary sources that you will use in your speeches include reference works such as dictionaries, encyclopedias, yearbooks and almanacs, and books of quotations; books, which can be found in the computerized catalog system or in the card catalog; magazines and journals, which can be found in general and specific computerized and noncomputerized indexes; and newspapers, which can be found in computerized and noncomputerized indexes.

Reference Works

Most libraries have a reference room or reference area that includes several different kinds of materials. We cannot describe every reference source, but some of those that you are most likely to use are dictionaries, encyclopedias, yearbooks and almanacs, and books of quotations. We will consider the usefulness of each of these.

Dictionaries

Need help pronouncing a word? Wonder what a technical term means? Want to know where a word came from? Dictionaries—desktop, comprehensive, and specialized—are the resource to use.

For most of your speeches, the collegiate dictionary is sufficient to find spelling, meaning, and pronunciation, but sometimes you may need more. A comprehensive dictionary, such as the *Oxford English Dictionary,* can tell you most of the known meanings and origins of a word. A related reference work, the thesaurus, can provide you with lists of words with the same (synonyms) or opposite (antonyms) meanings.

Still another kind of dictionary, a dictionary of usage, can tell you how words are used in actual practice. Do you know when to use *affect* and *effect*? A dictionary of usage can tell you. Some examples of these references are

> Black, Henry C., *Law Dictionary*
>
> Comrie, John Dixon, *Black's Medical Dictionary*
>
> Fowler, H. W., *A Dictionary of Modern English Usage*
>
> Partridge, Eric, *Dictionary of Slang and Unconventional English*
>
> *Roget's International Thesaurus*
>
> *Webster's New Dictionary of Synonyms*

Encyclopedias

Encyclopedias are great for finding background information. If you want to give an informative speech about any subject except the most current, you can find some information in a general encyclopedia, such as *Encyclopaedia Britannica,* or a specialized encyclopedia, such as the following:

> Buttrick, George A., and Keith R. Crim, eds., *Interpreter's Dictionary of the Bible*
>
> *Dictionary of American History*
>
> *Encyclopedia of Philosophy*
>
> *Encyclopedia of World Art*
>
> Illing, Robert, *Dictionary of Musicians and Music*
>
> Mitzel, Harold, ed., *Encyclopedia of Educational Research*
>
> Munn, Glenn G., *Encyclopedia of Banking and Finance*
>
> Turner, John, ed., *Encyclopedia of Social Work*

Yearbooks and Almanacs

Yearbooks and almanacs provide facts and figures on a large range of subjects. What songs were popular in the 1960s? Who owns the Minnesota Twins? When did the last earthquake rock Los Angeles? Who is the leader of Japan? How many Native American tribes reside in the United States? How much iron ore was produced in 1990? How many CEO's of Fortune 500 companies are women? Who are some of the famous living women in America today? Topics as different from each other as these can all be found in yearbooks and almanacs. The following list of books of facts, statistics, and details may be helpful to you as you prepare your speech.

Americana Annual

The Annual Register of World Events

Current Biography

Dictionary of American Biography

Dictionary of National Biography

Economic Almanac

Facts on File

Information Please Almanac

New International Year Book

Rand McNally Cosmopolitan World Atlas

Statesman's Year-Book

Statistical Abstract of the United States

Who's Who of American Women

Who's Who in America

World Almanac and Book of Facts

Books of Quotations

Have you ever noticed how excellent speakers often have just the right quotation to begin or end their speeches? Individuals who speak frequently seem to be particularly adept at summarizing their ideas with the pithy words of famous people. Do these people have good memories or private collections of quotations? Maybe so, but they might also rely on the many different kinds of books of quotations that are available for speakers and writers.

What are some of the possible sources of quotations? Probably the best-known collection is *Bartlett's Familiar Quotations*. This mainstay in the market contains well over 20,000 quotations from both contemporary and historical figures. Similarly, *Respectfully Quoted: A Dictionary of Quotations Requested from the Congressional Research Service* features over 2,000 quotations that are routinely requested or asked to be verified by the Congressional Research Service of the Library of Congress. The *Oxford Dictionary of Quotations* and the *Home Book of Quotations* are also large collections of quotations that have existed for nearly sixty years.

Paperback books of quotations are also available. The *Pocket Book of Quotations* is printed regularly. Specialized paperback books such as *The Quotable Woman* might also be useful to you.

Similarly, books of anecdotes might be helpful to you. These books include longer stories told by famous people or about famous people. Some of these include the large volume *The Little Brown Book of Anecdotes,* and smaller books like *The Oxford Book of American Literary Anecdotes* and *Presidential Anecdotes.* Most of the quotation and anecdote books are indexed so you can find a quotation or anecdote by topic or author.

Most libraries now offer dictionaries, encyclopedias, yearbooks, almanacs, and books of quotations in an electronic form. You may be able to request an actual CD ROM, which you can insert in a computer. Or, you may be able to request encyclopedia, dictionary, thesaurus, or quotation materials within an existing program that has already been installed on a computer. The second edition of the *Oxford English Dictionary* is available on CD ROM and can be searched in a variety of ways. A common encyclopedia data base is the *New Grolier Multimedia Encyclopedia,* which includes the text of the *Academic American Encyclopedia* and adds to it pictures, sounds, movies, and other visuals. *Time Almanac: 1990* contains the complete text of all issues of *Time* magazine since 1989, and also includes an almanac of facts and figures. The library staff can assist you in finding these and other such materials electronically.

Figure 2

An explanation of one computerized catalog system.

```
About ALICE

ALICE includes listings for:
     MOST  books, music scores, periodicals (magazines &
           journals), sound recordings, and video recordings
     SOME  government documents, manuscript collections,
           maps, and microforms

     *              *              *              *              *

ALICE does NOT include listings for:
     individual articles in magazines, journals and
     newspapers; some older books (use the card catalog on
     the 4th floor to find them).

To be sure of doing a complete search on a topic, consult
staff members in the appropriate library department(s).

To return to the list of Help Screens, type /HELP and press
the RETURN key. Or, proceed with a search.
```

Books

Very few speeches will be prepared without the assistance of non-reference books. Where do you find books in the library? The answer seems both obvious and trite—books are everywhere in the library.

Where do you find exactly the *right* books for your speech? Most likely you will use a computerized library catalog system.[7] Each library refers to this electronic aid with a different name, but most computerized catalog systems work the same way. You will be able to search for sources if you know the author, title, or subject of your search. We will examine one specific computerized catalog system, but you should check at your own library to determine exactly how you can access information. Most computerized library systems can be accessed within the library, as well as from remote locations with the assistance of a modem and a telephone line. One of the first screens that is provided to new users is an explanation of the system (see figure 2 for a typical screen display).

New users can learn more specific information about the computer system by requesting it. Figure 3 explains how one system works. Essentially, if you are interested in a book and you know the title of it, you would type "T" and then the title to access information about the book. If you had an author in mind, you would type "A" followed by the author's name. If you had only a subject in mind, you would type "S" followed by that subject.

Imagine, for example, that you are interested in a book that you know is entitled *Love,* but you have no additional information about it. You would type the symbol for a title search (most often "T") and then type "love." On this system, when this step was completed, eleven sources came on the screen and a prompt suggested that more sources were available (see figure 4). You decide that listing 10 is the book you are looking for. You then type "10" in order to gain more information on this book. When that was done, the computer provided circulation information on the book, including the call number for the book, it's location, the date when it was added to the library, and the date when it was last checked back into the library (see figure 5).

Figure 3

An explanation of how to use one computerized catalog system.

```
Welcome to the university's computerized library system.

A list of Help Screens for the system is given below. For more
information type a line number and press the RETURN key.
     1. About ALICE
     2. General COMMANDS used by the system
     3. Setting SEARCH LIMITS by LANGUAGE, FORMAT, or DATE
     4. AUTHOR search                      A/
     5. TITLE search                       T/     Be sure to use
     6. SUBJECT search                     S/     the / and not
     7. CALL NUMBER search                 C/     the \.
     8. KEYWORD search: single word        W/
     9. KEYWORD search: two or more words  B/
    10. RESERVE ROOM searches              P/ or Q/
    11. Library hours and telephone numbers
    12. Library circulation policies
    13. Searching databases of other O.U. campuses
In all searches on ALICE, spelling and spacing are VERY important;
punctuation and capitalization are not.


For detailed information on one of these topics, type a line number
and press the RETURN key. Or, proceed with a search.
```

Figure 4

Titles listed on a computerized catalog system when titles containing the word "love" were requested.

```
 1. Love.
 2. Love: a novel.
 3. Love: a novel/Angela Carter.
 4. Love: a play in five acts/by James Sheridan Knowles.
 5. Love, by Gilbert Cannan.
 6. Love, by Leo F. Buscaglia.
 7. Love/Elizabeth von Arnim; with a new introduction by
     Terence de Vere White.
 8. Love. Italian
 9. Love: poems/by Danielle Steel.
10. Love: the foundation of hope: the theology of Jurgen
     Moltmann and Elisabeth Moltmann-Wendel/edited by Frederic
     B. Burnham, Charles S. McCoy, M. Douglas Meeks.
11. Lovebeast: a parable. Wordvision [by] Stephen Levine;
     mandalahand [by] Miriam Arguelles.
```

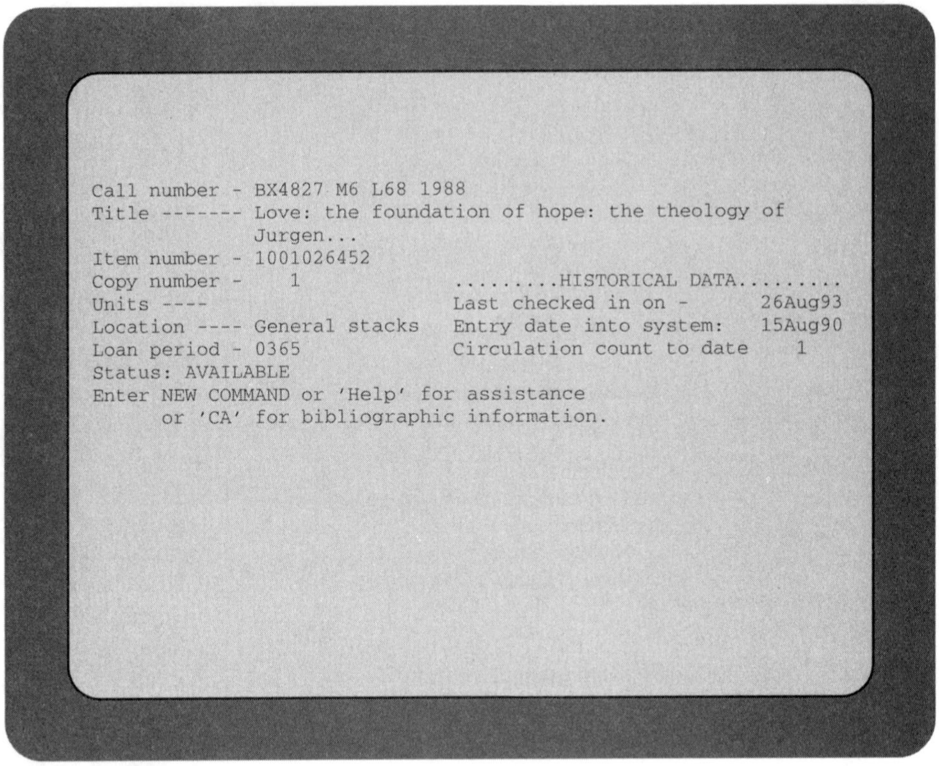

Figure 5

Circulation information for the tenth listing generated by the title search T/love.

```
Call number - BX4827 M6 L68 1988
Title ------- Love: the foundation of hope: the theology of
              Jurgen...
Item number - 1001026452
Copy number -    1              ........HISTORICAL DATA........
Units ----                      Last checked in on -      26Aug93
Location ---- General stacks    Entry date into system:   15Aug90
Loan period - 0365              Circulation count to date    1
Status: AVAILABLE
Enter NEW COMMAND or 'Help' for assistance
       or 'CA' for bibliographic information.
```

Another student was interested in the topic of the aging Hispanic American population. She began her search by typing "S/Hispanic American aged." She found that only three sources on this topic existed in her library (see figure 6). The title that looked most useful to her was the first one listed. She typed "1" to learn more about that source (see figure 7). She found that the book was available in the general stacks and what the call number was to find it more efficiently. She also noted that no one had ever checked the source out of the library.

A final student wanted to learn if Barbara Boxer had ever written any books that were available in the library. He typed "A", since he was doing an author search, and then typed "Boxer, B." He learned that two books by Barbara Boxer were available, and that the library also contained a book by Baruch Boxer (see figure 8). He chose the first listing and found the two titles by Barbara Boxer (see figure 9). Seeking the location and call number of the second book, he typed that line number and found the information provided in figure 10.

If your library does not have a computerized catalog system, you may need to use a card catalog, which consists of 3 × 5″ cards alphabetized in rows of file card drawers. Before the development of computerized catalog systems, all library book searches were conducted with the card catalog. Today, most colleges and universities have switched to computerized systems.

If you need to use a card catalog, you should know that most card catalogs are organized by author, title, and subject. One section of the card catalog will contain an alphabetically arranged set of author cards. Another section will include an alphabetically arranged set of title cards. A final section will provide an alphabetically arranged set of subject cards. An example of each of these kinds of cards is provided in figure 11.

After you have found the information you need, you still need to find the book. You will notice that the call number for the book is provided on the computer screen or on the 3 × 5″ notecard. This number will tell you where you can find the book in your library.

```
3 Subject:      Hispanic American aged.

1. MAIN TITLE - Final report/White House Mini-Conference on
                Hispanic Aging, February, 1981; prepared by
                La Asociacion Nacional
   AUTHOR ----- White House Mini-Conference on Hispanic Aging
                (1981: Los Angeles, California)
   PUB. DATA -- Los Angeles: La Asociacion Nacional Pro
                Personas Mayores

2. MAIN TITLE - Hispanic elderly: a cultural signature/Marta
                Sotomayor, editor; Herman Curiel,co-editor.
   PUB. DATA -- Edinberg, Tex.: Pan American University Press,
                1988.

3. MAIN TITLE - The Hispanic elderly: a research reference
                guide/Rosina M. Becerra, David Shaw.
   AUTHOR ----- Becerra, Rosina M.
   PUB. DATA -- Lanham: University Press of America, c1984.

Enter NEW COMMAND or LINE # of selection or 'HELP'.
```

Figure 6

Sources listed on a computerized catalog search when the topic or subject "Hispanic American aged" was requested.

```
Call number - HV1461 W49 1981x
Author ------ White House Mini-Conference on Hispanic Aging
              (1981 :
Title ------- Final report/White House Mini-Conference on
              Hispanic...
Item number - 1001211310
Copy number - 1                ........HISTORICAL DATA.......
Units -------                  Last checked in on -   04Feb92
Location ---- General stacks   Entry date into system:04Feb90
Loan period - 0365             Circulation count to date 0
Status: AVAILABLE
Enter NEW COMMAND or 'HELP' for assistance
      or 'CA' for bibliographic information.
```

Figure 7

Circulation information for the first source generated by the subject search S/Hispanic American aged.

Figure 8

....

Listings generated by a computerized catalog search when the author "Boxer, B." was requested.

```
1.      2 Boxer, Barbara.
2.      1 Boxer, Baruch.
```

Figure 9

....

More specific information on writings authored by Barbara Boxer.

```
2 Author        Boxer, Barbara.

1. MAIN TITLE - AIDS education activities aimed at the
                general public implemented slowly: report
                to the Honorable Barbara Boxer,
   AUTHOR ----- United States. General Accounting Office.
   PUB. DATA -- [Washington D.C.]: The Office, [1988]
                              Format — MICROFICHE

2. MAIN TITLE - Strangers in the Senate: politics and the
                new revolution of women in America/Barbara
                Boxer with Nicole Boxer;
   AUTHOR ----- Boxer, Barabara.
   PUB. DATA -- Washington, D.C.: National Press Books, 1994.
```

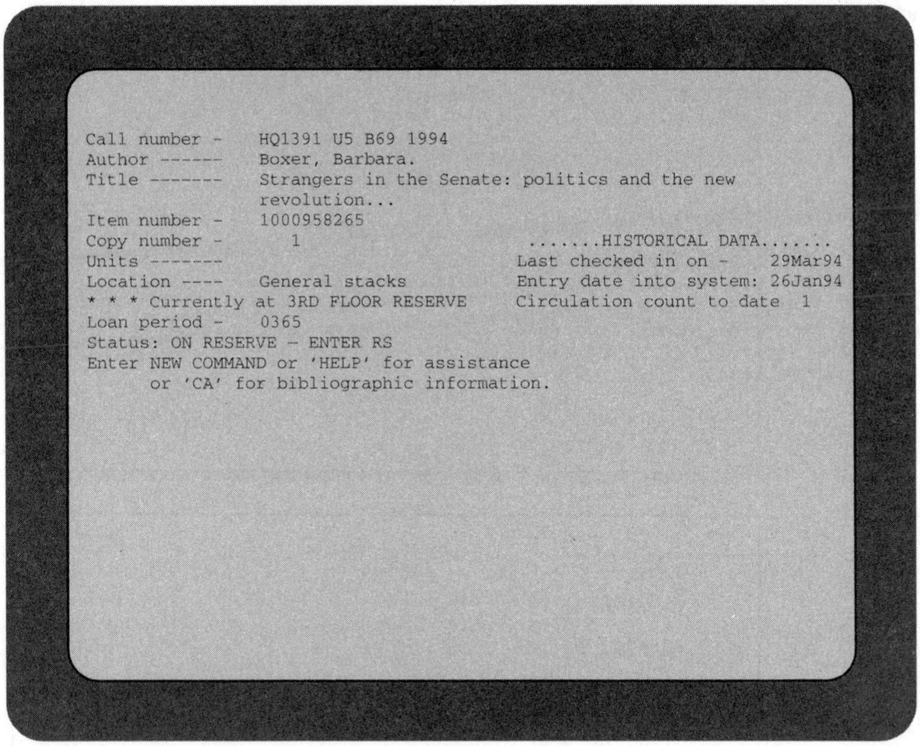

```
Call number -    HQ1391 U5 B69 1994
Author ------    Boxer, Barbara.
Title -------    Strangers in the Senate: politics and the new
                 revolution...
Item number -    1000958265
Copy number -       1                       .......HISTORICAL DATA.......
Units -------                               Last checked in on -    29Mar94
Location ----    General stacks             Entry date into system: 26Jan94
* * * Currently at 3RD FLOOR RESERVE        Circulation count to date  1
Loan period -    0365
Status: ON RESERVE - ENTER RS
Enter NEW COMMAND or 'HELP' for assistance
      or 'CA' for bibliographic information.
```

Figure 10

Circulation information on a book authored by Barbara Boxer.

You will, of course, need to familiarize yourself with where books with specific call numbers are housed in your library. Most libraries have signs and pamphlets providing this information.

In the last two decades, a few libraries have networked their online public access catalogs (OPACs) so that individuals at one university could learn what sources were available at a nearby university library. Such an arrangement was established between the University of North Carolina at Chapel Hill, North Carolina State University, and Duke University. In California, the various branches of the University of California were linked so people at any one of the institutions could electronically examine the "card catalog" of another institution.

Even more recently, the development of Internet and the introduction of specific research tools have allowed researchers who own computers and modems access to large data bases that include libraries throughout the world.[8] While you may not be using Internet at the present time, it is highly likely that you will be before you graduate from college or soon after graduation.

Magazines and Journals

Magazines and journals are also staple sources of speech writers. How can you easily find information in popular magazines such as *Newsweek, Sports Illustrated, Consumer's Guide, Vital Speeches, Glamour, Car and Driver, Time, Psychology Today, Runner's Magazine, Cosmopolitan, U.S. News and World Reports, Details, Modern Maturity, TV Guide,* or *Ebony*? How about journals such as *Sex Roles, Communication Education, Journal of Marriage and the Family, Deviant Behavior, Journal of Social and Personal Relationships, Public Health Reports, American Behavioral Scientist, Communication Quarterly, American Journal of Sociology, Philosophical Quarterly, Journal of Personality and*

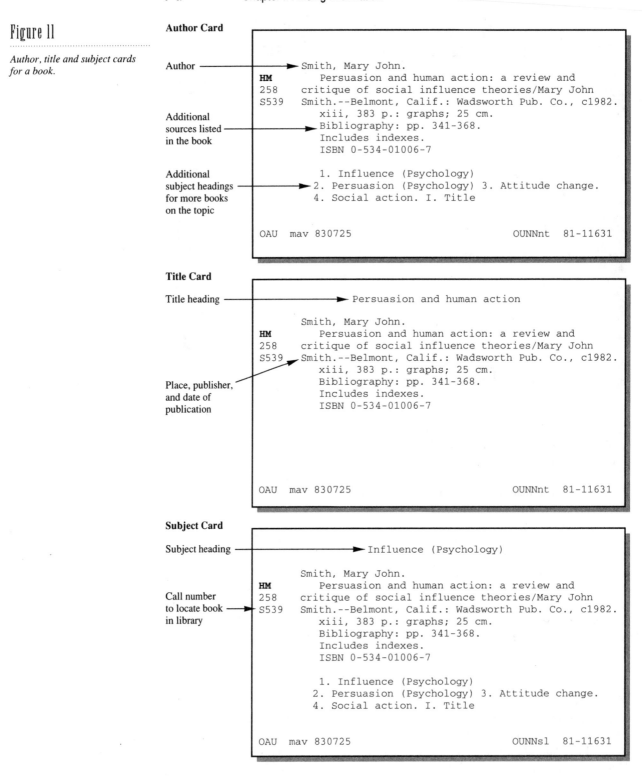

Figure 11

Author, title and subject cards for a book.

Author Card

Author
> Smith, Mary John.
> HM   Persuasion and human action: a review and
> 258   critique of social influence theories/Mary John
> S539   Smith.--Belmont, Calif.: Wadsworth Pub. Co., c1982.
>   xiii, 383 p.: graphs; 25 cm.

Additional sources listed in the book
>   Bibliography: pp. 341-368.
>   Includes indexes.
>   ISBN 0-534-01006-7

Additional subject headings for more books on the topic
>   1. Influence (Psychology)
>   2. Persuasion (Psychology) 3. Attitude change.
>   4. Social action. I. Title
>
> OAU   mav 830725   OUNNnt   81-11631

Title Card

Title heading
> Persuasion and human action
>
>   Smith, Mary John.
> HM   Persuasion and human action: a review and
> 258   critique of social influence theories/Mary John

Place, publisher, and date of publication
> S539   Smith.--Belmont, Calif.: Wadsworth Pub. Co., c1982.
>   xiii, 383 p.: graphs; 25 cm.
>   Bibliography: pp. 341-368.
>   Includes indexes.
>   ISBN 0-534-01006-7
>
> OAU   mav 830725   OUNNnt   81-11631

Subject Card

Subject heading
> Influence (Psychology)
>
>   Smith, Mary John.
> HM   Persuasion and human action: a review and

Call number to locate book in library
> 258   critique of social influence theories/Mary John
> S539   Smith.--Belmont, Calif.: Wadsworth Pub. Co., c1982.
>   xiii, 383 p.: graphs; 25 cm.
>   Bibliography: pp. 341-368.
>   Includes indexes.
>   ISBN 0-534-01006-7
>
>   1. Influence (Psychology)
>   2. Persuasion (Psychology) 3. Attitude change.
>   4. Social action. I. Title
>
> OAU   mav 830725   OUNNsl   81-11631

Social Psychology, Family Issues, Human Relations, Violence Victims, American Psychologist, Journal of Sex Research, Adolescence, or *Family Relations?* Obviously, thumbing through the various magazines and journals would take too much time. Even examining the index within a specific journal or magazine would take far more time than most people have to complete the research for their speech.

In order to effectively and efficiently find material in magazines and journals, general and specific indexes are used. The most familiar general index is the *Reader's Guide to Periodical Literature,* which includes a current listing of between 180 and 190 of the most frequently read magazines published in the United States. The *Reader's Guide* dates back to 1900, and most libraries carry all of the volumes back to this date.

The *Reader's Guide to Periodical Literature* is now also available in an electronic form. All of the issues of the index published since January of 1983 are now available on the Internet and on CD ROM. In either form, the *Reader's Guide* provides author, title, and subject indexes. You may look up material if you know the author or title of the article, or just the subject matter.

You may also need to use a more specialized index for your topic. A properly narrowed topic often requires specialized information. For example, if you decide to attack the grading system, you might find some information in the *Reader's Guide,* but you would find more in the many periodicals and journals that specialize in education. The *Education Index,* for instance, can lead you to articles in 150 magazines and journals.

Remember that specific indexes lead you to specialized periodicals written for professionals and experts. You may find that you have to simplify the articles for your audience's understanding.

Some of the special indexes to periodicals are

Applied Science and Technology Index (author, title, subject)

Art Index (author, subject)

Bibliographic Index (subject)

Biography Index (subject)

Biological and Agricultural Index (subject)

Book Review Index (author, title, subject)

Business Periodicals Index (subject)

Catholic Periodical Index (subject)

Education Index (author, subject)

Engineering Index (subject)

Index to Book Reviews in the Humanities (author, subject)

Index to Legal Periodicals (author, subject)

Music Index (author, subject)

Public Affairs Information Service (subject)

Quarterly Cumulative Index Medicus (author, subject)

Social Sciences and Humanities Index (author, subject)

Technical Book Review Index (author, subject)

Some of these general and specific indexes have been computerized. We already mentioned that the *Reader's Guide to Periodical Literature* has been computerized since 1983. In addition, a variety of others are available. In figure 12, we list some of the indexes that might be most helpful to you, along with an explanation of what they include.

Title	Dates of coverage	Notes
General: all subjects		
Books in Print Plus	Current	Includes full text of book reviews of some titles. Updated monthly.
Broadcast News	1992–	Full text transcripts of news and public affairs programs on ABC, CNN, NPR and PBS.
CD NewsBank	1993	Full text of articles selected from 30+ American newspapers.
InfoTrac	Last 3–4 years	Indexes 1100 general interest, business, and scholarly periodicals, plus the most current two months of the *New York Times*, *Wall Street Journal* and *Christian Science Monitor*.
Monthly Catalog of U.S. Government Publications	1976–	An index to publications from the Government Printing Office. Updated every two months.
New York Times Ondisc	1990–	Full text of articles. Updated monthly.
Newspaper Abstracts	1985–	Indexes articles in nine major American newspapers.
Readers' Guide	1983–	Indexes articles on all subjects from general interest magazines. Updated monthly.
U.S. Government Periodicals Index	1993–	Indexes the contents of periodicals published by the U.S. government.

Figure 12

Computerized general and specific indexes.

None of these electronic indexes is difficult to use. In some cases, you need to type a key word, the author's name, the title of the article, or the subject matter of interest, and press "search" or "enter." In other cases, the procedure is only slightly more complicated. Ask a library staff member to help you during your first attempts to use these electronic resources. You will find that they save you valuable time, and they oftentimes provide more complete information.

Most college and university libraries are updating their indices with information retrieval services available in an electronic format. These services are sometimes referred to as SearchNets or data bases. They are known by several different product names. You will want to learn if your library has such services and how to use them.

One such service, the SearchNet, includes a large number of indexes. For example, they may include all of those mentioned in figure 12 and even more. Most SearchNets allow you to type in single words or combinations of words connected by the word "and." The word "and" allows you to find articles that include all of your topics within them. For instance, if you typed in "gender differences," you would be inundated with hundreds of possible sources that deal with differences between women and men. If you added "and self-disclosure," you would narrow your search, but you might still find far more

Medicine and Health

AIDSLine	1980–	Comprehensive coverage of AIDS research. Updated quarterly.
CancerLit	1986–	Comprehensive coverage of cancer research. Updated monthly.
Health	1975–	Indexes articles on health planning and administration. Updated monthly.
Medline	1966–	Comprehensive index to medical literature.
Nursing & Allied Health	1983–	Comprehensive index to articles on nursing and other health-related fields. Updated monthly.

Science and Technology

Applied Science & Technology Index	Oct. 1982–	Good for basic literature searches.
Biological Abstracts	Jan. 1990–	Comprehensive index for the life sciences.
Biological Abstracts /RRM	Jan. 1991–	A companion database to the above, covering reviews, reports, and meetings. Both databases should be used.
Biological and Agricultural Index	July 1983–	Good for basic literature searches.
CASSIS	Current	Database for U.S. patents. Abstracts of the last two years of patents; index to all prior years. Updated bimonthly.
Compendex	1986–	Comprehensive index for engineering.
Computer Select	Latest year	Covers computer science. Includes full text (no graphics) of articles from selected journals. Updated monthly.
General Science Index	May 1984–	Good for basic literature searches.
GeoRef	1785–	Comprehensive index to earth science literature.
History of Science and Technology	1976–	Indexes journal articles, conference papers, books, book reviews, and dissertations.

Figure 12 (continued)

studies than you want. You might try "gender differences and self-disclosure and adolescents" in order to get a list of sources of manageable size. You will need to experiment with how broadly or narrowly you define your topic in order to maximize or minimize the number of sources that you find. Later in this chapter we will take you through two SearchNet searches to clarify the process.

Newspapers

Finally, you will want to examine newspapers, particularly if you are speaking on a current event. Just as you cannot look at all magazines or journals, you will not have time to examine all issues of a newspaper, or all issues of several newspapers for the same day. Instead, you can begin your newspaper search with a newspaper index. The following newspapers are indexed.

Chicago Tribune (1972–present)

Los Angeles Times (1972–present)

The New York Times (1851–present)

Wall Street Journal (1958–present)

Washington Post (1972–present)

Business

ABI/Inform	1971-	Indexes articles from about 800 business publications. Updated monthly.
Business NewsBank	1985-	Indexes a collection of newspaper articles on companies and industries selected from several hundred U.S. newspapers and reprinted on microfiche. The microfiche themselves are in the Microforms Collection.
Business Periodicals Index	June 1982-	Good for basic literature searches.

Humanities

Art Index	Oct. 1984-	Good for basic literature searches.
Avery Index to Architecture Periodicals		Indexes more than 1,000 periodicals.
Billboard/Phonolog Music Reference Library	1992	Indexes musical recordings by title, artist, label, etc.
Columbia Granger's World of Poetry	1993	Indexes 90,000 poems in 550 anthologies; full text and quotations of some poems.
Contemporary Authors	1993	Biographical and bibliographical information on authors active since 1960.
Film Index International	1993	Details on films and film personalities, plus reference to periodical articles on film.
Historical Abstracts	1982-	Includes citations for books, articles, and dissertations on world history (excluding the U.S. and Canada) since the year 1450.
Humanities Index	Feb. 1984-	Good for basic literature searches.
Music Index	1981-	Indexes music periodical literature.
MLA International Bibliography	1981-	Indexes articles on modern languages and literature, and folklore.

Figure 12 (continued)

You can also use the electronic retrieval system called the *National Newspaper Index* to find a source in *The New York Times,* the *Wall Street Journal,* or the *Christian Science Monitor* from 1970 to the present; or the *Los Angeles Times* or the *Washington Post* from 1982 to the present. Ask a library staff person if your library has this electronic index. Again, it could save you valuable time.

Back issues of newspapers appear in two forms. Your library may have the actual newspaper if it is recent, or it will carry back issues on microfilm, which requires a microfilm reader available in the library.

If you get confused about these available reference works, then remember only one thing: Members of the library staff can help you find the information you need.

Researching Effectively

People like to know more about a subject. A game entitled Trivial Pursuit has been a best seller for several years. The game is based on wide knowledge of many disciplines. The winners are the ones who know the most about the most subjects. The game is popular because people think it is fun to pit one team's knowledge against another's.

You will find that doing research can also be very interesting. At first, you may find it frustrating because you have to learn how to find information, record it, and adapt it for your speech, but you will also find that research can be distracting. As you look for the

```
                    Social Sciences

Anthropological Literature              Indexes articles and essays in English
                                        and other European languages.

EconLit                    1969-        Indexes journals on economics.

ERIC                       1966-        Indexes journal articles and research
                                        reports on education and related fields.

Handbook of Latin                       Indexes books, book chapters, articles,
American Studies                        and conference papers.

Hispanic American                       Citations from more than 400 scholarly
Periodicals Index                       journals.

PsycLit                    1974-        Indexes articles on psychology.

Social Sciences            April 1983-  Good for basic literature searches.
Index

Sociofile                  1974-        Indexes articles on sociology.

Sport Discus               1975-        Covers exercise physiology, coaching,
                                        counseling, sports medicine, biomechanics
                                        and related areas.
```

Figure 12 (continued)

things you need for your speech, other items attract your attention. This section is designed to help you become an effective researcher by providing helpful hints about finding material for your speech.

Begin the Research Process

In order to research effectively, you must get started. It is important to find a topic without delay. Too often people waste most of their time finding a topic, and then spend very little time researching it. A more effective strategy is to choose a topic early and leave yourself maximum time for research.

Researching Effectively

1. Begin the research process.
2. Record potential sources.
3. Make index cards.
4. Learn as you look.

Figure 13

SearchNet areas of research.

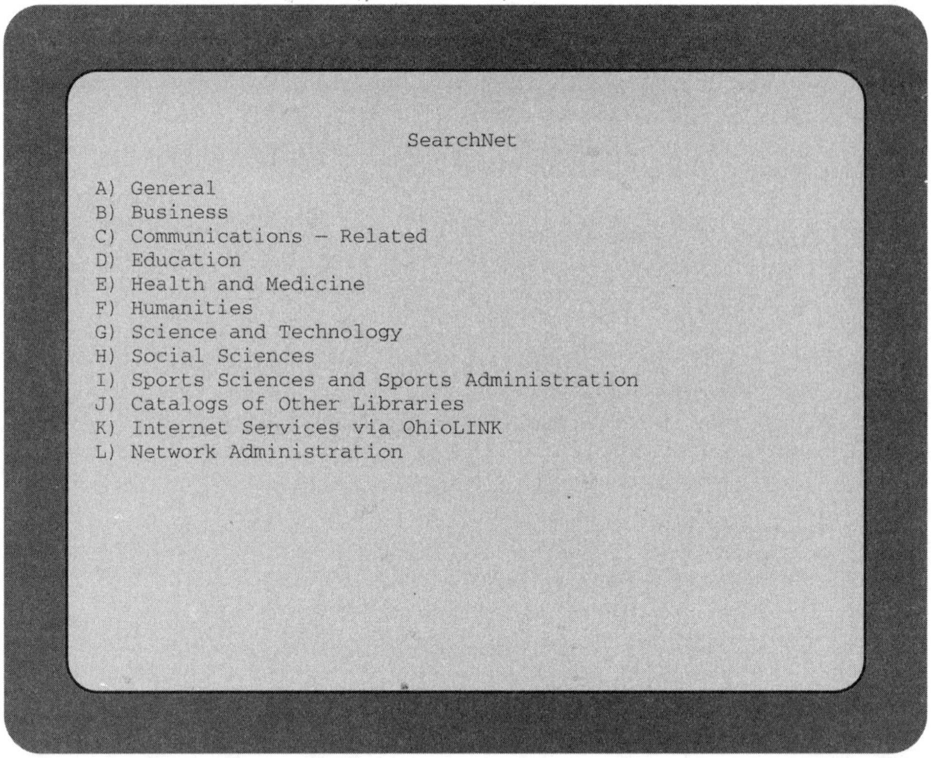

```
                              SearchNet
     A) General
     B) Business
     C) Communications — Related
     D) Education
     E) Health and Medicine
     F) Humanities
     G) Science and Technology
     H) Social Sciences
     I) Sports Sciences and Sports Administration
     J) Catalogs of Other Libraries
     K) Internet Services via OhioLINK
     L) Network Administration
```

In addition to finding a topic early, you should narrow it to fit the time allowed. The body of a five-minute speech is rarely more than three or four minutes long because the introduction and conclusion take about one to two minutes. The body includes transitions and organizational moves that take time. Thus, you actually have a limited amount of time to present the supporting material of your speech.

Let us follow the progress of three students as they research their speeches at the library. The first student, Tomoko Kawashima, wanted to do her speech on gender issues in education. She went to the SearchNet, and encountered twelve areas of research on the first screen (see figure 13).

If Tomoko had chosen the general index of the SearchNet, she would have found eleven possible interfaces (see figure 14). One of them, FirstSearch, requires a password and is accessible by paid subscription only. All of the other interfaces are available to the general public in this particular library.

Instead, Tomoko decided that the area of education (choice D on the first screen) would best fit her needs, so she scrolled down to that choice and pushed "enter." This led her to the next screen, which offered several education interfaces. She chose the "Education Index," and then conducted a multiple subject search, with the word "education" as one subject and the word "gender" as the second. Tomoko immediately learned that 77,140 sources contained the word "education," that 1,196 sources used the word "gender," and that 303 sources contained a combination of the two key words. She realized immediately that her topic was too broad.

Tomoko knew that she really wanted to examine communication, as well as gender and education, so she did a second search. This time she used three key words in her multiple subject search—"gender," "education," and "communication." By using the combination of all three key words, she found thirteen articles that dealt with her topic. She knew that she had sufficiently narrowed her topic for a short speech.

```
                      General

A)  InfoTrac
B)  Periodical Abstracts [OhioLINK]
C)  Readers' Guide
D)  Broadcast News
E)  Dissertation Abstracts {OhioLINK}
F)  New York Times
G)  Newsbank
H)  Newspaper Abstracts [OhioLINK]
I)  Monthly Catalog of U.S. Government Publications
J)  WorldCat
K)  FirstSearch (REQUIRES PASSWORD)
```

Tomoko began to look at the thirteen articles, and found an interesting article in *Education Canada* suggesting that the underachievement of girls was due to societal issues rather than gender issues. She decided not to use an article on gender and publications in core higher education journals that was available in the *Journal of College Student Development.* Probably the most useful article, she thought, was one in *Communication Education* that discussed a gender-balanced curriculum in basic speech communication courses.

Tomoko selected ten of the thirteen articles that she found and printed the entries for later reference. The SearchNet only provided the bibliographical information, so Tomoko still had to go to the stacks to actually find the articles. With her printouts, she went to her library's computerized library catalog system. She had the titles of the journals she wanted, so she typed in T/*Communication Education,* for example, to find the call number and location of this journal.

While Tomoko was at the computerized library catalog system, she also decided to see if there were any books in the library that considered gender and education issues. Her good fortune held, and she found two additional sources. She made a note of their call numbers and locations, too, and went off to find both her journal articles and her books.

Another student wanted to learn about college sports. A controversy over the firing of a basketball coach at his campus stirred his interest. Rich Hoce chose the Sports Sciences and Sports Administration category on the SearchNet. He found that he had several interface possibilities, including ABI/Inform, which indexes articles from about 800 business publications, and the *Business Periodicals Index,* which Rich knew was good for basic literature searches within the business area. He also found ERIC (Educational Resources Information Center), which consists of the Resources in Education (RIE) file of document citations and the Current Index to Journals in Education (CIJE) file of journal article citations from over 750 professional journals. Other choices ranged from a sports discussion group to a medical express line.

Since Rich was interested in college sports, he selected ERIC. ERIC then offered the option of searching through journals from 1966 through 1981 or journals from 1982 through 1994. Because he wanted the most current information, he chose the more recent journals. Rich then entered a multiple subject search using "college" and "sports" for his two key words. This search yielded sixty-one entries, which Rich knew was too broad. He added the word "scholarships" as a third key word, but found that no entries included a combination of the terms "college," "sports," and "scholarships." He had narrowed his topic too far.

Rich thought about his topic for awhile and decided that he really did not select key words that reflected his interests. He actually wanted to focus on basketball. He went back to ERIC and typed "college" and "basketball." His efforts were rewarded, as he found nine entries for this combination.

The bibliographic entries were varied. One article featured Ryneldi Becenti, star of the Arizona State women's basketball team, who discussed how she balanced the demands of college basketball with her academic work. Another article provided information on how Cam Henderson invented the zone defense. Rich also found a highly technical article that considered reinforcement, adversity, and responses to adversity in the videotape play of fourteen college basketball teams. Rich's search also uncovered articles about the broadcasting of basketball games in rural areas, loyalty, alumni giving, and college basketball programs. After he had reviewed the nine articles, he identified six that he wanted to examine in more depth. Rich, like Tomoko, went to the library's computerized library catalog system to find the call numbers and locations of the articles.

Teresa Rojas-Gomez was not in the same situation as her classmates, Tomoko and Rich. When she went to the library, she did not have a particular speech in mind. She had no strong feelings about a topic, but she knew that she wanted to talk about something of current interest. As an international student, she was not sure what issues were of contemporary interest in the United States. She spoke to a member of the library staff, who told her about a periodical known as the *CQ Researcher,* which was published by Congressional Quarterly Inc. She learned that this weekly publication had begun in 1990, and that it had formerly been known as *Editorial Research Reports.* Each week, the periodical featured a different issue of current interest. In examining a few of the back issues, Teresa found the following topics:

Racial tensions in schools	Prozac controversy
Religion in America	Electing minorities
Blood supply safety	Genetically engineered foods
Economic sanctions	Birth control choices
Arts funding	Crime victims' rights
Religion and politics	Foreign policy and public opinion
Regulating tobacco	Dietary supplements
The courts and the media	Nuclear arms cleanup
Welfare experiments	Public land policy
Home schooling	

Teresa observed that each issue was divided into sections identifying the problem; the background of the problem; the chronology of events surrounding the problem; the current status of the problem; the future outlook of the problem; current bibliographical sources including books, reports, and studies; and a section entitled "The Next Step," which included additional information from a newspaper and periodical abstracts data base of current research divided according to relevant topics.

Figure 15

A bibliography card for a book.

> Dorothy C. Holland, <u>Educated in Romance: Women, Achievement, and College Culture</u>. Chicago: The University of Chicago, 1992.
>
> This provocative book is a close-focus ethnography of higher education. The authors study the academic culture of the university and find that "the official grading of academic attainment goes on in eerie counterpoint to the unofficial grading of sexual attractiveness in peer-group life" (p. ix). These researchers found out that although most of the young women they studied were good students and about half of them stated they would seek a career in math or science when they began college, less than a third of them "met their own expectations for the future" (p. 3). The book explains why this appears to be true.

Teresa found the issue on Prozac to be particularly interesting, and decided to do her speech on this topic. She went directly from the *CQ Researcher* to the library's computerized library catalog system to look up books and articles that were included in the *CQ Researcher* and to find additional books. She had eight excellent sources for her speech about the harmful side effects of Prozac and related anti-depressant drugs. Her audience seemed especially interested in learning about the negative effect such drugs have on sexual functioning and behavior.

Students sometimes ask how many sources they should have for their speeches. The guideline that most successful speakers use is the "three per minute" rule, which suggests that they examine at least three sources for every minute they are speaking. For example, if you are to give a five-minute speech, you should examine at least fifteen different sources. You generally end up using about one source per minute from this larger bibliography. Most speech teachers would probably approve of using five sources for a five-minute speech, or eight sources for an eight-minute speech; however, you should discuss the number of sources expected with your instructor.

Each of these students chose a slightly different way to explore a topic. The students narrowed their topics appropriately—partly through electronic means and partly through their own considerations of the topics of interest. You, too, will want to narrow your topic appropriately and conduct your research efficiently. Let us consider some other steps in researching effectively.

Record Potential Sources

Your next step in research is to make a bibliography card for each book, magazine article, or newspaper article that appears to relate closely to your topic. A bibliography card for a book should list the author, title, place of publication, publisher, date of publication, call number (to locate the book in the library), and any notes you might want to make about the specific information in the book or its importance. A bibliography card for a book would look like figure 15. Notice that the name of the author is written in normal order and that the title of the book is underlined. Underlining with a typewriter or in handwritten copy is a way of indicating that it appears in italics when printed.

Figure 16

A bibliography card for a periodical.

Steve Duck, Kris Pond, and Geoff Leatham. "Loneliness and the Evaluation of Relational Events." Journal of Social and Personal Relationships 11 (1994): 253-76.

These authors show that people who are lonely do not evaluate their own or other people's conversations negatively; however, they do "draw negative global conclusions about their own relationships" (p. 253). The authors suggest that lonely people may have general dissatisfaction with their own social performance in their relationships.

Figure 17

A bibliography card for a newspaper article.

J. Troiden, "Green Thumb Helps Nay Ah Shing Kids Grow and Mature," Mille Lacs Messenger, May 11, 1994, p.3.

This article tells about a company called Green Thumb Inc. which employs older people to do a variety of tasks. In this particular instance, the story is about three women in Green Thumb Inc. who are helping in an Ojibwe lower school known as Nay Ah Shing. The three women range in age from 67 to 84. The article suggests that older people are important resources that are sometimes overlooked.

A bibliography card for a periodical has slightly different information (see figure 16). It should include the name of the author, the title of the article, the name of the periodical (underlined), the volume if indicated, the date of publication in parentheses, and the pages on which the article appears in the periodical.

A bibliography card for a newspaper includes the name of the reporter (if available), the headline, the name of the newspaper (underlined), the exact date, the section, and the page number. See figure 17.

A final suggestion concerns the survey of sources and the gathering of a potential bibliography for your speech. You should have more sources in your potential bibliography than you can use, but not so many that you have wasted time writing them. With a potential bibliography of ten sources, only about half are likely to yield material that you can use in your speech. In short, survey with your eyes a large number of potential sources, record on notecards the bibliographic information for those you think will be relevant for your speech topic, and record information only from the ones that prove related to your ultimate goal and the immediate response you seek from your audience.

Figure 18

An index card with a direct quotation.

```
                Fashion and Status

Lure, The Language of Clothes, p. 145.

"Certain concessions have been made to female
emancipation..., but any woman who is honest will admit
that the full-length mink coat that advertises her
husband's wealth is heavier and harder to manage than
the down jacket she wears in the country, and that her
diamonds and gold jewelry are a constant invitation to
mugging and murder."
```

Make Index Cards

Your first temptation might be to take a notebook to the library, start writing down the bibliographic information, and enter all the information from that source in your notebook. Doing that would be a serious mistake.

Writing your sources and information in a book will make the information difficult to retrieve. Writing them on index cards is like entering them in a computer—they can be easily rearranged, organized, and discarded.

The recommended method of recording ideas, quotations, and information from both interviewed and written sources is to use index cards. Buy $3 \times 5''$ or $4 \times 6''$ index cards with or without lines. Use them to record the potential sources and to record the information you find in them. Following are some hints about writing notes on index cards:

1. Exercise extreme care to record your sources and write your notes legibly. Nothing is more irritating than being unable to decipher your own notes when you need them for the speech.

2. Write one idea, quotation, or bit of information on each card. Do not try to write as much as possible on each card, because you will have difficulty retrieving and reorganizing the information.

3. Get in the habit of recording the subject, author, title, and page on the top of each card so you do not forget where you found your information (see figure 18).

4. Take more notes than you need but not so many that you have wasted time. If some information looks relevant and interesting, write it on a card. However, do not try to write down everything you see, or you will have to discard much of what you wrote.

Notice that the index card in figure 18 is a direct quotation limited to a single idea: how women's clothing continues to be a burdensome signal of social standing. Notice also that the direct quotation has three spaced dots, called an ellipsis, indicating that words were edited out to save space on the card and time in the speech.

An index card from a telephone interview might resemble figure 19. The lack of quotation marks indicates that this index card contains a paraphrase rather than a direct quotation from the source.

Figure 19

An index card from a telephone interview, with paraphrased content.

```
                Topic: Men's Clothing and Status

Dr. Emily Williams
Director, School of Home Economics
Cortlander Community College

Dr. Williams told me that men's clothing changes less
radically than does women's clothing but that, in recent
years, bold and fine-striped shirts; wider and more
colorful ties; loose-fitting pleated pants; and
double-breasted, wide-lapel jackets have joined the
two-piece suit in the executive suite.


Telephone interview 1/12/95
```

You are very likely to use electronic means of gathering information for your speech. You may want to consider the most efficient, yet accurate, way of recording this information. Index cards remain the recommended method, but how can you put the information from the computer in index card form? If you can download information on your own disks, you can format the information for notecard size. You can also cut out the data from the computer printouts and paste it on notecards, or you may be able to print it from a computer word processor. You will find that the index cards facilitate the alphabetization and creation of bibliographic materials.

Learn As You Look

Every person who prepares a speech by doing research learns that it is good to keep an open mind about the topic. Your early notions about the topic may change as you learn more about the subject. It is appropriate to do the following:

1. Narrow your topic as you discover its true scope.
2. Modify your own position on an issue consistent with what you now know about the topic.
3. Pursue new directions on the topic that you did not know when you began your research.

Doing research is learning; let it make you more intelligent, more informed, and more confident.

Creating a Bibliography

After you have completed your interviews, used the library, and narrowed down your sources, it is time to create a bibliography. If you have done a good job recording complete information on your bibliography cards, this task will be simple. If you have only captured partial information, you may have to go back to your original sources to find volume numbers, page numbers, the years of publication, the first names or initials of the authors, and so on.

The bibliography of your speech includes a list of the sources consulted or the sources actually used in the speech. Your instructor will tell you whether you should include all of your sources or only those you actually cite in your speech. In any case, you will want to provide them in correct bibliographic form.

Two common bibliographic forms are those provided by the American Psychological Association (APA) and the Modern Language Association (MLA). In order to become familiar with the differences in these two style guides, you should consult the original sources.[9] Alternatively, you may wish to purchase a reference book that includes both of these styles or the style preferred by your instructor.[10]

Three basic bibliographic formats are the entries for a book, a periodical, and a newspaper article. We provide examples of these three for both APA and MLA styles. For other types of bibliographic entries, you are again encouraged to seek a reference book.

APA Style

Books:

Boshu, Z. (1994). *Marxism and human sociobiology: The perspective of economic reforms in China.* Albany: State University of New York Press.

Magolda, M. B. B. (1992). *Knowing and reasoning in college: Gender-related patterns in students' intellectual development.* San Francisco: Jossey-Bass.

Periodicals:

Cumberford, R. (1995, January). Design of the year: Ferrari 456GT. *Automobile,* pp. 54–55.

Dowd, A. R. (1994, December 12). What the vote means to business. *Fortune,* pp. 129–136.

Putnam, J. J. (1994, December). Buenos Aires. *National Geographic,* pp. 84–105.

Waisbord, S. R. (1994). Television and election campaigns in contemporary Argentina. *Journal of Communication, 44,* 125–135.

Newspaper articles:

Goodman, E. (1994, June 21). Conservatives oppose change, then carp about compromise. *The Messenger,* p. 4.

Howlett, D. (1994, June 24). Stonewall: Kicking the closet open: Gay rights marks 25th anniversary. *USA Today,* p. 4A.

Humans, crocodiles share address at Mozambique zoo. (1994, June 15). *The Japan Times,* p. 6.

MLA Style

Books:

Eckert, Alva. *A sorrow in our heart: The life of Tecumseh.* New York: Bantam Books, 1992.

Holland, Dorothy C. *Educated in romance: Women, achievement, and college culture.* Chicago: The University of Chicago, 1992.

Periodicals:

Burgoon, Michael. "To dream the impossible dream: The rhetoric of Gerald R. Miller." *Human Communication Research* 20 (1994): 431–436.

Duck, Steve, Kris Pond, and Geoff Leatham. "Loneliness and the evaluation of relational events." *Journal of Social and Personal Relationships* 11 (1994): 253–276.

Gleick, Elizabeth. "The Beauty Quest." *People Weekly* 5 (December 1994): 65–66.

Johnson, Nils. "King of Bingo." *Ohio Magazine* (December 1994): 39–43, 48–50.

Newspaper articles:

"Humans, crocodiles share address at Mozambique zoo." *The Japan Times* 15 June 1994: 6.

"Native Americans battle to save sacred lands." *The Columbus Dispatch* 11 July 1993: F5.

Troiden, Jason. "Green thumb helps Nay Ah Shing kids grow and mature." *Mille Lacs Messenger* 11 May 1994: 3.

You have probably noticed that the sources are listed in alphabetical order by the last name of the first author or by the name of the article if no author is given. Generally, you also place all of your sources together rather than dividing them up into books, periodicals, and newspaper articles. The following bibliography would be typical. Can you determine if the style is APA or MLA?

Bibliography

Brush, S. (1989, September 24). The Scientific REMifications of an afternoon nap. *Washington Post,* pp. F1 & F8.

Goleman, D. (1989, September 12). Feeling sleepy? An urge to nap is built in. *New York Times,* pp. C1 & C5.

Gorman, J. (1994, March). Go ahead, take a nap. *Reader's Digest,* pp. 143–44.

Hunt, M. (1989, January 29). What a difference a nap makes! *Parade Magazine,* p. 16.

Monroe, D. (1990, July 30). A nap in time. *The Atlanta Constitution,* p. E5.

Nap Break. (1991, July 2). *Wall Street Journal,* p. A1.[11]

Oral Footnotes

When you deliver your speech, you will not read your bibliography to the audience. Instead, you will indicate to them with oral footnotes where you found your information. These oral footnotes will be placed throughout the speech, not at the end of your talk. They only appear at the end of the speech in the formal outline.

The following incident illustrates clearly the importance of oral footnotes. On the front page of the *Boston Globe* appeared an article with a picture of the dean of the College of Communication at Boston University. The headline read: "BU Dean Used the Words of Another: Source Not Given During Speech." The lead paragraph explained that "In his May 12 commencement address before a crowd of future journalists and filmmakers . . . the dean of the College of Communication at Boston University, repeated nearly word for word portions of an article by a nationally known film critic but never acknowledged the source."[12] Nearly word for word? The article exhibited six paragraphs that were either direct quotations or closely paraphrased sections. The article reported fourteen passages repeated nearly word for word.

This speaker, who had joined the faculty as a professor of international relations and journalism, should have known better. His own college provided students with guidelines about plagiarism and the penalties for it. All he would have had to do to avoid this serious breach of ethics is to say that the words and ideas were first printed in Michael Medved's article, "Popular Culture and the War Against Standards," in the February 1991 edition of *Imprimis,* a scholarly journal published by Hillsdale College. He probably would have been safe if he had used an abbreviated oral footnote crediting Medved with the words and ideas. Instead, he was dismissed as dean for his indiscretion and his violation of ethical standards.

A few years ago, a candidate for President of the United States had to drop out of the race for using portions of a British politician's speech, and a candidate for president of a major university dropped out of the race for using portions of another person's publication in a speech without attribution. The moral of these true and tragic stories is clear: you must credit the words and ideas of others with oral footnotes.

What is an oral footnote, and when should you use one? A footnote is used in written works to indicate where information was found. Usually it includes the name of the author, the name of the article, the name of the magazine or paper, the date of publication, and the page on which the quotation or idea was found. In public speaking, an oral

Table 1
Oral Footnotes for Public Speaking

Citing a source for paraphrased information:

According to the July 1991 *Motor Trend,* the 1991 Acura Legend LS can go 0 to 60 mph in 8.3 seconds.

Citing a source for a direct quotation:

Theodore White, in his book entitled *In Search of History,* states, "What I learned was that people accept government only if the government accepts its first duty—which is to protect them."

Citing a magazine, a reference work, and a speech:

In his speech on campus one month ago, Andrew Young . . .
Last week's *Time* magazine reported . . .
According to the 1995 *World Almanac,* the number of people in . . .

footnote is much briefer but equally important. It may be just the name of the person or the publication or speech that is being quoted or paraphrased, or it might include the year or date of publication or the place where the speech was delivered. However brief the citation, the important thing is that the audience understands that the words or ideas came from a source other than the speaker.

What needs to be cited by an oral footnote? Anything that is taken from a source should be cited. It could be a direct quotation, in which you state the exact words of another person from print or a speech. It could be a paraphrase—that is, the words of a source not directly quoted but put in your words. The dean used an author's exact words, and he followed the same idea so closely that he practically filled in the blanks with his own information. That he took the idea from someone else was indisputable.

What do oral footnotes look like? In table 1, you will find the proper form for oral footnotes.

Before leaving the subject of oral footnotes, you should be aware of the connection between oral footnotes and the ethics of public speaking. Following the Golden Rule—"Do unto others as you would have them do unto you"—is an ethical guide for public speakers. Would you want others to use something you wrote or said as if it were their own? In our society, using the words of another person, whether those words were in a speech or a newspaper article, is regarded as a serious offense, so serious that people's careers and opportunities have floundered on that single charge of plagiarism. In citing sources, it is much better to be too careful than to be careless, because the consequences are rough and avoidance is easy. Part of gaining confidence as a public speaker is the certainty that you have avoided plagiarism by using oral footnotes.

Summary

This chapter on finding information stressed the importance of using your personal experience as a resource—as long as it is directly related to the topic or shows your relationship to the topic. The interview is a valuable means of securing information for your speeches, especially if the interview is well planned, well executed, and followed up with accurate notes and quotes. Mentioned also was the possibility of gaining information through phone calls and mail requests.

A third place to find information—besides yourself and other people—is the library. The library staff should be a partner in your plan to produce superior speeches. The library section surveyed the resources available in computerized catalog systems, card catalogs, indexes, dictionaries, encyclopedias, yearbooks and almanacs, and newspapers. You will find that electronic research possibilities will continue to enhance your ability to find pertinent information. New developments are emerging continually.

Effective research requires careful planning. Start your research as soon as you select and narrow a topic, leave time for interviews and for surveying library sources, record your sources and the information in them, and modify your plan as you learn more about your chosen subject.

Finally, this chapter revealed the importance of citing your sources with oral footnotes. Some colleges and universities expel students who use the words of others without citation. Some others give a failing mark in the course or on the assignment. All educational institutions require, as a rule of scholarship, that the words and ideas of another person be attributed to the original author. Anything less is regarded as a breach of ethics.

 # Applications

Application Exercises

Evaluating Personal Experience

1. Write the name of your topic in the top blank and list below it three aspects of your personal life or experience that could be used to enhance your credibility or to provide supporting materials for your speech.

Topic _____
Personal Experience

    1. _____

    2. _____

    3. _____

Evaluate your personal experience by checking off each item as you use it to examine the experience.

_____ Was your experience typical?

_____ Was your experience so typical that it will be boring or so unusual that it was a chance occurrence?

_____ Was your experience one that this audience will appreciate or from which the audience can learn?

_____ Does your experience constitute proof or evidence of anything?

Library Scavenger Hunt

2. You are much more likely to use reference works if you know where they are in the library and if you know what kind of information is in them. The following exercise is designed to better acquaint you with the library and its reference works.

1. From the computerized catalog system or the card catalog, find the author and title of one book that deals with your topic.

Author _____ Title _____

_____

2. Using an electronic periodical index, find the name and author of an article that deals with your topic.

Author _____ Title _____

_____

3. From the *Reader's Guide to Periodical Literature,* find the title and author of one article on your topic.

Author _____ Title _____

_____

4. Using the *Education Index* or other specialized index, give the author, title, and name of publication for an article on the topic you have selected.

Author _____ Title _____

_____ Publication _____

5. Using an encyclopedia, yearbook, or almanac, find specific information about your topic. In one sentence, explain what kind of information you found.

_____

_____

Source _____

6. Using an almanac or a government publication, state some information about a topic in correct form on an index card.

7. Using an electronic newspaper index, look for a current article that is related to your topic.

Author (if provided) _____

Title _____

Newspaper _____

Bibliographic Form

3. See if you can state your sources accurately by placing these sources in proper form for a bibliographical entry.

Source A: The name of the book is *At Home: The American Family 1750–1870.* The book was published in 1990. The author is Elisabeth Donaghy Garrett. The place of publication is New York, New York. The publisher is Harry N. Abrams, Inc.

Source B: The name of the periodical is the *Western Journal of Speech Communication.* The date of publication is Spring 1991. The article runs from page 159 through 179. The authors are Daniel J. Canary, Herry Weger, Jr., and Laura Stafford. The name of the article is "Couples' Argument Sequences and Their Associations with Relational Characteristics." The volume number is 55.

Source C: The name of the reporter is Jessica Lee. The name of the newspaper is *USA Today.* The article appears on page 1. The title of the article is "Hostages Pour Out of Iraq."

To check your answers, compare them to the examples in the chapter.

Endnotes

1. This speech was given by Laura Kovatch during Spring Quarter 1994 at Ohio University in Interpersonal Communication 103: Public Speaking, taught by Kim Varey.
2. This speech was given by Rena D. Campbell during Spring Quarter 1994 at Ohio University in Interpersonal Communication 103: Public Speaking, taught by Dan Shapiro.
3. This speech was given by Jessi Smith during Winter Quarter 1994 at Ohio University in Interpersonal Communication 103: Public Speaking, taught by Kim Varey.
4. These speeches were given by Rachel Planisek during Fall Quarter 1993 at Ohio University in Interpersonal Communication 103: Public Speaking, taught by Marsha Clowers.
5. This speech was given by Steven M. Bailey during Spring Quarter 1994 at Ohio University in Interpersonal Communication 103: Public Speaking, taught by Dan Shapiro.
6. This speech was given by Elizabeth Tyre during Spring Quarter 1994 at Ohio University in Interpersonal Communication 103: Public Speaking, taught by Kim Varey.
7. Lucy M. Rowland, "Libraries and Librarians on the Internet," *Communication Education* 43 (1994): 143–50 observes that "As librarians became leaders in the creation of bibliographic data bases, by the mid-1970s they began to utilize mainframe computers to convert library card catalogs into machine-searchable files. The familiar wooden catalog cases were replaced with computer terminals, but, in actuality, little in the use and retrieval results had changed at all" (p. 143).
8. D. L. Wilson, "Array of New Tools is Designed to Make it Easier to Find and Retrieve Information on the Internet," *Chronicle of Higher Education* 39 (1993): A17–A19.
9. *Publication Manual of the American Psychological Association,* 3rd ed. (Washington, DC: American Psychological Association, 1983); Joseph Gibaldi and Walter S. Achtert, *MLA Handbook for Writers of Research Papers,* 2nd ed. (New York: The Modern Language Association of America, 1984).
10. One excellent reference is Diana Hacker, *A Writer's Reference* (New York: St. Martin's Press, Inc., 1989).
11. This bibliography is taken from a speech entitled, "Naps," which was written and delivered by Heather Tritle, during Spring Quarter 1994 at Ohio University in Interpersonal Communication 103: Public Speaking, taught by Kim Varey.
12. Anthony Flint and Muriel Cohen, "BU Dean Used the Words of Another: Source Not Given During Speech," *The Boston Globe,* July 2, 1991.

Arrange whatever pieces come your way.

Virginia Woolf

SPEECH ORGANIZATION AND OUTLINING

QUESTION OUTLINE

I. Why is speech organization important to the speaker and to the audience?

II. What are the three steps involved in organizing the body of the speech?

III. What are some suggestions that a speaker should use in identifying and writing the main points of a speech?

IV. What are some of the organizational patterns that can be used in ordering your main points?

V. How can the speaker connect main points and subpoints during the speech?

VI. What are the three principles of outlining and what does each principle mean?

VII. What are the three types of outlines most speakers create and when are they created?

VIII. What is included in a formal outline?

Introduction

Sam Cohen had forty-eight notecards full of information, but he didn't have the foggiest notion of what to do with them. He had narrowed the topic of abortion to a prochoice stance, since that was the position his parents had believed in and so did his Rabbi. The Rabbi had given him at least a third of the sources and an interview. Unfortunately, his task now was to make sense of the information by organizing it in a reasonable fashion.

The speech was supposed to be persuasive, and it would have to be, because many students in the class were fundamentalist Christians who believed strongly in the prolife position on abortion. Should he say in the beginning what his position was? Should he state their side of the issue too? Where should he place his best arguments, his most important points, and his best evidence? Sam decided he had better read the chapter on organization and outlining and find answers to his questions.

To help you increase your confidence in public speaking, this chapter will focus on how to organize and outline a speech. You have already found information on your topic, now you need to understand how best to organize that material. In this chapter we will begin by discussing the importance of speech organization.

The bulk of this chapter will discuss how to organize and outline the body of a speech. We will consider how to divide the body into main points, how to determine the order of the main points, and how to incorporate supporting materials.

We will also consider how speakers can show the connections between their main points and subpoints. We will examine the role of transitions, signposts, internal previews, and internal reviews.

Finally, we will turn our attention to outlining, where we will discuss the three principles of outlining—subordination, division, and parallelism, and the three types of outlines—the preparation outline, the formal outline, and the key word outline.

The Importance of Organization

Imagine that you have spent a great deal of time writing a carefully organized speech. After you have finished, you try an experiment. You deliver your speech as you have planned it to one group of people. For another group of people, you organize the speech randomly, moving sentences and ideas around haphazardly. Although you used all of the same words and, indeed, all of the same sentences, your speech has no structure to it. How do you think the two audiences would respond? Do you think both audiences would see you as a competent speaker? Do you think the two audiences would be able to recall a similar amount of information from your speeches?

Researchers have conducted experiments similar to the one we are describing. Speakers who gave well organized speeches—compared to those who were not well organized—found a number of benefits. First, audience members could understand the organized speeches better.[1] Second, audience members perceived speakers who delivered organized speeches more competent and trustworthy than speakers who delivered disorganized speeches.[2] Clearly, audiences appreciate well organized speeches.

Speakers also benefit from taking the time to carefully organize their speeches. First, speakers state that they are more confident when their messages are more (rather than less) organized.[3] Second, they believe that they deliver their speeches more smoothly.[4] Third, Paul Fritz and Richard Weaver found that to the extent that students can learn and master the ability to organize ideas, they will be better analytical thinkers.[5] Organizational skills probably generalize in positive ways beyond the speaking situation. In short, learning how to organize ideas for a speech will help you as a speaker and in a variety of other future endeavors.

The introduction, body, and conclusion are the three main components of any speech. In this chapter we consider the organization of the body of the speech. Generally, the body of the speech is organized and created before the introduction and conclusion.

Organizing the Body of the Speech

Divide the Body into Main Points

The first task in organizing the body of the speech is to identify the main points that you will discuss. Examine the material that you have gathered and consider the key issues you want to address. If you have written your specific purpose, you may be able to identify your main points easily. For example, one journalism student gave a speech on writing books.[6] Her specific purpose was to have her audience learn the steps involved in writing a book. Her main points included the following:

> **I.** How to get started on writing your book.
> **II.** How to do research.
> **III.** How to do the actual writing of the book.
> **IV.** How to publish your book.

In another speech this same student had a more difficult time determining her main points from her specific purpose. Her purpose was to inform her audience about the lifestyle of Native Americans who formerly lived in the Eastern Woodlands of the U.S. and to dispel myths about them. She finally decided on these main points:[7]

> **I.** The Native Americans inhabited an area of North America known as the Eastern Woodlands.
> **II.** Eastern Woodland Native Americans lived in wigwams and longhouses.
> **III.** The Eastern Woodland Native Americans were distinctive in appearance because of their attire and ornaments.

These sets of main points divide the topic into main ideas that can be explained and discussed further. The main points, as we see here, provide the skeleton for the body of the speech. They will be fleshed out with supporting materials, examples, evidence, and further divisions of subpoints and sub-subpoints.

As you are considering your speech topic, your specific purpose, and the main points that you will develop from them, you should keep in mind some other advice about main points. First, you should consider having between two and five main points. Second, you should word your main points in a parallel manner. Third, your main ideas should be approximately equal in importance. Let us consider each of these suggestions in more depth.

Limit Your Main Points to Between Two and Five Points

Most speeches have three main points, but any number between two and five is fine. Some topics are difficult to divide, and you may come up with only two main points. For example, imagine that you are going to speak on the way husbands and wives view marriage. A topic like this one has only two obvious main points:

> **I.** Husbands' views of a traditional marriage are often more positive than wives' views of marriage.
> **II.** Wives' views of a traditional marriage are often less positive than husbands' views of marriage.

Other topics are more easily divisible into a greater number of points. For instance, if you are talking about some process, you could divide your talk up into the five main steps of the process. Imagine that you are giving a speech on growing your own vegetables. You could organize your speech with these five main points:

> **I.** Prepare the soil with surface tilling.
> **II.** Plant the seeds or starter plants in measured rows.
> **III.** Protect the plants from chemicals, insects, and drought.
> **IV.** Harvest the crops by picking or cutting at the correct time.
> **V.** Prepare your garden for the next year by clearing weeds, turning the soil, and covering it with mulch.

You might be tempted, sometimes, to divide your topic into more than five main points. For example, if you are going to talk about breeds of dogs that are good house pets, you may have a dozen or more breeds that could each be a main point. When this occurs, you want to examine your list of several main points and determine if there are ways to group these points under broader, more generic categories. For instance, the long list of dogs may be able to be subsumed under the main points of small dogs, medium-sized dogs, and large dogs. Or, you might be able to divide them into short-haired, medium-haired, and long-haired dogs.

Word Your Main Points in a Parallel Manner

A second suggestion is to word your main points in a manner that is as parallel as possible. Parallel construction in speaking and writing increases clarity, sounds more engaging, and lingers longer in memory. Parallel construction means that you repeat words, phrases, and sentences. Which of the following would be easier to hear and easier to remember?

No Parallel Construction

I went to the Promised Land where I found that people did not fear each other.

The people had homes.

There was food enough for everyone.

Jobs were available for people who wanted them.

Parallel Construction

I went to the Promised Land where people do not fear each other.

I went to the Promised Land where people had a roof over their heads.

I went to the Promised Land where people had food for their kids.

I went to the Promised Land where people had jobs if they wanted them.

Let us re-examine the main points on the speech about how to write a book.

> I. How to get started on writing your book.
> II. How to do research.
> III. How to do the actual writing of the book.
> IV. How to publish your book.[8]

While these main points clearly define four steps in the writing of a book, they are not parallel. They might be rewritten as follows:

> I. Getting started on the book.
> II. Doing research for the book.
> III. Writing the book.
> IV. Publishing the book.

They could also be written this way:

> I. How to get started on writing your book.
> II. How to do research on your book.
> III. How to write your actual book.
> IV. How to publish your book.

Similarly, the speech on the Eastern Woodlands may have benefitted from being rewritten with parallel structure. The speaker might have more appropriately had these three main points:

> I. The geography of the Eastern Woodlands.
> II. The homes of the Eastern Woodland Native Americans.
> III. The people of the Eastern Woodlands.

While these changes in wording may appear to be subtle, they affect the way subsequent subpoints and sub-subpoints will be written. In general, using parallel construction in your main points encourages more parallel development of supporting ideas. When your main points are organized similarly, the audience is more likely to remember them.

Ensure That Your Main Points Are All Relatively Equal in Importance
Another important consideration to keep in mind as you write your main points is whether or not they are relatively equal to each other in importance. Your main points should be about the same in magnitude. One way that you can check this as you develop the main points is to consider how much subdividing you are doing for each point. If one main point has several subdivisions, but the others have almost no subdivisions, that point must be far more important than the others.

Similarly, when you practice your speech later on, you may find that you do not spend equal time on each main point. It is not essential that each main point be granted exactly the same amount of time, but the time you spend discussing each point should be relatively similar. If you have three main points, you should probably spend between 20 and 50 percent of your total time allotted for the body of the speech on each one. If you have five main points, you might spend between 10 and 30 percent of your total time allotted for the body of the speech on each one. In the speech on the Eastern Woodland Native Americans, for example, the speaker spent about 30 percent of her time defining and describing the Eastern Woodlands, about 25 percent of her time describing the types of homes of the Eastern Woodland Native Americans, and 45 percent of her time describing the appearance of the Eastern Woodland Native Americans.

In the speech about writing a book, the speaker spent about 20 percent of her time on how to get started, nearly 50 percent of her time on how to do research, and about 15 percent of her time on the last two main points (doing the actual writing of the book and publishing the book). Her time allotments for each main point were not identical, but it was not too extreme to cause notice. Further, her allotments might reflect the actual proportion of time involved in each of these activities when one writes a book.

Determine the Order of the Main Points

Sometimes the order of your main points seems obvious. For example, in the speech on writing a book, the speaker arranged the main points in chronological order. In other words, she talked about what occurs first in the writing of a book, what occurs next, and so on. The speech would have seemed bizarre if the publication of the book preceded how to get started on writing a book.

At other times, the organizational pattern is not quite so clear. In this section we provide you with some alternatives you can consider for the organization of your main points. As you will see, you actually have several options for organizing your main points.

The general purpose of your speech will suggest potential ways to organize it. Among the possible organizational patterns for your speech are the time-sequence and spatial relations patterns, which are often used in informative speaking; the cause-effect and topical sequence patterns, which are used both in informative and persuasive speaking; and the problem-solution and Monroe Motivated Sequence patterns, which are often used in persuasive speaking. A seventh pattern, climactic or anticlimactic, describes a way to order arguments, ideas, or supporting materials so they can be superimposed over other patterns.

The topic of your speech and the specific purpose will also affect your organizational pattern. For example, if you are giving a speech on a step-by-step process, you will probably rely on the time-sequence pattern. If you are attempting to persuade an audience to sign a petition, you might use a climactic pattern. The effective and ethical public speaker develops a large repertoire of organizational possibilities that can be applied appropriately to the general purpose, specific purpose, and topic.

Time-Sequence Pattern

The **time-sequence pattern** states the order of events over time. It reveals when something occurred. You should use this pattern when your primary purpose is to tell your audience how something came about over a period of time. Examples would be stating the steps in constructing a cedar chest, in making French bread, in growing an eastern white pine from seed to maturity, or in recounting the watershed events leading to the Civil War. This pattern is commonly used in "how to do it" speeches because the audience will be unable to "do it" unless steps are followed in the correct order. A speech outline using the time-sequence pattern is shown in figure 1.

Patterns of Organization

Usually Informative	Either Informative or Persuasive	Usually Persuasive
Time-Sequence	Cause-Effect	Problem-Solution
Spatial Relations	Topical Sequence	Monroe's Motivated
	Climactic	Sequence
	Anticlimactic	

Immediate purpose: To instruct class members about registration procedures for the next session so that they can complete the process without difficulty

Statement to gain audience's favorable attention

Introduction:

I. Registration for classes is a process that can be completed without difficulty by following certain steps.

Thesis sentence

Body:

II. The steps for completing registration include selecting forms, securing signatures, and turning in papers at the correct place.

Main points

   A. Go to Central Administration to pick up your registration forms.

   B. Complete your own registration forms, including all of the classes you wish to take.

   C. Find your advisor for a signature.

   D. Turn in your registration at Window 3 in the Central Administration Building.

Conclusion:

Conclusion

III. After you complete the appropriate steps cited above, you must wait for two weeks until the computer sorts out all of the class requests.

Figure 1

An example of the time-sequence pattern of organization.

Spatial Relations Pattern

The **spatial relations pattern** demonstrates how things are related in space. You would use this pattern when you have to show an audience where places are located on a map; where the tachometer, odometer, and speedometer are located on a dashboard; or how to select choices on a menu-driven computer screen with a mouse. Your purpose, not the topic, determines your choice of organizational pattern. So if your purpose is to show the audience how to arrange lighting for fashion photography, you would use a spatial relations pattern to show them the lighting design and location of the subject. The example of spatial relations in figure 2 shows how a speaker could use a detailed map to show location of historical sites.

Problem-Solution Pattern

The **problem-solution pattern** tends to be used more often in persuasive than in informative speeches. The statement of the problem is difficult to describe without framing it in some way that indicates your own perspective that you want the audience to adopt. For example, let's say you describe the problem of crime in terms of pickpockets and muggings.

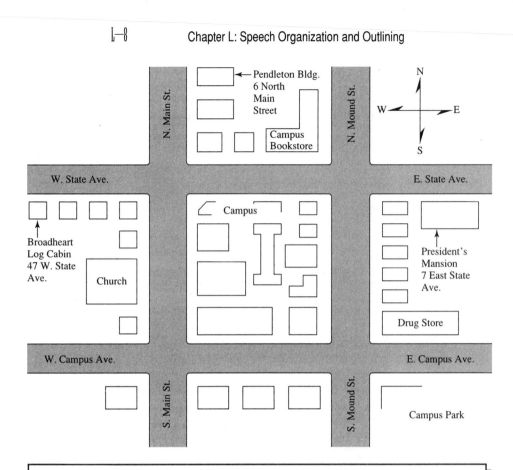

Immediate purpose: To show the audience how to locate historically important sites in our area.

Introduction:

   I. Unknown to many students, this area has a number of historically important sites.

   II. Knowing how to find these sites will increase your appreciation for this area of the country.

Body:

   III. As indicated on the map, there are three historically significant sites within walking distance of the university.

      A. The Broadheart Log Cabin was discovered under clapboard siding on West State Avenue.

      B. The President's mansion was built by a coal baron in the 1800s.

      C. The Pendelton Building on Main Street was the scene of the area's most dramatic murder.

Conclusion:

   IV. All three buildings are open year-round and admission is free.

   V. I encourage all of you to learn more about the local area by visiting these historic sites.

Figure 2

An example of the spatial relations pattern of organization.

That is your perspective. One could just as easily define crime as the millions of dollars lost in white collar crimes like fraud, embezzlement, and scams. That is a different perspective. The point is that to describe a problem reflects a point of view that you want your audience to adopt.

The solution is even more likely to be perceived as persuasive because your solutions to problems ordinarily advocate some policy or action that you want your audience to embrace. In the case of person-on-person crimes, you might, for example, advocate closer control over who has weapons or stronger penalties for using them. In the case of white collar crime, you might advocate closer surveillance by the Attorney General, more widespread warnings about scam artists, or jail time for so-called victimless crimes. In both cases, you select a particular solution that you end up persuading your audience to adopt.

The problem-solution pattern raises one serious question for the speaker: how much should you say about the problem or the solution? Usually you can work out a proper ratio based on what the audience knows about the issue. If the listeners are unaware that a problem exists, you may have to spend time telling them about it. On the other hand, if the problem is well known to all, you can spend most of your time on the solution. This pattern lends itself nicely to outlining, with the problem being one main head and the solution the other. An example of the problem-solution pattern of organization is shown in figure 3.

Cause-Effect Pattern

The **cause-effect pattern** of organization describes or explains a problem and its ramifications. Some examples include the cause of Parkinson's Disease and its effects on the body; the causes of urban blight and one local government's solution; and the causes of low- and high-pressure weather systems and their effect on ground temperature. As with the problem-solution pattern, this one lets you decide how much time you should spend on the cause(s) and how much on the effect(s). A cause-effect pattern of organization is shown in figure 4. This outline suggests that the speaker will spend about two-thirds of the allotted time talking about the causes of social drinking and about one-third talking about the effect of those factors.

Climactic and Anticlimactic Patterns

The **climactic** and **anticlimactic patterns** can be seen as a way to organize an entire speech, or as an overlay—a pattern that can "go over" or be superimposed over other organizational patterns. For example, you could organize a problem-solution speech in which you use a climactic pattern to describe the problems and an anticlimactic pattern to describe the solution. Or you could have a time-sequence pattern in which your entire speech builds toward a climactic ending about how you survived a traumatic event, what brought a big dispute to an end, or where your journey will end. The climactic speech, like a good story, builds toward some exciting conclusion. The anticlimactic speech starts with the excitement and then proceeds to unravel the story behind the excitement. An example of a climactic pattern is shown in figure 5.[9] For further information on the climactic and anticlimactic patterns, see figure 6.

Topical Sequence Pattern

The **topical sequence pattern** is a highly versatile organizational pattern. Seen by some as the pattern of last resort and by others as the most important form of organization, using the topical sequence pattern simply means that you divide up your topic. For instance, the following organizational patterns are all topical: a speech showing advantages and disadvantages, a speech citing different qualities of some object or thing, a speech on the pros and cons on an issue, four qualities of a leader, or three types of local transportation. Figure 7 shows an example of the topical sequence pattern.

Figure 3

An example of the problem-solution pattern of organization.

Statement to gain audience's favorable attention

Thesis sentence

Main points

Review

Immediate purpose: To convince my audience to discontinue practices that invite credit card fraud

Introduction:
I. Thousands of credit card holders are bilked each year by thieves.
II. Today, you will find out more about the problem of credit card fraud and some solutions to the problem.

Problem:
III. The problem of credit card fraud is stolen cards, unauthorized copies, and telephone phonies.
   A. When your credit card is taken by a pickpocket or robber, you may be charged for a spending spree by the thief.
   B. When you pay with a credit card, an employee might keep an unauthorized copy of the carbon so your number can be used for phone purchases.
   C. Telephone crooks trick you into revealing your credit card number on the phone to use it themselves for purchases.

Solution:
IV. The solution to credit card fraud is to follow the rules on stolen cards, take carbons, and avoid revealing your number to strangers.
   A. Report stolen cards immediately by keeping phone numbers for your cards in a list off your person.
   B. You should take your customer's copy and any full-length carbons or copies at the time of purchase.
   C. Never tell someone your credit card number on the phone unless you placed the call for a purchase.

Conclusion:
V. You can avoid credit card fraud by being a cautious customer.
   A. Treat your plastic as if it were worth your line of credit because that is what you can lose—and more.
   B. Watch, guard, and protect your credit card with vigilance and maybe even insurance.
VI. Your credit card may be worth a fortune to you and those who would prey on you: use it defensively.

Another example of the topical sequence pattern that can be used in persuasive, legal, or logic-based speeches is the "speech of reasons." In the speech of reasons the body is divided into a series of arguments for or against some proposition. The speech is persuasive because the main points, the reasons or arguments, move the audience toward concurrence or acceptance. Such a speech could also have an overlay of climactic organization with each argument increasing in strength, relevance, or potency.

Monroe's Motivated Sequence

Monroe's Motivated Sequence[10] was developed by Alan Monroe, who applied John Dewey's work on reflective thinking to persuasion. This organizational pattern includes five specific components: attention, need, satisfaction, visualization, and action.

Figure 4

An example of the cause-effect pattern of organization.

Immediate purpose: To persuade the class that social drinking leads to alcoholism

Statement to gain audience's favorable attention

Thesis sentence

Introduction:

I. Jobs, school, and families bring stress, which many of us try to reduce with alcohol.

II. For some the social drinking will become problem drinking, which will become alcoholism.

Main points

Body:

III. Why an individual becomes chemically dependent on alcohol remains a mystery, but the reasons seem rooted in nature and nurture.

    A. Children of the chemically dependent have a much greater chance of becoming chemically dependent themselves.

    B. Persons who drink at all risk becoming chemically dependent.

IV. Social drinking can become problem drinking.

    A. The person who cannot seem to stop drinking is already a problem drinker.

    B. The person who passes out, blacks out, or cannot remember what occurred has a serious drinking problem.

    C. The person whose relationships with others begin to fail with regularity has turned from people to alcohol.

V. The problem drinker becomes an alcoholic.

    A. The person who is unable to stop drinking has become chemically dependent.

    B. The person who is alcoholic must usually be helped by others to stop.

    C. The most common way to avoid recurrence is to never drink again.

Review

Conclusion:

VI. The best illustration that social drinking leads to alcoholism is that a nondrinker will never become an alcoholic.

    A. Persons with a family history of chemical dependence can protect themselves by abstinence.

    B. Persons whose families see a person becoming dependent might want to encourage nondrinking before the problem becomes worse.

Following this sequence, you would first attempt to capture the attention of your audience. You want your audience to decide that it is important to listen to you.

Second, you establish the need for your proposal. You want to describe a problem or show why some need exists. You want your audience to believe that something must be done.

Third, you present the solution to the problem or show how the need can be satisfied. You want your audience to understand how your proposal will satisfy the need.

Fourth, you go beyond simply presenting the solution by visualizing it for the audience. You want the audience to see themselves enjoying the benefits of your proposal.

Last, you state the behavior that you expect of your audience. In this step, you request action or approval. You want your audience to respond by saying that they will do what you have asked. Your speech should have a strong conclusion that asks for specific, but reasonable, action.

Figure 5

An example of the climactic pattern of organization.

Immediate purpose: To have classmates recognize the difference between media-perpetuated views of the attitudes of college students and the actual attitudes shown in a recent study

Introduction:

Statement to gain audience's favorable attention

   I. Our elders often think that college students are seeking high-paying jobs and the life of single bliss.
     A. The press headlines stories about the materialistic goals of youth.
     B. Books and magazines emphasize the lives of the swinging singles.

Thesis sentence

  II. A new study indicates that these views of today's youth may be incorrect.

Body:

Main points

  III. A national survey of first-year students indicates that their top goals focus on relationships.
     A. The Institute for Social Research at the University of Michigan finds that 80 percent of the students sought a good marriage and family life.
     B. Seventy percent of the first-year students cite strong friendship as a top goal.
  IV. The Michigan study shows that nearly 100 percent of the first-year students want to marry and have children.
   V. The study reveals at least one possible contradiction in student attitudes toward top goals.
     A. Two-thirds of the students say the mother of preschool children should be at home with them.
     B. Only 4 percent of the women expect to be full-time homemakers at age thirty.

Conclusion:

Review

  VI. First-year students seek good marriages and strong friendships as their top goals in life.
  VII. First-year students do not live up to the stereotype portrayed in the media.

Figure 6

Climactic or anticlimactic patterns depend on where you place your best or most important material.

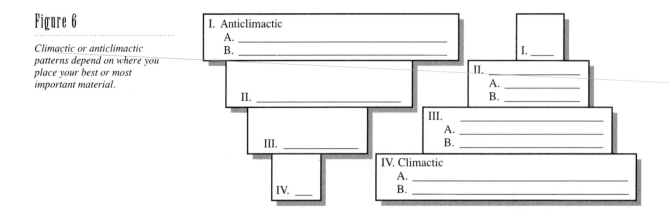

Immediate purpose: To invite prospective students to measure themselves against the criteria for being a communication major by stating whether or not they qualify to be admitted on their evaluation of the speech

Introduction:

Statement to gain audience's favorable attention

I. Crowded conditons and shortage of faculty have resulted in new admission standards.
  A. The College of Communication has 2200 majors.
  B. The College of Communication has eighty faculty members.

Thesis sentence

II. The new admission standards are more rigorous than those of the past.

Body:

Main points

III. Direct admission to the College of Communication depends on class rank and SAT scores.
  A. Direct admission students must be in the top one-third of their high school graduating class.
  B. Direct admission students must have SAT scores of at least 1000, combined verbal and quantitative.

IV. Transfer students must have a 2.5 cumulative grade point average after forty-five quarter credits for admission.

Conclusion:

Statement encouraging listeners to act on speech's ideas

V. Use your evaluation form to indicate whether or not you qualify for direct or indirect admission to the College of Communication.

Figure 7

An example of the topical sequence pattern of organization.

One student was upset by the second-hand smoke that he was forced to breathe each day. His speech, which followed the steps of Monroe's Motivated Sequence, is shown in figure 8.[11]

We have surveyed seven organizational patterns you can use in your public speeches. The one you select for your own speech should be determined largely by the topic you select, the purpose of your speech, how much the audience knows about the topic, and which arguments or evidence the *audience* will perceive as strongest or best.

Do not conclude from this discussion that these are the only ways to organize a speech. A recent article in a speech journal tells how storytelling is used in criminal trials by lawyers who need to convince jurors to make sophisticated judgments about complex information.[12] In another case, a student delivered a highly effective speech by telling a series of five stories about himself, interspersed with a refrain that was his main point. His organization was effective, but the speech defied the principles of outlining. The number of ways in which you can organize your speech is limited only by your imagination.

Incorporate Supporting Materials

As we stated, the main points create the skeleton of the body of the speech. The speaker must flesh out this skeleton with subpoints and sub-subpoints. These subordinate materials include examples, illustrations, proof, and other supporting materials.

Figure 8

An example of Monroe's Motivated Sequence.

A Law Against Smoking in Public

I. Introduction:
A. Twice a day I walk to Bentley Hall for class, and just as I get to the doors, I am engulfed by a cloud of smoke from a group of people who insist on smoking before class. Something must be done about this.
B. In the book entitled <u>Passive Smoking</u> by Susan Neumister[1], second-hand smoking is defined as the phrase associated with the inhalation by nonsmokers of tobacco smoke produced by smokers.
C. A study in <u>Current Science</u> by Ingrid Wickelgren reports that cigarette smoking kills 419,000 Americans every year.[2]
D. There are three reasons why I am credible on this subject.
    1. I have lived with smokers and asthma sufferers for much of my life.
    2. I have been locked on the 6th floor of the library studying smoking for the past week.
    3. I take classes in Bentley Hall.
E. Today I'll begin speaking about the problem of smoking in public places. Secondly, I will present my solution and prove that it must be enacted. Finally, I'll speak about what will happen if my solution is not enacted and what will occur if it is enacted.

II. Need:
A. First of all, the problem is that 40 million Americans smoke.[3]
B. Germs and poison live in second-hand smoke, and this smoke is everywhere.
    1. It lurks in front of Bentley Hall and every other hall across campus.
    2. You can't go out for a night of boot scootin' country dancing at a club uptown without coming home saturated with the stench of smoke.
    3. Even restaurants are filled with smoke.
C. Smokers poison themselves, and when they smoke in public, they poison everyone else as well. Second-hand smoke kills.
D. The World Health Organization says that unless people are encouraged to quit smoking, the number of deaths due to smoking will reach half a billion.[4]

III. Satisfaction:
A. My solution is to enact a law forbidding cigarette or any other drug smoking in public.
B. Smokers can have as many cigarettes as they want in the privacy of their own homes. However, in public places, smoking would be prohibited.
C. My proposal would bring many benefits.
    1. It would decrease the number of hospitalized asthma victims.
    2. It would promote purer air.
    3. It would greatly diminish deaths due to passive smoking.
    4. It would take away the odor on clothes and the watery eyes caused by smoke.
D. Veronica Johannesen was awarded workers' compensation benefits for asthma developed on the job in New York City from second-hand smoke.[5]
E. Even corporate giants like GM and Texas Instruments are tightening policies on smoking or banning it entirely to save money.
F. Smokers object to this proposed law.
    1. Smokers claim that this is America and the government may make no law to abridge their freedom to smoke.
       a. It is true that it is their right to smoke, but they do not have the right to put the health of nonsmokers at risk.

Figure 8 (continued)

  b. According to a 1994 <u>Wall Street Journal</u> report, the EPA used studies on the risk of second-hand smoke to ban smoking from all office buildings.[6]

  2. Another argument by smokers' rights advocates claims that second-hand smoke in no way jeopardizes the health of nonsmokers.

  a. The <u>Journal of the American Medical Association</u> reports that active and passive smoking causes immediate physiological changes and illnesses in children.[7]

  b. The American Heart Association recommends reducing children's exposure to tobacco hazards.[8]

IV. Visualization:

A. Let's imagine what will happen if my proposal is not accepted.

  1. If it is not enacted, we will continue to unnecessarily suffer from burning eyes, coughing attacks, and smoke-stained skin.

  2. <u>U.S. News and World Report</u> says children are getting hooked on nicotine in alarming numbers.[9]

B. Finally, let's flip the coin and imagine a cigarette smoke free environment.

  1. Unsuspecting victims of second-hand smoke will no longer perish.

  2. Smokers' children will no longer be as prone to suffering.

  3. We can once again feel free to breathe in public.

V. Action:

A. Today we looked at the problem of smoking in public places. Secondly, I proposed the solution that smoking be outlawed in public places. Finally, we imagined two scenarios: one in which my proposal is not accepted and nonsmokers serve as targets for death, and the other scenario in which the law is enforced and living conditions improve.

B. On a personal level, I do not hesitate to ask someone to put a cigarette out. I refuse to silently wait as I become a statistic.

C. Remember, smoking is a colorful habit. Your teeth turn yellow, and your lungs turn black. Though you may not smoke, this could happen to you just because you go country dancing, out to eat, or even to Bentley Hall.

In this section we draw your attention to the idea that speakers do not stop the organizing process once they have identified their main headings. Let us take, for an example, the speech on the Native Americans of the Eastern Woodlands. This informative speech was very straightforward. The speaker supported the main points by including the following subpoints, as well as some presentational aids that are not shown here.[13]

I. The Native Americans inhabited an area of North America known as the Eastern Woodlands.

  A. The geographic region where these Native Americans lived can be seen on a map of the United States.

  B. The principal tribes inhabiting the area are listed on my poster.

II. Eastern Woodland Native Americans lived in wigwams and longhouses.

  A. Tribes or bands that preferred individual or family living quarters chose the wigwam.

  B. Tribes or bands that preferred a more communal arrangement chose the longhouse.

III. The Eastern Woodland Native Americans were distinctive in appearance because of their attire and ornaments.

  A. The accompanying pictures of males show them in everyday and battle dress.

  B. The accompanying pictures of females show them in informal and ceremonial attire.

Developing the supporting materials may not be quite so straightforward. Persuasive speeches are often more complicated than are brief informative speeches like the one outlined above.

You may be an expert researcher who is able to find far more information on your topic than you can possibly use in your speech. Which information do you use and which do you discard? Two authors state that in an ideal situation, the speaker chooses "the most important facts and figures," "the most authoritative judgments about a situation, made by sources the audience will respect," and "at least one interesting story or example that helps humanize and clarify the situation."[14]

For the speech on second-hand smoke, the speaker found facts and figures that showed the harm caused by second-hand smoke. He could have found facts and figures on the harm caused by first-hand smoke, but that would have been less relevant to his thesis. He cited the authors of books and magazine articles who were experts on second-hand smoke. He also began and ended his speech with circumstances with which his audience was familiar—walking to classroom buildings, eating at restaurants, and going to bars. He personalized it further by observing that everyone in his audience was a second-hand smoker. This speaker probably received high marks for highly appropriate supporting materials.

Before we conclude this section, we need to look at the ways that speakers manage to hold their speeches together. If you identify and organize two to five main points and appropriate supporting materials, your job is still not completed. You also need to devise methods of moving from one point to another, of telling the audience where you are in the overall speech, where you are going next, and where you have been. This "glue" is critical in a speech because audience members cannot "reread" a speech as they can reread an essay if they get lost in the organization.

Consider the Connections

Transitions, signposts, internal previews, and internal reviews are the mortar between the bricks. Together they allow the audience easy access to the information you are presenting. Audience members appreciate being informed that you are finished with one point and moving on to another. They show high regard for the speaker who lets them know where he or she is within the organization of the speech. They value previews, which tell them what lies ahead, as well as reviews, which tell them what they have just heard. Let us consider each of these four devices.

Transitions

Transitions are statements throughout the speech that relate back to what has already been said and forward to what will be said. For instance, a transition might sound like this:

Now that you have seen the consequences of smoking, consider some methods of kicking that habit.

This transition might well appear in the middle of a speech about lung cancer, heart trouble, and high blood pressure in the first half and "cold turkey," behavioral modification, and substitutions in the second half of the speech.

Transitions also move the speech and the speaker toward, then away from visual aids.

We know that cancer is a vicious consequence of smoking; just how vicious cancer is can be seen on this graph, which indicates how likely you are to contract the disease if you smoke.

After explaining the figures on the visual aid, another transition moves you back into the speech:

> *The graphs are grim evidence of how smoking is correlated with cancer, but cancer is not the only terrible consequence: pulmonary emphysema affects smokers more than any other group.*

As with all transitions, the statement reflects back to what was said and forward to what will be said. Such transitional statements appear throughout the speech as you move from main point to main point and into and out of support material.

Signposts

Signposts are often briefer than transitions because they do not have to point backward and forward; they have only to tell the listener where the speaker is in the speech. Some examples include the following:

My first point is that . . .

Another reason you should . . .

One of the best examples is . . .

To illustrate this point, I will . . .

Let us look at this picture . . .

A second, and even more convincing argument is . . .

One last illustration will show . . .

Signposts are the guides that help the audience follow your movement through the speech. Skillful use of signposts and transitions will clarify your organization and help you become a confident speaker.

Internal Previews

Internal previews inform listeners of your next point or points, and are more detailed than transitions. They are similar to the statements a speaker makes in the introduction of his or her speech, but they occur within the body of the speech. Examples of internal previews include the following:

I will tell you next about how you can prevent skin cancer in four different ways.

My next point is that depression can be prevented, and I will tell you how you can prevent it in your own life.

Share an image with me as we explore the beauty of the Canadian Rockies next.

The speaker who discussed the Eastern Woodland Native Americans might say, "I would like to tell you next about the types of homes that were built and inhabited by people living in the Eastern Woodlands. As you will determine, two distinctive types of homes predominated." She would be introducing her second main point and suggesting how she was going to subdivide it.

Suppose the speaker said, "We have just discussed the geography of the Eastern Woodlands, and we will now turn our attention to the types of homes that predominated in the Eastern Woodlands." In this instance, she would be offering a transition. If she added to this transition, "As you will determine, two distinctive types of homes predominated," she would be providing both a transition and an internal preview.

Internal Reviews

Internal reviews remind listeners of your last point or points and are more detailed than transitions. They are similar to what a speaker does in the conclusion of his or her speech, but they occur within the body of the speech. Examples of internal reviews include the following:

I have just told you about three reasons you should not drink and drive.

My four main points concerning suicide among children were . . .

Let me remind you of what I just told you . . .

We have considered the importance of speech organization and discussed the three steps that are involved in organizing the body of a speech. We also discussed some suggestions for identifying the main points of a speech, and offered seven patterns you can use to arrange your main points. Finally, we discussed ways that the speaker can connect main points. We turn now to the second major topic of this chapter: outlining the speech.

Principles of Outlining

The organization of a speech is generally shown in an outline form. Outlining is relatively easy to learn. There are three principles that govern the writing of an outline—subordination, division, and parallelism. The following sections are devoted to helping you understand these three principles so you can learn how to compose an outline.

Subordination

If you follow the **principle of subordination,** your outline will indicate which material is more important and which is less important. More important materials usually consist of generalizations, arguments, or conclusions. Less important materials consist of the supporting evidence for your generalizations, arguments, or conclusions. In the outline, Roman numerals indicate the main points, capital letters indicate the subpoints under the Roman numeral statements, and Arabic numbers indicate sub-subpoints under the subpoints. Figure 9 shows a typical outline format. Notice, too, that the less important the material, the greater the indentation from the left-hand margin.

Principles of Outlining

1. Subordination
2. Division
3. Parallelism

Figure 9

Symbols and margins indicating subordination.

I. Generalization, conclusion, or argument is a main point.
  A. The first subpoint consists of illustration, evidence, or other supporting material.
  B. The second subpoint consists of similar supporting material for the main point.
    1. The first sub-subpoint provides additional support for the subpoint stated in "B."
    2. The second sub-subpoint also supports subpoint "B."
II. The second generalization, conclusion, or argument is another main point in the speech.

The principle of subordination is based not only on the symbols (numbers and letters) and indentations, but also on the content of the statements. The subpoints are subordinate to the main points, the sub-subpoints are subordinate to the subpoints, and so on. Therefore, you need to evaluate the content of each statement to determine if it is broader or narrower, more important or less important than the statements above and below it. The student outline in figure 9 illustrates how the content of the statements indicates levels of importance.

Division

The second principle of outlining is the **principle of division,** which states that, if a point is to be divided, it must have at least two subpoints. For example, the outline illustrated in figure 10 contains two main points (I, II), two subpoints (A, B) under main point I, and three sub-subpoints (1, 2, 3) under subpoint A. All items are either undivided (II) or divided into two or more parts. The principle of division can, however, be applied too rigidly: sometimes a main point will be followed by a single example, a solo clarification, or an amplification. Such cases can be regarded as exceptions to the general rule: points, if divided, must be separated into two or more items of approximately equal importance.

Parallelism

The third principle of outlining is the **principle of parallelism,** which states that main points, subpoints, and sub-subpoints must use the same grammatical and syntactical forms. That means that in a sentence outline you would use all sentences, not a mixture of sentences, dependent clauses, and phrases; and that the sentences would tend to appear the same in structure with subject followed by verb followed by object, for instance. Figure 11 illustrates a sentence outline using parallel form.[15]

An outline can use parallel construction without consisting entirely of sentences. For example, a key word outline on notecards might consist of single words used to remind you of the content as you deliver your speech.

To review the information on the principles of outlining, you should examine figure 12, which briefly explains each of the three principles.

In the preparation and delivery of a speech, you will generally make three different kinds of outlines. First, you will create a preparation, or working outline. Next, you will probably be required to provide your instructor with a formal outline. Finally, you may want to create a key word outline on notecards, which you can use when you actually deliver your speech. Although these three outlines are related, their functions and formats are different.

Types of Outlines

Figure 10

Content should show division into two or more categories.

I. Jumping rope is a cardiovascular (CV) activity.
   A. A cardiovascular activity is defined by three main requirements.
      1. Large muscles must be used in rhythmic, continuous motions.
      2. The heart beat per minute must be elevated to an intensity that is approximately 85 percent of a person's maximum rate.
      3. The elevated heart rate must be maintained for twenty to thirty minutes to achieve a CV "training effect."
   B. Other CV activities include running, swimming, and handball.
II. Jumping rope requires simple, inexpensive equipment.

Figure 11

Form and content unite through subordination, division, and parallelism.

An Informative Speech on Automobile Tires

Specific purpose: My audience will be able to decode the information printed on their tires.

Understanding Your Tire Symbols

I. "Original equipment" tires tend to be generally good for ride, endurance, traction, and noise, but they are not outstanding in any of these features.

II. Upgrading your tires requires that you understand the new system of symbols printed on tires: 205/60R13 85H, for example.
- A. The 205 stands for "section width," or 205 millimeters wide.
- B. The 60R is 60 percent aspect ratio with radial construction.
  - 1. A "low aspect" tire has a smaller diameter.
  - 2. A radial tire rides soft and looks underinflated.
- C. The 13 means that the tire fits on a 13-inch diameter wheel, which is what you had better have on your car if you expect to use this tire.
- D. The 85 is "load index," which means the tire can handle 1135 pounds.
- E. H is a speed rating that means the tire can handle a speed of up to 130 miles per hour.

III. Before you upgrade your original equipment, you should decide if you want to have a wider tread, to increase the aspect, to buy larger or smaller wheels, to increase or decrease the amount of weight the tire can carry, or to buy a tire that can handle more speed.

Figure 12

Outlining principles of subordination, division, and parallelism.

Subordination	Division	Parallelism

I. _____ .
  A. _____ .
  B. _____ .
    1. _____ .
    2. _____ .
      a. _____ .
      b. _____ .
        i. _____ .
        ii. _____ .
II. _____ .
	Every "I" must have a "II."
	Every "A" must have at least a "B."
	Every "1" must have at least a "2."
	Every "a" must have at least a "b."
	Every "i" must have at least a "ii."
		Each entry must be a complete sentence, a phrase, or a single word; entries may not be a mixture of sentences, phrases, and words.

The Preparation Outline

After you have selected the topic for your speech and have gathered information for it, you will begin to sketch out the basic ideas you wish to convey to your audience. The **preparation outline** is your initial or tentative conception of your speech. It is your original plan showing what you intend to say in the speech.

For example, imagine that you want to speak on Native American religious beliefs and their implications in current American issues. You might start out by identifying some of the Native American religious beliefs and some of the current issues that involve those beliefs. Your preparation outline might look something like this:

Native American religious beliefs
    Belief in a Supreme Being
    Belief in guardian spirits
    Belief in afterlife
    Belief that the earth and nature are sacred
Current issues that infringe upon Native American religious beliefs
    Use of peyote
    Destruction of shrines
    Destruction of burial sites[16]

As you conduct more research, you might add to this working outline, or you may delete subpoints for which you can find no proof or examples. You may also rearrange it or add additional main points. Since this is a preparation, or working, outline, it is always in process. After you have spent some time researching your topic and trying a variety of ways to organize your information, you will create a formal outline.

The Formal Outline

A **formal outline** is a final outline in complete sentence form. It includes the following elements:

1. The title
2. The specific purpose
3. The thesis statement
4. The introduction of the speech, which may be outlined or written out in full
5. The body of the speech in outline form
6. The conclusion of the speech, which may be outlined or written out in full
7. A bibliography of sources or references consulted

An example of a formal outline from a student speech about Native American religious freedom rights can be found in figure 13.[17]

Now that you have seen an example of a formal outline, let us consider briefly each of its seven parts.

Title

The title of the speech may be optional within the classroom setting, but a title is necessary if you are going to speak in most other situations. In formal speaking situations, another person will introduce you. Usually he or she will tell the audience about your credentials and will conclude by stating the title of your speech.

A speech title should be relatively short. It may contain a clever play on words, alliteration, or other stylistic features. It may also be a simple set of words that describe your speech. For example, one student gave a speech on Tecumseh entitled "Tecumseh: Shawnee Warrior and Leader." Other examples of titles from student speeches follow.

Figure 13

An example of a formal outline with scripted introduction and conclusion.

Title: The Religious Freedom Rights of Native Americans
Specific purpose: To inform my audience of the beliefs of the religions of the Native Americans and how those beliefs have been violated in current American decisions
Thesis statement: Native Americans have specific religious beliefs that have been violated in several recent decisions.

Introduction:

I will begin with a short passage from the First Amendment of the U.S. Constitution: "Congress shall make no law respecting an establishment of religion, or prohibiting the free exercise thereof. . ."

Our forefathers, many of them, originally came to America in search of religious freedom. Yet still today, the first inhabitants of this land, the Native Americans, are fighting for this religious freedom that most of us take for granted. States Oliver Thomas, an attorney at Georgetown University, "'The Native Americans'. . . are unique because they predate the Constitution. There's something troubling about our government's coming in and telling Native Americans who have carried on for centuries with their faiths that you can't do this or you can't do that." If the government suppresses religious freedom, what other rights that affect us and that we hold dear might the government endanger? Just how secure are our religious beliefs and practices from governmental tyranny? It is a question few of us have considered and few can answer, including myself. I have long been interested in Native American culture and I have done research into their lives and beliefs. Thus, today I would first like to speak to you on various Native American beliefs and then to discuss current religious issues surrounding Native practices. By doing so, I hope to increase your awareness of the problem that Native Americans have in securing the same religious rights we so ignorantly enjoy.

Transition

Body:

I. There are many rich beliefs in the religion of the Native Americans.
   A. Most Native American tribes believed in a Supreme Being.
   B. Many native tribes believed guardian spirits manifested themselves in animals.
   C. All tribes believed in an afterlife.
   D. All tribes believed the earth and nature were sacred.
   E. Native American beliefs are not entirely different than those of the other religions of the world.

Transition

II. Many current issues involve Native American religious practices.
   A. Peyote use by Native Americans has come under fire.
      1. I will define the word peyote.
      2. I will define a typical peyote service and its goals.
      3. The 1965 Drug Control Act hampers the legal use of peyote.
   B. Also threatened is the Native American belief that holds the land as sacred.
      1. The Forest Service wants to build a ski lift through an Indian shrine.
      2. A burial site may be leveled so motorists can see a Wal-Mart.
      3. The Supreme Court's ruling in 1988 threatens Native American sacred sites.
      4. Walter Echohawk urges support of Native American religious rights.

Figure 13 (continued)

Conclusion:

Today, we have briefly looked at various Native American beliefs and current issues involving their religious practices. We all must realize that we take our religious freedom for granted while others are still fighting for their rights. All I ask is that you remain aware of the difficulties facing Native Americans today in their battle for religious freedom. Please continue to educate yourselves; read books; and attend lectures here at the university about Native Americans. November is Native American Heritage Month, and I suggest you visit Follette's Bookstore, which has dedicated an entire window and book section to Native Americans in honor of the month. I would like to close on a note from Native American Pat Lefthand: "We are in a battle for survival of our very way of life. We've had 500 years of attacks on our way of life. The land is gone. All we have left is our religion." I believe we at least owe Native Americans the right to practice their religion freely. Thank you.

Bibliography:

Axtell, J. (1987). Colonial America without the Indians: Counterfactual reflections. Journal of American History, 73, 995.

Eckert, A. (1992). A sorrow in our heart: The life of Tecumseh. New York: Bantam Books.

Hagen, W. (1985, Winter). Full blood, mixed blood, generic and ersatz: The problem of Indian identity. Arizona and the West, 27, 310.

Meier, P. (1986). The American people: A history. Lexington, MA: D.C. Heath and Company.

Native Americans battle to save sacred lands. (1993, July 11). The Columbus Dispatch, p. 5F

Nichols, R. (1988). Indians in the post-termination era. Storia Northamericana, 5, 74–77.

Oswalt, W. (1988). This land was theirs: A study of North American Indians. Mountain View, CA: Mayfield Publishing Company.

Svingen, O. (1987, Fall). Jim Crow, Indian style. American Indian Quarterly, 11, 277.

Welager, C.A. (1972). The Delaware Indians: A History. New Brunswick, NJ: Rutgers University Press.

The Benefits of Compact Discs

Remembering the Holocaust

Native Americans of the Eastern Woodlands

How to Write a Book

Laws Against Smoking in Public

Preventing Child Abuse

Titles do not have to be clever, but they must be an accurate portrayal of the speech. If they go beyond the scope of the talk, the audience will be disappointed. If they are misleading, people may be frustrated with the speech. If you spend more time working on a provocative and interesting title than you do on creating an engaging speech, your audience's high expectations will not be realized.

Specific Purpose

The general purpose of a speech simply states whether your intention is to inform, to persuade, or to entertain. The specific purpose is more precise because it also includes the audience. For example, a specific purpose might be "To inform my audience of methods to stop smoking." A **specific purpose** thus includes your general purpose, your intended audience, and your precise goal. Some additional examples of specific purpose statements follow.

My audience will be able to explain the religious importance of the Jewish celebration of Passover.

My audience will be able to identify common herbs that can be used to remedy minor medical problems.

My audience will be able to recite the different "benefits" offered to employees who work by the hour, month and year.

My audience will be able to state three arguments that show why more women should major in chemistry.

Thesis Statement

The **thesis statement** is a one sentence summary of the speech. The thesis statement is similar to the topic statement or central idea of a written composition. It is a complete sentence that tells exactly what your speech is about. Some examples of thesis statements follow.

Compact discs are superior to other audio recordings in at least three major ways.

The United States Holocaust Memorial Museum is a dramatic tribute to the testimony "Never forget, never again."

Tobacco should be declared an addictive drug like cocaine because of the health problems it creates for this country.

Introduction

The introduction of a speech should comprise about 15 percent of the total speech time. It should fulfill four functions: gaining and maintaining attention, relating the topic to the audience, relating the speaker to the topic, and previewing the message by stating the purpose and forecasting the organization of the speech. Many speakers write out their introductions and virtually memorize them so they feel secure in how they will begin their talk. Others outline their introductions and deliver them extemporaneously.

Body

The body of the speech comprises the bulk of the speech. It generally consists of about 75 to 80 percent of the entire talk. The body should be outlined using the principles of subordination, division, and parallelism discussed earlier.

Conclusion

The conclusion is even shorter than the introduction. If the introduction to the speech is about 15 percent of the entire speech, then the conclusion should be about 5 percent of the speech, and certainly no longer than 10 percent. The functions of the conclusion include forewarning the audience of the end of the speech, reminding your audience of the main points, and specifying what the audience should do as a result of the speech.

Bibliography or References

The formal outline includes a list of the sources consulted and the sources actually used in the speech. Your instructor will tell you whether you should include all of your sources or only those you actually cite in your speech. In any case, you will want to provide them in correct bibliographic form.

Two common bibliographic forms are those provided by the American Psychological Association (APA) and the Modern Language Association (MLA). In order to become familiar with the differences in these two style guides, you should consult the original sources.[18] Alternatively, you may wish to purchase a reference book which includes both of these styles or the style preferred by your instructor.[19]

Three basic bibliographic formats are the entries for a book, a periodical, and a newspaper article. We provide examples of these three for both APA and MLA styles. For other types of bibliographic entries, you are again encouraged to seek a reference book.

APA Style

Book:

> Eckert, A. (1992). *A sorrow in our heart: The life of Tecumseh.* New York: Bantam Books.

Periodical:

> Axtell, J. (1987). Colonial America without the Indians: Counterfactual reflections. *Journal of American History, 73,* 995–1003.

Newspaper Article (with no author):

> Native Americans battle to save sacred lands. (1993, July 11). *The Columbus Dispatch,* 5F.

MLA Style

Book:

> Eckert, Alva. *A sorrow in our heart: The life of Tecumseh.* New York: Bantam Books, 1992.

Periodical:

> Axtell, John. "Colonial America without the Indians: Counterfactual Reflections." *Journal of American History* 73 (1987): 995–1003.

Newspaper Article (with no author):

> "Native Americans battle to save sacred lands." *The Columbus Dispatch* 11 July 1993: F5.

The Key Word Outline

Finally, you will want to make a key word outline on notecards. The **key word outline** is a brief outline that you can use during the delivery of your speech. It may include words that will prompt your memory, sources that you are citing within the speech, or even the complete quotations of material you are repeating. The key word outline may look very messy or unclear to someone other than the speaker. See figure 14 for an example of a key word outline.

Summary

This chapter on speech organization and outlining began with a discussion of the importance of speech organization. Speakers who present organized speeches are perceived as more competent than are speakers who present less organized speeches. Further, their messages are more memorable. In general, audiences give higher marks to well-organized speakers.

When you organize the body of a speech, you should first divide the body into main points. You should probably have between two and five main points. These main points should be worded in a parallel manner and should be approximately equal in importance.

After you have identified the main points for your speech, you need to determine the order in which you will present them. Some typical ways to order or pattern your speech

Figure 14

An example of a key word outline.

Working Off Fat

Introduction:

Do you have a "body by Jake," a slinky torso by Susan, or a video-shaped profile by Jane? Well, I don't. I know it. And I show it. But I'm doing something about it, and so should you. Here is what I learned about weight control through exercise—and twenty-five years of trying.

Transition

Body:

    I. Why exercise?
      A. Beauty
      B. Everyday health
      C. Long life
    II. How to exercise
      A. Motivation
      B. Routine
      C. Invest in self
    III. How to keep going
      A. Self-rewards
      B. Good habits
      C. Fun

Conclusion:

Don't buy expensive equipment and don't hurt yourself trying. Instead, do as I told you: improve your looks, your heart, and your lungs by investing in yourself. Get in the good health habit by exercising often. And don't forget to reward yourself—with something other than fattening food.

---

include the time-sequence, spatial relations, problem-solution, cause-effect, climactic, anticlimactic, and topical sequence patterns, and Monroe's Motivated Sequence. Finally, the speaker needs to incorporate the supporting material into his organizational plan.

The effective and ethical public speaker also considers the connections between ideas. Among the connecting devices available are transitions, which are brief linkages in the speech; signposts, which tell the audience briefly where the speaker is within the speech; internal previews, which forewarn the audience of that which is to come; and internal reviews, which remind the audience of what has already been covered.

Next we turned to outlining the speech. Outlining includes three important principles. The principle of subordination means that the symbols and indentation of your outline should show which material is more important and which material is less important. The principle of division states that when points are divided, they must have at least two subpoints. The principle of parallelism states that main points, subpoints, and sub-subpoints must use same grammatical and syntactical forms.

During the speech preparation process, you will probably create three types of outlines. The preparation outline is your initial or tentative conception of your speech. A formal outline is a final outline in complete sentence form. It includes the title, specific purpose, thesis statement, introduction of the speech, body of the speech, conclusion of the speech, and a bibliography of sources consulted. The key word outline is a brief outline—often on notecards—created for you to use during the delivery of your speech.

Vocabulary

anticlimactic pattern An organizational arrangement in which the strongest arguments and supporting materials are presented first and then descend in order of importance

cause-effect pattern An organizational arrangement in which part of the speech deals with the cause(s) of a problem or issue, and part of it deals with the effect(s) of the problem or issue

climactic pattern An organizational arrangement in which the arguments and supporting materials are presented in increasing order of importance, with the strongest arguments and evidence presented last

formal outline A final outline in complete sentence form which includes the title, specific purpose, thesis statement, introduction of the speech, body of the speech, conclusion of the speech, and a bibliography of sources consulted

internal previews Statements that inform listeners of your next point or points and are more detailed than transitions

internal reviews Statements that remind listeners of your last point or points and are more detailed than transitions

key word outline A brief outline created for you to use during the delivery of your speech

Monroe's Motivated Sequence An organizational arrangement based on reflective thinking that includes five specific steps: attention, need, satisfaction, visualization, and action

preparation outline The initial or tentative conception of a speech in rough outline form

principle of division An outlining principle that states that every point divided into subordinate parts must be divided into two or more parts

principle of parallelism An outlining principle that states that all points must be stated in the same grammatical form

principle of subordination An outlining principle that states that importance is signaled by symbols and indentation

problem-solution pattern An organizational arrangement in which part of the speech is concerned with the problem(s) and part with the solution(s) to problem(s)

signposts Direct indicators of the speaker's progress; usually an enumeration of the main points: "A second cause is . . . "

spatial relations pattern An organizational arrangement in which events or steps are presented according to how they are related in space

specific purpose The purpose of your speech, which includes your general purpose, your intended audience, and your precise goal

thesis statement A one sentence summary of the speech that is similar to the topic statement or central idea of a written composition

time-sequence pattern An organizational arrangement in which events or steps are presented in the order in which they occur

topical sequence pattern An organizational arrangement in which the topic is divided into reasonable parts, such as advantages and disadvantages, or various qualities or types

transitions The links in a speech that connect the introduction, body, and conclusion, as well as main points and subpoints; they provide previews and reviews, and lead into and away from visual aids

 # Applications

1. Think of a speech topic not mentioned in this chapter that would be best organized into each of the following patterns. Write the topic in the appropriate blank.

Application Exercises

Time-sequence

Topic: _____

Spatial relations

Topic: _____

Problem-solution

Topic: _____

Cause-effect

Topic: _____

Climactic and anticlimactic

Topic: _____

Topical sequence

Topic: _____

Monroe's Motivated Sequence

Topic: _____

Can you explain why each pattern is most appropriate for each topic?

2. Go to the library and find the publication called *Vital Speeches of the Day,* which is a collection of current speeches. Make a copy of a speech and highlight the transitions, signposts, internal previews, and internal reviews.

Application Assignments

1. On a sheet of paper, write your name, the title of your speech, and your general and specific purposes. Then organize the body of your speech using between two and five main points that are worded in a parallel manner and are approximately equal in importance. Develop at least one of the main points with subpoints and sub-subpoints. Identify which organizational pattern you are using.

2. On a sheet of paper, write your name and your preparation outline. This initial rough outline should illustrate your first thoughts on organizing your talk.

3. On a piece of paper, write your name and the title, specific purpose, and thesis statement of your speech. Given these three elements, what subdivisions might your speech include? Suggest at least three main points that should be included.

4. On a sheet of paper, write your name and a key word outline that you could use to deliver your speech. Practice with the key word outline until you feel confident about your delivery.

Endnotes

1. Ernest C. Thompson, "An Experimental Investigation of the Relative Effectiveness of Organizational Structure in Oral Communication," *Southern Speech Journal* 26 (1960): 59–69.
2. Harry Sharp, Jr. and Thomas McClung, "Effect of Organization on the Speaker's Ethos," *Speech Monographs* 33 (1966): 182–83.
3. John O. Greene, "Speech Preparation Processes and Verbal Fluency," *Human Communication Research* 11 (1984): 61–84.
4. Greene, 1984.
5. Paul A. Fritz and Richard L. Weaver II, "Teaching Critical Thinking Skills in the Basic Speaking Course: A Liberal Arts Perspective," *Communication Education* 35 (1986): 177.
6. This speech was given by Rachel Planisek during Fall Quarter 1993 at Ohio University in Interpersonal Communication 103: Public Speaking, taught by Marsha Clowers. The outline is reprinted with permission from the student.
7. This speech was given by Rachel Planisek during Fall Quarter 1993 at Ohio University in Interpersonal Communication 103: Public Speaking, taught by Marsha Clowers. The outline is reprinted with permission from the student.
8. This speech was given by Rachel Planisek during Fall Quarter 1993 at Ohio University in Interpersonal Communication 103: Public Speaking, taught by Marsha Clowers. The outline is reprinted with permission from the student.

9. The information about the national survey of freshmen came from Jerald G. Bachman and Lloyd D. Johnston, "The Freshmen, 1979," *Psychology Today* 13 (September 1979): 79–87.

10. Douglas Ehninger, Bruce E. Gronbeck, and Alan H. Monroe, *Principles of Speech Communication—9th brief edition* (Glenview, Illinois: Scott, Foresman and Co., 1984), 249.

11. This speech was given by John R. Reindel during Fall Quarter 1993 at Ohio University in Interpersonal Communication 103: Public Speaking, taught by Kim Varey. The outline is based on Reindel's outline and is reprinted with permission from the student. The speech contained the following endnotes: 1. Susan Neumister, *Passive Smoking* (Monticello, IL: Vance Bibliographies, 1985); 2. Ingrid Wickelgren, "Are Smokers Addicts?" *Current Science* (September 9, 1994): 10–12; 3. Walecia Konrad, "Smoking Out the Elusive Smoker," *Business Week* (March 16, 1992): 62–63; 4. From a World Health Organization report on ABC World News Tonight (number 4186) September 19, 1994; 5. "Is Secondhand Smoke Illness Compensable?" *Occupational Hazards* 56 (no. 8) (August 1994): 67; 6. "Secondhand Cancer?" from a television program entitled Wall Street Journal Report (number 628) October 8, 1994; 7. Andrew A. Skolnik, "Firts AHA Statement on Tobacco and Children," *Journal of the American Medical Association* 272 (no. 11) (September 21, 1994): 841; 8. Skolnik, 1994; 9. "Kids are Getting Hooked," *U.S. News and World Report* 117 (no. 12) (September 26, 1994): 24.

12. W. Lance Bennet, "Storytelling in Criminal Trials: A Model of Social Judgment," *Quarterly Journal of Speech* 64 (February 1978): 1–22.

13. This speech was given by Rachel Planisek during Fall Quarter 1993 at Ohio University in Interpersonal Communication 103: Public Speaking, taught by Marsha Clowers. The outline is reprinted with permission from the student.

14. Michael Osborn and Suzanne Osborn, *Public Speaking,* 3rd ed. (Boston: Houghton Mifflin Co., 1994), 184.

15. Based on an article by Ron Grable, "The Do's and Don'ts of Upgrading Tires," *Motor Trend* (July 1991): 112–15.

16. This speech was given by Rachel Planisek during Fall Quarter 1993 at Ohio University in Interpersonal Communication 103: Public Speaking, taught by Marsha Clowers. The outline is reprinted with permission from the student.

17. This speech was given by Rachel Planisek during Fall Quarter 1993 at Ohio University in Interpersonal Communication 103: Public Speaking, taught by Marsha Clowers. The outline is reprinted with permission from the student.

18. *Publication Manual of the American Psychological Association,* 3rd ed. (Washington, DC: American Psychological Association, 1983); Joseph Gibaldi and Walter S. Achtert, *MLA Handbook for Writers of Research Papers,* 2nd ed. (New York: The Modern Language Association of America, 1984).

19. One excellent reference is Diana Hacker, *A Writer's Reference* (New York: St. Martin's Press, Inc., 1989).

THE ETHICAL AND EFFECTIVE USE OF EVIDENCE, PROOF, AND ARGUMENT

You raise your voice when you should reinforce your argument.

Dr. Samuel Johnson

QUESTION OUTLINE

I. How are the four kinds of evidence used effectively and ethically in persuasive speeches?

II. What decisions should be made about the four kinds of proof in persuasive speeches?

III. What are the components of an argument?

IV. What are the three types of claims?

V. How does one construct an effective argument?

VI. How should the ethical and effective persuader use the four kinds of argument?

VII. What are some common fallacies or faulty arguments?

VIII. What questions should the ethical persuader ask?

Introduction

Lydia Gompertz had been thinking about her persuasive speech for the entire academic term. She had decided that this would be the speech in which she would attempt to convince others about her feelings about homosexuality. Lydia had gathered information from research studies that compared heterosexual and homosexual choices and behaviors. She interviewed some lesbian women and gay men. She interviewed some clergy people and business people who held strongly conservative attitudes about the topic.

Lydia thought about her audience. Some people were completely opposed to homosexuality on moral or religious grounds. At least three people—two men and one woman—in the class were openly gay and lesbian. She did not know of the opinions of others in her potential audience.

Lydia's problem was not a shortage of research. She had logical and scientific arguments, as well as the emotional and inspirational statements of others. Lydia was also not sure if her membership in the Roman Catholic Church would be seen as a plus or a minus in her persuasive speech. Should she let the audience know about this affiliation? What arguments should she use? Which ones should come first? How could Lydia demonstrate both ethical and effective choices in her persuasive attempt?

In this chapter you will learn how to use evidence, proof, and argument in an effective and ethical way. You will learn about a variety of forms of evidence which will be defined and explained. You will learn how to apply the four kinds of proof—personal proof, emotional proof, logical proof, and mythic proof—to the persuasive speech. The chapter includes information on how to structure arguments, including the components of an argument, the types of claims, the types of argument, and common fallacies or faulty arguments. Finally, you will learn more about ethical issues that are essential to the speaker who wishes to alter the feelings, attitudes, or behaviors of others.

How Can Evidence Be Used Ethically and Effectively in the Persuasive Speech?

Evidence consists of supporting materials used in a persuasive speech. Supporting materials include information that "backs up" or reinforces your arguments. They include—but are not limited to—statistics, facts, opinions, examples, illustrations, tests (e.g., DNA or blood tests), objects (e.g., a weapon with finger prints), and analogies. When supporting materials are used to argue for a position, they become evidence.

Evidence may be viewed as the building blocks or basic elements of the persuasive process. If the evidence you use is viewed as irrelevant or insufficient, then your entire persuasive effort can fail. Let us take an example. Imagine that you are going to give a persuasive speech encouraging cultural diversity at American universities. Furthermore, you are going to argue that universities should encourage international students to study on their campuses.

You have done research on international students on college campuses. You have interviewed others, and you have done research in the library. How do you use this information in your speech?

Amy Morehead at Ohio University had this task.[1] She said, in part,

According to a publication entitled *International Perspectives,* there are over 11 million students in American Universities, and 300,000 of them are from other countries.[1] My first reason for encouraging your support and that of our government is that the presence of these students promotes international understanding. Our education is enriched by their academic and cultural contributions. We experience this cultural diversity every day at this university by living with people from nearly 100 countries. They bring their culture to us in the dormitories, in the cafeterias, during the international street fair, on their independence days, and especially in the classroom.

How do international students foster world understanding? Both parties benefit when American students study with students from around the globe. International students, for instance, say that they benefit from the experience. A study published by the American Institute for Foreign Study reveals the benefits. One hundred percent of the exchange students report higher levels of maturity, over 70 percent report increased adaptability, and over 85 percent gained important knowledge of another culture.[2] But American students also gain from the relationship with students from other cultures. Nichole Baker, a junior who has cultivated friendships with international students for the last three years, says, "International students are quite an asset to our university. They make students in the United States aware of the life-styles led in other countries."[3]

Besides this first benefit of better global cooperation, the presence of international students on campus brings a second benefit. Their presence whets American students' competitiveness both in admissions and in overall achievement. Of the 16,374 students enrolled last fall on this campus, 1345 students were from other countries according to the International Student Report.[4] This number was a 13 percent increase over the previous year. The important point is that students from this state must compete with intelligent students from around the world to gain admission and to maintain high grades.

I know from my own experience that I work harder when I am competing for success. Some recent studies suggest that students from other countries perform better than American students in school. I see these results as a challenge, a motivator for achievement.

Global cooperation and college competition are just two of the benefits of having international students. A third point is what international students do to encourage world peace. A statement in the Quarterly Report notes "a growing perception of America's interdependence within the world and hence our need to interact with other countries to achieve basic economic, political and security goals. It has also been stimulated by periodic studies indicating the lack of global awareness on the part of the American polity."[5]

Claims that international students can benefit schools, indirectly showing what the speaker believes is wrong with the status quo; *instead of showing what is wrong, the speaker shows what needs to be improved*

Uses two different modes of support for claim: statistics and testimony

A possible fallacy in reasoning: the speaker failed to provide evidence that the increase in international students caused *the American students to push for higher grades.*

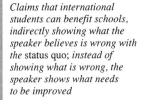

Over 11 million students attend American universities, and 300,000 of them are from other countries.

Amy's evidence consisted of the facts and figures, examples, and testimony she used to attempt to convince her audience of the importance of increasing the number of international students on campus. Some pieces of evidence she used were undoubtedly more convincing than others. She may have even made a fallacy in her reasoning when she noted that a 13 percent increase in international students had occurred at Ohio University in the past year and then suggested that because of this, the American students were studying and working more diligently. The example is not perfect, but it illustrates the importance of effective evidence in the persuasive speech.

In order to clarify how evidence is used both ethically and effectively, we will consider each of the four forms of supporting material: facts and figures, examples, narratives, and testimony.

Facts and Figures

Facts and figures are statements or numbers about which people agree because they are verifiable. In the informative speech, facts and figures are used to illustrate and clarify the points you wish to make. In the persuasive speech, they provide a foundation from which you argue your case. Facts and figures are often given early in a persuasive speech, and they frequently serve to forewarn the listeners about your position on a topic.

An example of facts and figures that could be used early in a speech encouraging men to participate to a greater extent in household chores follows.

Surveys indicate that women do most of the household chores, although more women are working outside the home.

Nearly three times as many women as men do most of the household cleaning, according to surveys.

At the same time, more women are working outside the home; the number of full-time working women has increased by 1 million each year since 1960.

In Ohio, 82 percent of women surveyed did most of the cleaning and the housekeeping, according to an October survey commissioned by Merry Maids Inc., a cleaning service. Twenty-six percent of the men in the survey said household chores were their primary responsibility.

In addition to the 30 to 40 hours a week spent working outside the home, women spent 40 to 44 hours a week on housework, said a study done in July at the University of Missouri. Their husbands or male partners spent about 13 hours a week on household chores, the survey said.[2]

Facts and figures are verifiable statements or numbers from reliable sources that can be used to support your arguments in a persuasive speech.

Examples

An **example** is a specimen, an instance that represents a larger group. For instance, Amy Morehead, in the speech reprinted in part earlier, used herself as an example when she said, "I know from my own experience that I work harder when I am competing for success." Another example is provided in the information about women doing more household chores than men. Nancy L. McGrath of Loveland, Ohio wrote, "Yes, I do all the housework at home—from the bathrooms to laundry to kitchen and everything in between. Granted, my husband does clean the gutters, mow the lawn, and maintain the cars, but these are seasonal; my job is every day."[3]

Examples come in a variety of forms. A brief example, like the ones above, are a mere sentence or two. Extended examples are three sentences or more. Examples may also be categorized as actual examples or hypothetical examples. Actual examples are based on reality, like the two examples above. Hypothetical examples, by contrast, are plausible, but

David L. Archambault, President, Standing Rock College.

they are created by the speaker in order to make a point. An ethical persuader reveals to the audience which examples are reality-based and which are hypothetical.

Narratives

Narratives are stories told to illustrate a point. In the informative speech, narratives serve to illustrate or to make obvious the major or subpoints the speaker is providing. In the persuasive speech, narratives serve a variety of functions. They encourage a positive relationship between the speaker and the listeners, they make abstract ideas concrete and they help to create memorable messages.

An example of a narrative is provided by David Archambault, former President of the American Indian College Fund, in a speech to the Rotary Club in Murray, Utah, on April 6, 1992. The speech was entitled, "Columbus Plus 500 Years: Whither the American Indian." Archambault reminded the audience of the Massacre of Wounded Knee.

More than 100 years ago, our great Chief Sitting Bull was murdered. His people—frightened that they too would be killed—set out on foot across South Dakota along with Chief Big Foot. Carrying their children, they fled across the frozen prairie through the bitter sub-zero cold 200 miles to seek refuge on the Pine Ridge reservation in southwestern South Dakota.

On December 29, 1890, near a creek now known to all the world as Wounded Knee, Chief Big Foot and his followers were massacred. No one knows who fired first, but when the shooting was over, nearly 300 Indians—men, women, and children—lay dead and dying across the valley. Their bodies were dumped into a mass grave. The survivors were unable to hold a burial ceremony, a ceremony we call the wiping away of tears. It meant the living could never be free.[4]

Archambault's moving description in this narrative gave non-Native Americans a glimpse at the pain he and his people felt.

Testimony

Testimony consists of opinions that support the speaker's claims. You can use your own opinions, but audiences are frequently more impressed with the words of an expert. Testimony can also be used in an informative speech, but its role is more crucial in the development of a persuasive speech.

An example of testimony was provided by Marc Maurer, then President of the National Federation of the Blind, in the banquet speech he delivered in Denver, Colorado, on July 8, 1989. Maurer was explaining to the audience that thought and speech are one. He said, "Thoughts cannot occur without being verbalized (either physically or in the mind), and words cannot be spoken or imagined without expressing thought. The words and the thoughts are the same."[5]

He then provided testimony from a wide range of characters.

The historian and essayist Thomas Carlyle once noted that language is not the garment of thought but the body of it. Modern anthropologists have advanced the Whorf-Sapir hypothesis, which declares that all of human culture is fabricated by language. The poet Percy Bysshe Shelley said that man was given speech, "and speech created thought." Samuel Taylor Coleridge observed that "language is the armory of the human mind, and at once contains the trophies of its past and the weapons of its future conquests." Socrates asserted that language is the guiding spirit of all human endeavor. "Such as thy words are," he said, "such will thine affections be; and such as thine affections will be thy deeds; and such as thy deeds will be thy life." If the language is modified, the thought is also altered. If the thought is shifted, the deed cannot remain the same. Therefore, to change a pattern of behavior, we must change the habit of speech.[6]

Maurer's words about the power of language and the link between language and thought are testimonial evidence. Within his speech are more testimonials from Carlyle, modern anthropologists, Shelley, Coleridge, and Socrates. His speech illustrates the power of testimonial evidence.

Evaluating Evidence

If you have done your research properly, you will have an abundance of evidence to use in your speech. How will you decide which materials to use and which to discard? You will need to apply some criteria of effectiveness and ethical standards.

What Are Some of the Characteristics of Effective Evidence?

First, *effective evidence is always relevant to your argument*. You will find lots of evidence for most arguments, but the evidence will vary considerably in its relevance to your argument. For example, you might argue that grocers close to campus are taking advantage of students by charging higher prices. You chose the topic because the same grocery chain has a store in your hometown, and you believe that they overcharge there as well. Your opinion about the hometown grocery store is less relevant than more substantial proof, such as a comparison of prices in the city where your campus is located with prices of groceries in an off-campus mall. Another more relevant piece of evidence would be a quotation, testimonial evidence, by the manager of the campus grocery, who admits that she charges more to make up for shoplifting, bad checks, and breakage. Always choose the evidence that is most relevant to your argument.

Second, *effective evidence is easily understood by the audience*. DNA tests, blood tests, and fingerprints may be evidence that lawyers can use in a jury trial where the

Characteristics of Effective Evidence

As a speaker, have you considered whether your evidence
1. is relevant,
2. is easily understood by the audience,
3. is striking or remarkable,
4. is novel,
5. is of the appropriate length,
6. is significant, and
7. is credible.

lawyers have as much time as they need to educate the jurors, but in a one-shot public speech you will not have time to educate the audience about such complicated forms of evidence. Instead, choose evidence your audience will understand. An educated audience is likely to understand statistics if you put them in context and explain their importance. An audience of small children might be partial to stories that illustrate your point. All evidence may not be useful in your persuasive speech, but evidence that the audience can understand will be more persuasive.

Third, *effective evidence is striking or remarkable.* This quality will make your evidence more memorable. You might say, for instance, that "More Americans die by car than by warfare" and that "It is safer to fly on any commercial airline—including commuter flights—than it is to drive to the airport." Striking or remarkable facts capture audience attention and provide impressive support for your argument.

Fourth, *effective evidence is novel.* The speaker who uses ordinary or well-known evidence will be less persuasive. The speaker who uses evidence the audience has never heard before will be more effective. A student speaking on the National Rifle Association (NRA) made a novel point. He said that the NRA argues that everyone needs weapons for protection against potential enemies, an armed citizen militia. But, he added, a list of members of the NRA in enemy hands would provide the names and addresses of most gun owners in this country. Novel evidence attracts audience attention and supports the persuader's argument.

Fifth, *effective evidence makes your case without losing your audience.* In other words, you should present the evidence in enough detail to enhance clarity, but you should not make your evidence so extensive that the audience loses both interest and understanding. At a trial dependent on DNA, the defense lawyer's exhaustive efforts to get ordinary people to understand genetic markers and testing could result in a jury overcome by complex detail.

Sixth, *effective evidence is significant, and thus more persuasive.* Significance means importance. Your evidence can be relevant but insignificant. Discovering that a can of mushroom soup costs more at the campus grocery than at the grocery store in the mall is relevant, but not significant. Finding that all soups, crackers, canned goods, bread products, meats, and produce cost more at the campus grocery is significant because it is larger in importance.

Seventh, *effective evidence is highly credible.* "Who said it?" is an important question about testimonial opinions, because the audience might find their union president much more credible than the president of the company. "Who found the evidence?" may be an important question to ask about surveys, alleged facts, and other information gleaned from research. If the survey of customers' preferred clothing styles was done by a textile manufacturer, then it is less credible than if it was done by a more neutral party like a university or professional polling service. Finally, "What did they find?" can be an important question because the findings could be an aberration, an accidental blip in

Characteristics of Ethical Evidence

As a speaker, have you considered whether your evidence
1. is true, or is clearly identified as hypothetical,
2. is recent, or is clearly identified as from another period of time,
3. is provable,
4. is complete, and
5. is not overdramatized for effect.

statistics. Findings that are inconsistent with other known evidence invites questions about accuracy. The credibility of your sources is always important when you consider evidence for a persuasive speech.

What Are Some of the Characteristics of Ethical Evidence?

First, *ethical evidence (if it consists of facts and figures, actual examples, true narratives, or testimony) is true*. If you are using hypothetical examples or narratives, you should clearly indicate that to your audience, probably both before and after you provide the evidence.

Second, *ethical evidence is recent*. If you are providing evidence from long ago, you should carefully qualify your evidence. Circumstances from another era or century may have less application for current events than do more recent findings.

Third, *ethical evidence is provable*. If your evidence is known only to you and no interviewee, printed source, or video will back you up, then your audience cannot assess its accuracy or credibility. Your truthfulness could be called into question.

Fourth, *ethical evidence is understandable to an audience*. Explain statistics so the audience can put them in context and understand them. Always clarify your arguments and evidence, because your case is proven only if the audience understands it.

Fifth, *ethical evidence provides complete information to the audience*. Do not omit evidence that casts doubt on your position. Instead, you should admit to contrary evidence but try to explain it. If you give your audience statistics on how many people get killed with handguns each year and you are only using the states of North and South Dakota, but you fail to reveal that you are using two relatively low population states, you are not behaving ethically.

Finally, *ethical evidence is not overdramatized for effect*. Ethical persuaders do not "inflame the passions." Do not treat the audience as pawns in a chess game. The student who faked a pulsating wound with animal blood in front of class to emphasize the need for first aid training upset the students so much that the teacher gave the speech a failing grade.

Using Proof Ethically and Effectively

Proofs are the means by which speakers support their claims. Proofs were originally proposed in the Golden Age of Greece, which began in approximately 500 B.C. Although earlier rhetoricians had discussed proof, Aristotle was the first to systematically examine and discuss the nature of proof.

Aristotle distinguished proofs into **extrinsic proofs,** which support claims by referring to objective evidence such as confessions, contracts, and existing laws. The residence hall director who says you are being removed from the hall for possessing illegal drugs in your room can use your dormitory contract and the university policies on illegal drugs as extrinsic proofs for her claim that you should be removed. The lawyer can say your confession of guilt is grounds for conviction. And the traffic cop can fine you by imposing the extrinsic proof of local law.

Intrinsic proofs consist of the evidence in communicative messages that "authorizes, sanctions or justifies belief, attitude, or action."[7] The listener must understand and agree that the evidence is compelling and requires a change in his or her feelings, beliefs, attitudes, or behavior.

Aristotle further categorized intrinsic proofs into ethos (personal), pathos (emotional), logos (logical), and mythos (mythic). These proofs are important to you as a persuasive communicator who wants listeners to believe your propositions and to be influenced by your message. We will consider each of these types of intrinsic proof in depth.

Personal Proof

Ethos, or personal proof, is "the audience's perceptions of the character of the speaker."[8] Aristotle saw ethos as a combination of the speaker's knowledge, good will, and moral character. Today this aspect of intrinsic proof is called speaker credibility, and contemporary communication research suggests that it includes five aspects: competence, character, sociability, composure, and extroversion.[9]

Competence refers to the degree to which listeners perceive you as knowledgeable and informed about your topic. In order to be viewed as competent, you will need to read and learn as much about your topic as you can. You should learn about the arguments of both proponents and opponents to your proposition. When you are finished conducting your research, you should have far more information than you are able to present in your persuasive speech. You should be able to answer questions after your speech in an informed and reasoned way. You should also be able to meet the objections of those who hold contrary beliefs. Professors are an example of a category of people who signal competence by knowing more than others do about a subject.

Character means that listeners see you as trustworthy, honest, and sincere. How can you be viewed as a person of high character? You should show that you follow ethical practices in the communicative process. You can be honest in your dealings with others. In general, you can show that you are a person of integrity. Priests, rabbis, and ministers are an example of a category of people whose character is a mainstay of their credibility.

Sociability refers to the idea that your audience sees you as friendly, pleasant, and likeable. In the classroom setting, you can encourage others to see you as sociable by coming to class early to talk with others, by initiating interactions, and by being warm in your interpersonal encounters with other students. You can also be cordial during the presentation of your persuasive speech. People in sales and nearly all service-oriented businesses depend to some degree on their sociability for their credibility.

Composure means that the listeners view you as being in control, poised, and relaxed. Although you can be too tightly in control, it is more likely that you will need to control your tension and anxiety in the public speaking setting. In your interpersonal interactions with audience members, show that you are confident. Broadcasters, public relations spokespersons, and beauty contestants are among the groups in American society whose composure is an important feature of their credibility.

Extroversion refers to the audience's perception that you are outgoing, energetic, and talkative. Television evangelist Jimmy Swaggart of Baton Rouge, Louisiana, is an example of a speaker who exudes extroversion: he paces about, he sings, he plays the piano and electric organ, and he preaches with so much energy that he sweats, cries, and shakes during his Sunday morning services.

Clearly, extroversion is a dimension of credibility that is culturally determined. Very few Episcopalian rectors, Presbyterian ministers, Orthodox Jewish rabbis or Roman Catholic parish priests act like Jimmy Swaggart. Extroversion is probably exhibited more on the streets of New York City than in small towns in the Midwest. African Americans,

Speaker Credibility

As you prepare your speech, consider the following qualities of a credible speaker. To be effective, consider how you can encourage your audience to see you in these ways. To be ethical, be sure you are not misrepresenting yourself.

1. **Competence:** Will your listeners perceive you as knowledgeable and informed about your topic?
2. **Character:** Will your listeners see you as trustworthy, honest, and sincere?
3. **Sociability:** Will your listeners see you as friendly, pleasant, and likeable?
4. **Composure:** Will your listeners see you as being controlled, poised, and relaxed?
5. **Extroversion:** Will your listeners see you as outgoing, energetic, and talkative?

Italians, and Puerto Ricans seem to value extroversion more than people who came from England, Finland, and Vietnam. In other words, the value of extroversion varies by co-culture, region, and ethnic origin—to name a few of the possibilities.

In order to better understand credibility, the introduction of a speech presented by David Archambault, a member of the Native American tribe Lakota, to a Rotary Club is provided. As you read this excerpt, consider how Archambault established his credibility.

Hau Kola. That is how we Lakota say "Greeting, Friends." I am happy to be here today to represent Native American people. I am a Ikoeya Wicaska—an ordinary man. We think of an ordinary man as not superior to anyone else or, for that matter, to anything else. We—all people and all things—are related to each other.

We begin our spiritual ceremonies with the phrase "Oni takuya Oyasi," which means all my relations. We believe that all people are ultimately part of one nation—the nation of mankind, but that this nation is only one of many nations that inhabit the Mother Earth. To us all living things are nations—the deer, the horses, things that crawl, things that fly, things that grow in and on the ground. All of these nations were created by the same Power, and none is superior to another. All are necessary for life. We are expected to live and work in harmony.[10]

How did David Archambault establish his credibility? First, Archambault is a Lakota speaking to a Rotary Club, so his own ethnicity is a visible sign of his competence on this topic. Second, Archambault speaks Lakota, so he is rooted in his ethnicity by language, which adds to his competence. Third, he says he represents Native American people, so he sees himself as a spokesperson, a sociability characteristic. Fourth, he levels the relationship between himself and his audience by calling himself at the outset "an ordinary man" related to all living things and linked to all nations. This statement speaks to his character, the audience's perception of honesty, trustworthiness, and sincerity. In very few words, David Archambault establishes a number of credibility factors that encourage his audience to heed his words.

If you wish to establish positive credibility with your audiences, you, too, will wish to demonstrate these five characteristics as well as you can. Also remember the ethical dimension of ethos: the ethical communicator does not represent himself or herself falsely. You do not pretend to be sociable while disliking the audience; you do not act as though you know more about the topic than you really do.

Nelson Mandella.

Emotional Proof

Pathos, or emotional proof, involves attempts to persuade an audience with emotional appeals. If you attempt to evoke pity, sympathy, or other such strong emotions, you are using pathos. Your audience has both emotions and reasoning abilities. If you ignore the emotions of your audience, you will probably be unable to persuade them. As one writer put it:

> *The creature man is best persuaded*
> *When heart, not mind, is inundated;*
> *Affect is what drives the will;*
> *Rationality keeps it still.*[11]

Some of the emotional appeals you might use include idealism, transcendence, determination, conviction, and the dramatic example. **Idealism** is communicating the highest expectations of humanity, however rare their practice in reality. Mother Theresa is an example of an idealist whose work among the poor in India made her famous throughout the world. Maggie Kuhn, leader of the Gray Panthers, was an idealist who sought a better life for America's aging population. The persuasive appeal using idealism argues for peace among nations, harmony among races, and elimination of poverty to name a few. An appeal to idealism projects the world as it should be.

Transcendence is another positive emotional appeal, similar to idealism, that attempts to rise above or transcend people's differences in search of bonding similarities. Malcolm X, in the time before his assassination, saw in Islam a religion that appealed to people of all colors, a unifying force that he missed in the Black Muslim movement. Nelson Mandella believed that South Africa could transcend its racial, economic, and tribal differences to achieve a democratic government. In a persuasive speech using transcendence, the speaker picks a perspective that rises above conflict to find unifying similarities.

Determination is a positive emotional appeal characteristic of long-term movements. Republicans exhibited determination in their twenty-year struggle to gain control of the Senate and the House of Representatives in 1995. Cesar Chavez spent years in determined effort to organize low-paid laborers. A persuasive speaker can show determination by arguing in favor of causes thought to be lost, by joining minority voices in movements against the dominant position on issues, and by trying in speech after speech to gain ground on an issue that most others oppose.

Conviction is a positive emotional appeal characterized by a deep feeling of certainty in the righteousness, truth, and virtue of your cause. Union leaders have strong convictions about the right to organize for better pay, better benefits, and better working conditions. Corporate leaders have strong convictions about capitalism, the virtue of profits, and the vice of government intervention. The Pope proclaims the convictions of the Roman Catholic faith for 900 million believers around the world. In a persuasive speech, you use the positive emotional appeal of conviction when you speak about the importance of your education in securing a living wage, the need for an economy that welcomes entry-level workers, and the right to have health benefits even for employees who earn low wages.

One final type of positive emotional appeal is the **dramatic example,** a narrative or story that illustrates a message in a manner that stirs the emotions. In the Bible such stories are called parables, in children's stories they are called fables, and in speeches they are called dramatic examples. Most TV programs about cops or emergency rooms are built around dramatic examples. Religious leaders often use them to illustrate their point about adopting their faith. Students tell stories about car accidents, drug abuse, family conflict, and athletic prowess to persuade their audiences about their topic.

An example of emotional appeals is provided in a speech written by Solomon Moore in 1989. Solomon was then a high school senior at Wooster High School in Ohio. He began his speech entitled, "The Elusive Peace":

> *In the Middle East, as the war between Iran and Iraq supposedly dies down the world begins to see that whatever they were fighting for has been drowned by the blood of people. In Central America, thousands upon thousands perish as communist and democratic puppet masters cry, "Freedom!" and fill their lands with guns instead of education, soldiers instead of teachers. In South Africa, the government sits high upon the scarred backs of the Bantus, who see nothing but the dusty road to fascism beneath them.*

He concluded with another set of powerful emotional appeals.

> *In order to grasp peace the world must want it. The nations and the peoples of the world must have some reason to embrace peace. Perhaps the whole world will have to squirm under a tyrannical government, not just Haiti or Libya. Perhaps the whole world will have to feel hunger's bite, not just Ethiopia or Sudan. Perhaps then peace will be craved. But never will it be too late for peace. Nothing people can do can thwart peace. Peace is inevitable. . . . When the peoples of the world realize this, the earth will be but one nation, and humankind, its citizens.*[12]

Moore appeals largely to the audience's idealism as he discusses the possibility of peace for the world. He shows determination as he notes that "Nothing we can do can thwart peace. Peace is inevitable." Moore's conviction is obvious throughout the introduction and conclusion. Finally, he provides dramatic examples in discussion of the Middle East, Central America, and South Africa. Moore's speech is a fine example of the powerful role of emotional proof within a persuasive speech.

What should you do if you want to use emotional proof effectively and ethically? You will want to ensure that your audience understands the relationship of the emotional appeal to your proposition or main point. You will also want to choose an emotional appeal that is vivid and memorable. Ethically, you need to be sure that the feeling, attitude, or behavior that you want to change in your audience warrants an emotional appeal. You do not want to incite your audience to riot or leave them all in tears for no compelling reason.

Registering to vote is an example of an action goal.

Logical Proof

Logos, or logical proof, occurs when you try to persuade an audience with logical appeals, reasoning, and arguments. In other words, logical appeals tend to be rational evidence. Logical appeals are not the opposite of emotional appeals, but another distinctive mode of proof.

Logical appeals include the "finding of arguments necessary to prove the validity of a proposition."[13] This fairly technical definition suggests that three elements are necessary in logical appeals. First, we have a statement or proposition that must be proven. Second, we have evidence that suggests the statement is true. Finally, we have a conclusion that binds the proposition and the evidence.

Julia Hughes Jones, then auditor of the state of Arkansas, delivered a speech on August 26, 1992, on the anniversary of women's suffrage in the United States. Her speech entitled, "A Greater Voice in Action: Women and Equality," included the following section:

Why is a vote important? Many times, a single vote has changed the course of history.

More than a thousand years ago in Greece, an entire meeting of the Church Synod was devoted to one question: Is a woman a human being or an animal?

It was finally settled by vote, and the consensus was that we do indeed belong to the human race. It passed, however, by just one vote.

Other situations where one vote has made a difference:

• In 1776, one vote gave America the English language instead of German.

• In 1845, one vote brought Texas and California into the Union.

• In 1868, one vote saved President Andrew Johnson from impeachment.

• In 1923, one vote determined the leader of a new political party in Munich. His name was Adolph Hitler.

• In 1960, one vote change in each precinct in Illinois would have defeated John F. Kennedy.

History has proven the enormous power of one single vote.[14]

In this excerpt, Jones asserts and then must prove her statement that a single vote is important, indeed, that "a single vote has changed the course of history." Then she provides factual evidence that illustrates the importance of one vote. She finally concludes, tying her evidence to her initial statement by repeating, "History has proven the enormous power of *one single vote."*

If you want to use logical proof effectively, be sure that your evidence demonstrates your statement or proposition. You also need to be sure that the audience understands the conclusion that ties the evidence to the statement. In order to be ethical, you will not provide untrue pieces of evidence, nor will you use evidence that does not prove your statement. Finally, you will not go beyond your evidence in your conclusion.

Mythic Proof

You probably know what a myth is: a tale or legend of unknown origin that reveals how or why something occurred in the past. You might not know the word **mythos,** a related but somewhat different concept that summarizes attitudes and beliefs that characterize a group or society. For example, Manifest Destiny was part of American mythos that guided our behavior for a century and justified taking lands from Mexicans and Native Americans. Mythos said the dominant American culture had the God-given right to take land from the Atlantic to the Pacific, and from Canada in the north to the Rio Grande River in the south. Slavery was justified by the mythos that the Bible justified dominance over the sons of Ham; Hitler's aggressive military and genocide against the Jews was justified by the mythos of a pure Aryan race; and several American wars have been justified by the American mythos that says "We are the police force for the world."

The reason that mythos has been added to our repertoire of persuasive proofs is that America includes cultures from many lands that each have their own mythos. America has co-cultures with their own mythos. These co-cultures range from the fundamentalist Christian mythos that everyone needs to be Christian to be saved, to the Black Muslim idea that African Americans should be united in self-protection and faith, to the White Supremacist and Skinhead idea that America should be for white people only. To illustrate the concept further, let us turn to a less divisive mythos concerning our concept of time.

An African American expatriate from Paris lectured at Harvard to university administrators about time. Time, he said, has a different meaning to European Americans than it does to African Americans, largely because of their countries of origin. Europeans lived for centuries in harsh climates where timing of planting, cultivation, and harvest was a matter of life and death. Doing things "on time" was of crucial importance to survival. Africans lived for thousands of years in places where food was simply picked, not planted or harvested, and where time was not crucial to survival. One of the results is a different mythos about time. At the Frankfurt, Germany international airport, the large flight schedule for world-wide flights says over and over: Lufthansa (the German airline) "on time." Nearly every African flight said "delayed" or had a sign on the airline desk saying "tomorrow." Is this an oversimplified theory about differences in ideas about time? Perhaps, but such ideas about time are not unheard of among German Americans and African Americans who have been away from their countries of origin for generations.

The persuasive power of mythos is important in a diverse society. Some Native Americans see time as renewable seasons with no real beginning and no real end.[15] The Hopis have no words to designate time, but view it as "a smooth flowing continuum in which everything in the universe proceeds at an equal rate, out of a future, through a present, into a past."[16] Some Christian groups believe that every word in the Bible is literally true, while other Christian groups see stories like the one in Genesis as being a metaphorical explanation about the origins of humans. Yes, mythos may not be what is taught as logical reasoning, but who would deny that mythos about races and marriage between races was somehow confounded in the famous O. J. Simpson case? In a country like America where hundreds of cultures converge in one larger society, our respect for and knowledge of the mythos that guide peoples' thoughts becomes one of the ways we influence each other.

Mythic proof, traditional ideas and stories, is conveyed mainly through the use of metaphors and narratives. When Bill Clinton became President, he used the metaphor of the seasons both to portray his program and that of his predecessor. Read carefully these excerpts from his inaugural address:

> This ceremony is held in the depth of winter. But, by the words we speak and the faces we show the world, we force the spring.
>
> A spring reborn in the world's oldest democracy, that brings forth the vision and courage to reinvent America. . . .
>
> So today, we pledge an end to the era of deadlock and drift—and a new season of American renewal has begun. . . .
>
> Yes, you my fellow Americans, have forced the spring. Now, we must do the work the season demands. . . .
>
> And so my fellow Americans, as we stand at the edge of the 21st century, let us begin with energy and hope, with faith and discipline, and let us work until our work is done. The scripture says, "And let us not be weary in well-doing, for in due season, we shall reap, if we faint not." [17]

The speech is replete with references to a European American mythos about time, work, progress, seasons, planting, and harvest. Unstated is the idea that the Bush administration must have represented winter, while the new President represents the renewal of spring. Scripture is invoked to resonate with the large number of Americans who believe in the Bible. He suggests that Americans will reap a great harvest if they plant and work hard in the spring. The use of mythos to persuade is the best explanation for what is happening in these passages. It is not a string of arguments with evidence; it is a systematic appeal to age-old mythos resident in American culture.

Mythos is difficult to manage for the ethical communicator in our contemporary diverse society. Americans from Mexico, Cuba, Puerto Rico, Vietnam, Columbia, Canada, China, Japan, India, and hundreds of different countries of origin bring to us their own mythos. So do Baptists, lesbian women and gay men, musicians, veterans, union members, and Republicans. The ethical persuader must consider the particular audience members to know which mythos might appeal. Certainly one group's mythos might be less ethical than another's. The ideas that Americans must speak English, that all conceptions should result in children, and that one religion is better than another, are based in different mythos that invite ethical evaluation in our national discussions.

You learned earlier that evidence consists of supporting materials used for a persuasive purpose. These basic elements of the persuasive process are used to support your propositions or positions. Certain rules guide the way we combine evidence and propositions to create conclusions. **Argument** consists of the presentation of a claim or conclusion and the evidence which supports it. [18] Certain inferences or assumptions often go unstated in arguments.

Arguing in an Ethical and Effective Way

If you want to convince an audience that your idea meets their needs, you will be interested in learning about arguing. If you wish to demonstrate the benefits of your plan, you will need to understand the information in this section. If you want to show that your idea is consistent with the audience's present beliefs, attitudes, and values, this information will be helpful to you.

Components of an Argument

As you have been reading about evidence and proofs, you may have already discerned the components that form an argument. Essentially, the components are only two in number: a claim and evidence. The **claim** is the conclusion you wish your audience to accept. **Evidence** consists of supporting materials used in a persuasive context. When you make an argument, you need to provide a claim and evidence for it. Sometimes the relationship between the two is fairly obvious; at other times, you may have to explain to your audience how they are related.

Before we consider the nature and types of argument, we need to consider in more depth the notions of claims. In the next section, we will distinguish between claims of fact, claims of value, and claims of policy.

Types of Claims

Public speeches, especially speeches intended to persuade others, are full of claims that the advocate wants the audience to accept. This section provides you with terms to describe those claims: claims of fact, value, and policy. Why should you know, understand, and use these terms? First, the terms provide you with language to describe what you use in your own speeches and hear in those of others. Second, the terms allow you to think critically about their use. When you hear a speaker claiming a fact, you know that you have a right to know where the speaker found that fact and if the source is credible. Third, the terms help you to know what kinds of evidence or proof are necessary for the different claims. For example, no one can absolutely demonstrate that a policy will work as claimed because it tries to predict how it will work in the future. There are always unintended results. In order to understand them, we will consider each of the three types of claims in more detail.

Claims of Fact

Claims of fact deal with truth and falsity. They are concerned with the occurrence, the existence, or the particular properties of something. Examples of claims of fact include:

The United States does not have enough water to meet normal needs.

The most likely way for a child in the United States to die is at the hands of another child.

Small amounts of marijuana are not harmful to the human body.

Women do not have equal opportunities for employment in the United States.

California has suffered more natural disasters in the last decade than any other state.

Claims of Value

Claims of value require judgments of good and bad. Such claims are grounded in the participant's motives, beliefs, and cultural standards. Desirability and satisfaction are often central to claims of value. Examples of claims in this category include:

A college education is desirable for everyone.

Forensics competitions provide a positive experience for young women.

The most important issue facing America is that of increased violence in our neighborhoods and our homes.

Claims of Policy

Claims of policy concern future action. The purpose of a policy claim is to argue that a course of action should be taken or supported in a specific situation. The word *should* is generally included in a claim of policy. Examples of claims of policy include the following:

Types of Claims

Claims of fact deal with truth and falsity.
Claims of value require judgments of good and bad.
Claims of policy concern future action.

What claim will you use in your persuasive speech? Remind yourself of the three types of claims identified here. State the claim you will make in your speech. Explain why it is a claim of fact, value, or policy.

Rules against nepotism should be dropped.

People over the age of seventy should not be allowed to work.

Husbands who rape their wives should face the same penalties strangers face when they are found guilty of rape.

College students should have no required courses.

The age for drinking alcohol legally should be raised to twenty-five.

The Construction of a Sound Argument

The components of argument are few in number, which may suggest to you that constructing an argument is fairly easy to do. On the contrary, the construction of an effective and ethical argument is complex. Here is an example of an argument provided by a student speaker from a speech entitled "Keep the Elderly at Home." In this speech, Julie L. Cook argues that nursing homes have inherent problems. She said, in part,

> This country has 20,000 nursing homes but over half of them are substandard. According to Nursing Home Life: What It Is and What It Could Be, *nursing homes focus on the physical and medical aspects of geriatric care. Little is being done to satisfy any nonmedical needs, to make patients' lives meaningful, livable, or natural. Even though all nursing homes have to balance care and costs, our elderly should not be required to live an existence that is not worthwhile.*[19]

Would you accept the speaker's argument? She has made a claim and she has offered in evidence some paraphrased testimony. Some people might conclude that her evidence is sufficient and that she has made the link between the claim and the evidence. Others might find her support inadequate.

In his speech on world peace, Solomon Moore provided a claim and evidence. Moore said,

> *The biggest problem caused by the building up of armaments is not their destructive power, but instead the drain of available resources, which many nations could put to better use.*
>
> *For instance: the amount of money spent on researching new forms of death is seven times what is spent on new ways to prolong life. The training of military personnel in the United States costs twice as much as the budget for the education of 300 million South Asian children. At present levels, everyone during his or her lifetime will sacrifice three to four years of income to the arms race. With under one percent of the world's military budget, almost twenty-five million lives could be saved by vaccinating all children against polio, measles, tetanus, and by draining swamps and providing medicine to rid the world of malaria. The present nuclear arsenal contains the explosive power of over 6000 World War II's. Every two days the world spends $4 billion on military*

expenditures, and every two seconds four people starve to death. And when the world does finally put the money into the 930 million people who are hungry all of the time, it's like a grimace of kindness on a murderer's face.[20]

In this argument, Moore links his claim to both logical and emotional evidence. He uses facts and figures and examples. He also uses metaphor to make his evidence more striking. Do you find this argument stronger or weaker than the one provided by Cook? Why?

When Julie Cook gave her speech, she was a sophomore in college majoring in business administration. Julie is a middle-class European American female. When Solomon Moore gave his speech, he was a seventeen-year-old high school senior. A native of Ohio, Solomon is African American. Does this information change the way you see their arguments? How does this small amount of personal information contribute to the speaker's ethos, or personal proof?

Aristotle observed that, "A speech has two parts. Necessarily, you state your case, and you prove it."[21] Both speakers used the two components of an argument: a claim and evidence. As we have seen, however, these two elements can be put together in a variety of ways. In order to be an effective persuasive speaker, you will need to consider all of the elements in public argument, including the kinds of evidence and the types of proof available to you.

Types of Argument

Although all arguments make a claim and provide evidence, arguments can be made on different bases. Let us consider the four most common types of argument: the argument by analogy, the argument from cause, the argument by deduction, and the argument by example or induction.

Argument by Analogy

An **argument by analogy** points out similarities between two things, comparing something that the audience knows well to something it does not. To say that our society is analogous to a stew suggests that all of the ethnic groups in our pot retain their original flavors, but are enhanced by being mixed together. To say that our society is a melting pot suggests that ethnic groups lose their individual identities to become something else—Americans. To clarify the concept of argument by analogy further, you should know that some analogies are figurative and others are literal.

A **figurative analogy** takes two fundamentally different things and compares their common properties. For example, this is how one student described her family.

My family is a football team. My father's position is the quarterback who calls his own plays. He decides what strategy to take and then implements it. My mother could be considered my dad's right arm and, therefore, is placed in the position of running back, the star running back. She is the consistent one who will always get at least four yards. My "little" brother resembles the entire front line. Not only by his physical size, but by his concern for our family. He would never let anyone penetrate through the line to get to any of us. My sister holds the position of second string quarterback. She's a lot like my father as far as attitudes and values. She is very independent and believes "her way" is always best. My position on the team would be on the sidelines. I am the biggest fan, the loudest cheerleader and, at times, the head referee. I am not as involved in the play by play because of geographical barriers. However, when I am able to be with my family I play an active role. Regardless of victory or defeat my family remains strong and united, our spirit never faltering. Together we are definitely a winning team![22]

This analogy comparing the student's family to a football team clarified the relationships and roles of her family members. Audience members with some knowledge of American football understood reasonably well what her family was like.

A **literal analogy** is a comparison of two similar things, instead of two fundamentally different things. The city of Columbus solved its traffic flow problems by creating a grid of one-way streets. Should the city of Cleveland do the same thing? A speech favoring the plan of one city for another would use a literal analogy.

A real-life example of a literal analogy occurred when National Public Radio correspondent, Nina Totenberg, was summoned before the Senate Special Independent Counsel for reading portions of Anita Hill's affidavit to the Senate Judiciary Committee to nine million listeners. Republican supporters of Clarence Thomas, a nominee for the Supreme Court, were angry about leaks to the press. The purpose of the hearing was to force Totenberg to reveal her sources, which she regarded as a violation of journalistic ethics. Here is part of her response:

> At the beginning of our Republic, in 1798, one party, the Federalists, sought to silence its critics in the upcoming election by making it a crime punishable by up to two years in prison and a fine of $2000 to "write, print, utter or publish" any material that would bring government officials into "contempt or disrepute." (See A. Lewis, Make No Law, 1991.) Under the Sedition Act, editors and publishers of opposing Republican party papers were jailed and fined. But many of our most famous Founding Fathers were outraged by the Act—James Madison and Thomas Jefferson called it a blatant violation of the First Amendment. Jefferson, after being elected President, pardoned those convicted under the act and within less than half a century the law (which lasted only three years) was in such disrepute that Congress paid back many of the fines that had been imposed under it. In 1964, the Sedition Act was, at long last, held unconstitutional.
>
> I suspect that Congress may one day look back on these press subpoenas with equal disdain.[23]

Totenberg's defense is a literal analogy comparing the hated and ineffective Sedition Act of 1798 with the legal subpoenas of 1992. Incidently, she never did reveal her sources, but Clarence Thomas did become an Associate Justice of the United States Supreme Court.

The key to determining just how ethical an analogy is depends on how parallel the compared cases are. By definition, both figurative and literal analogies compare different things, but the appropriateness and ethical value of an analogy depends on the similarities. If the Sedition Act of 1798 and the forced appearances of journalists at hearings in 1992 are sufficiently similar in comparison, then the analogy can be said to be appropriate and ethical. If the Sedition Act and the subpoenas are sufficiently different in comparison, then the analogy can be attacked as "apples and oranges" and found ethically suspect. Always, the speaker and listeners as critical thinkers need to analyze, compare, and decide.

Argument from Cause

An **argument from cause** occurs when you reason from a cause to an unknown, but likely, effect.[24] You are arguing that one event caused, or was responsible for, a second event. Some common examples of argument from cause include the following:

Smoking causes cancer.

Drinking while you are pregnant causes birth defects.

Excessive exposure to the sun causes skin cancer.

Unsafe sex causes the spread of disease or pregnancy.

Skipping classes causes lower grades.

Yo-yo dieting causes heart problems.

Achieving high grades in undergraduate schools causes easier admission to graduate school.

An example of an argument from cause is provided in a speech by Cheng Imm Tan, a Buddhist Unitarian Universalist minister, who works with Cambodian, Vietnamese, and

Chinese women in the Asian American Task Force Against Domestic Violence. Her speech is about the plight of Asian women who find themselves alone in American cities when they leave the men who abuse them. See if you can find the arguments from cause in her speech.

> *Since 1970, the Asian American population has doubled each decade. It is the fastest growing group in the United States. Today, 60 percent of the Asian American population are immigrants.*
>
> *. . . . Although much has been done in the last fifteen years since the battered women's movement began to address domestic violence in the United States, for most Asian women, the gains made have not been accessible.*
>
> *. . . . The relative isolation of the Asian communities . . . has meant marginalization and invisibility. Violence in the home continues to be seen as a private family matter. Most Asian women are not aware of available resources or of their legal rights. Many also fear reporting abuse because of their fear and distrust of governments and authorities. Like other people of color, they also fear discrimination and unfair treatment.*
>
> *. . . . Asian refugee and immigrant women are particularly isolated. Many do not speak or understand English. Even those who do speak English are not confident in using the language. Since shelters and hotlines do not have staff who speak Asian languages, this language barrier ensures isolation. In fact, few battered women's shelters serve Asian women. Many battered women who have fled to a shelter have returned because the unfamiliarity of the shelter environment, language difficulties, and cultural differences make separation from their community unbearable. . . .*[25]

Cheng Imm Tan's speech cites numerous causes—isolation, language and cultural barriers, and ignorance—for the effect: battered Asian women do not receive help in American society.

How does the ethical and effective persuader assess arguments from cause? First, you must consider whether the cause and effect presented are linked at all; in other words is there a relationship between the two? Second, you need to determine whether the cause and effect are strongly related. Third, you need to determine if the effect may be related to a different cause.

For example, you might decide to give a persuasive speech in which you encourage people not to drink and drive an automobile. You argue, in your speech, that people who drink and drive are far more likely to have accidents than do those who do not drink. In this instance, the cause is drinking and the effect is an automobile accident.

If your argument is to be successful, you will have to convince your audience that the cause and effect you are describing are related to each other. Your audience will have to agree that drinking and accidents are related.

Second, you will have to show that the link between drinking and automobile accidents is an important one. If someone can demonstrate that only 5 percent of people who drink and drive have automobile accidents, your argument may be defeated. People may agree that drinking causes accidents, but the percentage of this incidence within the total number of accidents is too low to be of much concern.

Third, you need to determine if the effect may be related to a different cause. For example, if multiple causes for automobile accidents—age, sex, personality characteristics, distance from home, speed of vehicle, etc.—can be shown to be just as relevant as drinking, the audience may see the cause-effect link, but dismiss it because the effect is related to other causes.

Similarly, someone might argue that drinking is actually the effect of another phenomenon—say age or personality or predisposition to alcoholism. They could argue that it is really one's age, personality, or predisposition that is the cause of automobile accidents and that drinking and accidents are both effects.

Argument by Deduction

An **argument by deduction** occurs when you reason from a general proposition, or from a generally accepted truth, to a specific instance or example.[26] In deductive argument you have a **conclusion** deduced from a major and a minor premise. Instead of resulting in a probability, as inductive reasoning does, *a deductive argument results in a conclusion that necessarily follows from the two premises.* A deductive argument looks like this:

Major premise: All insects have six legs.

Minor premise: Ants are insects.

Conclusion: Therefore, ants have six legs.

Notice that, if the premises are true, then the conclusion must necessarily be true also, because in a sense the two premises are the same as the conclusion.

In conversation and even in most speeches, a deductive argument usually does not sound or look quite as formal as it appears in our example. In fact, the argument cited would more likely appear in a speech like this: "Since all insects have six legs, ants must too." The reasoning is still deductive, except that the minor premise is implied rather than openly stated. At other times, the conclusion is implied and the major and minor premises are provided in words. An **enthymeme** is a deductive argument in which either the minor premise or the conclusion is implied rather than stated. Since deductive arguments most oftentimes appear as enthymemes in speeches, they are difficult to detect and even more difficult to analyze. For this reason, it is necessary to listen closely to the reasoning in speeches, in order to determine what has been implied—or *seemed* to be implied, but actually wasn't—in addition to what has been stated openly.

Here are some examples of enthymemes. If you say "Henry Wong is Republican because he is Chinese" then you have a conclusion that's premises are: All Chinese are Republicans; Henry Wong is Chinese; therefore, Henry Wong is Republican. In other words, part of the deductive argument is omitted. If you say "All fraternity men are drunks," then you have a major premise for a deductive argument that can say: All fraternity men are drunks; Fred is a fraternity man; therefore, Fred is a drunk. The key to recognizing an enthymeme is to know that it is incomplete reasoning, that some of the deductive argument is omitted.

If you feel you have particularly strong arguments by deduction in your own speech, you might consider taking the time to state them clearly and completely rather than providing them less completely as enthymemes. Well reasoned deductive arguments can have great persuasive power, because once the audience has accepted the validity of the premises, *the conclusion is inescapable*. Mathematical proofs commonly take the form of deductive arguments, and the reasoning in your own speech should have all the clarity and impact of such proofs: if A equals B, and if B equals C, then A equals C.

How does the ethical and effective persuasive communicator test deductive arguments? The tests are straightforward. First, you ensure that both the major premise and the minor premise are true. Second, you ascertain that the premises are actually related to each other.

An example of an argument by deduction occurs in this speech by Nannerl O. Keohane, president of Wellesley College, entitled "Educating Women for Leadership: Drawing on the Full Human Race." Examining Keohane's deductive argument will allow us to illustrate the tests for the effective and ethical persuader. Keohane states,

> *We know that a society cannot flourish, indeed cannot survive, without at least a minimal sense of shared ethical standards and goals. To renew this sense among our own people we need students educated on our campuses who are familiar with the great moral examples provided by men and women in the past who have wrestled with their own*

Women hold an increasing number of leadership positions in the United States and around the world.

ethical dilemmas. We need to be sure they have read deeply in philosophy and literature, religion and biography, to understand how human beings develop a sense of truthfulness and compassion and how such attributes advance our common goals.[27]

Keohane's major premise is that a society cannot flourish without a minimal sense of shared ethical standards and goals. Her minor premise, which is unstated, is that people will have a sense of shared ethical standards and goals if undergraduate students become familiar with moral examples and read in the areas of philosophy, literature, religion, and biography. Her conclusion is that undergraduate students should become familiar with such examples and read in these areas.

If Keohane's major and minor premises are related to each other and are true, then the conclusion must also be true. In most speeches, matters of truth are not so easily ascertained, however. Someone might disagree with the major premise. They could point to societies that flourished without a sense of shared ethical standards. They could also disagree that the minor premise is true. They might argue that people who are familiar with moral examples and well-read in philosophy, literature, religion, and biography do not necessarily have a sense of shared ethical standards. The truth of her conclusion is based on the truth of her premises. Again, if the premises are agreed upon as true, then the conclusion is inevitably true.

Argument by Induction

An **argument by induction,** or example, is argument from specific instances to a general conclusion. The conclusion is not necessarily true, but it is highly probable. An argument by example was provided in the section on logos in the excerpt of a speech by Julia Hughes Jones. Jones argued that one vote has changed the course of history. She proved her proposition by providing example after example of instances when one vote decided major issues.

Another example is provided in the following speech excerpt by Nannerl O. Keohane. In this excerpt Keohane argues that women are holding an increasing number of leadership positions around the world. She stated,

Types of Argument

Argument by analogy: Arguing that if two cases are alike in known ways, they are similarly alike in unknown ways.

Argument from cause: Reasoning from a cause to an unknown, but likely, effect.

Argument by deduction: Reasoning from a general proposition, or from a generally accepted truth, to a specific instance or example.

Argument by induction: Arguing from specific instances to a general conclusion.

There are women generals and women judges, women neurosurgeons and opera conductors and newspaper editors, and even, occasionally, a woman CEO.

Such new leaders join the legions of strong women who have traditionally been leaders in more familiar fields: in early childhood education, on the boards of symphonies and art museums, in the soup kitchens and in the peace movement, in all kinds of non-profit organizations that so enrich our lives.

There are more women in politics, as well, more women governors, mayors, even presidential and vice-presidential candidates these days. If someone had said ten years ago that the mayors of several of America's largest cities in 1990 would be women, or that one-half the cabinet, one-half the legislature, and the prime minister of Norway would be female, they would have been laughed out of court.[28]

Keohane's list of examples is extensive. She cites women in leadership in a variety of careers. These examples allow her to conclude that women have a greater number of leadership positions today than in the past. She begins with specific examples and ends with a generalization.

In Keohane's case, as in all cases of argument by example, the conclusion is not necessarily true. This argument provides evidence that allows an "inferential leap" to the generalization. Since the argument requires an inference, the generalization that is drawn may be false, but it is viewed as generally, or probably true.

How can we determine the likeliness that the generalization is true? Some specific tests can be applied to the inductive argument to test its validity. First, we need to ensure that the examples are true. Second, we need to be sure that the examples are recent. Third, we consider whether the examples are relevant. Fourth, we need to determine if an adequate number of examples were provided. Finally, we consider whether the examples are typical.

In Keohane's speech, the generalization that women have attained more leadership roles remains only a probability, even with the large number of examples that she presented. Are her examples true? We might have to cite her sources or cite independent sources of our own. In our search we can also determine the recency of Keohane's examples. We need to consider if her examples are relevant. What if women held other leadership roles in the past that have now been taken over by men? What if these leadership positions are not very important ones? Next we need to consider if she has provided an adequate number of examples. Finally, we need to decide if the examples that Keohane has presented are representative of all, or most, leadership positions. Similar questions allow us to see that the generalization, while probably true, can always be questioned by a reinterpretation of other evidence or by the introduction of contrary evidence.

You now know about four types of argument and the specific tests that the ethical and effective communicator uses to examine each. In addition, four general questions should be asked to ensure that your reasoning and evidence is generally sound.

1. *Is your evidence consistent with other known evidence?* An example is the controversy over insurance rates. Cities, counties, and even transit authorities are facing rates they cannot afford to pay. The federal government claims that those high rates are partly because of all the lawsuits, a claim that they back with evidence. The lawyers counter with their evidence that the actual number of lawsuits involving insurance have increased only with the increase in population. The point is that the amount of evidence you have that consistently supports your position can help you persuade an audience. At this juncture in the lawyer-government-insurance controversy, none of the combatants have really won the public's endorsement with their evidence.

2. *Is there any evidence to the contrary?* When you try to reason with evidence, you must always be aware of any evidence that does not support your cause. An opponent can do much damage to your arguments and your credibility if she can find contrary evidence that you did not mention. Usually you are better off mentioning any conflicting evidence, especially if you can argue against it in your presentation.

3. *Does your generalization go beyond your evidence?* Speakers always face the danger of overstating what their evidence shows. A small study that shows grade inflation is treated like a universitywide problem. Evidence of a local problem becomes a national problem in the speech. Always be careful that you do not go beyond what your evidence demonstrates.

4. *Is your evidence believable to the audience?* In persuasive speaking, you need to provide only enough evidence to have the audience believe and act as you wish. More than that is too much; less than that is too little. A large amount of evidence that the listeners find unacceptable will not persuade them; a small amount that the audience finds acceptable will be sufficient to persuade.

Fallacies of Argument

In addition to the tests that should be considered if you want your arguments to be effective and ethical, a number of standard fallacies or faulty arguments have been identified. These fallacies are based on plausible, but invalid reasoning. We will consider some of the most common fallacies. If you wish to consider additional fallacies, you may wish to consult resources on argumentation and discussion.[29]

The **hasty generalization** violates the rules of inference by coming to a conclusion with too little evidence. Some examples would include the following: The last woman I hired was calling her kids on the phone all the time, so I stopped hiring women; I'll never trust college students because several of them have taken items from my store without paying; My last ride with an Iranian taxi driver convinced me never to ride with an Iranian taxi driver again. In all cases, a conclusion was drawn based on a sample of one, which was generalized to all women, college students, and Iranians. Coming to a conclusion with very little evidence is regarded as faulty reasoning.

The **post hoc, ergo propter hoc** fallacy literally means "after this; therefore, because of this." The faulty reasoning involved is that of false cause: just because one thing occurs after another does not mean that it was caused by the first thing. Here are some examples: I had a car accident immediately after I saw a black cat, which everyone knows is bad luck; I got a headache after eating at an Italian restaurant, so I am going to avoid headaches by avoiding Italian restaurants; I get sick at work a lot because it is a "sick building." Just because two events correlate does not mean they necessarily cause each other. The car accident was not caused by a black cat, the headache was a hangover, and the illness at work was from a chronic condition that had nothing to do with the workplace. The lesson of the post hoc fallacy is to not confuse correlation with causation.

The **equivocation** fallacy means that the same word is used in different ways to result in an incorrect interpretation. Some examples of equivocation in action are the following: The Constitution says that "All men are created equal," so women must not be equal to men; We say that "America is the land of the free," so we must be free to do anything we like; I have an open door policy, but you will have to wait two weeks for an appointment. The words "men," "free," and "open door" are words that are used in two different ways resulting in an incorrect interpretation.

The **faulty analogy** fallacy means that the analogy has gone too far. An analogy compares two fundamentally different things, and the comparison can be carried over some—but not all—characteristics. Here are some examples: most English police do not carry weapons, and that country has substantially fewer murders, so we should disarm our police to achieve a lower murder rate; America is like ancient Rome in its fascination with violence, nudity, and drinking, so our society is about to meet the same fate as Rome; many animals kill each other to establish territoriality just as humans do, that is why we will never have peace. English society and American society are similar in some respects, but not all, so disarming the police may or may not work in American society. America and Rome are centuries apart and fundamentally different, so there is no assurance that our current behavior will have the same result that it did in ancient Rome. Animals and people are different enough, so there is no guarantee that we will be unable to settle territorial disputes peacefully. The faulty analogy carries the comparison too far.

The **red herring** fallacy occurs when extraneous issues are introduced to distract attention away from the argument. Examples of the red herring fallacy come from the political arena. When Clinton's political opponents attacked him by saying that his brother Roger had drug problems, the intent was to detract from Clinton's political agenda. When Newt Gingrich's political opponents falsely accused him of asking his first wife for a divorce when she was suffering from cancer, they were trying to detract from Gingrich's being named Speaker of the House of Representatives. When Democratic Representative Ted Strickland appeared on a TV promotion for his opponent saying over and over again that "it would take new taxes," few knew until after his opponent won the election that the opponent had taken those few words out of context to get what sounded like a pro-tax statement, which he instant replayed over and over on his political commercials. The faked pro-tax message was a red herring, a distraction from the real issues, that won the election for the feckless opponent. The red herring fallacy, a claim irrelevant to the main issues, is a common ploy in American politics.

The **slippery slope** fallacy is erroneous reasoning that suggests that if one event occurs, then a chain of other events will follow. It is similar to the "domino theory," which suggests that if the first event happens (the first domino falls), it will create a second event (the second domino falling), and then another (the next domino will fall), until a series of events have occurred (all of the dominos will eventually be knocked down).

The slippery slope fallacy often occurs around the issue of gun control. People argue that if large automatic weapons such as AK-47s and Uzis are controlled, then hand guns will be controlled next. After hand guns, they believe that all types of shotguns and rifles will be banned, and soon people will be defenseless in their own homes. They thus argue that people should have the right to own powerful, automatic weapons originally designed for wartime.

The **argumentum ad hominem** fallacy occurs when you attack the other person rather than the issue. It is similar to the tactic of name-calling. An example of ad hominem occurs when people who espouse the right to life and oppose abortion call people who espouse the right to choice "murderers," and "criminals." Similarly, when Rush Limbaugh labels women who want equal rights as "femi-Nazis," he is using an ad hominem fallacy rather than considering the validity of their arguments.

Fallacies in Argument

1. Hasty generalization
2. Post hoc, ergo propter hoc
3. Equivocation
4. Faulty analogy
5. Red herring
6. Slippery slope
7. Argumentum ad hominem
8. False dilemma
9. Bandwagon or appeal to popular opinion
10. Begging the question

The **false dilemma** fallacy exists when listeners are provided with only two choices even though a variety of options are available. For instance, if you support a particular political candidate and tell your audience that the choice is simple—either your candidate or four more years of despair, depression, and down-sizing—you are committing this fallacy.

The **bandwagon,** or **appeal to popular opinion,** fallacy is present when a phenomenon is viewed as true or right because a majority of people believe it to be. The clichéd parental remark to teenage children, "If your friends jumped off a bridge, would you jump off it, too?" is parents' way of letting their children know that they have committed this fallacy. Although the parental response is tired from overuse, it does suggest that none of us should engage in a behavior simply because a majority of other people are engaged in it.

Begging the question is a fallacy that occurs when someone uses language to make claims that they have not proven. One way this may be done is if someone argues in a circular fashion. For instance, if you argue that education is important because well-educated people are generally better off than are people who are not well-educated, you have not really proven your claim that either education is important or that well-educated people are better off. Another way you can beg the question is by using "devil terms" or "angel terms" in association with a concept that you oppose or propose. When Dr. Jack Kevorkian discussed "issues of human dignity" when he considered the right to die, he was essentially begging the question. If you believe in human dignity (and who would say that they do not), then you are obligated to agree with Kevorkian's circular reasoning.

Additional Ethical Concerns

Persuasive speaking offers ample opportunities for ethical mischief. Certainly persuasive speaking can be used for positive purposes: stop smoking, start exercising, do not overuse your credit card, and avoid AIDS. However, persuasive speaking can also be used to sell you unwanted insurance, unneeded repairs, overpriced products, and ineffective diets. Distinguishing between ethical and unethical persuasive appeals is a challenging task for which there are some general guidelines.

1. Be careful whom you trust. The smooth-talking individual can be a pathological deceiver, whereas an unattractive, inarticulate person can have your best interests in mind. When buying or selling, dating or mating, you should look at past behavior and the testimony of others who have had more experience with the person with whom you are dealing. In short, source credibility should always be an issue.

2. Analyze and evaluate messages for reasonableness, truth, and benefit to you or humankind. Our social norms discourage acceptance of messages for purely

emotional reasons ("I bought the $3000 ring because I wanted it"; "I married him because of his cute little nose"). Instead, our society encourages us to accept messages because they meet our standards of reason, because we find them to be true, or because the message seems to benefit us or others more than it will harm us.

3. You and your messages will be more persuasive if you have a long, positive history ("The thing you only get to lose once is your reputation"); if your past invites others to trust you and your word; and if others tend to benefit from your messages as much or more than you do (that is, you don't seek compliance for selfish purposes). A nationally known evangelist was caught for the second time in the company of a prostitute. Will the money keep flowing to a person who cannot be trusted to stay on the straight and narrow himself? Are you building a history that will help or harm you when you attempt to persuade others?

Summary

In this chapter you learned how to use evidence, proof, and argument in an effective and ethical way. You first learned that four kinds of evidence can be used in an ethical and effective way in persuasion. They include facts and figures, examples, narratives, and testimony. After considering some ethical and effectiveness criteria for evidence, we turned our attention to proof. The modes of proof include personal proof, emotional proof, logical proof, and mythic proof.

We then shifted to a discussion of effective argument. In order to understand argument, we need the foundation of understanding evidence and proof. In addition, we need to know that claims are of three types: claims of fact, claims of value, and claims of policy. Although arguments consist only of evidence and claims, the construction of a sound argument is complex.

What types of argument are most common? We considered the argument by analogy, the argument from cause, the argument by deduction, and the argument by induction, or example.

If we consider public discourse today, we know that many people use argument inappropriately. We thus devoted some attention to understanding the fallacies associated with argument. We considered the hasty generalization; post hoc, ergo propter hoc; equivocation; faulty analogy; red herring; slippery slope; argumentum ad hominem; false dilemma; bandwagon or appeal to popular opinion; and begging the question fallacies. The chapter concluded with some additional ethical considerations.

Vocabulary

argument The presentation of a claim or conclusion and the evidence which supports it

argument by analogy The argument that occurs when you argue that if two cases are alike in known ways they are similarly alike in unknown ways

argument by deduction The argument that occurs when you reason from a general proposition, or from a generally accepted truth, to a specific instance or example

argument by induction An argument from specific instances to a general conclusion

argument from cause The argument that occurs when you reason from a cause to an unknown, but likely, effect

argumentum ad hominem A fallacy which occurs when you attack the other person rather than the issue

bandwagon or appeal to popular opinion A fallacy which is present when a phenomenon is viewed as true or right because a majority of people believe it to be

begging the question A fallacy which occurs when someone uses language to make claims that they have not proven

character A dimension of speaker credibility that means that listeners see you as trustworthy, honest, and sincere

claim The conclusion you wish your audience to accept

claims of fact Claims that deal with truth and falsity

claims of policy Claims that concern future action

claims of value Claims that require judgments of good and bad

competence A dimension of speaker credibility that refers to the degree to which listeners perceive you as knowledgeable and informed about your topic

composure A dimension of speaker credibility that means that listeners view you as being in control, poised, and relaxed

conclusion The result of deductive reasoning, which is valid if it is correctly arranged

conviction A positive emotional appeal based on a deep feeling of certainty in the righteousness, truth, and virtue of your cause

determination A positive emotional appeal based on single-minded will power to achieve a purpose

dramatic example A positive emotional appeal based on a story or narrative that illustrates a message in a manner that stirs the emotions

enthymeme A deductive argument in which either the minor premise or the conclusion is implied rather than stated

equivocation Faulty reasoning based on shifting one meaning of a word to another meaning

ethos A mode of proof also known as personal proof that refers to the audience's perceptions of the character of the speaker

evidence Supporting materials used in a persuasive context

example A specimen, an instance, that represents a larger group

extrinsic proofs Proofs that support claims by referring to objective evidence such as confessions, contracts, and existing laws

extroversion A dimension of speaker credibility that refers to the audience's perception that you are outgoing, energetic, and talkative

facts and figures Statements or numbers about which people agree because they are verifiable

false dilemma A fallacy which exists when listeners are provided with only two choices when a variety of options are available

faulty analogy A generalization based on insufficient evidence

figurative analogy A comparison of the common properties between two fundamentally different things

hasty generalization A generalization based on insufficient evidence

idealism A positive emotional appeal based on communicating the highest expectations of humanity, however rare their practice in reality

intrinsic proofs Proofs that consist of the evidence in communicative messages that justifies belief, attitude, or behavior

literal analogy A comparison of the common properties between two similar things

logos A mode of proof also known as logical proof that occurs when you try to persuade an audience with logical appeals, reasoning, and arguments

mythos A mode of proof also known as mythic proof that occurs when you try to persuade an audience with stories and statements that depict the values, beliefs, and feelings of a group of people

narratives Stories told to illustrate a point

pathos A mode of proof also known as emotional proof that involves attempts to persuade an audience with emotional appeals

post hoc, ergo propter hoc A fallacy based on mistaking correlation for causation: just because one thing happens after another does not mean that the second event was caused by the first

proofs The means by which speakers support their claims

red herring A fallacy which occurs when extraneous issues are introduced to distract attention away from the argument

slippery slope A fallacy which suggests that if one event occurs, then a chain of other events will follow

sociability A dimension of speaker credibility that refers to the idea that your audience sees you as friendly, pleasant, and likeable

testimony Opinions that support the speaker's claims

transcendence A positive emotional appeal based on rising above differences in search of bonding similarities

 # Applications

Claims

1. Can you distinguish between the variety of claims that a persuasive speaker can make? Mark each claim with **F** for fact, **V** for value, or **P** for policy.

_____ 1. The best place to live in America are the Twin Cities of Minneapolis and St. Paul, Minnesota.

_____ 2. Everyone should take Vitamin E, Vitamin C, and beta-carotene each day.

_____ 3. We must stop America's children from turning to crime.

_____ 4. You must turn your stress into energy.

_____ 5. Spirituality is the answer to your problems.

_____ 6. You should use ATM's (Automated Teller Machines) for more than banking.

_____ 7. If you want more understanding from your parents, try to be more understanding of them.

_____ 8. For total health, you must limit your activities so you do not try to do too much in too little time.

_____ 9. Cindy Crawford is the highest-paid model today.

_____ 10. The press should not try people in the media before they are allowed their day in court.

_____ 11. The genital mutilation of girls in Africa must be viewed as torture, not tradition.

_____ 12. Americans spend too much money on housing.

_____ 13. The holocaust never occurred.

_____ 14. The information superhighway is a myth.

_____ 15. You can contract AIDS without having sex and without using a contaminated needle.

_____ 16. Rap music has become too violent.

_____ 17. Most Americans claim to be religious, but few people take their faith seriously.

_____ 18. _Mrs. Doubtfire_ taught us about family values.

_____ 19. JFK was killed by a single person who was probably mentally ill.

_____ 20. Children's literature teaches sexism and racism.

_____ 21. Pornography should be prohibited.

_____ 22. X-rays of the head and neck cause cancer of the thyroid.

_____ 23. People's social standing is directly related to their wealth.

_____ 24. America should spend less money on weapons.

_____ 25. Women should retain their unmarried names when they marry.

_____ 26. All educational institutions should be co-educational.

_____ 27. Employees should determine their own work schedules.

_____ 28. The federal government should regulate the use of energy.

_____ 29. Abortion laws are too liberal.

_____ 30. Unemployment falls disproportionately on the young.

Types of Argument

2. Do you understand the four types of argument presented in this chapter? To demonstrate your knowledge, find or write one example for each of the four types of argument. You might examine news magazines, newspapers, or televised news programs.

Fallacies in Argument

3. Once you become familiar with the fallacies that are used in argument, you will begin to see them and hear them in public discourse. Examine a talk show, a televised news magazine, a radio opinion program, or editorials in the print media. Find at least five fallacies. What kind of fallacy seems most prevalent?

Why do you believe that people with large audiences (millions of television viewers, thousands of newspaper readers) are not held accountable for the fallacious reasoning they use? If respected television, radio, and news people are allowed to make fallacious arguments, how does this affect the ethical standards of our society? What can we do to insist that people in responsible positions use valid arguments?

Endnotes

....

1. This speech was composed by Amy Morehead, an Ohio University student. The endnotes for the speech: 1. Bill Getz, *International Perspectives* (Greenwich, CT: American Institute for Foreign Study, 1988); 2. Getz; 3. Alan W. Boyd, *International Student Report* (Ohio University: International Student and Faculty Services, fall 1990); 4. Getz; 5. Ricard C. Remy and Robert B. Woyach, *Quarterly Report* (Ohio State University: Mershon Center, autumn 1983).
2. "Surveys Say Women Still Do Most of Household Chores," *The Messenger* Athens, Ohio (January 16, 1994): B8. Reprinted with permission of the editor.
3. Ibid.
4. David Archambault, "Columbus Plus 500 Years: Whither the American Indian," delivered to the Rotary Club, Murray, Utah, April 6, 1992. Reprinted in *Vital Speeches* 58.16 (1992): 491–93. Courtesy of David Archambault, 1992.
5. Marc Maurer, "Language and the Future of the Blind: Independence and Freedom," delivered at the Banquet of the Annual Convention of the Federation of the Blind in Denver, Colorado, July 8, 1989. Reprinted in *Vital Speeches* 56.1 (1989): 16–22. Courtesy of Marc Maurer.
6. Maurer, 1989.
7. Walter R. Fisher. "Toward a Logic of Good Reasons," *The Quarterly Journal of Speech* 64 (1978): 378.
8. Joseph A. DeVito, *The Communication Handbook: A Dictionary* (New York: Harper & Row, 1986), 109.
9. See, for example, James C. McCroskey, "Scales for the Measurement of Ethos," *Speech Monographs* 33 (1966): 65–72; J. C. McCroskey, P. R. Hamilton, and A. N. Winer, "The Effect of Interaction Behavior on Source Credibility, Homophily, and Interpersonal Attraction," *Human Communication Research* 1 (1974): 42–52; and J. C. McCroskey, W. E. Holdridge, and J. K. Toomb, "An Instrument for Measuring the Source Credibility of Basic Speech Communication Instructors," *Speech Teacher* 23 (1974): 26–33.
10. Archambault, 1992.
11. From Marvin Karlins and Herbert Abelson, *Persuasion: How Opinions and Attitudes Are Changed,* 35. Copyright © 1970 by Springer Publishing Company, Inc., New York. Used by permission.
12. Solomon Moore, "The Elusive Peace," written in 1989 at Wooster High School, Wooster, Ohio, for forensic competition in original oratory. The speech was provided by Diana Tucker, an Ohio University undergraduate student and forensics team member.
13. DeVito, 1986.
14. Julia Hughes Jones, "A Greater Voice in Action: Women and Equality," delivered at Charlotte, North Carolina, August 26, 1992. Reprinted in *Vital Speeches* 59 (1992): 109–11. Courtesy of Julia Hughes Jones, former State Auditor, Arkansas.

15. For an excellent and relevant article on this topic, see, Randall A. Lake, "Between Myth and History: Enacting Time in Native American Protest Rhetoric," *Quarterly Journal of Speech* 77 (1991): 123–51.
16. B. L. Whort, "An American Indian Model of the Universe," in *Teachings from the American Earth: Indian Religion and Philosophy,* D. Tedlock and B. Tedlock, eds. (New York: Liveright, 1975), 121.
17. Reprinted in "Americans Challenged to Embrace Change and Sacrifice," *The San Francisco Chronicle* (January 21, 1993): A12.
18. DeVito, 1986.
19. From a speech composed by Julie L. Cook, a junior accounting major in the College of Business Administration at Ohio University. The endnote for this particular portion is a reference to Clifford Bennett, *Nursing Home Life: What It Is and What It Could Be* (New York: The Tiresias Press, Inc., 1980), 17–18.
20. Moore, 1989.
21. *The Rhetoric of Aristotle,* trans. Lane Cooper (New York: Appleton, 1931), 220.
22. From Judy C. Pearson, *Communication in the Family: Seeking Satisfaction in Changing Times,* 2nd ed. Copyright © 1993, HarperCollins Publishing Co., New York, NY.
23. Nina Totenberg, "Statement Before the Senate Special Independent Counsel," in *Women's Voices In Our Time: Statements by American Leaders,* Victoria L. DeFrancisco and Marvin D. Jensen, eds. (Prospect Heights, Illinois: Waveland Press, Inc., 1994), 202–03.
24. DeVito, 1986.
25. Cheng Imm Tan, "Women's Fund Talk," in *Women's Voices in Our Time: Statements by American Leaders,* Victoria L. DeFrancisco and Marvin D. Jensen, eds. (Prospect Heights, Illinois: Waveland Press, Inc., 1994), 224–25. Courtesy of Cheng Imm Tan, 1994.
26. DeVito, 1986.
27. Nannerl O. Keohane, "Educating Women for Leadership: Drawing on the Full Human Race," delivered at the City Club of Cleveland, Cleveland, Ohio, April 26, 1991. Reprinted in *Vital Speeches* 57.19 (1991): 605–08. Courtesy of Nannerl O. Keohane, 1991.
28. Keohane, 1991.
29. See, for example, Monroe C. Beardsley, *Thinking Straight: Principles of Reasoning for Readers and Writers* (Englewood Cliffs, NJ: Prentice-Hall, 1956), 29.

Chapter M

INTRODUCING AND CONCLUDING YOUR SPEECH

It is with eloquence as with a flame; it requires fuel to feed it, motion to excite it, and it brightens as it burns.

Tacitus

QUESTION OUTLINE

I. What are four functions of the introduction?

II. What are some ways to gain and maintain audience attention?

III. What are some ways to relate the topic to the audience?

IV. What are some methods of relating the speaker to the topic?

V. What suggestions will help you improve your introductions?

VI. What is mid-speech sag and how can you prevent its occurrence?

VII. What are three functions of the conclusion?

VIII. What are four conclusionary techniques?

IX. What suggestions will help you improve your conclusions?

Introduction

No one is taking care of our children.

Seven million children are "latchkey" kids who are under thirteen and who care for themselves for at least part of every workday.

No one is taking care of our children.

The turnover rate in child care centers was 42 percent because of low pay, poor benefits, and stressful working conditions.

No one is taking care of our children.[1]

Mothers and fathers both have to work these days just to have the standard of living the last generation enjoyed with one wage earner.

Today we are going to explore the issue of day care to see why no one is taking care of our children.

This introduction grabbed the audience's attention. The audience was full of working men and women, all of whom felt that they took care of their children. Most of them also knew that their children had to take care of themselves while they worked.

In this chapter, you will find out how to begin and end your speech. We will begin with the introduction. Why is your introduction so crucial to an effective speech? The answer is that much of the audience's impression of you is determined in the first fifteen seconds of the speech.[2] To learn how to develop an introduction, we will examine the four functions of an introduction, review some strategies that you can use in your introduction, and see some examples of introductions from student speeches. Later in the chapter, we will look at some of the same aspects in the conclusion of your speech.

The beginning of a speech is where most speakers feel the most stress, and the ending often determines whether or not the audience responds as you wish. This chapter will help you learn how to start and finish your speeches with confidence.

The Functions of an Introduction

Outside the classroom, you may be introduced by someone else. In the classroom, you will probably introduce yourself and your topic to the audience in that part of the speech called the introduction. An introduction serves four functions. You will examine these along with examples from student speeches. The four functions are (1) to gain and maintain favorable attention, (2) to relate your topic to your audience, (3) to relate yourself to the topic, and (4) to preview the message by stating the purpose and forecasting the organization of the speech.

Gaining and Maintaining Favorable Attention

The first function of an introduction is gaining and maintaining attention. Have you ever watched someone try to teach a group of very small children? As the teacher talks, the children turn around and look at each other. Sometimes they start talking to each other. Occasionally they touch someone. Getting children to pay attention is a very difficult job. Adults are no different. True, adults have learned to look as if they are listening. Their eyes are correctly directed, and their bodies may not move as much as children's bodies do, but the adults have replaced their overt physical activities with mental activities. When you speak to your classmates, their minds may be flitting from your speech to plans for the weekend, to the test the next hour, or to the attractive person in the next seat. You will have to gain and maintain their attention.

Spend some time planning your introduction. Your introduction often determines whether the audience listens to your message. The introduction and conclusion are the bookends of your speech. If either or both fail, then the core of the speech may very well fail too.

Functions of an Introduction

1. Gaining and maintaining favorable attention
2. Relating the topic to the audience
3. Relating the speaker to the topic
4. Previewing the message by stating the purpose and forecasting the organization of the speech

There are many ways you can gain and maintain attention. Here you will learn about ten of them. Which method should you select? How will you decide the way you will use it to gain and maintain the attention of your audience? It is critical at this point that you understand the principles of audience analysis and adaptation. If everyone in your class has used facts and statistics, for instance, you may want to choose a different method. If your class meets near lunch time, you may want to consider bringing food they can eat.

Present a Person or an Object

This method is used more often for informative speeches than for persuasive ones, but it can be used for both. A student speaking on health food may give everyone a granola bar to eat while listening to the speech. A student who works at a bank may begin a speech about the dangers of a checking account by distributing one blank counter check to each member of the audience. A student who informs the audience about classical ballet may bring a ballerina to class to demonstrate a few turns on point during the speech. All of these can be effective ways to gain and maintain attention.

Invite Audience Participation

Inviting audience participation early in your speech attracts their attention and interest in your topic. One student who was speaking about some of the problems of poverty asked his audience to sit crowded elbow-to-elbow during his presentation. Another asked the audience three questions about energy and requested they indicate by a show of hands whether they knew the answers. Because most members of the audience were unable to answer the questions, they listened carefully for the answers. One energetic student wrote an Internal Revenue Service notice for every person in class, which summoned each one to an audit. As the student began his speech, each person in the audience opened up a plain white envelope with the unwanted message inside. Such audience participation gained and maintained their attention.

Some Methods of Gaining and Maintaining Attention

1. Present a person or an object.
2. Invite audience participation.
3. Imagine a situation.
4. Use audio and video equipment.
5. Arouse audience suspense.
6. Use slides or film.
7. Read a quotation.
8. State striking facts or figures.
9. Tell a story.
10. Use humor.

One method of gaining and maintaining attention is to present an object.

Imagine a Situation

You might have the audience imagine that they are standing on a ski slope, flying through the air, burrowing underground, and so on. As one student wrote in her plan for an introduction: "In order to gain audience attention, I will ask them to picture in their minds a hospital scene in which each of them is the patient on the operating table. They must watch their own death and subsequent resuscitation. This picture will prepare them for my topic on a second existence and raise the question in their minds of what actually happens in the interim." Inviting the audience to imagine a hypothetical situation is an effective method of gaining and maintaining attention.

Use Audio and Video Equipment

A student's speech on alternative music began with a one-minute excerpt from a song. A deputy sheriff who was taking public speaking played two minutes of an audiotape confession from an illegal drug dealer. A theater major specializing in costuming used videotape of the play cast in costume—a silent videotape for which she provided the commentary in her speech—in an informative speech about technical theater. For focus on sounds and words, audiotapes are difficult to beat. For more total involvement and visualization, videotapes are the answer. Remember when using audio and video that they are support for your speech, not the speech itself.

Arouse Audience Suspense

One student began his speech by saying, "A new sport has hit this state, yet it is a national tradition. It is held in the spring of the year in some of our most beautiful timbered areas. It is open to men and women alike, with women having the same chance of success as men. It is for responsible adults only and requires common sense and patience. This sport of our ancestors is . . ." Arousing curiosity captures the audience's attention.

Use Slides or Film

A student who was speaking on big city slums began with a rapid series of twelve slides, showing trash heaps, crowded rooms, rundown buildings, and rats. An international student from the Philippines showed attractive photographs of her native land. A varsity football player, who was speaking on intentional violence in the sport, showed a film of two kickoff returns in which he and others were deliberately trying to maim their opponents with their face guards. The audience—seeing the slums, the tropical beaches, and football violence—was attentive.

Read a Quotation

The reading can be hypothetical, literary, poetic, dramatic, or real. It can even be an inspirational passage from a speech delivered by a famous person. One student who was giving a speech about some of the delights of being middle-aged quoted President Reagan's speech to the Washington Press Club dinner when he turned seventy. "Middle age," Reagan told the Press Club, "is when you're faced with two temptations and you choose the one that will get you home at 9 o'clock."[3]

You can find quotations in newspapers, news magazines, and collections of speeches such as *Vital Speeches of the Day*. You can find collections of quotations in resource books such as *Bartlett's Quotations* or *Respectfully Quoted*, a dictionary of the quotations most often requested by Congress and high government officials for their speeches. There are even specialized books of quotes by women, African Americans, and other ethnic groups. Although you can find quotations by using all of the shortcuts mentioned above, nothing really replaces wide and deep reading, watching, and listening about an issue. To simply nab a quotation out of a book without really knowing the context behind the quotation is a bit like pretending to be a musician because you recognize an electric guitar when you see one. Always be sure to cite your sources when you use a quotation.

State Striking Facts or Figures

A student delivering a speech on the death penalty provided these interesting facts and figures:

> According to Anna Quindlen's article on *"The High Cost of Death"* in last week's New York Times: *"Black men are disproportionately represented on death row," "almost all capital cases involved white victims,"* and several years ago a notable execution took place: *"it was the first time in nearly half a century that a white American was put to death for killing a black one."*

The speaker went on to say (using the same source):

> Florida spent $60 million in fifteen years when eighteen executions occurred for a $3 million per prisoner average. And Texas spends $2 million per death penalty prosecution, which is, according to last Saturday's Times, *"about three times the cost of sending someone to prison in a high-security facility for 40 years."* [4]

The racial aspect of the death penalty may have been known to a few, but the stark reality that black men often die for killing white victims while white men rarely die for killing black victims was attention-getting—as were the high costs of maintaining death row.

Tell a Story

Telling a story to gain the audience's attention is one of the oldest and most commonly used methods. Your story can be actual or created, as long as you tell your audience which kind of story you are using. Often the story can be humorous. The following story is an analogy from the introduction of a student speech. It is not humorous, but it is a clever way to enlighten an audience about greed.

> I'd like to share with you a story about a man who, every morning, took his horse and wagon out into the woods to gather firewood. He would later take the wood to a nearby town and sell it for his only income. He was by no means wealthy, yet he lived a comfortable life. One day, in his greed, the man found that if he doubled his load of wood each day, he could earn twice as much money. He also found that if he spent half as much on feed for his horse, he could save even more money. This worked fine until one day the extra loads and the reduced food proved too much for the horse, and it collapsed from exhaustion and hunger.

One method of gaining and maintaining attention is to tell a story.

The student revealed in his speech that the man represented farmers who find that they are expected to produce more and more goods despite government controls limiting their capacity to do so. The analogy got the audience involved in a speech that might have drawn less attention if it had been an openly announced speech on government control of farmers.

Use Humor

Although often overused, jokes or humor to gain and maintain attention can be effective, especially if the humor is related to the topic. Too often jokes are told for their own sake, whether they have anything to do with the subject of the speech or not. Another word of caution: if you are not good at telling jokes, then you ought to practice before your speech in front of the class. On the other hand, if you are quite good at telling jokes or using humor in conversation, then humor related to your topic might be a good option for you. Finally, be careful that your humorous story is not so long or so compelling that the audience focuses only on the funny story and not on your speech.

Some speakers are not good at telling jokes, but they are witty. When you think of humor in public speaking, you should think of the term *humor* in its broadest sense to include wit and cleverness. Test your humor on friends before delivering it to an audience—this reduces anxiety and increases the chance that it will work.

An example of a speaker who shocked her audience with her wit is Dr. Johnetta Cole, who is president of Atlanta's Spelman College. She was invited to address the National Press Club, a group that probably had never heard from a black female college president. Dr. Cole won over her audience by proposing a toast in black English: "We bees fur 'lowin difurnce an' 'spectin difrunce til difrunce don make no mo difrunce," a toast that she translated for the crowd: "We are for allowing difference and expecting difference until difference doesn't make any more difference."[5] That toast was a clever way for Dr. Cole to say I am black and I can speak the language of the streets, but I am also a woman who is a college president, which I would like to become so common that it is not unusual.

One word of warning: always make sure your attention-getter is related to the topic. Jokes told for their own sake are a weak way to begin a speech. Another undesirable way to start is to write a provoking word on the board and then say, "I just wanted to get your attention." All of the examples in the ten methods of gaining attention are from student speeches. They show that students can be creative in order to gain and maintain audience attention.

These ten methods of gaining and maintaining attention in the introductory portion of a speech are not the only ones. There are dozens of other ways. Just think of imaginative ways to involve the audience. You can start by stating a problem for which your speech is the solution. You can create dramatic conflict between seemingly irreconcilable forces: business and government, teachers and students, parents and children, grading systems and learning. You can inform the listeners about everyday items they do not understand: stock market reports, weather symbols, sales taxes, savings accounts, and automobiles.

The speaker must adapt the message to all listeners.

Relating the Topic to the Audience

The second function of an introduction is relating the topic to the audience. You can relate almost any topic to an audience, preferably in the introduction of a speech. This assures the audience that there is a connection between them and the topic. You should find many helpful examples in the previous section on audience attention. A student gave a speech on women's rights, a topic the audience cared little about. However, in her introduction she depicted the plight of married women who have fewer job opportunities and receive less pay than their male co-workers. She asked the audience how they would feel under such circumstances. How would the men like their wives and girlfriends to earn less than male co-workers in the same jobs? Most of the men wanted their girlfriends and wives to be able to earn as much money as men in the same jobs. The audience listened to the speech with more interest because the speaker took pains to relate the topic to both the men and the women in class.

To relate your audience to your topic, you can introduce your speech with a brief case study for which your speech is an analysis and your conclusion is a solution. Cheng Imm Tan, who used the case study opening, began her speech like this:

> I would like to start by telling you a story. This is the story of Sothi, a Cambodian refugee woman. Sothi is a Cambodian refugee woman who survived the disruption of war as well as violence in the home.
>
> Sothi did not come from a rich or well known family. But life was good. She was married to a man who treated her well, and they had a son together. They lived near her parents who had a plot of land on which her husband worked. Then the war broke out. Her husband was drafted into the army, and she was moved to another province to work on a communal farm. Before too long news came that he had been killed in action. It got increasingly hard. There was not enough food to eat, her son became sick, and medical care was not readily available. Separated from her parents and unsure of what the future might bring, she decided to escape to Thailand to get medical care for her son.

> *One day while she was getting her twenty-liter daily ration of water at the refugee camp in Thailand, she noticed a man staring at her. She had caught his fancy. He pursued her. He came to the house, brought her little gifts, and tried to get her attention. When she refused his advances, he became increasingly violent and threatened to blow the family up with a grenade if she refused to marry him. She married him, and together they had three more children, but the violence did not stop. In 1982 they were resettled in Boston, Massachusetts. Under the pressure of adjusting to a new environment, his drinking and gambling increased and so did the threats and the beatings. He would beat her because he could not find a job, because he lost in gambling, because he felt humiliated at the unemployment office.*
>
> *Isolated in a foreign city, Sothi bore the abuse in silence. . . .*[6]

This case study of what happens to immigrant women who are victims of spouse abuse became an analysis of the issue, and concluded with recommendations for reforms. A case study that poses a problem that captures the audience's attention gets the audience involved in the issue, and encourages the audience to get involved in the solution.

Relating the Topic to the Speaker

The third function of an introduction is relating the topic to the speaker. In the previous section, you related the topic to the audience. In this section, you will look at three strategies for relating the topic to you, the speaker.

Dress for the Topic and Occasion

You can wear clothing that will signal your credibility on a topic. That shows your relationship to the topic and the occasion. One student aroused the audience's interest in the topic and the speaker by showing up with a hardhat on his head, a sweat rag around his neck, and a flashlight in his hand. He was encouraging his classmates to take up the questionable activity of exploring the university's steam tunnels.

Other ideas for using appropriate clothing to signal your relationship to the topic are to wear a warmup suit for a speech on exercise, a laboratory coat for a speech on chemistry experiments, or a dress or suit for a speech on how to interview for a job. In all of these cases, the speaker's attire reminds the audience of the topic and makes the speaker look like an authority.

Invite the Audience to Participate

A student at Iowa State University figured out a clever way to get his audience to understand how cramped he was in the university's married student housing. Before class he had outlined the floor space of his apartment with masking tape. Before his speech began, he had everyone move their chairs inside the tape boundaries. The twenty-two chairs barely fit. During the five-minute speech, the audience felt the cramped conditions the speaker described. They were participants in his main message.

Use Self-Disclosure

A third strategy for relating yourself as a speaker to your topic requires no special clothing and no audience participation. Instead, all you have to do is reveal yourself, especially how you have knowledge about the topic. Sometimes **self-disclosure** is confessional: "I had malaria," "I am an alcoholic," or "I was the victim of a mugger."

Self-disclosure must be honest information. Don't invent an occurrence or exaggerate an experience beyond recognition. You will not be viewed as a trustworthy speaker if you practice deception and dishonesty in your speeches. One student began his speech by telling a story of how his friend had set his body on fire to protest U.S. involvement in conflicts in other parts of the world. He went on to say that the friend had suffered first-, second-, and third-degree burns and that he had to have plastic surgery later. When the students in the class expressed their regrets to him after the speech, he laughed and said he had made up the story and the friend. The classmates felt betrayed. The speaker earned their scorn for his deceit, and he found that they would not believe what he said in his later speeches.

This method has considerable impact on the audience, mainly because it violates the audience's expectations. A daring disclosure in a public speaking class occurred when a mild-mannered young man revealed that he had been in a Louisiana prison on a drug offense—for six years. He spoke with great feeling about the effects of our penal system on an individual.

Not all self-disclosures have to be so dramatic. Indeed, some of the best examples pose a common problem, such as this one:

> I am a Catholic girl and I have a Baptist boyfriend. Our different religions have
> challenged us both but have strengthened, rather than weakened, our relationship
> because we have to explain our faiths to each other. With that in mind, I'd like to share
> with you the similarities between two seemingly different religions.

Another student spoke on structural barriers to people with physical disabilities and revealed that she knew about the subject because of a hip operation that forced her to learn how to walk all over again. Both of these students disclosed information that the audience had not known; it enhanced their credibility and captured the audience's attention.

Self-disclosure must be used carefully in public speech. Most self-disclosure occurs in interpersonal communication, when only two or three people are engaged in conversation. Be sure that you can handle the disclosure. One woman decided to tell a class about her sister's recent death from leukemia, but she found she could do nothing but cry. The speaking situation is one that is already filled with a certain amount of tension, and you do not want to overload yourself with more emotion than you can handle. To avoid this problem, you may wish to check your emotions by practicing your speech in front of close friends. Practicing the emotional portions over and over may help you control your feelings when you deliver the speech in front of an audience.

Self-disclosure must be considered carefully for a second reason. As stated, self-disclosure generally occurs when one person provides personal information to one or two others. In general, we do not tell highly personal information to a large number of people. Perhaps the story of your unwanted pregnancy will gain the attention of the audience, but do you want twenty of your peers knowing such information? Do not self-disclose information that is potentially embarrassing to yourself or to people who care about you.

Previewing the Message by Stating the Purpose and Forecasting the Organization

The fourth function of an introduction is stating the purpose and forecasting the organization and development of your speech. This step should be taken late in the introduction because it reveals for the audience the length and direction of your speech.

The *specific purpose statement* tells the audience of the informative or persuasive intent of your speech. It is optional in persuasive speeches where the purpose is not revealed until the end of the speech. **Forecasting** tells the audience how you are going to cover the topic. Here is an example that clearly indicates both the specific purpose and the organization:

> *You should start buying your books at the student co-op bookstore because the textbooks are less expensive, the used books receive a higher price, and the profits go for student scholarships.*

The type of speech is persuasive. The specific purpose is to have the listeners stop their book trade at the commercial bookstore and to start buying and selling books at the student co-op. The speech will have three main points.

Here are some additional examples of statements of purpose and forecasting from student speeches. The specific purpose statement is underlined in each for emphasis:

> *Follow my advice this evening and <u>you can earn ten dollars an hour</u> painting houses, barns, and warehouses. First, I will show you how to locate this kind of work. Next, I will teach you how to bid on a project. And, last, I will give you some tips on how to paint well enough to get invited back.*

> *<u>You can understand your own checking account.</u> I will help you "read" your check by explaining the numbers and stamps that appear on the face; I will help you manage your checking account by showing you how to avoid overdraw charges; and I will demonstrate how you can prove your check cleared.*

Forecasts and statements of specific purpose can take many forms. They do not have to state blatantly that you wish "to inform" or "to persuade," but your intentions should be clear to you and to your audience.

Demonstrating the Functions in a Speech

To see how the four functions operate together in a single introduction, examine the student introduction in figure 1. The side notes indicate which function is being fulfilled. Notice that the speaker gains and maintains attention, relates the topic to himself and to the audience, and forecasts the development of the speech. Remember that using a story is just one strategy that can be used in an introduction. There are many more equally effective types of introductions.

Let us turn next to some suggestions for introducing your speech.

Suggestions for Introducing Your Speech

Even though you now know the four functions of a speech introduction, some additional tips will help you deliver an appropriate and effective speech introduction. You need to recognize time constraints, capitalize on your own abilities, create an appropriate mood, prepare the body of the speech before you prepare the introduction, experiment with your introduction, and prepare your introduction precisely, but deliver it casually. In this section, we will explain each of these suggestions further.

1. *Recognize time constraints.* In any speech, the introduction should comprise about 15 percent of the total speech time. In a classroom situation, you are asked to deliver relatively short speeches. Therefore, the introduction to your speech should be relatively brief, as well. For example, if you are giving a ten-minute speech, the introduction should last between one and two minutes.

   If you go on to give longer speeches, your introduction may be extended. Speakers who talk for an hour may have introductions that are five minutes in length, for example. In all cases, the speaker needs to consider the relative amount of time to spend on the introduction in relation to the length of the entire speech.

2. *Capitalize on your own abilities.* As you have observed in this section of the chapter, many techniques can be used to capture and maintain audience attention. You need to consider the techniques that work best for you. You may be a great story teller, but not very good at using audio or visual equipment. You may be an expert at arousing suspense, but uncomfortable when telling a joke. Consider your own strengths and play to them in the introduction of your speech.

Figure 1

An example of an introduction.

Death Race

Begins with a narrative, a story to gain attention

Role plays a veteran checking out his gear to maintain attention

Story is a subtle means of relating himself to the topic: he has had the experience

Arouses curiosity about the topic to maintain attention

Story employs drama, adventure, and conflict

Begins to announce the topic

Relates topic to audience Announces topic, forecasts development, and states specific purpose

With sweat beading on my forehead and adrenalin gushing through my body, I solemnly survey my mission. Gusting winds cut through my jeans as a cloudy sky casts shadowy figures on the surroundings. I check through my gear one final time, for a failure of any item can spell certain death for me. Let's see. Good tread on tennis shoes. Check. Flourescent vest turned on. Check. I take time to reflect on my previous missions. Yes, you could say that I am a veteran. I've been there and back many times. Two hundred or so successful assignments without a serious injury. A good record. A couple of close calls, but never anything more than a sprained ankle or a hurt ego. But today is a new day. I must not let my record lull me into carelessness. I'm ready. The time is now, for, if I wait one minute longer, I'll be late for class!

The thoroughfare is crowded and I can barely see my destination. Cautiously I look both ways, up and down the street, once, twice, three times before I venture out. An opening breaks and I begin to hurry. Wait! A Mack truck just pulled out and is rushing toward me. Will he see the flashing warning lights? Will he read the big yellow sign proclaiming my right of way? As he rumbles recklessly toward me, I realize that the answer is no. I cover the remaining twenty feet in a couple of leaps and bounds. Exhausted, my mission is complete. I have successfully crossed a campus street.

Does this story sound familiar to you? How many times a day do you have to risk life and limb to cross a campus street? How often have you been angered by the drivers who ignore the pedestrians, the crosswalks, and the warning lights? We have all had the experience.

Today I want to discuss with you what can be done to end this terror for the innocent pedestrian on campus. I want to talk about three suggestions that I have for alleviating the problem of crosswalk warfare: closing certain streets, increasing off-campus parking, and installing lights and crosswalks in strategic areas.

3. *Create an appropriate mood.* If you are going to attempt to persuade the audience to be more sensitive in their use of language, you should not antagonize them first by showing them how clumsily they use it now. If you are an after-dinner speaker and humor is expected, you do not want to provide a speech filled with facts and figures and void of amusing material. You cannot expect an audience to be crying one moment and laughing the next. Consider the mood of your audience and the tone you want to set. Begin to set that tone in your introduction.

4. *Prepare the body before planning the introduction.* When you begin preparing your speech, do not start with the introduction. If you begin your speech by looking for appropriate introductory materials, you may have difficulty. Instead, do the research necessary for the body of your speech first. As you read materials and interview people, consider the stories, facts, figures, quotations, and humor that you find. Determine if any of your gathered materials might contribute to your introduction as you continue to gather and file information.

5. *Experiment with your introduction.* Within the first few seconds of your speech, your audience will decide if they should pay close attention to your message or if they are going to provide you with little more than a cursory hearing. Your introduction, therefore, is critical. Rehearse more than one possible introduction. Consider whether each is appropriate for your audience, your purpose, your topic, and you. Which introduction sets the mood you want to establish? Do not adopt the first introduction you construct. Experiment with different possibilities and be open to other alternatives.

6. *Prepare your introduction precisely; deliver it casually.* Your instructor may ask you to script your introduction or to provide an outline of your introduction. In either case, you want to be confident about the first words that you will say to an audience without reading them. Many speakers feel more confident if they have planned their introduction exactly as they will deliver it. They also feel less anxious if they deliver it from relatively few notes. The more familiar your introduction is to you without memorizing it, the more poised you will appear to the audience. In the first few seconds of your speech, the audience will see you as a credible speaker who is worthy of their complete attention.

Mid-Speech Sag

At this transition point in the chapter—between information on introductions and information on conclusions—let us pause for a moment and think about what comes between the introduction and the conclusion.

The chief justice of the state supreme court gave a luncheon address.[7] He started with a story of a young lawyer who was out in the countryside on a call when he ran low on gas and had to stop at a one-pump "station" that looked more like a shack. Outside the shack was an old man sitting on a chair with a large junkyard dog at his feet. "Does your dog bite?" asked the lawyer cautiously as he slowly opened his car door. "Nope," said the old man. The lawyer jumped from the car and stepped to the pump when the dog snarled and growled so loud that the lawyer leaped into his car and slammed the door. "I thought you told me that your dog doesn't bite," said the lawyer with undisguised anger in his voice. "He don't," said the old man, "but this dog does." The speech started off strong and it ended with an upbeat conclusion, but the rest of the speech—like so many—suffered from **mid-speech sag.** That is, all the energy, humor, and excitement were built into the beginning and the ending. The middle was like a tape recording of legal cases and decisions that mainly inspired sleep. In the middle of the speech, the body became largely a collection of evidence delivered with a minimum of enthusiasm.

At this midpoint in the chapter, remember that most of the time in a speech is spent in the middle, the body. Keeping the audience interested in that part of the speech is a continuing challenge. You can do it by repeatedly revealing how the speech is related to the audience, because, if it isn't related, you shouldn't be saying it. You can do it by using many of the attention-gaining-and-maintaining techniques that are mentioned earlier in this chapter; they are not for exclusive use at the beginning of a speech. Finally, you can keep in mind that it is easier to get an audience's attention than it is to keep it, easier to arouse the audience at the beginning and end than in the body of the speech, and simplest to keep the listeners' attention throughout a speech if the content speaks to them.

You should talk to audience members about what is vital to them—their jobs, their kids, their neighborhood, the threats to their existence, the opportunities that meet their aspirations—and they will listen to you. They will not fall asleep. The content should be the most captivating aspect of a speech. The humor, the gestures and movement, and the attention-gaining techniques are simply allies in the speaker's attempt to impart information and influence behavior.

Functions of a Conclusion

1. To forewarn the audience that you are about to stop
2. To remind the audience of your central idea or main points
3. To specify what the audience should do in response to your speech

We have discussed the introduction of the speech very thoroughly. Let us now consider the ending, or conclusion, of the speech. Just like the introduction, the conclusion of a speech fulfills certain functions: (1) to forewarn the audience that you are about to stop; (2) to remind the audience of your central idea or the main points in your message; and (3) to specify what the audience should think or do in response to your speech. Let's examine each of the functions of a conclusion in greater detail.

The Functions of a Conclusion

Forewarning the Audience of the End

The **forewarning function** warns the audience that you are about to stop. Can you tell when a song is about to end? Do you know when someone in a conversation is about to complete a story? Can you tell in a TV drama that the narrative is drawing to a close? The answer to these questions is usually yes, because we get verbal and nonverbal signals that songs, stories, and dramas are about to end. How do you use the brake light function in a speech?

The most blatant, though trite, method of signaling the end of a speech is to say, "In conclusion . . ." or "To summarize . . ." or "In review . . ." Another way is to physically move back from the lectern. Also, you can change your tone of voice to have the sound of finality. There are hundreds of ways to say, "I'm coming to the end." For instance, as soon as you say, "Now let us take my four main arguments and bring them together into one strong statement: you should not vote unless you know your candidates," you have indicated an impending conclusion.

Reminding the Audience of Your Main Points

The second function of a conclusion—to remind the audience of the thesis of your message—is the **instant-replay function.** You could synthesize a number of major arguments or ideas into a single memorable statement. A student giving a speech on rock music concluded it by distributing to each classmate a sheet of paper that had the names of local rock stations and their locations on the radio dial. You could also simply repeat the main steps or points in the speech. For instance, a student who spoke on the Heimlich Maneuver for saving a choking person concluded his speech by repeating and demonstrating the moves for saving a person's life.

Specifying What the Audience Should Do

The third function of a conclusion is to clearly state the response you seek from the audience, the **anticipated response.** If your speech was informative, what do you want the audience to remember? *You* tell them. If your speech was persuasive, how can the audience show its acceptance? A student who delivered a speech on periodontal disease concluded by letting her classmates turn in their candy for a package of sugarless gum. Other students conclude by asking individuals in the audience to answer questions about the

A dramatic conclusion can make a speech memorable.

content of the speech: "Judy, what is the second greatest cause of lung cancer?" Whether your speech is informative or persuasive, you should be able to decide which audience behavior satisfies your goals.

Methods of Concluding Your Speech

We have considered the functions of a conclusion. You know that you need to forewarn the audience that you are about to end your speech, that you should remind them of your main points, and that you should specify what they should do in response to your speech. How do you accomplish these functions? In this section we will consider four conclusionary techniques: ending with a quotation, asking a question, telling a story, and closing with a striking statement.

Ending with a Quotation

Quotations provide an effective end to your talk. Most speeches that you will present in the classroom will be less than fifteen minutes in duration. You should confine yourself to a brief quotation or two. A good example of concluding a speech with a quotation follows.

Benjamin E. Mays, an important individual in the Civil Rights Movement and a mentor to the late Dr. Martin Luther King, Jr., gave the eulogy at King's funeral. After a moving speech, Mays concluded,

> *I close by saying to you what Martin Luther King, Jr. believed: "If physical death was the price he had to pay to rid America of prejudice and injustice nothing could be more redemptive." And to paraphrase the words of the immortal John Fitzgerald Kennedy, permit me to say that Martin Luther King, Jr.'s unfinished work on earth must truly be our own.**

Mays' quotations—from the man he eulogized and from the President of the United States who was assassinated only four and a half years earlier—were powerful. He soothed the audience by suggesting that King's death was not in vain, and he urged listeners to action.

*Source: A. L. Smith, *The Voice of Black Rhetoric: Selections,* Allyn and Bacon, Inc., Needham Heights, MA, 1971.

Some Methods of Concluding a Speech

1. Ending with a quotation
2. Asking a question
3. Telling a story
4. Closing with a striking statement

In longer speeches, extended quotations can be used. In an inspirational speech on how older couples managed to have long and happy marriages, one of the co-authors used a quotation from a children's book. Since the speech was one hour in length, the introduction, as well as the conclusion, were longer than they would be in most classroom speeches.

> Margery Williams, in The Velveteen Rabbit, *has the last word: "It doesn't happen all at once," said the Skin Horse. "You become. It takes a long time. That's why it doesn't often happen to people who break easily, or who have sharp edges, or who have to be carefully kept. Generally, by the time you are Real, most of your hair has been loved off, and your eyes drop out and you get loose in the joints and very shabby. But these things don't matter at all, because once you are Real you can't be ugly, except to people who don't understand."* [8]

This conclusion was especially effective because the introduction of the speech used the same book and a slightly longer excerpt. The parallelism between the introduction and the conclusion gave the speech a sense of closure.

Asking a Question

Speakers use questions to open their talks to invite listeners into their topics; they use them to close their talks to encourage them to learn more about the topic or to take action. Katie Haas, a college sophomore of German heritage, gave a speech on the Holocaust. She concluded her informative speech with a question and an answer to the question.

> In conclusion, the Holocaust can only be understood when one understands the history behind the horror, the actions taken, and the aftermath. You might ask, "But why study it?" A large part of the world seems to want to forget it, which can be seen in last April's USA Today *survey in which 22 percent of adults and 20 percent of high school students say it seems possible that the Holocaust never happened. Another 38 percent of adults and 53 percent of students did not know what the term "Holocaust" referred to. As members of the human race we must not forget because only in learning about the past can we free ourselves of repeating our errors.* [9]

You may conclude your speech with a question and an answer or you may leave your question unanswered. Evangelists and politicians sometimes use the technique of the unanswered question in order to motivate congregations or voters to answer the question for themselves and to act upon their answer.

Telling a Story

Audience members enjoy hearing stories. Stories are especially apt in a conclusion when they serve to remind the audience of the purpose of a speech. In a speech on the equality

of all human beings, one speaker concluded with a story about the Greek orator, Diogenes. Diogenes believed that the satisfaction of people's basic needs was all that was necessary for happiness; he discouraged the quest for wealth and success.

> *Alexander the Great was puzzled to find Diogenes examining a heap of human bones. "What are you looking for?" he inquired.*
>
> *"I am searching for the bones of your father," replied the philosopher, "but I cannot distinguish them from those of his slaves."* [10]

The stories that you tell may be real or hypothetical. The ethical speaker is careful to distinguish between actual events and those that are created for the speech.

Closing with a Striking Statement

President Bill Clinton's inaugural address was concluded with these remarks. Because the speech was much longer than the speeches you will present in the classroom, it was appropriate that it was as long as it was.

> *And so my fellow Americans, as we stand at the edge of the 21st century, let us begin with energy and hope, with faith and discipline, and let us work until our work is done. The scripture says, "And let us not be weary in well-doing, for in due season, we shall reap, if we faint not."*
>
> *From this joyful mountain top of celebration, we hear a call to service in the valley.*
>
> *We have heard the trumpets. We have changed the guard. And now—each in our own way, and with God's help—we must answer the call.* [11]

Clinton's conclusion is memorable because of his use of metaphor. He invoked scripture and he referred to God. He contrasted the mountains with the valleys and joyfulness with service. Both Biblical and military images are provided in his allusion to trumpets, changing of the guard, and answering the call. In a classroom speech, your conclusion will be much shorter.

A student many years ago gave a speech with a clever ending that summarized his arguments and gave it a memorable ending. His speech was on car accidents, the wearing of seat belts, and the disproportionately large number of college-aged people who die on the highways. He talked about how concerned we are that an accident not be our fault. His conclusion: "It does not matter who is right in the case of an automobile accident. It is not who is right that counts in an accident; it is who is left." It was a grim conclusion that made the main point memorable.

Even though you have learned about the functions of a speech conclusion, some additional tips will help you deliver an appropriate and effective conclusion. You need to recognize time constraints, conclude with strength, and experiment with your conclusion. Let us consider each of these suggestions in more detail.

Suggestions for Concluding Your Speech

1. *Recognize time constraints.* Earlier you learned that the introduction to the speech should be brief; we observe now that the conclusion should be even shorter. Nothing is more frustrating to an audience than to listen to a long speech and hear the words, "And, in conclusion . . . ," and then listen to you talk for several more minutes.

2. *Conclude with strength.* You might be tempted to pay little attention to your conclusion because it is so brief. Even though the conclusion should be short on time, it should be long on impact. If you have begun with a strong introduction and have avoided mid-speech sag, you have created a favorable impression in the minds of your listeners. Do not lose their respect in the last few moments of your speech.

   The conclusion is the last message you provide to your audience. You want their last impression of you to be as powerful as their first impression. Just as in the introduction, you want to prepare a precise message. You may want to practice your conclusion without memorizing it until you feel comfortable delivering it with minimal notes, but don't read it.

3. *Experiment with your conclusion.* As you research your topic, consider whether any of the materials you come across are appropriate for your conclusion. Can you offer a conclusion that is parallel to your introduction? In other words, if you have used a quotation in the introduction, use a quotation in the conclusion. If you have begun with a question, conclude with another question. A humorous anecdote in the beginning of the speech might be matched with another witty story at the end.

   Do not automatically use the first conclusion you considered. Try several different approaches. Just as in the introduction, consider your audience, the purpose of your speech, the mood you are attempting to create, and your own strengths. Feel free to experiment. Your goal is to create a last, and a lasting, impression with the audience.

Summary

This chapter has concentrated on beginnings and endings, the skills necessary for developing the introduction and the conclusion of a public speech.

In the first section, you learned that there are four functions of an introduction: to gain and maintain attention, to relate the topic to the audience, to relate the speaker to the topic, and to preview the message by stating the purpose and forecasting the organization. You were given ten strategies for gaining and maintaining attention, some ideas for relating the topic to the audience and three strategies for relating the speaker to the topic. You were also given some suggestions on how to prepare an effective introduction for your speeches.

Before we turned to conclusions, we considered mid-speech sag, which may occur when the introduction and conclusion are very strong and the body sags in the middle of the speech. You were encouraged to pay as much attention to the body of the speech as you do to beginning and ending it.

In the last section of this chapter, you learned that there are three functions of a conclusion: forewarning the audience of the end, reminding the audience of your main points, and specifying what the audience should do. You also learned about four methods of concluding a speech: ending with a quotation, asking a question, telling a story, and closing with a striking statement. Finally, you learned some suggestions that might improve your public speeches.

Vocabulary

anticipated response Revealing to an audience what you want them to think, know, or do as a result of your speech

forecasting A function of the introduction that reveals to the audience the organization and development of the speech

forewarning function A function of the conclusion of a speech in which the speaker indicates an impending ending by verbal and nonverbal means

instant-replay function A function of the conclusion of a speech, in which the speaker summarizes, synthesizes, or repeats the main points of the message

mid-speech sag A phenomenon that occurs when the speaker places too little emphasis on making the body of the speech as captivating as the introduction and the conclusion

self-disclosure A speaker's revelation of a characteristic that the audience is unlikely to know already; a device used in public speaking to gain and maintain an audience's attention

 # Applications

Application Exercises

Gaining and Maintaining Attention

1. Think of a speech topic. Then use any three of the ten methods of gaining and maintaining attention listed in the text to introduce your topic.

Signaling the Conclusion

2. Watch your professors for a few days. How do they indicate that classes are over? How many of them use ordinary ways to signal the end, such as saying, "For tomorrow read pp. 229–257"? What are some more imaginative ways that your teachers conclude their classes and lectures? Do any of them use methods that you could imitate in a public speech?

Concluding a Speech

3. Between class sessions, develop a conclusion that can be tried on a small group of classmates. See if you can fulfill the four functions given in the text. Try especially to develop skill in summarizing, synthesizing, and stating the main point of your message in language that will be striking and memorable.

Performance

1. Deliver a two- to four-minute introduction to a speech. Be sure your introduction fulfills the functions explained in this chapter. The criteria for evaluation are the extent to which you

1. Gain and maintain the audience's attention through some means relevant to the topic
2. State the topic of the speech and its relationship to the immediate audience
3. Describe your qualifications for delivering a speech on this topic (i.e., the relationship between you and the topic)
4. Preview the message by stating the purpose and forecasting the organization of the speech.

Do not go beyond the introduction in this performance; instead, try to make the audience eager to hear more.

Written Script or Outline

2. Write a script or outline of your introduction. Include side notes that indicate how it fulfills its functions.

Ethical Questions

3. Listening to a speech in class, try to identify the source for every direct quote or restatement (paraphrase) to see if oral footnotes are used appropriately. For one of the direct quotations, seek the source to discover to your satisfaction whether the quotation was accurately quoted and whether the context of the quotation invites a different interpretation.

1. "Child Care Fact Sheet," in *Women at Work,* published by the National Commission on Working Women, 2000 P St. N.W., Suite 508, Washington, DC 20036, Fall 1985.
2. L. S. Harms, "Listener Judgments of Status Cues in Speech," *Quarterly Journal of Speech* 47 (1961): 168.
3. The student found the Reagan quotation in "Reagan's One Liners," *New York Times,* February 6, 1981, A13.
4. Anna Quindlen, "The High Cost of Death," *New York Times,* November 19, 1994, 15.
5. Dr. Johnetta Cole's toast was quoted in Bill Wallisch, "20 Seconds to Profundity: How to Handle the Broadcast Media," *Educational Record: The Magazine of Higher Education* (Spring 1988): 16.
6. Cheng Imm Tan, "Women's Fund Talk," a speech delivered at a workshop titled "Women's Organizing for Freedom and Justice" on April 25, 1992. The speech is included in *Women's Voices In Our Time,* edited by Victoria L. DeFrancisco and Marvin D. Jensen (Prospect Heights, Illinois: Waveland Press, 1994), 223. Courtesy of Cheng Imm Tan, 1994.
7. This speech was delivered by the Honorable Chief Justice Thomas Moyer of the Ohio Supreme Court to a meeting of Rotary International, Athens, Ohio, December 13, 1988.
8. *The Velveteen Rabbit,* by Margery Williams, © 1983. Reprinted by permission of the publisher, Simon and Schuster Books for Young Readers.
9. From a speech presented by Katie Haas in Winter Quarter 1994, at Ohio University in Interpersonal Communication 103: Public Speaking, taught by Marsha Clowers.
10. Originally printed in *The Little, Brown Book of Anecdotes,* Clifton Fadiman, ed. (Boston: Little, Brown, and Company, 1985), 169.
11. Text was reprinted in "Americans Challenged to Embrace Change and Sacrifice," *The San Francisco Chronicle,* January 21, 1993, A12.

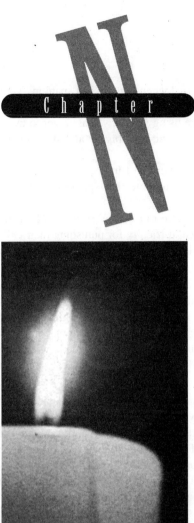

LANGUAGE IN PUBLIC SPEAKING

Chapter N

The Eskimo has fifty-two names for snow because it is important to them; there ought to be as many for love.

Margaret Atwood

QUESTION OUTLINE

I. How do the politically correct movement and hate speech codes affect your language choices in public speaking?

II. How do First Amendment rights influence what you can say in public speaking?

III. Why should you be concerned about sexist and racist language in your public speeches?

IV. How does written style compare with spoken style?

V. How does your language affect your perception?

VI. What meanings do you attribute to language characteristics such as denotative and connotative, abstract and concrete, direct and indirect, and vivid and dull language?

VII. What effect do figures of speech and forms of speech have on your public speeches?

VIII. What ethical questions could be raised about your language choices in public speaking?

Introduction

Speaker: Well, I don't think you can call it "child abuse" when you are just spanking your kid for doing something wrong!

Audience Member: It is child abuse because you are using your physical power to overcome the kid instead of using reasoning. When your child gets bigger and stronger, he will use the same methods on you: might makes right!

Speaker: You're wrong! My parents used the belt on me, and I'm going to use the belt on my kid. No mamby-pamby soft-heart is going to tell me that spanking is "child abuse." I call it "discipline!"

Audience Member: Your child rearing practices come out of the Stone Age! In the Scandinavian countries parents can get in serious legal difficulty for punishing their children the way you do. You don't get to vent your anger on your children. You need to grow up yourself.

This exchange of views following a public speech demonstrates why you need to learn about language. The speaker and the audience member have different understandings of "child abuse" and "discipline." Words are symbols representing thought. Human beings interpret those symbols differently. As a result, they have to negotiate meanings of words after which they might still disagree, but at least both parties will know exactly what they are arguing about.

Language and Power

Language is powerful. Language is uniquely human. Some animals can communicate, but none can talk about what they did yesterday and what they are going to do tomorrow. Language is also something that people argue about. In the 1980s an entire movement sprang up regarding **politically correct language.** That movement centered on language used to describe nondominant individuals and groups in American society. On campuses across the land the controversy extended from what to call people to what to include in the curriculum. Hundreds of campuses established **hate speech codes** to root out undesirable language and behavior. Americans found themselves discussing their own language as they rarely had before.

The Politically Correct Movement

One of the reasons that students became concerned about politically correct language was the great change in the student population. More people were going to college. More women, African Americans, Hispanics, Asians, and international students filled American classrooms. Consider the facts in figure 1 concerning higher education and diversity.

The politically correct movement went far beyond determining what we should call each other. In a publication entitled "War of Words" sponsored by The Freedom Forum, Arati R. Korwar depicted the push for politically correct speech like this:

> *Some critics define political correctness as the forced study and acceptance of leftist ideas on politics, race and sex, originally promoted on campus by college professors who were radicals in the 1960s and 1970s. Evidence of political correctness, critics say, is in the changing curriculum at many universities which requires students to study not only the well-known white male authors but also those of relatively unknown woman and minority-group members. Educational traditionalists believe the new, broader curriculum compromises solid, established educational values and say the mood of political correctness prevents them from expressing criticism of the new curriculum; such criticism is inevitably viewed as racism, sexism or other-isms, they say.*[1]

In 1870 when the Office of Education first kept records, only about one percent of the 18- to 24-year olds went to college. By 1993 about 33% of this group sought higher education.

Fifteen percent of degrees in 1870 went to women; Fifty-three percent went to women in 1990.

By the middle 1980's well over 1.3 million students with disabilities were in postsecondary education.

Total enrollment of Asian students doubled over the past ten years.

Between 1982 and 1992 the total enrollment of Hispanic students increased by nearly 84%.

Between 1982 and 1992 the total enrollment of African Americans increased by over 26%.

In 1992–93 3% of the total student population was international students mainly from China, Japan, Taiwan, India, Korea, Canada, Malaysia, Hong Kong, Indonesia, and Pakistan.

In 1991 over 21% of the college student population consisted of minorities.

Figure 1

Facts about higher education and diversity.

Sources: Deborah J. Carter and Reginald Wilson, *Minorities in Higher Education,* 1993, American Council on Education, Washington, DC; Education section of *Time,* April 13, 1992, p. 60; *Digest of Education Statistics 1993,* Thomas D. Snyder, project director, National Center for Education Statistics, U.S. Department of Education, October 1993; *Estimates of Fall 1992 Enrollment at Public, Four-Year Institutions,* National Association of State Universities and Land-Grant Colleges and American Association of State Colleges and Universities, July 1993, Washington, DC; *Open Doors 1992–93: Report on International Educational Exchange,* Marianthi Zikopoulos, editor, Institute of International Education, 1993, New York; and *120 Years of American Education: A Statistical Portrait,* Thomas D. Snyder, editor, National Center for Education Statistics, U.S. Department of Education, January 1993.

College students are more diverse today than in the past.

Whatever the origins of the PC movement, one of its outcomes was that many Americans became highly conscious of the language they used in regard to women, people of color, lesbian women, gay men, people in wheelchairs, immigrants, Jewish people, and even people who were unusually tall, short or wide.

The power and flexibility of language was especially apparent in how women and African Americans were treated. "Girls" was out, "women" was in. "Negro" was ancient, black was passé, "people of color" was correct, and "African American" was preferred for Americans of African descent. An important change was taking place: until now the dominant culture decided which name was correct. The PC Movement changed that by declaring that people had the right to decide what they should be called. So it was that "queer" was out, "homosexual" started to sound clinical, "gay" was acceptable, and "lesbian women" and "gay men" became preferable. On campus the PC movement took another turn—hate speech codes.

College Hate Speech Codes

On hundreds of campuses "hate speech" codes were written into the student catalogs and handbooks. The National Institute Against Prejudice and Violence reported that one-quarter of all minority students were victimized by prejudice annually.[2] Administrators, faculty, and students across the land sought to protect the targets of hate speech by "out-lawing" threats of violence, taunts, harassment, caricatures, offensive events, sexist songs, and distasteful messages scrawled on doors and walls.[3] The war of words pitted the First Amendment right of free expression against the Fourteenth Amendment right of equal protection so forcefully that the American Civil Liberties Union had some affiliates defending the hate speech codes and others defending civil liberties. The ACLU was confused, and so was most of America.

Sexist Speech and the First Amendment

While many people were confused about which Amendment of the Constitution to uphold, communication and law professors went about the task of clarifying some of the potential positions on the issue. For example, Franklyn S. Haiman, the John Evans Professor of Communication Studies at Northwestern University, rendered his opinion. A professor who has studied freedom of speech for decades, Dr. Haiman wrote an article entitled "Sexist Speech and the First Amendment" in the January 1991 volume of *Communication Education*. In his article he reveals to us which kinds of language are prohibited by law and which kinds of language or expression need to be regulated by social pressure, persuasion, or instruction. You should know what he says so you can express yourself within the rules. Notice, however, that the rules can be different in public colleges and universities, which must adhere to all local, state, and federal laws, and private schools, which are given more latitude to make rules against certain behavior—including what is said in the classroom.

Both obscenity and child pornography are against federal law. Direct harassment of individuals concerning their sexual identity by an authority figure like a teacher is not protected by the First Amendment. This includes any demeaning or derogatory references that intimidate a student from speaking, that make a student fear for his/her grade, or suggest sexual advances.[4] The same kind of abusive comment by a peer does not violate the First Amendment, but it does violate the student codes of conduct in most universities.[5]

Obscenity, pornography, and sexual harassment are rarer in the classroom than **sexist language,** derogatory, demeaning, or offensive utterances toward and about women. Haiman provides phrases like "A woman's place is in the home" or "They are only good for having babies," as examples of sexist language. This kind of talk is regarded as social discourse and is not restricted by law in public universities, though it can be in private colleges and universities. Teachers can face disciplinary consequences for such remarks, but students would more likely hear only about the flaws in their thinking.[6]

Korwar thoroughly analyzed 384 student handbooks from colleges and universities and found the following statistics that could relate to language in the public speaking classroom.[7]

- **Threats of violence** are not protected as expression and over half of the universities had rules prohibiting threats.
- Only 15 percent of colleges had a "breach of peace" clause referring to offensive or outrageous speech that might inflame the listeners.
- Nearly 80 percent of schools had rules against disruption of teaching, which includes heated or hateful conduct.
- Obscenity has no First Amendment protection, and nearly 40 percent of the schools in the survey had rules against obscenity, though it was rarely defined.

- Intentionally inflicting emotional distress—severe embarrassment, humiliation, shame, or grief—is prohibited in 14 percent of the schools surveyed.[8]
- State and national laws regulate **slander**—verbal statements that impeach the honesty, integrity, virtue, or reputation of another person.
- Fighting words that are likely to provoke an immediate violent reaction are not protected by the First Amendment.
- Nearly half of all schools surveyed specifically prohibited lewd, indecent or profane language.
- Of the schools surveyed, 60 percent banned verbal abuse or verbal harassment, and over one-third punished verbal abuse based on membership in specific groups like race or ethnic origin.[9]
- Some schools have rules against incitement to violence, riot, illegal acts, overthrow of the government, and advocacy of biased ideas. These rules include some items that appear to punish protected expression. For example, the First Amendment protects the right to say "Asians are genetically superior to all other races." The point might inspire argument, but it is not illegal by federal law.

These statistics reflect an increasing awareness of the responsibility we all have to encourage and enforce the use of respectful language. Franklin Haiman summed it up best when he said "A classroom is preeminently a place where a high value is supposed to be given to reasoned discourse and where the teacher should serve as a role model for such communication."[10] Knowing what you know now, you can help make your public speaking classroom such a place.

Using Appropriate Language

It is important to consider the issue of language and cultural sensitivity in any communication context, but it is particularly crucial in public speaking. In our culturally diverse world, we must take care to be sensitive to language that could be viewed as exclusionary or hurtful to audience members. You need to know how people prefer to describe themselves and the language that is acceptable in communicating with people in a diverse world. We will now discuss some suggestions for avoiding cultural insensitivity.

First, *avoid sexist language.* Sexist language includes **"man-linked" terms** such as *repairman, salesman, serviceman,* and *chairman.* It also includes using traditional generics such as *he, his,* and *him* when the gender of the antecedent is ambiguous (e.g., "Each student stated his name").

In 1979, William Strunk, Jr. and E. B. White wrote in the third edition of their popular style manual, *The Elements of Style,*

> *The use of* he *as pronoun for nouns embracing both genders is a simple, practical convention rooted in the beginnings of the English language.* He *has lost all suggestion of maleness in these circumstances. . . . It has no pejorative connotations; it is never incorrect.*[11]

This advice was largely carried over from the first edition of the book, which was published in 1959. Over thirty years later, many organizations and institutions have issued statements recommending or requiring writers to substitute "he or she" or "they" for the historically correct "he" form.[12]

These groups relied on extensive research which showed that when the term "he" is used, people envision a man, but when "he or she" or "they" are used, people envision both women and men.[13] Theorists and researchers argued that the exclusive use of the term "he" perpetuated a male bias and reinforced sexist attitudes and behaviors.[14] Consequently, most educators today recommend that a more gender-neutral term such as "he and she" or "they" be substituted for the male biased "he." Or, perhaps even better, the sentence construction can be changed to eliminate the sex biased language.

Most recently, John Gastil, at the University of Wisconsin in Madison, discovered that the term "he" produced mostly male images for both women and men. The term "he/she" was also viewed by men as being primarily male but was seen by women as creating mixed images of women and men. The term "they" produced mixed images for both women and men.[15] Gastil's study suggests that "they" may be the preferred form for the speaker who wishes to avoid biased generics and who wishes to include everyone in the audience.

Our recommendation, then, is to *substitute plural forms for singular generics*. In most cases you can talk about *they, them,* and *their*. We also encourage you to *eliminate the use of man-linked terms*. You can substitute the word *person* for *man* in many cases—*salesperson, repairperson*. Furthermore, in some instances you can eliminate the word *man* altogether by using *chair* instead of *chairman,* for example. Finally, you can some-times find an alternative word to use instead, such as *mail carrier* for *postman*.

Similarly, you should *avoid calling attention to someone's demographic characteristics when such information is largely irrelevant*. When you describe someone as a *female* judge, an *Hispanic* professor, a *woman* doctor, or the city council member *in a wheel chair,* you are emphasizing impertinent qualifiers about them. The implication might be that people who are female are rarely judges or doctors, that people of Hispanic origin are generally not professors, and that individuals in wheel chairs are typically not elected to city council. Or, even worse, a listener might assume that you do not believe that people from such groups ought to be in such positions.

You should also *avoid humor that is sexist or racist*. A great deal of humor is based on in-group, out-group relationships. For example, people in one state of the United States will construct elaborate sets of jokes about people in an adjacent state. People in Minnesota tell stories about people in Iowa. In Ohio, West Virginia is the target state. Similarly, men tell jokes about women, or European Americans may create stories about African Americans. Such "joke-telling" is taboo for the public speaker. The potential humor is more than offset by the probable harm.

Similarly, *avoid naming another co-culture with a name that is not of their choosing*. People ought to have the right to be called by labels they find acceptable. These names change over time. The word *Negro* was replaced with *black,* which has been altered to *African American* in many places. Some people find the term *lady* unacceptable, while others eschew the word *girl* for adult human females. What should you do as a sensitive public speaker? Find out what terms are acceptable and appropriate from members of your audience. Use the words that people within the particular co-culture prefer.

Finally, as you consider your language choices with regard to cultural sensitivity, you might also *consider whose language you quote*. Do you incorporate the words of women, African Americans, or other co-cultures in your speech? Do you look for words of wisdom in sources that include quotations, speeches, and the writings of people other than white males? When you cite individuals who are Native American, Hispanic American, or in wheel chairs, you are telling your audience that you value the contributions of everyone in the culture, not just those who have been traditionally privileged.[16] See figure 2 for a summary of these suggestions on how to avoid undesirable language choices.

A Comparison of Spoken and Written Language

The man was President of the university. He gave dreadful speeches. His audiences usually consisted of people who were told that they were expected to be there: vice presidents, deans, department heads, and some retirees who seemed to have little better to do. He read every word, mostly without looking up. His sentences were highly complex, his ideas abstract, and his words long. He thought he spoke for posterity, not for the audience in front of him, and he published all of his speeches in a book that was little read and quickly forgotten.

Figure 2

*Suggestions for avoiding
undesirable language choices.*

1. Do use terms preferred by the people you are describing. For example, if the person or group wishes to be called <u>sight impaired</u> instead of <u>blind,</u> you should choose their preference.

2. Do use plural pronouns like <u>they, them, and their</u> instead of the generic <u>he</u> to refer to people.

3. Do use <u>person</u> and other gender-neutral terms instead of man-linked terms. For example, say <u>chairperson</u> or <u>chair</u> instead of <u>chairman</u>, and <u>worker</u> instead of <u>workman</u>.

4. Do not use humor that demeans a person because of gender, sexual preference, ethnicity or religion.

5. Do not refer to a person's race, gender, or sexual preference when it is irrelevant (e.g., the lesbian athlete, a black physician, the female engineer).

6. Do use a variety of sources for different voices so your speech does not simply reflect a single perspective.

The speaker had a problem. He did not know the difference between written and spoken style. He was a brilliant person who truly thought that a well-composed essay made a fine speech. He was wrong. His audiences did not understand what he was talking about, they could not follow his organization, and they ended up fighting sleep as he read his speech from a script.

What is the difference between **written style** and **spoken style?** Speaking requires short sentences so you can take a breath, while written sentences can be long and complex because they can be read more than once. Speaking is immediate. If the audience didn't get it, it is gone and it must be repeated if they look mystified. Speaking is personal: it uses personal pronouns and personal stories to make a point. Written work has only the words to convey the message. The speech has gestures, facial expressions, vocal intonation, and body movement. Written work lies flat on the page and has no voice, while the spoken word can be shouted, whispered, or spoken slowly for dramatic effect.

Table 1
A Comparison of Speaking and Writing

The language of speaking	The language of writing
Uses short, simple sentences with action verbs and one idea per sentence	Uses longer, complex, compound, and compound-complex sentences
Uses contractions, sentence fragments, short words, slang	Uses few contractions, no fragments, difficult words
Tends to use personal stories, experiences	Tends to use an impersonal voice
Uses concrete, specific, picture-producing words	Often uses abstract words, difficult to picture
Uses personal pronouns: *I, me, we, us, you, they*	Uses *one, a person, he or she*
Receives immediate feedback	Receives delayed or no feedback
Tends to say the same thing several ways—repetitive	Tends to be concise, with little or no repetition
Reinforces words with facial expression, voice, gesture	Reinforces words by bold type, pictures, punctuation
Reinforces transitions by gesture and movement	Restricts transitions to words
Vocalized pauses distract	Does not use vocalized pauses
Uses pauses and silence for dramatic effect or emphasis	Dashes, dots, and empty space indicate pause or silence

From *Speak With Confidence: A Practical Guide,* 5th Edition, by Albert J. Vasile and Harold K. Mintz. Copyright © 1989, 1986 Albert J. Vasile and Associates, Inc. and Harold K. Mintz. Reprinted by permission of HarperCollins Publishers, Inc.

The author of a written work does not know how you react to the words. The speaker who observes the audience while speaking knows your reaction to every word, phrase, and sentence. The writer cannot adapt to your inattention or misunderstanding, but the speaker can see when your attention wanes and rephrase when you misunderstand. You are a passive receiver of the written word and an active receiver of the spoken word. The reader does not know the writer, but the speaker becomes part of the message received by the listener. As the reader, you can give life to the written word, but you largely rely on the speaker to give life to the words of a speech.

You can avoid speaking like the hypothetical president of the university by watching how good speakers speak, by choosing to deliver an extemporaneous speech from an outline or a few notes rather than reading from a script, and by practicing your words with an ear to how they will sound to an audience. You can be a much better speaker just by recognizing the differences between written and oral style. See table 1 for a comparison of the two styles.

Language and Thought

Your words are a reflection of your mind. If you can't think it, you can't say it. If you do not have a concept in mind and understand it, you cannot express it with words. In fact, most first and second year college classes teach you the language of biology, sociology, political science, history, and philosophy. The lower level courses are loaded with vocabulary, with words that represent concepts, that you must understand to know the field of study.

Language Shapes Perception

Two language theorists, Benjamin Whorf and Edward Sapir believed that your language shapes your perceptions.[17] The person who knows knitting sees and feels a cotton/rayon

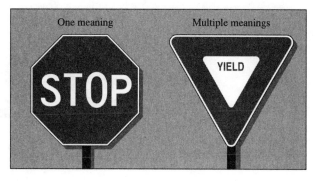

blend with a touch of cashmere in a cable-knit design, while the person who knows little about knitting sees only a sweater. The person who knows little about cars sees a red car, while the person with automobile knowledge and vocabulary sees a mid-size Acura with a 24-valve V-6 with Z-rated 15-inch all-weather tires, a dual exhaust in a ruby red sedan. What you know is reflected in the language that shapes what you see.

Another way to state the **Whorf-Sapir hypothesis** is "if you can't say it, you probably don't see it, and most likely you don't know it." Someone who has not studied plants does not recognize the bark, leaves, shape, and size of a tree enough to identify it. Language is important, then, as a direct indicator of what you know. Your ability to give a public speech about a topic depends on your knowledge of the subject and your capacity to put that knowledge into words.

Words and Things

People made up words and decided what they should mean. Dictionaries are merely histories of what people have used words to mean. But words are only partly able to represent that which they stand for. For example, if you lose a good friend in an accident, there are no words that can really describe how you feel. You are the one who gives meaning to words and the meanings are highly individual. That is why you can think of the world having as many languages as it has people: everyone's meanings are individual.

Over time, people have reached agreements about what words should mean. When you see an eight-sided red sign that has the letters STOP on the front, you know that society has agreed that this sign means you should come to a full stop. But meanings are unique to individuals, so not everyone really stops. A triangular sign that says YIELD is more ambiguous in its meaning because you might come to a full stop, you might speed up, or you might creep through. Your actions are supposed to depend on what you see coming toward you. The point about the two signs is that (a) society has agreed-upon meanings for words, (b) sometimes those meanings are ambiguous, and (c) the individual's interpretation of the sign's meaning is still what determines the resulting behavior.

Definitions and Meaning

Because words can mean so many different things, people must negotiate what they mean by a word. In the opening of this chapter two people were in conflict over the possible meanings of "child abuse" and "discipline." In this section you will learn some ways that you as a public speaker can reveal to an audience your intended meaning of terms in your speech.

You are likely to use some words in your speeches that the audience does not understand. After all, you should choose a topic that you are willing to learn more about than your classmates. If you speak about aerobics, there is nothing incorrect about using terms like "arteriosclerosis," "cardiovascular-pulmonary system," or "cardiorespiratory endurance." However,

The term "home" may elicit many different images for listeners.

ordinary people may not know what you are talking about unless you make the effort to define your terms. One simple way to define a term is to use the denotative meaning provided by a dictionary. Many terms, however, require further explanation. Here you will briefly examine six of the many ways that you can clarify terms for your audience: comparisons, contrasts, synonyms, antonyms, etymology, and the operational definition.

Comparisons

Something unfamiliar can be defined by showing how it is similar to something the audience is more familiar with. A student who was defining *wassailing* explained that the term meant "going on a spree or a binge" or "painting the town red." As the Bible puts it, "eat, drink, and be merry."[18]

The idea is to compare the unknown (that which the speaker saw) with the known (that with which the audience is familiar), as a student did when she said that "two G's" are the same as you would feel "on the big hill of the tornado rollercoaster."

As a public speaker, you must be careful to avoid comparisons that have been overused. Clichés such as "smooth as silk," "pretty as a picture," or "hard as a rock" are so common that they carry little impact. Instead, try to create comparisons that help the audience envision what you describe—such as the speaker who said that a basketball viewed from a distance of one centimeter looks "like the pebbly bottom of a backwood stream" or the speaker who described snow as a "soft, rolling white carpet."

Contrasts

Something unfamiliar can be defined by showing how it is different from something else the audience is more familiar with. A speaker who was attempting to communicate the meaning of assertiveness explained the concept like this:

> *Assertiveness can be contrasted with the more familiar idea of aggressiveness. Aggressiveness is characterized by pushiness and threats, while assertiveness is characterized by clarity. The aggressive person might say, "Get over here and help me"; the assertive person might say, "I need your help."* [19]

Synonyms

To define a term with synonyms is to use words that are close to or similar in meaning and more familiar to the audience. "Being spaced out," said a speaker who was defining the term, "is similar to having the mind go blank, being dumbfounded, or being disoriented."[20]

Antonyms

To define a term with antonyms is to use words that are opposite in meaning and that are more familiar to the audience. Hence, being "spaced out" is "not being alert, keen, or responsive."[21]

Etymology

To define a term by means of its etymology is to give its origins, or history. A desk dictionary reveals the language or languages from which a word is derived. Specialized sources, such as the *Dictionary of Mythology,* the *Oxford English Dictionary,* and the *Etymological Dictionary of Modern English,* provide more detailed accounts. In a speech of definition, a speaker used the etymology of a word to explain its significance:

> *What does* rhinoplasty *mean? Well, without a dictionary, you might feel that you're lost. But if you break up the word into its two parts,* rhino- *and* -plasty, *the meaning becomes clearer. You might not know the meaning of* rhino- *itself, but if you think of an animal whose name bears this prefix, namely the rhinoceros, and of the most distinctive feature of this beast, its rather large snout, you would probably guess correctly that* rhino- *refers to the nose. The meaning of the suffix* -plasty *also seems elusive, but a more common form of it,* plastic, *reveals its meaning of "molding or formation." Put together, these meanings have been modified to create the current medical definition of* rhinoplasty: *"a plastic surgical operation on the nose, either reconstructive, restorative, or cosmetic." Put quite simply, a* rhinoplasty *is a nose job.*[22]

Operational Definition

An operational definition reveals the meaning of a term by describing how it is made or what it does. A cake can be operationally defined by the recipe, the operations that must be performed to make it. A job classification, such as secretary, can be operationally defined by the tasks that the person in that job is expected to perform: a secretary is a person who takes dictation, types, and files papers. Following is an operational definition from a student speech:

> *Modern rhinoplasty is done for both cosmetic and health reasons. It consists of several mini-operations. First, if the septum separating the nostrils has become deviated as a result of an injury or some other means, it is straightened with surgical pliers. Then, if the nose is to be remodeled, small incisions are made within each nostril, and working entirely within the nose, the surgeon is able to remove, reshape, or redistribute the bone*

and cartilage lying underneath the skin. Finally, if the nose is crooked, a chisel is taken to the bones of the upper nose, and they are broken so that they may be straightened and centered.[23]

Remember that defining your terms can improve your communication.

Language and the Public Speaker

The public speaker needs to know how to use language to communicate. That means that the speaker has to know how to put thought into words and how to choose words that will evoke a similar thought in the minds of the audience. This section gives you some ideas about how to achieve high fidelity communication between you and your audience.

Denotative and Connotative

The **denotative meaning** of a word refers to what the word describes, its definition. It could even be thought of as a word's dictionary meaning, since dictionary entries mainly try to express through description how the word has been used by people in the past. For example, the denotative meaning of the word *degree* has twelve descriptions in *Webster's New World Dictionary,* and you have to get to the seventh meaning before you get to the one that most students are aiming for: "7. Educ. a rank given by a college or university to a student who has completed a required course of study. . . ." You will find in public speaking that you have to define your terms in a speech. If an audience is unfamiliar with your topic, you will find yourself providing them with definitions, mainly denotations, of the words.

Another characteristic of language is **connotative meaning.** This refers to the emotionality, the color, the feelings evoked by the word. Consider these words describing a student's experience in earning a college degree.

> *I worked my tail off. I held down two minimum wage jobs while I worked my way through college. One was at a greasy fast-food joint; the other was moving boxes to a conveyer belt in the back room of a warehouse. I was doing thirty-five hours of labor while I was carrying twelve hour loads. I was lucky to stay awake in class and ended up being proud of my dismal gpa. I got my degree, but it took me five years and lots of sweat.*

This passage is more than the sum of its denotative meanings. Instead, these words express feelings and emotions that you did not experience with the descriptive meaning of the word *degree.*

Abstract and Concrete

Words can also be described as abstract or concrete. **Abstract language** is usually more ambiguous in the same way that "yield" is more ambiguous than "stop." People who study language use the metaphor of the **ladder of abstraction** to help others understand levels of abstraction (see figure 3). They would say that words like *animal, climate, home furnishings,* and *vehicle* are examples of highly abstract words. The more abstract a word is, the less control the speaker exerts over what the audience will think. There is nothing wrong with using abstract language, but concrete language tends to evoke a more predictable response.

Concrete language tends to be specific or particular, and is more likely to evoke in the minds of the audience a highly individual but specific thing from their own experience. If you were to write down everything that came to mind when you heard the word *animal,* you might think of many animals. That is because *animal* is abstract. But if I said, "Think right now about your dog," then your own particular dog is most likely to come to mind. Public speakers tend to favor concrete words over abstractions because the former produce a more predictable audience response.

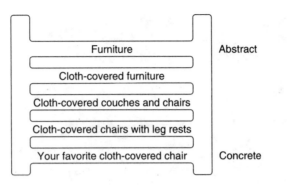

Figure 3

The ladder of abstraction shows how words can have degrees of abstractness or concreteness depending on their rung of the ladder.

Direct and Indirect

Because time is limited in a public speech, you should make every word count. Use **direct language** by choosing words that the audience is sure to understand. Instead of saying, "One of the things you could do with the information I have given you about candidate Rosen is to vote Republican this year—a straight ticket—with Rosen on your list." That long, indirect sentence can be reduced to "Vote for Rosen."

Malcolm X, a 1960's civil rights activist, was known for his direct speech. According to biographer Peter Goldman in *The Death and Life of Malcolm X:* "He *wanted* whites to be frightened and blacks to be brave, and to those ends he spoke to both in a visceral language he assumed we could both understand. He did this at the risk of seeming violent himself and so forfeiting that new regard he wanted."* An example of direct language from Malcolm X occurred when he said, "I am not a racist. I don't believe in any form of segregation or anything like that. I'm for the brotherhood of everybody, but I don't believe in forcing brotherhood upon people who don't want it."*

Indirect language is the use of words to avoid stating the socially unacceptable. For example, in American society we use one kind of language to describe bodily functions when we talk with same-sex friends and quite another when we give a public speech. Same-sex friends may use graphic language among themselves, but more publicly the language becomes less direct.

One kind of indirect language is the **euphemism,** an inoffensive word substituted for an offensive one. Certainly a public speaker can use euphemisms in a speech, but directness is expected when an entire speech covers a subject that Americans like to treat indirectly. Consider the topic of death. In a speech about death and dying, the speaker will be better served by using those direct terms than to continuously speak in euphemisms about "passing on," "going to the great beyond," and "passing away."

Direct and Indirect Language

Direct Language	Indirect Language
Assisted suicide	Euthanasia
Dead body	Remains
Kill	Terminate
Sex	Making love
Fat	Plump
Talkative	Friendly
Crazy	Mentally disturbed

*Source: Peter Goldman, *The Death and Life of Malcolm X,* 2d ed., pp. 187 and 264, 1973. University of Illinois Press, Champaign, IL.

Malcolm X.

Vivid and Dull

Some people speak in words that capture your attention. They use **vivid language** or words that have color, energy, and insight. An example is the "sound bite"—a quick sentence or phrase that captures an idea in a few words. Joe Schildmeyer from Cincinnati's WNKR was asked if he wanted his office computer linked to the station's mainframe. His reply: "On the information super highway, I'm roadkill."[24] The opposite is **dull language** or the use of many words to describe very little. Vivid language is memorable; dull language is forgettable.

Imagine you are giving a speech about safety. To make the point about the importance of following safe procedures when working in a chemical plant, you say: "A careless move can turn you into a smoldering cinder in less than two minutes." That vivid language will grab the audience faster and longer than saying something like: "Working around chemical vats can be very dangerous, so it is best if you follow procedures and observe safety precautions." Governor George Voinovich of Ohio exhibited vividness when he said: "I want to make crystal clear that if you kill a cop in Ohio, you are either going to die in the electric chair or spend the rest of your life in prison."[25]

The language of public speaking, then, can be either denotative or connotative, with denotations being used to define and connotations being used to include emotion. Informative speeches tend to be more denotative; persuasive speeches tend to be more connotative.

The language of public speaking can be abstract or concrete, but the effective public speaker is more likely to use concrete than abstract language because the latter results in more predictable effects. The language of public speaking can be direct or indirect, but directness tends to be more economical and higher in impact. Finally, the language of public speaking can be vivid or dull. Dullness repels an audience while vividness tends to attract attention and enhance memory.

One of the ways that you can make your public speaking attractive and memorable to the audience is to use figures and forms that bring attention to your ideas. You want your audience to respond to your words, to see what you describe, to feel your sadness or joy, to taste the bread, to smell the polluted air, and to pull back at the touch of hot metal. You elicit these responses through the use of **imagery,** vivid language that evokes pictures in the mind. Let's examine two types of imagery in closer detail.

Figures and Forms of Language

Simile and Metaphor in Speaking

One kind of imagery is accomplished through the simile. A **simile** is a figure of speech that compares two different things linked by "like" or "as." For instance, consider this sentence: "He had a voice like a bubble from the bottom of the ocean—deep, heavy, and bursting with energy." Two unlike things—the voice and a bubble from the bottom of the ocean—are compared by linking the two with the word "like."

See if you can find the simile in this student speech about the Shawnee warrior, Tecumseh:

> Let me read a passage from The Indian Tribes of Ohio by Warren King Morehead. "Of commanding figure, nearly six feet in height and compactly built; of dignified bearing and piercing eye . . . brave as a lion, but humane and generous withal—in a word, an aboriginal knight. . . .[26]

This passage develops a visual image of the Shawnee warrior, in part by using the simile comparing him to a lion.

A **metaphor** is an implied comparison between two unlike things, sometimes in a word or phrase and sometimes extended throughout a longer passage or entire speech. When Shakespeare said "All the world's a stage and we're but players in it," the Elizabethian playwright was using a metaphor. You might see your own life in metaphorical terms: are you on a "fast track" in a race toward a finish line? Or are you running over the hurdles through life, sometimes falling or tripping and sometimes clearing the boards with ease? Or, maybe you are on a slow boat to nowhere with destinations unknown and time no object. Our metaphors are powerful guides to how we think about ourselves.

In public speaking the apt metaphor helps the audience to see the connections between the familiar and the unfamiliar. Note how the student in the following speech depicted the elusiveness of world peace by using similes and an overall metaphor from the animal kingdom.

> But still some countries act like wolves; while frothing at the mouth, fur matted with blood, and fangs stripping the flesh from some other wolven nation, they will look upon their prey and exclaim, "I do this for peace!" And the whole world will echo this wolf, "Peace! Peace!" . . . On a collective basis the nations of the world act much like wolves: fangs dripping, snarling, hating, protecting their own sacred territories at any cost and risking everything to gain more resources for their respective nations.[27]

The vivid imagery, the use of simile and metaphor, demonstrate the power of language. The comparison of warring nations and wolves serves as an effective metaphor because it helps solidify the speaker's point in the minds of the listeners.

Parallelism and Repetition in Speaking

Moving from content oriented similes and metaphors to forms like parallelism and repetition will show you how structure brings force to language.

Parallelism is the repetition of syntax or structure, the repeating of certain words, phrases or sentences. Parallelism has striking effects in speaking because the audience gets caught up in the cadences, or rhythms, of linguistic structure. Usually, parallelism is accompanied by increased volume, increased energy, and increased forcefulness as the repeated forms build toward some climactic ending.

An example of parallelism in action comes from a eulogy delivered by civil rights leader Benjamin E. Mays at Martin Luther King, Jr.'s funeral.

> *If Amos and Micah were prophets in the eighth century B.C., Martin Luther King, Jr., was a prophet in the twentieth century.*
>
> *If Isaiah was called of God to prophesy in his day, Martin Luther was called to prophesy in his day.*
>
> *If Hosea was sent to preach love and forgiveness centuries ago, Martin Luther was sent to expound the doctrine of nonviolence and forgiveness in the third quarter of the twentieth century.*
>
> *If Jesus was called to preach the Gospel to the poor, Martin Luther was called to bring dignity to the common man.*
>
> *. . . If a prophet is one who does not seek popular causes to espouse but rather the causes which he thinks are right, Martin Luther qualifies on that score.*[*]

Mays' eulogy uses parallel form by repeating the use of "if . . . then" sentence construction to compare his friend Martin Luther King with a host of Biblical figures.

A second form commonly used in public speaking is **repetition,** the use of the same words or sets of words repeated at the beginning or end of each sentence. Parallel form uses repeated sentence structures, while repetition changes the content very little so the emphasis goes to the few words that do change. Observe how repetition works in this excerpt from a speech by Julia Hughes Jones, the Auditor for the state of Arkansas. The speech was entitled "A Greater Voice in Action: Women and Equality" and was delivered in Charlotte, North Carolina, on August 12, 1992:

> *As we look to the future, we must ask ourselves how many of those rights that women like Lucretia Mott, Elizabeth Cady Stanton, and Susan B. Anthony started fighting for back in 1848, have we achieved?*
>
> *—do we have complete political rights?*
>
> *—do we have complete economic rights?*
>
> *—do we have complete gender rights?*
>
> *—do we have complete marital rights?*
>
> *—do we have complete educational rights?*[28]

As the list goes on, the audience gets the distinct impression that the fight for women's rights is far from over. The repetitive structure has much stronger effect than simply asking: "Do we have complete political, economic, gender, marital, and educational rights?"

The use of figures like similes and metaphors and forms like parallelism and repetition are just a few examples of the way figurative language and the syntax or arrangement of words can increase the power of the spoken word. There are actually

---

*Source: A. L. Smith, *The Voice of Black Rhetoric: Selections,* 1971, Allyn and Bacon, Inc., Needham Heights, MA.

dozens of figures and forms used in public speaking, but a detailed look at these four illustrates their function in public speaking.

You already know that one of the central ethical issues in the use of language is to acknowledge through oral footnotes the use of another person's words. Violating that rule can result in failure of the class or even expulsion in most colleges and universities.

You might be less aware that language can be used unethically. Two examples here will illustrate the point: exaggeration and oversimplification.

Ethics and Language

Exaggeration and Oversimplification

Another word for exaggeration in language is **hyperbole** (hi-PURR-bull-ee), which is a kind of overstatement or use of a word or words that exaggerate the actual situation. To call a relatively normal fire "the biggest conflagration this city has ever seen" is an example. The ethical speaker exercises care in how events, people, and situations are described. It is perfectly acceptable to use vivid, concrete language as long as the words do not overstate or exaggerate. The warning appears here because in the heat of a persuasive speech you might be tempted to state your side of the issue with exaggerated or overstated importance.

A second error in language is **oversimplification,** describing a complex issue as if it were a simple one. Political campaign speeches are full of examples. The candidate for senate says, "We'll whip this crime problem with more prisons." The candidate for the state house of representatives says, "No new taxes." And the candidate for governor says "Welfare reform." Bumper sticker slogans rarely solve problems and neither do sound bites. Most social issues are highly complex and most solutions have unintended consequences. The candidate who says "Get rid of welfare" practically never means cutting the billions of dollars that big businesses save with tax loopholes or the millions that go to farmers in the form of crop subsidies. Instead, their slogan tends to mean "take money from those who have the least" and "leave those with the most alone." The ethical speaker tries to examine issues thoroughly, states them as descriptively as possible, and provides sound reasons for why the audience should adopt a certain position on the issue without exaggeration or oversimplification.

Language and Perspective

Your words reflect your **perspective,** your point of view or perception. The words you choose in public speaking indicate to others how you see the world, whether you intend them to or not.

Imagine you are giving a speech about taxation. If you choose to talk about "rich people," "poor people," and "middle class people," you are using language that divides America into economic classes. That is a particular perspective. If you talk about the "struggling young people" and "the social security set," you are dividing Americans by age—another perspective. Talk of the "marriage penalty" and high taxes on single wage earners divides the adult population into those who are married and those who are not. No matter how you discuss the issue, you use language that indicates your perspective.

How is this concept related to ethical speaking? Consider the connotations of the words that you can use to describe individuals who earn over $100,000 annually: "top 10 percent in income," "rich people," "wealthy individuals," "fat cats," or "privileged class." Each description indicates a perspective, but some of them—like the last two—indicate a medium to strong negative connotation that may or may not be fair to high earning individuals. In other words, the words you choose can indicate prejudice, bias, or unfairness toward individuals or groups.

Unless you are careful with your language, you can make serious errors in your depictions of people. Consider the word *Hispanic*. That word can be used to describe millions of people. Some of them are European Americans (Spanish), some of them are people of color (e.g., South Americans of African or Indian origin), some of them are Cuban Americans, some of them are Mexican Americans, and some of them are Puerto Rican. Here again, the ethical speaker uses the description preferred by the people described.

Suggestions About Language in Public Speaking

While we have discussed some of the more theoretical aspects of language, we turn now to some practical suggestions. In this section, we will offer five suggestions. First, you should choose language that is at a level appropriate for your audience. Second, you should choose language that the audience can understand. Third, you should choose language that does not violate any laws, local ordinances, or the dignity of any audience members. Fourth, you should choose language that is consistent with who you are, the topic, and the situation. Finally, you should choose language that meets high ethical standards. Let us consider each of these suggestions in more detail.

1. *Choose language at a level appropriate for the specific audience.* The public speaker must choose to speak with relatively formal or relatively casual words. Nearly always, the language of public speaking is elevated above that which you would use on the street or in conversation with close friends. But the language choices need to be at the correct level of formality for the audience.

2. *Choose language that the audience will understand.* Using lots of words the audience cannot comprehend might impress the audience with your vocabulary, but language that is not understood by the audience neither informs nor persuades them. If you do use words that the audience is unlikely to understand, you are expected to define, explain, or provide examples.

3. *Choose language that does not violate the law, college or university policy, or hate speech codes, and avoid words that individuals or groups will find offensive.* One offended person in your audience can destroy the intended effect of your speech in the question and answer period. Violations of codes or even the social norms of your audience can result in a negative evaluation of your public speaking.

4. *Choose language consistent with the self, the topic, and the situation.* If you do not normally use legal or medical terms, you will feel and look uncomfortable using them in a public speech. Your language needs to be consistent with your level of knowledge and experience. The language needs to fit the topic: using overly dramatic words unwarranted by the topic constitutes exaggeration, and understating complex problems indicates a lack of analysis. The situation or occasion may dictate a certain kind of language—you don't speak the same way in a mosque, synagogue, or church as you do at a toxic dump site. The words need to fit the situation.

5. *Choose language that meets high ethical standards.* Your language needs to avoid exaggeration and oversimplification. Your language needs to recognize that words reflect a perspective. Avoid language that offends others because of their race, sex, sexual orientation, or physical or mental disability. Your task is to inform, persuade, or entertain, not to offend.

This chapter began with the power of language, especially as it is exhibited in the politically correct movement and the hate speech policies of colleges and universities. You learned what behavior is allowed and what is disallowed by the First Amendment, and the prohibitions against sexist and racist language.

You discovered many differences between written and spoken language, and you examined a list of differences between the two styles. You also found that words shape perceptions, that language and the meanings of words are social agreements among people. You found that the language of public discourse is characterized by words that have denotative or connotative meanings, that are abstract or concrete, direct or indirect, and vivid or dull.

The chapter then moved to a discussion of the figures and forms of language. You learned about similes and metaphors and how they manage through comparison to inspire the imagination and unify the audience's thoughts about a topic. While learning forms of language, you found that parallelism and repetition are two related ways to provide structure and enhance memory of your words. Finally, you learned the ethical dimension of language from blatantly offensive and illegal language to socially offensive language to the more subtle difficulties with language as a reflection of personal perspective. The chapter ended with five suggestions about the use of language in public speaking.

Summary

abstract language Words that are very broad and wide in their meaning, making the speaker less certain of the response they will evoke

concrete language Words that are quite specific and particular such that they evoke a more predictable response from the audience

connotative meaning The feelings and emotions evoked by words that go above and beyond its mere definition

denotative meaning A description of what a word means; definition

direct language Words that have impact on the audience, that get right to the point and do not "beat around the bush"

dull language Forgettable words that describe very little

euphemism An indirect word substituted for another word that might be socially undesirable to say to an audience, e.g., *rest room* instead of *toilet*

hate speech codes College and university rules concerning language and behavior directed at individuals or groups because of their ethnicity, race, sexual preference, religion, etc.

hyperbole Using a word or words to exaggerate or overstate a situation

imagery The use of language to evoke pictures in the mind

indirect language Words that approach a subject by circling it, by hinting, suggesting, and intimating instead of hitting directly

ladder of abstraction Listing words about the same concept vertically according to the level of abstractness or concreteness

man-linked terms Words that often include the suffix *man,* even though the label is placed on things both men and women do, e.g., chairman, repairman, workman, salesman, etc.

metaphor A brief or extended comparison implying similarities between two fundamentally different things

oversimplification Describing a complex issue as if it were a simple one

parallelism The repetition of syntax or structure; the repetition of certain words, phrases, or sentences

perspective Your point of view; the way you perceive the world reflected in the words you choose

politically correct language The words used to describe nondominant groups in American society such as women, people of color, gays and lesbians, and members of religious groups

repetition A form of language in which the same words are repeated either exactly as before or with slight variations

sexist language Derogatory, demeaning, or offensive utterances toward and about women

simile A brief comparison of two things linked by *like* or *as*

slander Verbal statements that impeach the honesty, integrity, virtue, or reputation of another person; called *libel* in writing

Vocabulary

spoken style Language in speech characterized by short, simple sentences, contractions, fragments, concrete words, personal stories and experiences, immediate feedback, and repetition
threats of violence Verbally threatening others with bodily harm; not protected by the First Amendment and described in college codes of conduct as "breach of peace" or "disruption of teaching"
vivid language Memorable words that have color, energy, or insight
Whorf-Sapir hypothesis The language theory that says language shapes perception—the words you know determine how you can think and talk about a topic
written style Language in writing characterized by longer, more complex sentences, few contractions and fragments, bigger words, more abstractions, delayed or no feedback, and little repetition

 # Applications

Application Exercises

Translating Terms

1. Translate the abstract terms in the column on the left into more specific, concrete terms in the blanks on the right.

1. A recent article _____

2. An ethnic neighborhood _____

3. A good professor _____

4. A big profit _____

5. A distant land _____

6. A tough course _____

7. A tall building _____

8. He departed rapidly. _____

9. She dresses poorly. _____

10. They are religious. _____

Now examine carefully each of the words you have placed in the blanks and place a check (✓) after each one that may be a poor moral choice because it skews the audience's response in a negative or unduly positive direction. In other words, it lacks honesty and accuracy.

Connotative and Denotative Meanings

2. Examine the words in the column on the left. Write in the blank after each word, (a) its denotative meaning and (b) its connotative meaning. Remember that the denotative meaning is a descriptive definition; the connotative meaning is the feeling or emotion evoked by the term.

Girl   a. _____

              b. _____

Redneck   a. _____

              b. _____

Racist   a. _____

              b. _____

230

Republican   a. _____

                    b. _____

Politician   a. _____

                    b. _____

Language Form

3. Write a paragraph of your own in which you illustrate the use of parallel structure or repetition as it might be used in a speech. Think of three or more parallel sentences that play to a single theme.

Figures of Speech

4. Look at the words in the left hand column. Try to write a metaphor or simile for each one. Is it more difficult to think of a metaphor or a simile?

Word	Metaphor or Simile
Love	Love is like a puppy dog that is always happy to see you.
Happiness	_____
Pride	_____
Anger	_____
Equality	_____
Sadness	_____
Optimism	_____
Humor	_____
Wealth	_____
Beauty	_____
Truth	_____
Poverty	_____

The Speech on Language Appropriateness

1. Deliver a two- to three-minute speech on your own feelings about the idea of politically correct speech. How do the laws, policies, and social rules on speech about women, race, and religion make you feel? What do you think is good or bad about appropriate language in public speaking?

Application Assignments

The Speech on Language and Thought

2. Deliver a two-to-three-minute speech on how language shapes perception. Start by determining some subject that you know more about than most people. Think of the language or words that you know about that subject. Talk about how knowing the terminology related to a topic changes how you can think about that subject. One option would be to think of courses you have taken that have provided language that you can use to think differently about a subject.

Endnotes

1. Arati R. Korwar, *War of Words: Speech Codes at Public Colleges and Universities* (Nashville, Tennessee: The Freedom Forum First Amendment Center, 1994), 3. Copyright ©1994 The Freedom Forum, Nashville, TN. Reprinted with permission. See also Margaret A. Blanchard, *Revolutionary Sparks: Freedom of Expression in Modern America* (New York: Oxford University Press, 1992), 485.
2. Lawrence R. Stains, "Speech Impediment," *Rolling Stone* 662 (August 5, 1993): 46–48; Korwar, 1994.
3. Korwar, 1994; Blanchard, 1992.
4. Franklin S. Haiman, "Sexist Speech and the First Amendment," *Communication Education* 40 (January 1991): 1–3.
5. Korwar, 1994.
6. Haiman, 1991.
7. Korwar, 1994.
8. Korwar, 1994.
9. Korwar, 1994.
10. Haiman, 1991.
11. W. Strunk and E. B. White, *The Elements of Style,* 3rd ed. (New York: MacMillian Publishing Co., 1979), 60.
12. See, for example, APA Publication Manual Task Force, "Guidelines for Nonsexist Language in APA Journals: Publication Manual Change Sheet 2," *American Psychologist* 32 (1977): 487–94.
13. See, for example, S. Bem and D. Bem, "Does Sex-Biased Job Advertising 'Aid and Abet' Sex Discrimination?" *Journal of Applied Social Psychology* 3 (1973): 6–18; W. Martyna, "What does 'he' Mean? Use of the Generic Masculine," *Journal of Communication* 28 (1978): 131–38; and J. Gastil, "Generic Pronouns and Sexist Language: The Oxymoronic Character of Masculine Generics," *Sex Roles* 23 (1990): 629–43.
14. See, for example, A. Hill, *Mother Tongue, Father Time* (Bloomington, IN: Indiana University Press, 1986); W. Martyna, "Beyond the 'he/man' Approach: The Case for Nonsexist Language" in *Language, Gender, and Society,* B. Thorne, C. Kramarae, and N. Henley, eds. (Rowley, MA: Newbury House, 1983); and J. Silveira, "Generic Masculine Words and Thinking," in *The Voice of Women and Men* C. Kramarae, ed. (New York: Pergamon Press, 1980).
15. J. Gastil, 1990.
16. See, for example, Karlyn Kohrs Campbell, "The Sound of Women's Voices," *The Quarterly Journal of Speech* volume 75 (1989): 211–20; Karlyn Kohrs Campbell, "Women Speaking: A Feminist Analysis of Rhetoric," a lecture at Tulane University, 1985; and Douglas Thomas, "Rethinking Pedagogy in Public Speaking and American Public Address: A Feminist Alternative," *Women's Studies in Communication* 14 (1991): 42–57.
17. Benjamin Lee Whorf, "Science and Linguistics," in *Language, Thought and Reality,* John B. Carroll, ed. (Cambridge, MA: M.I.T. Press, 1956), 207–19; Edward Sapir, *Culture, Language, and Personality: Selected Essays,* David G. Madelbaum ed. (Berkeley, CA: University of California Press, 1949).
18. From a speech delivered by Roberta Mau in the honors section of public speaking, Iowa State University.
19. From a speech delivered by Jergen Nelson in the honors section of public speaking, Iowa State University.

20. From a speech delivered by John Rector in the honors section of public speaking, Iowa State University.
21. From a speech delivered by Sandra Eckerman in the honors section of public speaking, Iowa State University.
22. From a speech delivered by Mark Dupont in the honors section of public speaking, Iowa State University.
23. Ibid.
24. "Backtalk," *Cincinnati Magazine* (November 1994): 112.
25. Ibid.
26. W. K. Moorehead, *The Indian Tribes of Ohio* (Columbus, Ohio: Ohio Archeological and Historical Publications, 1889), 87–88. The excerpt was used in a speech by Rachel Planisek in Winter Quarter 1994 at Ohio University in Interpersonal Communication 103: Public Speaking, taught by Marsha Clowers.
27. Solomon Moore, a seventeen-year-old high school senior from Wooster High School in Ohio, wrote this speech in 1989. It was contributed by Diana Tucker, an Honors Tutorial student in Interpersonal Communication at Ohio University.
28. Speech by J. H. Jones, "A Greater Voice in Action: Women and Equality," copyright © 1992, in *Vital Speeches of the Day* 59 (1992): 109–11, Mount Pleasant, SC.

Chapter 9

DELIVERING YOUR SPEECH

Words mean more than what is set down on paper. It takes the human voice to infuse them with the shades of deeper meaning.

Mrs. Bertha Flowers quoted by Maya Angelou in I Know Why The Caged Bird Sings[1]

QUESTION OUTLINE

I. What is effective delivery?

II. Under what circumstances would you use a manuscript, memorized, impromptu, or extemporaneous speech?

III. What are some vocal aspects of delivery, and how do they function in your public speaking?

IV. What are some nonverbal aspects of delivery, and how do they function in your public speaking?

V. What steps can you take to improve your delivery?

Introduction

Rhonda Strauss was cool and confident when she went to the front of the room to deliver her speech. She had practiced her speech once in front of a full-length mirror and twice in front of two friends. Her speech was on notecards, but in her first practice in front of the mirror she found herself looking at the cards too much. Also, her voice sounded unexpressive. During her second rehearsal, Rhonda's friends suggested some minor changes and encouraged her to put the notecards down so she could move and gesture. That second time her delivery was noticeably better. For a few seconds she felt a little nervous, but once she started her introduction she was so focused on her audience and their reactions that her anxiety disappeared and time seemed to fly as she delivered her speech.

Ralph Waldo Emerson said "All the great speakers were bad speakers first,"[2] but you never have to be a bad speaker if you know what you are doing. Rhonda Strauss knew her topic and her audience, and she knew what she was expected to do when delivering her speech. The best speakers make it look easy. They make it look easy by practicing their speeches until they feel confident, look poised, and sound conversational. This chapter is committed to helping you learn how you can be as convincing as Rhonda.

You will learn what makes delivery effective, when to use the various methods of delivery, how to use movement and gesture effectively, how to use your voice correctly, and how to take steps toward improving your delivery. You will find that speech delivery is not as difficult as you might think, and you should find good delivery easier to achieve with practice and experience.

Most politicians, preachers, and teachers make delivery look easy because they know their subject matter well and because they get lots of practice giving the same or similar messages. Similarly, you can learn to deliver your speech smoothly if you familiarize yourself with your subject matter before you give the speech and practice your speech to gain poise and confidence. The classroom is an ideal place to learn delivery because your teacher and classmates can give you suggestions and encouragement to improve with every speech. To paraphrase a statement in *PR Reporter:* The difference between a merely competent speaker and a really good speaker is the difference between a hamburger cook at McDonald's and the head chef at Lutece: both will provide you with a meal, but only one will make a memorable impression on you.[3] Your goal is to use this chapter to learn effective delivery.

What Is Effective Delivery?

Demosthenes, a famous classic orator, was asked "What are the three most important aspects of public speaking?" His answer: "Delivery, delivery, delivery." Most public speaking teachers would disagree, because great delivery cannot make up for a lack of strong content. An effectively delivered speech cannot overcome a lack of research and knowledge of your topic. As Ray Grigg writes in *The Tao of Relationships,* "Let speaking come from deep within, from the quiet place."[4]

Effective delivery is a way of presenting a speech that does not call attention to itself. Again, Ray Grigg writes, "Too loud and we are not heard. Too bright and we are not seen. Too fancy and we are hidden. Too much and we are obscured."[5] His advice is well taken for the public speaker. If your audience is watching your gestures, your body movements, and your pronunciation rather than the content of your speech, you should reconsider what you are doing. Delivery should never distract listeners from the message.

Effective delivery appears conversational, natural, and spontaneous. Your delivery should be comfortable for you and your audience. When you speak this way, your audience will believe that you are speaking *with* them, not *at* them.

How can you focus on your ideas rather than your delivery? How can you draw your audience's attention to your message rather than your delivery? How can you sound conversational and natural? The answers to all three of these questions are the same. Develop your message first; revising it for delivery comes later.

To keep the focus on your message, select a topic about which you have keen interest or deep convictions. Your involvement in your topic will allow you to speak about it with an appropriate amount of vocal and bodily enthusiasm. If you are committed to the ideas you present, your delivery will come naturally. An upset parent defending their child at a PTA meeting needs no notes. The delivery naturally follows from the message.

To begin practicing your speech, concentrate only on the basics—speaking intelligibly, maintaining eye contact, and avoiding mannerisms that will distract listeners. Make sure that you are pronouncing words correctly. Avoid nervous habits such as playing with a strand of your hair, rubbing your face, tapping a pencil, or pulling on an article of your clothing. If you are practicing in front of friends, use their feedback to help you discover problems, and correct them in subsequent performances.

As you continue to grow in experience and knowledge as a public speaker, you should observe how highly experienced public speakers deliver their messages. How do they appear conversational and yet inviting to their audiences through voice inflection and body movements? What do they do to enhance the impact of their ideas? Which of these techniques can you adapt to your own speeches? Which aspect of other people's speaking styles do you want to avoid? Both positive and negative examples will help you become more effective.

The four methods of delivering a speech are (1) manuscript, (2) memorized, (3) impromptu, and (4) extemporaneous. While each of these four methods is appropriate for different topics, audiences, speakers, and situations, your instructor will identify what is appropriate for your class.

What Are the Methods of Delivering Your Speech?

Manuscript Method

The **manuscript method** of delivering a speech occurs when a speaker writes out the complete speech in advance and then uses that manuscript to deliver the speech. The manuscript method is most useful when a speaker has to be precise. A President who delivers a foreign policy speech in which the slip of a word could start a war, a minister who carefully documents a sermon with biblical quotations, and a politician who releases information to the press are examples of speakers who might adopt this mode.

An example of the use of this method occurred one week on campus when the school invited several speakers to present their points of view on religion. Every lecture drew a huge audience. The speakers, all professors, were a humanist, a Protestant, and an atheist. The humanist presented his point of view in a speech virtually without notes. His speech was almost paternal, full of human virtue, and devoid of conflicting opinions. The Protestant, a Lutheran, delivered her speech a few days later. Many students in the audience were also Protestants, mainly Lutherans, and the speaker had considerable support from her audience. She, too, delivered her speech with few notes. A few days later, the atheist presented his speech. Instead of standing on the well-lighted stage, as the others had done, he delivered his speech seated in the middle of the auditorium with a single spotlight shining on him in the darkness. He read every word from a carefully argued manuscript. Though he argued well, he had few followers in the audience. The response was polite but restrained.

The following weekend, all three speakers faced each other and the audience in a discussion of their positions. Because the atheist's position was unpopular with both his fellow speakers and the audience, he was asked most of the questions. He received the audience's reluctant admiration because, in verbal combat, his previous mode of delivery enabled him to have a solid position on almost every question. The humanist and the Protestant had difficulty remembering exactly what they had said, whereas the atheist answered nearly every inquiry by referring back to the manuscript. It was difficult for anyone in the audience or on the stage to distort the atheist's position. It was clearly a case in which a manuscript delivery was the most appropriate method for the speaker, audience, and situation.

What are the advantages of the manuscript speech? Generally, the complete manuscript prevents slips of the tongue, miswording, and distortion. It often boosts the confidence of beginning speakers because they know that if worse comes to worse they can cling to their manuscript.

The disadvantages outweigh the advantages, however. While using a manuscript might make the beginning speaker feel more confident, generally the delivery suffers. Eye contact is greatly reduced because the speaker is looking at the script rather than at the audience. The speaker's use of gestures may also be minimal. Being bonded to the podium and the script prevents the speaker from gesturing to emphasize or illustrate points. Vocal variety may be lacking as well, and the rate of speech may be too rapid for the audience. The speaker will sound inappropriate because written style is markedly different from spoken style. Instead of sounding conversational, the speech will sound like an essay being read. The manuscript method also hinders audience adaptation. The speaker is not watching the audience, and the manuscript is inflexible. This makes it very difficult to observe and respond to audience feedback. In general, the manuscript method is not recommended for most public speaking situations.

Memorized Method

The **memorized method** of delivery is one in which a speaker has committed a speech to memory. It entails more than just knowing all the words; it usually involves the speaker's rehearsal of gestures, eye contact, and movement. The speaker achieves this mastery of words and movement by practicing or delivering a speech over and over in much the same way that an actor masters a dramatic script.

The memorized method is common in oratory contests, on the lecture circuit, and at banquets. It is appropriate for ceremonial occasions, where little audience or topic adaptation is expected or needed. Campus lecturers often earn $5,000 to $20,000 or more a night for merely filling in the name of a different college in their standard speech. Politicians usually have a stock speech that they have delivered so many times that they have memorized it. Some speakers have delivered the same speech so many times that they even know when and how long the audience is going to applaud.

What are the advantages of the memorized method of presenting a speech? The main advantage is that it permits maximum use of delivery skills: every variation in the voice can be mastered, every oral paragraph stated in correct cadence, every word correctly pronounced at the right volume. With a memorized speech, you have continuous eye contact and you eliminate a search for words. Because no notes are used, bodily movements and gestures are freer.

However, the memorized method has many disadvantages. It permits little or no adaptation during delivery. The speaker is likely to focus more on the internalized manuscript than on the listeners. If the audience appears to have missed a point, it is difficult for a speaker to explain the point in greater detail. A second disadvantage is that recovery is more difficult if you make a mistake: if you forget a line, you have to search for the exact place where you dropped your line. A third disadvantage, especially for beginning speakers, is that a speech sometimes *sounds* memorized: the wording is too smooth, the pacing too contrived, and the speech is too much of a performance instead of a communicative experience.

When you answer a question in class, you are giving a brief impromptu speech.

The beginning speaker is more likely to be disadvantaged than advantaged by using the memorized method. However, later on you may find a place for the memorized speech in your public speaking repertoire. In some formal situations that you may find yourself in later on in your speaking career, you may wisely turn to the memorized speech. Some formal situations, such as a commencement address, call for little adaptation, making this method a good choice.

Impromptu Method

The word *impromptu* means "in readiness." When you give an impromptu speech, you are speaking "on the spur of the moment." The **impromptu method** entails giving a speech without advance preparation. Unlike the extemporaneous method, which we will discuss next, the impromptu method involves no planning, preparation, or practice. You may be ready for an impromptu speech because of your reading, experience, and background, but you do not have any other aids to help you know what to say.

You have already delivered impromptu speeches. When your teacher calls on you to answer a question, your answer—if you have one—is impromptu. You were ready because you had read the assignment or had prepared for class, but you probably had not written out an answer or certain key words. When someone asks you to introduce yourself, explain something at a meeting, reveal what you know about a particular subject, or give directions, you are delivering your answer in an impromptu fashion.

What are the advantages of the impromptu method? One advantage is that it reveals what you are like in unplanned circumstances. In a job interview, you might be asked to answer some questions for which you had not specifically prepared. Your impromptu answers may tell a potential employer more about you than if you were given the questions ahead of time and had prepared your answers. Similarly the student who can give an accurate, complete answer to a difficult question in class shows a mastery of the subject matter that is, in some ways, more impressive than it might be in an exam or another situation in which he or she may give partially planned answers.

The extemporaneous method of speaking appears spontaneous in spite of all the speaker's preparation.

Another advantage of the impromptu method is that it provides you with opportunities to think on your feet. As you engage in impromptu situations, you learn how to quickly identify the important points in the information you wish to share or the major arguments in the persuasive appeals you are attempting to offer. Americans have a great need to be able to give impromptu speeches at everything from fraternity, sorority, or residence hall meetings to social clubs and committee meetings.

The impromptu speech also has disadvantages. The primary problem is that it is so spontaneous that it discourages audience analysis, planned research, and detailed preparation. Most people who are seeking to gain employment, trying to sell a product, or aspiring for academic honors should not risk delivering an impromptu speech. Such circumstances require greater preparation. An impromptu speech can consist of a poor answer as easily as a good one. The lack of planning makes the outcome of the impromptu method of speaking uncertain.

Extemporaneous Method

The **extemporaneous method** occurs when a speaker delivers a speech from an outline or from brief notes. This method of delivery is most commonly taught in the public speaking classroom. As we shall determine, the advantages far outweigh the disadvantages for the beginning public speaker. Indeed, for most speakers, this is the method of choice.

Extemporaneous speaking sounds conversational, looks spontaneous, and seems effortless. However, extemporaneous speaking is the result of much effort. A speaker selects a topic appropriate for the audience, completes research on the topic, organizes the main points and supporting materials, practices the speech with a working outline or key words, and then delivers the speech with maximum eye contact, gestures, and movement. The speaker may occasionally glance at notes, but the emphasis is on communicating a message to an audience.

Extemporaneous speaking is something that you may have done many times without realizing it. Have you ever prepared for a class by reading the assignment, caught the drift of the professor's questions, jotted a few words on your notes, and given an answer in class? Your answer was a brief, extemporaneous speech. Have you ever sat in a meeting about an issue you knew something about, written a few phrases to remind you of your line of argument, and then addressed the group with your point of view? Your "speech" was extemporaneous because it included your background preparation, an organization of your ideas, brief reminders, and a conversational delivery.

An extemporaneous speech is not practiced to the point of memorization. In fact, it is never repeated in exactly the same words, even in practice. The idea is to keep the content flexible enough to adapt to the audience. If the audience appears puzzled by something you say, then you can include a definition, a description, or an example to clarify your position. Audience members like to be talked to, not lectured at or read to.

The extemporaneous method is also different from the manuscript method of delivery. The individual who uses a manuscript has every word written down in a text that looks much like a written report. The person who uses the extemporaneous method has only brief notes, sometimes including little more than key words or phrases that remind the speaker of a story, a concept, or some historical information.

What are the advantages of the extemporaneous method of delivery? First, it is the most versatile method. The speaker, free from notes, can engage in excellent eye contact. This eye contact allows careful audience analysis and immediate audience adaptation.

Second, and unlike the impromptu speech, extemporaneous speaking demands attention to all aspects of public speaking preparation. The speaker has an opportunity to consider the important dimensions of selecting a topic, determining a purpose, doing careful research, identifying supporting materials, organizing the speech appropriately, and using language in a spoken style that best communicates the message. In short, the extemporaneous speech allows a high quality talk.

Third, extemporaneous speaking invites body movement, gestures, and rapid response to audience feedback. The speaker can add or delete information based on the audience's responses.

Fourth, the extemporaneous speech is more likely to sound conversational because the speaker is not reciting scripted words. The language, then, is more inviting because it is created by the speaker who is talking with the audience, not at the audience.

Fifth, it is easier for you to find your place, when lost, on an outline than on a manuscript of a speech.

What are the disadvantages of the extemporaneous speech? If the speaker must be careful that every word needs to be exact, it might be more appropriate to use the memorized or manuscript method. If the speaker has no time to prepare, then the impromptu speech may be preferred. Under most circumstances, however, the extemporaneous method is the speech method of choice.

Your method of delivery must be appropriate for you, your topic, the audience, and the situation. Memorizing five pages of print may not be your style. A manuscript speech is out of place in a dormitory meeting, a discussion among class members, or any informal gathering. Ultimately the method of delivery is not the crucial feature of your speech. In a study to determine whether the extemporaneous or the manuscript method is more effective, two researchers concluded that the method of delivery does not determine effectiveness. The speaker's ability is more important. Some speakers are more effective with extemporaneous speeches than with manuscript speeches, but others use both methods with equal effectiveness.[6]

An effective public speaker learns to speak in front of an audience as if having a conversation.

How Can You Use Your Voice Effectively?

When you converse with your friends on campus, do you focus on how loud you are talking, on whether or not you are looking directly at your listeners, on your hand and body movements, and on the rate and pitch of your voice? Probably not. These delivery features are all a natural part of conversing. You don't even think about them. An effective public speaker learns to speak in front of an audience as if having a conversation. The voice and movements are a natural accompaniment for the words. In fact, some teachers believe that the best way to improve delivery is not to emphasize it directly.[7] Instead, they encourage students to let effective delivery flow from the message.

As you study delivery, you will examine it in parts, but remember that delivery and the message comprise an organic whole. Both are interrelated parts of a system. If the "what you say" is important to you and to your audience, the "how you say it" will not demand your attention. Like Rhonda Strauss in the introduction to this chapter, you will be so busy trying to communicate your message that you will gesture, move, look, and sound like a very competent speaker.

We will examine eight vocal aspects of delivery, but the first four—rate, pause, duration, and rhythm—can all be subsumed under the aegis of time because they are related to the speed, tempo, and punctuation of a speech.

Rate

Rate, the first vocal characteristic of delivery, is the speed of delivery. Normally American speakers say between 125 and 190 words per minute, but audiences can comprehend spoken language much faster. Four psychologists, in an article entitled "Speed of Speech and Persuasion," noted that speech rate improves the speaker's credibility and that rapid speech improves persuasion.[8] In another study, students shortened their pauses and increased their speaking rates from 126 to 172 words per minute. Neither the audience's comprehension nor evaluation of the speakers' delivery was affected.[9] Thus, faster speaking can be better speaking.

Instructors often caution beginning speakers to slow down. The reason is that beginning speakers frequently vent their anxiety by speaking very rapidly. A nervous speaker makes the audience nervous as well. On the other hand, fluency comes from confidence. A speaker who is accustomed to audiences and knows the subject matter well may speak at a brisk rate without appearing to be nervous. Effective speakers sound natural, conversational, and flexible. They can speak rapidly or slowly, depending on the circumstances.

Vocal Aspects of Delivery

1. Rate	5. Pitch
2. Pause	6. Volume
3. Duration	7. Enunciation
4. Rhythm	8. Fluency

The essential point, not revealed by the studies, is that speaking rate needs to be adapted to the speaker, audience, situation, and content of the speech. First, become comfortable with your rate of speaking. If you normally speak rather slowly, you might feel awkward talking like a competitive debater. If you normally speak at a rapid pace, you might feel uncomfortable speaking more slowly. As you learn to speak publicly, you will probably find a rate that is appropriate for you. Second, adapt your rate to the audience and situation. A grade-school teacher does not rip through a fairy tale; the audience is just learning how to comprehend words. A public speaker addressing a large audience without a microphone might speak like a contest orator to make sure the audience comprehends her words. Martin Luther King, Jr., in his famous "I have a dream" speech, began his address at a slow rate under 100 words per minute, but as he became more passionately involved in his topic and as his audience responded he finished at almost 150 words per minute.

The content of your speech may determine your rate of delivery. A story to illustrate a point can be understood at a faster rate than can a string of statistics or a complicated argument. The rate should depend on the effect you seek. Telling a story of suspense and intrigue would be difficult at a high rate of speed. Rarely does speaking "too fast" refer to words per minute; instead, "too fast" usually means the rate at which new information is presented without being understood. Effective public speakers adjust their rate according to their own comfort, the audience, the situation, and the content of their speeches.

Pause

A second vocal characteristic is the **pause**—a brief silence for effect. Speeches are often stereotyped as a steady stream of verbiage, yet a public speaker can use pauses and silences for dramatic effect and to interest the audience in content. You might begin a speech with rhetorical questions: "Have you had a cigarette today? Have you had two or three? Ten or eleven? Do you know what your habit is costing you a year? A decade? A lifetime?" After each question, a pause allows each member of the audience to answer the question in his or her own mind.

Another kind of pause—the **vocalized pause**—is really not silent at all. Instead, it is a way of delaying with sound. The vocalized pause can adversely affect an audience's perception of the speaker's competence and dynamism. The "ahhhs," "nows," and "you knows" of a novice speaker are annoying and distracting to most audiences. Unfortunately, even some highly experienced speakers have the habit of filling silences with vocalized pauses. One organization teaches public speaking by having members of the audience drop a marble into a can every time a speaker uses a vocalized pause. The resulting punishment, the clanging of the cans during the speech, is supposed to break the habit. A more humane method might be to rehearse your speech for a friend who can signal you gently every time you vocalize a pause. One speech teacher helps her students eliminate vocalized pauses by rigging a small red light on the lectern. Every time a student speaker uses a vocalized pause, the instructor hits the light for a moment. Do not be afraid of silence; most audiences would prefer a little silence to a vocalized pause.

One way to learn how to use pauses effectively in public speaking is to listen to how professional speakers use them. Paul Harvey, a Chicago radio commentator, practically orchestrates his pauses. A long pause before the "Page Two" section of his news broadcast is one technique that has made him an attractive radio personality. David Letterman, Jay Leno and most TV anchor persons on the news also use pauses effectively.

Duration

Duration refers to how long something lasts, and, in a speech, on the micro level it can refer to how long the sounds last and on the macro level to how long various parts of the speech last. Whereas rate refers to speed of speaking, duration refers to how long you dwell on your words. A broadcaster who says, "Tonight, I am speaking to you from London" is likely to say it by caressing every word but might deliver other parts of the newscast in rapid-fire fashion. Dwelling on the sound of your words can have dramatic impact; it gives the words a sense of importance.

Similarly duration can refer to the parts of a speech: how long you spend on the introduction, the main points, the examples, the presentational aids. The duration of most introductions is usually relatively short, the body relatively long, and the conclusion shortest of all. The duration should be related to importance; you want to stay longest on the main parts of your message and their support material and only briefly on the least important parts.

Rhythm

Rhythm refers to the tempo of a speech. All of the linear arts seem to have this characteristic. A novel or play starts slowly as the author introduces the characters, establishes the plot, and describes the scene. Then the emphasis shifts to the development of the plot and typically accelerates toward a conclusion, which brings the novel to a close. A musical piece also has some of these characteristics, though it could be said to consist entirely of rhythm.

In a speech, the rhythm usually starts off slowly as the speaker gives clues about who she is, what she is going to speak about, and how she is going to cover the topic. During the body of the speech, the tempo is faster, with verbal punctuation indicating what is most important. The conclusion typically slows in review as the curtain draws to a close. You can practically hear the drum rolls and trumpets on the important parts as the speech marches through time.

The rhythm of a speech includes not only its overall rhythm—the tempo of the major parts—but also the words, sentences, and paragraphs. One example of rhythm is the use of repetitious sounds as in the case of alliteration, the repetition of the initial sounds of words. For instance, it is more memorable to say "color, clarity, and carets characterize a good diamond" than to say "brightness, transparency, and weight give a diamond value." Another example of rhythm is with sentences, an effect often produced by the repetition of initial words: "I served my country because I am a patriot; I served my country because I saw it as my duty; and I served my country because its protection is my first concern." Similarly you can achieve rhythm with rhetorical devices, such as antithesis: "Not because I loved Octavius less, but because I loved Rome more." Jesse Jackson of the Rainbow Coalition is a fine example of a speaker who uses repetition effectively in his speeches.

Pitch

Pitch is the highness or lowness of a speaker's voice, its upward and downward inflection, the melody produced by the voice. Pitch is what makes the difference between the "Ohhh" that you utter when you earn a poor grade on an exam and the "Ohhh" that you say when you see someone really attractive. The "Ohhh" looks the same in print, but when the notes become music, the difference in the two expressions is vast. The pitch of your voice can make you sound animated, lively, and vivacious, or it can make you sound dull, listless, and monotonous. As a speaker, you can learn to avoid the two extremes: you can avoid the lack of pitch changes that results in a monotone and the repetitious pitch changes that result in a singsong delivery. The best public speakers use the full range of their normal pitch. They know when to purr and when to roar, and when to vary their pitch between.

Pitch control does more than make a speech aesthetically pleasing. One of the more important features of pitch control is that it can be used to alter the way an audience responds to words. Many subtle changes in meaning are accomplished by pitch changes. Your pitch tells an audience whether the words are a statement or question, whether they are sarcastic or ironic, and whether you are expressing doubt, determination, or surprise.

You learn pitch control by constant practice. An actor who is learning to say a line has to practice it many times, in many ways, before he can be assured that most people in the audience will understand the words as he intends them. A public speaker rehearses a speech in front of a sympathetic audience to receive feedback on whether the words are being understood as she intends them. Perhaps you sound angry or brusque when you do not intend to. Maybe you sound cynical when you intend to sound doubtful. Possibly you sound frightened when you are only surprised. You may not be the best judge of how you sound to others. Therefore, place some trust in other people's evaluations of how you sound. Practicing pitch is a way of achieving control over this important aspect of delivery.

Volume

A sixth vocal characteristic of delivery is **volume,** the relative loudness or softness of your voice. In conversation you are accustomed to speaking at an arm's length. When you stand in front of an audience, some of the listeners may be quite close to you, but others may be some distance away. Beginning speakers are often told to project, to increase their volume so that all may hear the speech. Interestingly, students who only hours or minutes before were speaking loudly enough for taxi drivers, roommates, and family members to hear become quiet as churchmice in front of their classmates. Projection means adjusting your volume appropriately for the situation.

Volume is more than just projection, however. Variations in volume can convey emotion, importance, suspense, and subtle nuances of meaning. You whisper a secret in conversation, and you stage whisper in front of an audience to signal conspiratorial intent. You speak loudly and strongly on important points and let your voice carry your conviction. An orchestra never plays so quietly that the patrons cannot hear it, but the musicians vary their volume. Similarly a public speaker who considers the voice an instrument learns how to speak softly, loudly, and at every volume in between to convey his or her intended meaning.

Enunciation

Enunciation, the seventh vocal aspect of delivery, is the pronunciation and articulation of words. **Pronunciation** is the production of the sounds of a word. **Articulation** is the

Adjust your speaking volume to the audience and situation.

physiological process of creating the sounds. Because your reading vocabulary is likely to be larger than your speaking vocabulary, you may use words in your speeches that you have never heard spoken before. It is risky to deliver unfamiliar words. Rather than erring in public, practice your speech in front of friends, roommates, or family, who can tell you when you make a mistake in pronunciation or articulation, or check pronunciation in a dictionary. Every dictionary has a pronunciation key. For instance, the entry for the word *deification* in *Webster's New World Dictionary of the American Language* follows:

> *de-i-fi-ca-tion (dè ə-fi-kā´ sh ə n), n.[ME.; OFr.],*
> *1. a deifying. 2. deified person or embodiment.*[10]

The entry indicates that the word has five syllables into which it can be divided in writing and that carry distinct sounds. The pronunciation key says that the *e* should be pronounced like the *e* in even, the *ə* like the *a* in ago, and the *a* like the *a* in ape. The accent mark (´) indicates which syllable should receive heaviest emphasis. You should learn how to use the pronunciation key in a dictionary, but, if you still have some misgivings about how to pronounce a word, ask your speech teacher for assistance.

Another way to improve your enunciation is to learn how to prolong syllables. Such prolonging makes your pronunciation easier to understand, especially if you are addressing a large audience assembled outside or in an auditorium with no microphone. The drawing out of syllables can be overdone, however. Some radio and TV newspeople hang onto the final syllable in a sentence so long that the device is disconcertingly noticeable.

Articulation errors are so common that humorous stories are often based on them. Stories about misunderstandings that children might have are often the basis of such jokes. For example, "Willy, the cross-eyed bear" is one child's interpretation of "Willing, the cross I bear." Another child thought that part of the Lord's Prayer was "hollow be thy name."

Articulation problems are less amusing when they occur in your speech. Four common articulation problems are addition, deletion, substitution, and transposition. **Addition** occurs when an extra sound is added. For example, if a person says "picanic" instead of "picnic," or "athalete" instead of "athlete," he or she is making an error of addition.

Deletion occurs when a sound is dropped or left out of a word. Examples of deletion are "rassberry" for "raspberry," or "libary" for "library." Deletion also commonly occurs when people drop the final sounds of words such as "reveren'" for "reverend," "goin'" for "going," or "comin'" for "coming." Finally, deletion occurs when individuals drop the initial sounds of words such as "'possum" for "opossum."

Substitution occurs when one sound is replaced with another. When people use the word "ant" for "aunt," "git" for "get," "ruff" for "roof," "crick" for "creek," or "tomata" for "tomato," they are making substitution errors.

Transposition occurs when two sounds are reversed. College students who call their teachers "perfessor" instead of "professor" or say "axe" for "ask" make this error. Similarly, if you call one "hundred" one "hunderd," you are making an error of transposition.

Fluency

The eighth vocal characteristic of delivery is **fluency**—the smoothness of delivery, the flow of the words, and the absence of vocalized pauses. Fluency is difficult because it cannot be achieved by looking up words in a dictionary or by any other simple solution. Fluency is not even very noticeable. Listeners are more likely to notice errors than the seemingly effortless flow of words and intentional pauses in a well-delivered speech. You can, however, be too fluent. A speaker who seems too fluent is perceived as "a fast talker," or "slicker than oil." The importance of fluency is emphasized in a study which showed that audiences tend to perceive a speaker's fluency, the smoothness of presentation, as a main ingredient of effectiveness.[11]

To achieve fluency, you must be confident of the content of your speech. If you know what you are going to say, and if you have practiced it, then disruptive repetition and vocalized pauses are less likely to occur. If you master what you are going to say and concentrate on the overall rhythm of the speech, your fluency will improve. Pace, build, and time various parts of your speech so that in delivery and in content they unite into a coherent whole.

How Can You Use Your Body Effectively?

We have considered the vocal aspects of delivery. Let us now examine the bodily aspects. Eye contact, facial expression, gestures, movement and physical appearance are five bodily aspects of speech delivery—nonverbal indicators of meaning—that are important to the public speaker. In any communication, you indicate how you relate to the material and to other people by your gestures, facial expression, and bodily movements. When you observe two people busily engaged in conversation, you can judge their interest in the conversation without hearing their words. Similarly, in public speaking, the nonverbal aspects of delivery reinforce what the speaker is saying. Researchers have found that audiences who can see the speaker, and his or her behavior, comprehend more of the speech than audiences who cannot.[12]

Some persons are more sensitive to nonverbal cues than are others. Five researchers who developed a "Profile of Nonverbal Sensitivity" found that females as early as the third grade are more sensitive to nonverbal communication than males. However, men in artistic or expressive jobs scored as well as the women. The researchers' finding suggests that such sensitivity is learned. A second finding on nonverbal communication is that, until college age, young people are not as sensitive to nonverbal communication as older persons are.[13] This, too, supports the notion that we can and do learn sensitivity to nonverbal cues, such as eye contact, facial expression, gestures, and movement.

Nonverbal Aspects of Delivery

1. Eye contact
2. Facial expression
3. Gestures
4. Movement
5. Physical appearance

Eye Contact

The first nonverbal aspect of delivery that is important to the public speaker is **eye contact.** This term refers to the way a speaker observes the audience while speaking. Studies and experience indicate that audiences prefer maintenance of good eye contact,[14] which improves source credibility.[15] Eye contact is one way you indicate to others how you feel about them. You may be wary of a person who will not look at you in conversation. Similarly, in public speaking, eye contact conveys our relationship with the audience. If you rarely or never look at audience members, they may be resentful of your seeming disinterest. If you look over the heads of your audience or scan them so quickly that you do not really look at anyone, you may appear to be afraid. The proper relationship between you and your audience should be one of purposeful communication. You signal that sense of purpose by treating the audience members as individuals with whom you wish to communicate a message, and by looking at them for responses to your message.

Eye contact—the frequency and duration of looking at the person to whom you are speaking—varies with gender, personality, and culture.[16] Americans of European descent tend to use more eye contact than do Americans of African descent. African Americans tend to use less eye contact while listening than do European Americans. Such differences in behavior can lead to misunderstanding. The African American's averted eyes can lead the European American to interpret disinterest. The European American's more intent eye contact could be perceived by an African American as staring or as aggressiveness. Some cultural groups such as some Latin Americans, Southern Europeans, and Arabs tend to stand close and look directly into the other person's face. Many people from India, Pakistan, and Scandinavia, on the other hand, turn their bodies toward the person to whom they are speaking, but avoid steady focus on the other person's face.

How can you learn to maintain eye contact with your audience? One way is to know your speech so well and to feel so strongly about it that you have to make few references to your notes. A speaker who does not know a speech well tends to be manuscript-bound. You can encourage yourself to keep an eye on the audience by delivering an extemporaneous speech from an outline or key words. One of the purposes of extemporaneous delivery is to help you adapt to your audience. Adaptation is not possible unless you are continually monitoring the audience's reactions to see if your listeners understand your message. Other ways of learning eye contact include scanning or continually looking over your entire audience, addressing various sections of the audience as you progress through your speech, and concentrating on the head nodders. In almost every audience, there are some individuals who overtly indicate whether your message is coming across. These individuals usually nod yes or no with their heads. You may find that you can enhance your delivery by finding the friendly faces and positive nodders who signal when the message is getting through to them.

Facial Expression

Another nonverbal aspect of delivery is **facial expression.** Socrates, one of humanity's greatest thinkers, said: "Nobility and dignity, self-abasement and servility, prudence and understanding, insolence and vulgarity, are reflected in the face and in the attitudes of the body whether still or in motion."[17] Some experts believe that the brain connects emotions and facial expressions and that culture determines what activates an emotion and the rules for displaying an emotion.[18]

Ekman and Friesen believe that facial expression shows how we feel and that body orientation (leaning, withdrawing, turning) expresses the intensity of our emotion.[19] Pearson, West, and Turner in their book *Gender and Communication,* cite studies showing differences between male and female facial expressions. For instance, women use more facial expressions and are more expressive than men; women smile more than men; women are more apt to return smiles; and women are more attracted to others who smile.[20]

Because facial expressions communicate, public speakers need to be aware of what they are communicating. A good example is that smiling can indicate both goodwill and submissiveness. Animals, such as chimpanzees, smile when they want to avoid a clash with a higher-status chimpanzee. First-year students smile more than upper-class students.[21] Constant smiling may communicate submissiveness instead of friendliness, especially if the smiling seems unrelated to the content of the speech.

As a public speaker, you may or may not know how your face looks when you speak. You can practice in front of a mirror, videotape your practice session, or speak in front of friends who will help you. The goal is to have facial expressions consistent with your intent and your message.

Gestures

Gestures are "any visible bodily action by which meaning is given voluntary expression."[22] Although you probably are unaware of your arms and hands when you converse with someone, you may find that they become bothersome appendages when you stand in front of an audience. You may feel awkward because standing in front of an audience is not, for most of us, a natural situation. You have to work to make public speaking look easy, just as a skillful golfer, a graceful dancer, and a talented painter all make their performances look effortless. Beginners make golfing, dancing, painting, and public speaking look difficult. Professionals make physical or artistic feats look easy.

What can you do to help yourself gesture naturally when you are delivering your speech? The answer lies in your involvement with the issues and with practice. Angry farmers and irate miners appear on television to protest low prices and poor working conditions. Untutored in public speaking, these passionate people deliver their speeches with gusto and determined gestures. The gestures look very natural. These speakers have a natural delivery because they are much more concerned about their message than about when they should raise their clenched fists. They are upset, and they show it in their words and actions. You can deliver a speech more naturally if your attention is focused on your message. Self-conscious attention to your own gestures may be self-defeating: the gestures look studied, rehearsed, or slightly out of synchronization with your message. Selecting a topic that you really care about can result in the side effect of improving your gestures, especially if you concentrate on your audience and message.

Gestures differ with the size of the audience and the formality of the occasion. With a small audience in an informal setting, gestures are more like those you would use in ordinary conversation. With large audiences and in formal speaking situations, gestures are larger and more dramatic. In the classroom, the situation is often fairly formal and the

Gestures need to be adjusted to the size of the audience and the formality of the occasion.

audience relatively small, so gestures are ordinarily bigger than they would be in casual conversation but not as exaggerated as they would be in a large auditorium.

Another way to learn appropriate gestures is to practice a speech in front of friends who are willing to make constructive comments. Constructive criticism is one of the benefits your speech teacher and fellow students can give you. For example, actresses and actors spend hours rehearsing lines and gestures so that they will look spontaneous on stage. You may have to appear before many audiences before you learn to speak and move naturally. After much practice, you will learn which arm, head, and hand movements seem to help and which hinder your message. You can learn, through practice, to gesture naturally in a way that reinforces your message instead of detracting from it.

Movement

The fourth nonverbal aspect of delivery is **movement,** or what you do with your entire body during a speech presentation. Do you lean forward as you speak, demonstrating to the audience how serious you are about communicating your message? Do you move out from behind the lectern to show that you want to get closer to the audience? Do you move during transitions in your speech to signal physically to the audience that you are moving to a new location in your speech? These are examples of purposeful movement in a public speech. Movement without purpose is discouraged. You should not move just to work off your own anxiety like a caged lion.

Always try to face the audience even when you are moving. For instance, even when you need to write information on the board, you can avoid turning your back by putting your notes on the board before class or by putting your visual material on posters. You can learn a lot about movement by watching your classmates and professors when they speak. You can learn what works for others and for you through observation and practice.

Think of physical movement as another way for you to signal a change in emphasis or direction in your speech. In the same way that a new paragraph signals a directional change in writing, moving from one side of the podium to the other can signal a change in your speech. All of the movements mentioned so far have been movements with a purpose. Purposeful movement can reduce your anxiety and hold audience attention. Speakers have "nervous energy" that can be worked off with movement. On the other hand, you should avoid channeling your anxiety into purposeless movement—movement unrelated to the content. Examples of purposeless movement are rocking back and forth or side to side or the "caged lion" movement in which a speaker circles the front of the room like a lion in a zoo.

The environment in which you give your speech helps determine what kind of movements are appropriate. The presence of a podium or lectern affects the formality of a speech. When a podium is present, the speaker is expected to use it, and the result is a higher level of formality than would otherwise be the case. The podium or lectern suggests a speaker-superior relationship with the audience, whereas the absence of a podium suggests more of an equal relationship with the audience. You should ask your professor's opinion about the use of the podium.

The distance between the speaker and the audience is also significant. A great distance suggests speaker superiority. That is why pulpits in most churches loom high and away from the congregation. A speaker often has a choice about how closely to move toward or away from the audience. In the classroom, a speaker who clings to the far wall may appear to be exhibiting fear. Drawing close suggests intimacy or power. Large people can appear threatening or aggressive if they approach the audience too closely, and small people behind large podiums tend to disappear from sight. You need to decide what distances make you and your listeners most comfortable.

Physical Appearance

How you look can make a difference in public speaking. You can do little or nothing about some aspects of your **physical appearance.** You might be unusually tall, short, wide, or good looking, but you can't change those characteristics for a public speech. Neither can you change racial characteristics or scars or the wheel chair in which you might ride, but the audience may still observe and make judgments.

Almost anyone who has a noticeable difference from others can be faced with prejudice. Unusually short-statured people report discrimination in employment opportunities and suffer from anxieties about social stigmas such as the tendency to equate size with age.[23] Young adults exhibit hostile stereotypes toward obese individuals.[24] Functionally disabled people experience social discrimination that is similar to that experienced by minority individuals from a dominant majority.[25] Often people who look different are avoided, ignored, or sometimes even ridiculed.

In the public speaking classroom, a person who is different in appearance for any reason can choose to ignore their uniqueness or address it. For example, a woman in a wheel chair introduced herself to her classmates with a different perspective. She said she did not want them to think of her as "handicapped" because in nearly all ways she was not—any more than most of them were limited in some way. She referred to her classmates as "temporarily able bodied" because they never knew when they might end up as she had from an automobile accident. Facing the issue all her classmates wondered about gave them permission to listen to her and talk with her without the anxiety they might otherwise have felt.

Even so-called normal people have to consider the relationship between appearance and audience response. Christine Craft was one of the early successful anchorwomen on television. After years of successful reporting her employer told her: "The people of Kansas City don't like watching you anchor the news because you are too old, too unattractive, and you are not sufficiently deferential to men." Originally hired because they loved her "looks," she quickly found repeated attention to her "squarish jaw and somewhat uneven eyes."[26] Being a woman is another factor you cannot control, but, unfortunately, it does make a difference in how an audience perceives you.

In an article entitled "Personal Appearance: Is Attractiveness a Factor in Organizational Survival and Success" Nykodym and Simonetti questioned 662 managers and found that appearance ranked eighth out of twenty survival and success factors. They also found that internal promotions tended to go to "individuals who have an acceptable corporate image."[27] Schindler and Holbrook found a "critical-period phenomenon": men formed a lifelong preference for women's styles that were popular when the men were in their early twenties. Women's preferences and even men's preferences for other men's styles were not so specific.[28] Appearance makes a difference on the job, and the age and gender of audience members makes a difference in what styles are preferred.

Finally, Stuart and Fuller in a 1991 article in the *Journal of Business Research* found that salesmen dressed in different attire were perceived quite differently. Nearly 400 purchasing agents were asked to judge photographs of a model dressed as a salesperson. The result: the salespeople in traditional outfits were perceived as better, more ambitious, self-assured, and optimistic. Furthermore, the traditionally dressed male was seen as representing a larger, more ethical company with more products, better credit, and better service.[29] Apparently, the purchasing agents made a lot of judgments about the salesperson based on their clothing.

Just so you do not get the impression that clothing choices are an overwhelming factor, consider the study of young people (average age seventeen) who applied for seasonal employment at an amusement park. Eight interviewers interviewed 517 applicants and judged them on personal style, body movement, and speech characteristics. Speech characteristics like articulation and proper pauses proved more important than personal appearance.[30]

Your clothing and accessories do make a difference in how people perceive you, but there can be big differences between a classroom speech and a speech in another setting. Following are some suggestions for choosing appropriate attire for the classroom setting.

1. Wear clothing that is normative for your audience, unless you are wearing clothing that makes some point about your speech. An international student speaking about native dress could wear clothing unique to his or her country, for example.

2. Avoid wearing clothing or jewelry that is likely to distract your audience from your message: too many holes in the Levis in the wrong places, too revealing a neckline, or pants that are two sizes too small.

3. Wear clothing and accessories that contribute to your credibility, not that lower it in the eyes of the audience.

Public speaking outside the classroom is clearly more complicated because you have to dress for the topic, the audience, and the occasion. Violate audience expectations and they will tend to respond negatively. Wear a wild, Hawaiian shirt for an upper midwest audience, and they will consider you odd. When in doubt, ask the people who invite you to speak how you should dress.

How Can You Improve Your Delivery?

A student confessed that he had disobeyed instructions. Told to write a brief outline from which to deliver a speech, the student, instead, was afraid to speak in front of the class without every word written out. He practiced the speech by reading the whole manuscript word for word. After rehearsing the speech many times, he wrote the entire speech in microprint on notecards so it would appear to be delivered from a brief outline on the cards. However, as he began his speech, he found that he couldn't read the tiny print on his cards, so he delivered the whole speech without using the cards at all. All the practice had helped him; the micromanuscript had not.

Practice your speech in the room where you will deliver it.

To help you improve your own delivery, you might want to follow these steps, which many students find useful:

1. Start with a detailed working outline that includes the introduction, the body, and the conclusion. Remember to include all main points and supporting materials.

2. Distill the working outline into a speaking outline that simply includes reminders of what you intend to include in your speech.

3. Practice your speech alone first, preferably in front of a mirror so you will notice how much or how little you use your notes. Ideally, 80 to 90 percent or more of your speech should be delivered without looking at notes.

4. Next practice your speech in front of your roommate, your spouse, your kids, or anyone else who will listen. Try again to maintain eye contact as much as possible. After the speech, ask your observers to explain your message—and seek their advice for improving the speech.

5. Practice your speech with minimal notes in an empty classroom or a similar place that gets you accustomed to its size and the situation. Focus on some of the more sophisticated aspects of delivery, such as facial expression, vocal variety, gestures, and movement.

6. Use past critiques from your instructor or classmates to provide direction for improvement on delivery.

7. If possible, watch a videotape of your own performance for feedback. If practice does not make perfect, at least it will make you confident. You will become so familiar with the content of your speech that you will focus more on communicating it to your audience.

A common error among beginning speakers is that they finish composing their speech late the night before delivery, leaving no time for practice. The most beautifully composed speech can be a delivery disaster, so protect yourself by leaving time for three to five practice sessions. Then you will be self-assured, and your delivery will show that confidence.

Effective delivery has many advantages. Research indicates that effective delivery, the appropriate use of voice and body in public speaking, contributes to the credibility of the speaker.[31] Indeed, student audiences characterize the poorest speakers by their voices and the physical aspects of delivery.[32] Poor speakers are judged to be fidgety, nervous, and monotonous. They also maintain little eye contact and show little animation or facial expression.[33] Good delivery also tends to increase the audience's capacity to handle complex information.[34] Thus, your credibility and ability to convey complex information may be affected by the vocal and physical aspects of delivery.

To put this chapter on delivery in perspective, remember that eye contact, facial expression, gestures, and movement are important, but content may be even more important. The same researcher who found that poor speakers are identified by their voices and the physical aspects of their delivery also found that the best speakers are identified by the content of their speeches.[35] Two other researchers found that an audience's evaluation of a speaker is based more on the content of the speech than on vocal characteristics, such as intonation, pitch, and rate.[36] Still another pair of researchers found that a well-composed speech can mask poor delivery.[37] Finally, one researcher reviewed studies on informative speaking and reported that, although some research indicates that audiences who have listened to good speakers have significantly greater immediate recall, other findings show that the differences are slight. His conclusion was that the influence of delivery on comprehension is overrated.[38]

What are you to do in the face of the reports that good delivery influences audience comprehension positively but also that the influence of delivery on comprehension is overrated? What are you to do when one study reports that poor vocal characteristics reveal a poor speaker and another states that good content can mask poor delivery? Until more evidence is available, the safest position for you as a public speaking student is to regard both delivery and content as important. What you say and how you say it are both important—and probably in that order.

Summary

This chapter on delivery began with a discussion of what is entailed in effective delivery. This section was followed by a consideration of the four methods of delivery: extemporaneous, manuscript, impromptu, and memorized. The method of delivery that most speech professors prefer for classroom instruction is the extemporaneous mode, which allows for minimal use of notes but invites spontaneity and maximum focus on message and audience.

Next, we reviewed the vocal aspects of delivery: rate, pause, duration, rhythm, pitch, volume, enunciation, and fluency. These vocal characteristics need to be orchestrated by the speaker into a symphony of sound and movement that sounds attractive to the audience. Monotony and unintended verbal blunders, such as the dreaded vocalized pause and verbal fillers, are the enemies of effective delivery.

Nonverbal aspects of delivery was the fourth section in this chapter. It examined eye contact, facial expression, gestures, movement and physical appearance. The keys to delivery are naturalness, sincerity, and sensitive responsiveness to the audience. You learn to look and move in ways that you find comfortable and the audience finds inviting.

We concluded with some ideas about perfecting your delivery. Starting with a script of your speech or preferably a sentence outline, with practice you move toward fewer and fewer notes and more and more attention to your audience. The key word is *practice*. Too much practice can turn your extemporaneous speech into a memorized one, but too little can turn your well-composed speech into a comedy of errors. Allowing time to practice your speech is about as tough as finding a topic in a reasonable amount of time, but those who practice usually receive the best evaluations.

....

addition An articulation problem that occurs when an extra sound is added

articulation The physiological process of creating the sounds of a word

deletion An articulation problem that occurs when a sound is dropped or left out of a word

duration The amount of time devoted to the parts of a speech (e.g., introduction, evidence, main points) and the dwelling on words for effect

enunciation A vocal aspect of delivery that involves the pronunciation and articulation of words; pronouncing correctly and producing the sounds clearly so that the language is understandable

extemporaneous method A method of speech delivery in which the speaker delivers a speech from an outline or from brief notes

eye contact A nonverbal aspect of delivery that involves the speaker's looking directly at audience members to monitor their responses to the message; in public speaking, eye contact is an asset because it permits the speaker to adapt to audience responses and to assess the effects of the message

facial expression A nonverbal aspect of delivery that involves the use of eyes, eyebrows, and mouth to express feelings about the message, audience, and occasion; smiles, frowns, grimaces, and winces can help a speaker communicate feelings

fluency A vocal aspect of delivery that involves the smooth flow of words and the absence of vocalized pauses

gestures A bodily aspect of delivery that involves the movement of head, hands, and arms to indicate emphasis, commitment, and other feelings about the topic, audience, and occasion

impromptu method A method of speech delivery in which the speaker has no advanced preparation

manuscript method A method of speech delivery in which the speaker writes out the complete speech in advance and then uses that manuscript to deliver the speech

memorized method A method of speech delivery in which the speaker commits the entire manuscript of the speech to memory, by either rote or repetition; appropriate in situations where the same speech is given over and over to different audiences

movement A nonverbal aspect of delivery that refers to a speaker's locomotion in front of an audience; can be used to signal the development and organization of the message

pause An intentional silence used to draw attention to the words before or after the interlude; a break in the flow of words for effect

physical appearance The way we look, including our display of material things such as clothing and accessories

pitch A vocal aspect of delivery that refers to the highness or lowness, upward and downward inflections of the voice

pronunciation The production of the sounds of a word

rate A vocal aspect of delivery that refers to the speed of delivery, the number of words spoken per minute; normal rates range from 125 to 190 words per minute

rhythm The tempo of a speech, which varies by part (e.g., introductions are often slower and more deliberate) and by the pacing of the words and sentences

substitution An articulation problem that occurs when one sound is replaced with another

transposition An articulation problem that occurs when two sounds are reversed

vocalized pause A nonfluency in delivery characterized by such sounds as "Uhhh," "Ahhh," or "Mmmm" or the repetitious use of such expressions as "O.K.," "like," or "for sure" to fill silence with sound; often used by speakers who are nervous or inarticulate

volume A vocal characteristic of delivery that refers to the loudness or softness of the voice; public speakers often project or speak louder than normal so that distant listeners can hear the message; beginning speakers frequently forget to project enough volume

 # Applications

Application Exercises

Selecting a Method of Delivery

1. Examine each of the following topics, audiences, and situations and indicate which method of delivery would be best by placing the appropriate letter in each blank on the left.

A = Manuscript   B = Extemporaneous   C = Impromptu   D = Memorized
    Method   Method   Method   Method

_____1. You have to answer questions from the class at the conclusion of your speech.

_____2. You have to describe the student government's new statement of policy on student rights to a group of high-level administrators.

_____3. You have to deliver the same speech about student life at your college three times a week to incoming students.

_____4. You have to give parents a "walking tour" of the campus, including information about the buildings, the history of the college, and the background of significant places on campus.

_____5. You have to go door-to-door, demonstrating and explaining a vacuum cleaner and its attachments that you are selling.

Bodily Aspects of Delivery

2. Observe a talented public speaker—a visiting lecturer, a political speaker, a sales manager—and study his or her gestures, facial expressions, eye contact, and movement. Then answer the following questions.

1. Do the speaker's gestures reinforce the important points in the speech?

2. Does the speaker's facial expression reflect the message and show concern for the audience and the topic?

3. Does the speaker maintain eye contact with the audience, respond to the audience's reactions, and keep himself or herself from becoming immersed in the manuscript, outline, or notes?

4. Does the speaker's movement reflect the organization of the speech and the important points in it?

5. Are the speaker's gestures, facial expressions, and movements consistent with the occasion, the personality of the speaker, and the message being communicated?

6. Do the speaker's clothing and other adornments reinforce, rather than distract from, the message?

Evaluating Your Delivery

3. For your next speech, have a classmate, friend, or relative observe and evaluate your speech for delivery skills. Have your critic use this scale to fill in the blanks on the left.

1 = Excellent   2 = Good   3 = Average   4 = Fair   5 = Weak

Vocal Aspects of Delivery

_____ Pitch: highness and lowness of voice, upward and downward inflections

_____ Rate: words per minute, appropriate variation of rate for the difficulty of content

_____ Pause: intentional silence designed to aid understanding at appropriate places

_____ Volume: loud enough to hear, variation with the content

_____ Enunciation: correct pronunciation and articulation

_____ Fluency: smoothness of delivery; lack of vocalized pauses; good pacing, rhythm, and cadence without being so smooth as to sound artificial, contrived, or overly glib

Nonverbal Aspects of Delivery

_____ Gestures: natural movement of the head, hands, arms, and torso consistent with the speaker, topic, and situation

_____ Facial expression and smiling behavior: consistent with message, used to relate to the audience, appropriate for audience and situation

_____ Eye contact: natural, steady without staring, includes entire audience, and is responsive to audience feedback

_____ Movement: purposeful, used to indicate organization, natural, without anxiety, use at podium and distance from audience

_____ Physical appearance: appropriate for the occasion, speaker, topic, and audience

Practicing Delivery Through Oral Interpretation

Application Assignment

Select a poem, play, short story, or speech that will provide you with three to five minutes of content so you can focus on the delivery of your selection. As with your other speeches, this one should be practiced until you can deliver it without heavy dependence on your notes. Introduce your selection and deliver it. Have the teacher and audience say what aspects of delivery were best performed in your speech.

Endnotes

1. Maya Angelou, *I Know Why The Caged Bird Sings* (New York: Bantam Books, 1969), 82.
2. Ralph Waldo Emerson, "Power" in *The Conduct of Life, Nature, and Other Essays* (Dutton, 1860).
3. Paraphrased from Phillip Lesly, "Managing the Human Climate," a supplement of *PR Reporter* (Exeter, NH: PR Publishing Co., Inc., 1988), May–June 1988, p. 1.
4. Ray Grigg, *The Tao of Relationships* (New York: Bantam Books, 1988), 15.
5. Grigg, 1988.
6. Herbert W. Hildebrandt and Walker Stevens, "Manuscript and Extemporaneous Delivery in Communicating Information," *Speech Monographs* 30 (1963): 369–72.
7. Otis M. Walter and Robert L. Scott, *Thinking and Speaking* (New York: Macmillan, 1969), 124–83.
8. Norman Miller et al., "Speed of Speech and Persuasion," *Journal of Personality and Social Psychology* 34 (1976): 615–24.
9. Charles F. Diehl, Richard C. White, and Kenneth W. Burk, "Rate and Communication," *Speech Monographs* 26 (1959): 229–32.
10. *Webster's New World Dictionary of the American Language—College Edition* (New York: The World Publishing Company, 1957), 386–87.
11. Donald Hayworth, "A Search for Facts on the Teaching of Public Speaking," *Quarterly Journal of Speech* 28 (1942): 247–54.
12. Edward J. J. Kramer and Thomas R. Lewis, "Comparison of Visual and Nonvisual Listening," *Journal of Communication* 1 (1951): 16–20.

13. Robert Rosenthal et al., "Body Talk and Tone of Voice: The Language Without Words," *Psychology Today* 8 (1974): 64–68.

14. Martin Cobin, "Response to Eye-Contact," *Quarterly Journal of Speech* 48 (1962): 415–18.

15. Steven A. Beebe, "Eye Contact: A Nonverbal Determinant of Speaker Credibility," *Speech Teacher* 23 (1974): 21–25.

16. Virginia P. Richmond, James C. McCroskey, and Stephen K. Payne, *Nonverbal Behavior in Interpersonal Relations* (Englewood Cliffs, NJ: Prentice-Hall, Inc., 1987), 82–83.

17. Socrates, Xenophon, *Memorabilia III* in *Nonverbal Communication: Readings with Commentary,* Shirley Weitz, ed. (New York: Oxford University Press, 1974), vii.

18. Paul Ekman, "Pan-Cultural Elements in Facial Displays of Emotion," *Science* 164 (1969): 86–88.

19. Paul Ekman and Wallace V. Friesen, "Head and Body Cues in the Judgment of Emotion: A Reformulation," *Perceptual and Motor Skills* 24 (1967): 711–24.

20. Judy Cornelia Pearson, Richard L. West, and Lynn H. Turner, *Gender and Communication* (Dubuque, IA: Wm. C. Brown Publishers, 1995), 250.

21. Pearson, West, and Turner, 1995.

22. *Nonverbal Interaction,* Adam Kendon, "Gesture and Speech: How They Interact," John M. Wiemann and Randall P. Harrison, eds., vol. II of *Sage Annual Reviews of Communication Research* (Beverly Hills, CA: Sage Publications, 1983), 13.

23. James M. Moneymaker, "The Social Significance of Short Stature: A Study of the Problems of Dwarfs and Midgets," *Loss, Grief and Care* 3 (1989): 183–89.

24. Mary B. Harris and Chiyoko Furukawa, "Attitudes Toward Obesity in an Elderly Sample," *Journal of Obesity and Weight Regulation* 5 (1) (Spring 1986): 5–15.

25. Harlan Hahn, "The Politics of Physical Differences: Disability and Discrimination," *Journal of Social Issues* 44 (Spring 1988): 39–47.

26. Christine Craft, *Too Old, Too Ugly, and Not Deferential to Men* (Rocklin, CA: Prima Publishing and Communications, 1988), 9.

27. Nick Nykodym and Jack L. Simonetti, "Personal Appearance: Is Attractiveness a Factor in Organizational Survival and Success?" *Journal of Employment Counseling* 24 (June 1987): 69–78.

28. Robert M. Schindler and Morris B. Holbrook, "Critical Periods in the Development of Men's and Women's Tastes in Personal Appearance," *Psychology and Marketing* 10 (6) (Nov–Dec 1993): 549–64.

29. Elinora W. Stuart and Barbara K. Fuller, "Clothing as Communication in Two Business-to-Business Sales Settings," *Journal of Business Research* 23 (3) (November 1991): 269–90.

30. Charles K. Parsons and Robert C. Liden, "Interviewer Perceptions of Applicant Qualifications: A Multivariate Field Study of Demographic Characteristics and Nonverbal Cues," *Journal of Applied Psychology* 69 (4) (November 1984): 557–68.

31. Erwin Bettinghaus, "The Operation of Congruity in an Oral Communication Situation," *Speech Monographs* 28 (1961): 131–42.

32. Ernest H. Henrikson, "An Analysis of the Characteristics of Some 'Good' and 'Poor' Speakers," *Speech Monographs* 11 (1944): 120–24.

33. Howard Gilkinson and Franklin H. Knower, "Individual Differences Among Students of Speech as Revealed by Psychological Tests—I," *Journal of Educational Psychology* 32 (1941): 161–75; Marshall Prisbell, "Assertiveness, Shyness and Nonverbal Communicative Behavior," *Communication Research Reports* 2 (1985): 120–27; Valerie Manusov, "Perceiving Nonverbal Messages: Effects of Immediacy and Encoded Intent on Receiver Judgments," *Western Journal of Speech Communication* 55 (1991): 235–53.

34. John L. Vohs, "An Empirical Approach to the Concept of Attention," *Speech Monographs* 31 (1964): 355–60.

35. Henrikson, 1944.

36. Ronald J. Hard and Bruce L. Brown, "Interpersonal Information Conveyed by the Content and Vocal Aspects of Speech," *Speech Monographs* 41 (1974): 371–80.

37. D. F. Gundersen and Robert Hopper, "Relationships Between Speech Delivery and Speech Effectiveness," *Speech Monographs* 43 (1976): 158–65.

38. Charles R. Petrie, Jr., "Informative Speaking: A Summary and Bibliography of Related Research," *Speech Monographs* 30 (1963): 81.

PRESENTATIONAL AIDS

Chapter P

Light hath no tongue, but is all eye.

John Donne

QUESTION OUTLINE

I. Why should you use presentational aids?

II. What factors affect the use of presentational aids?

III. How can you relate your visual aids to your topic, situation, and audience?

IV. What types of presentational aids are available for the public speaker?

V. How can graphics be used in public speeches?

VI. What types of display boards are possible for the public speaker to use?

VII. Why should public speakers consider computer-generated graphics?

VIII. What are the dangers involved in using display equipment in public speeches?

IX. What suggestions can be offered to the public speaker who uses display persons or things?

X. What is the relationship between your presentational aids and your message?

Introduction

bdul Hamid had a problem with his public speech. As an international student, he wanted Americans to understand more about the country from which he came. Because his English was not the best, he didn't think his descriptions would be understood. How could he get Americans to understand the beauty of his homeland and the richness of Muslim traditions? He knew it would be difficult to have them understand the customs of a nation they probably couldn't locate on a map.

Abdul's solution was presentational aids. A local travel agent had a poster that he could hang in front of the classroom as he gave his speech. He could wear traditional clothing during the speech, and he had a dozen good slides that he could show the class as he explained, as best he could, what they showed about his country. It took a lot of work to get the slide projector, to get the extension cord, to write notecards for each slide, and to explain in English what each slide revealed about his country. However, Abdul received his highest grade in his informative speech—and the most comments from his classmates. They were much more interested in him and his country after the speech, and they seemed to appreciate learning about other parts of the world.

Ours is a visual world. The average student has spent more hours in front of a television than in the classroom. With the publication of *USA Today* and the advent of new color technology, newspapers have become more colorful and pictorial than ever before. Video cameras are a hot item, with families recording every important event, and lots of unimportant ones, with their own cameras. In this highly visual world, the importance of *showing* what you are talking about has developed into a fine art.

You will be able to speak with more confidence when you learn how to use presentational aids to communicate your message to an audience. This chapter will help you learn the possibilities and the problems with the most commonly used presentational aids.

Why Use Presentational Aids?

Presentational aids are important for at least five reasons. First, they *reinforce the message* you provide to the audience. Second, they *clarify your message*. Third, they may make your message *more interesting* to an audience. Fourth, they make your speech *more memorable*. Fifth, the use of presentational aids helps reduce speech anxiety. Oftentimes, presentational aids add these benefits to your speech and are, at the same time, economical.

Presentational aids can help reinforce your message. Bess Pittman reinforced her message as she began the body of her speech with an enlarged photograph she had obtained from a local insurance company. The presence of flashlights and car lights indicated that the picture had been taken at night. The picture showed shoes. The shoes were spread across the road and in the ditch as if boxes of them had fallen off a truck. They were the shoes of teenagers. Thirteen high school seniors had died in a head-on, two-car crash near the city limits. The impact of the two speeding cars had knocked the shoes off most of the victims and had blasted them across the road and into the ditch. Bess was discussing the unusually high number of car accidents among our youth. Her photo showed no mangled wreckage, no blood, and no bodies. The shoes told the story.

Presentational aids can also clarify a message. They are often clearer than words alone. A public speaker trying to show how our financial situation has changed over a five-year period could use hundreds of words and many minutes explaining the effects of inflation, but a bar graph could show it more clearly in a couple of minutes.

Another benefit of using presentational aids is that pictures, graphs, charts, maps, and other presentational aids are often more interesting to an audience than just using words. The newspaper *USA Today* was the subject of jokes when it was first published. Cynics called it "McNews" and said that it would win a Pulitzer prize for the most outstanding paragraph. However, *USA Today* revolutionized the newspaper business by illustrating the importance of graphics—pictures, drawings, maps, and color. The editors who thought the paper was superficial and simple found themselves scrambling to improve their own graphics. People found the highly visual newspaper more interesting than columns of print.

An additional reason to incorporate presentational aids into your speech is that audiences find visualization memorable. We learn much of what we know through sight. According to Elena P. Zayas-Baya in the *International Journal of Instructional Media,*[1] we learn 83 percent of all we know through sight. The effect of our senses on memory is equally dramatic. The same author reports that we are likely to remember

10 percent of what we read	50 percent of what we see and hear
20 percent of what we hear	80 percent of what we say
30 percent of what we see	90 percent of what we say and do

Finally, the use of presentational aids may actually result in lowered levels of speech anxiety. Perhaps speakers feel more confident as they focus on their aids rather than on their own nervousness. Presentational aids serve to reinforce the message, which encourages the speaker to feel more assured. Presentational aids also allow the speaker to look away from the audience, which can relieve the speaker of tension. Whatever the specific factors, visual aids appear to lower speech anxiety. Joe Ayres, at Washington State University, recently demonstrated that people who were generally apprehensive about speaking but used presentational aids reported less anxiety than those who were generally apprehensive but did not use presentational aids.[2]

Seeing is an important component of learning and retaining information. That is exactly what you are trying to do with presentational aids—help the audience see what you are talking about, concisely, clearly, interestingly, and memorably.

Some experimental studies support the use of presentational aids. In one study, university students were exposed to a series of words and/or pictures and were tested on their ability to recall what they had seen. When the students were exposed to two stimuli at a time (i.e., sound plus pictures or printed words plus line drawings), they remembered better than they did with just one stimulus.[3] Another study demonstrated that two-dimensional objects, simple figures against a background, are better remembered when they move than when they stand still.[4]

A third study used male and female subjects from junior high to college age and tested them for audio and visual cues. The experimenters determined that these audiences are more influenced by what they see than by what they hear.[5] For the public speaker, the message is clear: presentational aids reinforce your message and will probably be the part of your speech that the audience remembers.

Following are six questions to ask yourself before using presentational aids:

1. What is the composition of my audience?
2. What is the occasion?
3. What is the setting?
4. What is the message?
5. What is the cost?
6. What are the rules?

Your answers to these questions will help you decide if, what kind of, and how many presentational aids are appropriate for your speech.

Factors Affecting the Use of Presentational Aids

Audience

What is the composition of my audience? This question considers the audience members' ages, education, status, and reason for attending your speech. In other words, the question considers audience analysis.

The younger your audience, the more necessary presentational aids become. Preschool and elementary children are captivated by visual aids. That is why elementary teachers have to learn how to use them.

People who have had little formal education may be more dependent on graphic illustrations, whereas highly educated people are more accustomed to interpreting what they hear. Regardless of educational level, some materials, such as statistics, mathematical formulas, and weather maps, are very difficult to comprehend without accompanying visuals.

High-status people have to be treated carefully lest they feel that the speaker is "talking down" to them with a visual presentation, but boards of directors, developers, and fund-raisers find that architects, lawyers, and investors often use visual displays to influence their decisions. You may recall that U.S. Presidential hopeful Ross Perot relied on extensive pie charts and other visuals in the 1992 presidential race. Similarly, Norman Schwartzkopf showed the American public elaborate diagrams explaining the Desert Storm operation.

If an audience must learn something from a speaker, then presentational aids usually come into play. Thus, informative speeches to most groups invite the use of visuals for clarification and understanding. If the audience is expecting to be entertained, then the need for aids may be less imperative. Nonetheless, even in a special occasions speech, visual aids may be helpful.

Occasion

What is the occasion? Ceremonial occasions often call for decoration—political bunting, ribbons, flags—but not often for presentational aids. Similarly, rituals such as funerals, baptisms, or bar mitzvahs, call more for decoration than for presentational aids. Even evangelists and most visiting lecturers depend more on words than on visuals. However, some occasions cry for presentational aids.

Instruction is an occasion that practically demands presentational aids, whether it is elementary school, high school, college, or a place of business. Where the purpose is pedagogical and the idea is to impart knowledge to a group, the need for presentational aids is high.

Persuasive situations, too, invite presentational aids. When the military tries to make a case for more funding, Congress is treated to graphs, charts, pictures, and even the very objects of defense. When a speaker is trying to convince an audience to stop drinking, start exercising, and continue eating appropriately, that speaker usually tries to persuade the audience with facts and figures presented visually. In short, the kinds of speeches that predominate in the classroom—informative and persuasive speeches—are the ones that need visual reinforcement if the audience is to understand and remember the message.

Setting

What is the setting? The place where the speech is to occur helps determine if and what kind of presentational aids should be used. The size and shape of the room can forbid their use or make them appropriate. Huge rooms demand specialized gear: large screens, projectors, amplifiers, and light. Small rooms—such as classrooms—are appropriate for a wide variety of presentational aids.

The place where the speech is to occur helps determine if and what kind of presentational aids should be used.

Classrooms, lecture halls, or conference rooms are usually designed for visual display; they usually come equipped with viewing screens, chalkboards, and places to hang posters. At the same time, you should not assume that all classrooms have all, or any, of these. A church sanctuary, lounge, or private office may be ill equipped for visual presentation. You have to decide what is possible to do in the particular setting in which your speech is to occur.

The setting should not be seen as an absolute limitation. One speech communication professor tells of a student who said his visual aid was too large for the classroom. The student had designed a mini-car with award-winning mileage. Larger than a midget racer, the mini-car required a site out-of-doors. The teacher made an exception by permitting the speech to be delivered outside on the building patio, with the audience attending. After an inspiring speech about the mini-car, the speaker jumped into his self-designed auto and drove off. Speakers can—with permission—alter the setting for their presentational aid. Students should exercise caution and gain instructor permission in advance, however. Some instructors may feel that visual aids that overwhelm the speaker or take too much attention away from the speaker—like an automobile, horse, dog, or motorcycle—are inappropriate.

Message

What is the message? Some messages are so simple or so compelling that presentational aids are superfluous, but most messages have parts that are tough to comprehend without some visual assistance. The complexity of the material is the main variable that determines the appropriateness of presentational aids: the more complex or difficult the message is to understand verbally, the more necessary presentational aids become. Some speech professionals feel that any speech can be made more memorable and interesting with presentational aids—no matter how simple the topic. Even spelling out your main points on a poster may enhance a simple speech.

Most quotations, narrations, and examples do not demand visual reinforcement; most messages about economic changes over time, statistical trends, series of dates, financial reports, sales records, and weather predictions do demand visual reinforcement. To determine when presentational aids will be most helpful, exercise the interpersonal skill of empathy: what parts of your speech will be better understood by the audience if they are presented visually or on audiotape?

Cost

What is the cost? Poster board is cheap, film is more expensive, and videotape or quadra-phonic sound in the classroom could be prohibitively expensive. Expense has to do with both time and money: few students have the time to make slides, films, or videos. Fortu-nately, the chalkboard, flip-charts, posters, physical objects, and handouts—the most common presentational aids—are neither very expensive nor very time-consuming. You have to consider how much time and money you can afford to spend on your public speech. You should also keep in mind that expensive, professionally-produced aids are not necessarily more effective than homemade ones.

Rules

What are the rules? When you are pondering the use of presentational aids, you should consider their safety and legality. Students often ask teachers about using drugs, drug paraphernalia, alcohol, guns, and fire in the classroom. Teachers tell of students pulling out a gun when talking about banning handguns or about a student who brought a flaming wastebasket into the room to talk about the effectiveness of various fire extinguishers.

You should use your imagination and creativity when you plan your speech, but you need to consider also the safety and legality of your presentational aids. If you have any doubt about the safety or legality of something you plan for your speech, check first with your teacher.

Now that you know some of the broad questions to ask about your presentational aids, or PAs as some students call them, you are ready to consider the types of PAs avail-able for your use in a public speech.

Types of Presentational Aids

There are many kinds of presentational aids, but you will be able to use them more easily if you think of them in categories.[6] We begin with the kinds of visual aids used the most—graphics—and move through display boards and equipment to persons and things—which are used less often in public speeches.

Graphics

Graphics include photographs; pie, line, and bar graphs; charts and tables; drawings; and maps. All of these are in the public speaker's repertoire.

Photographs

Photographs are useful in a public speech if they are large enough for the audience to see. A student from the Philippines gave a speech about her native land accompanied by large travel posters borrowed from a travel agency. The large pictures of the beaches, the city of Manila, and the countryside reinforced what she told the audience about her country.

Avoid passing snapshots or small pictures because as they look at the snapshots, the audience will not be listening to your speech. Instead, use large pictures, like the student who showed a large satellite photograph of the region, with circles drawn to indicate how far various AM, FM, and TV signals would carry. Any picture that needs to be passed is too small for use in a public speech.

Graphs

Graphs are of three types—pie, line, and bar. A pie graph looks like a pie cut in slices. The entire pie equals 100 percent and each slice equals a smaller percentage. Although some people have difficulty determining percentages by looking at a pie graph, your pie

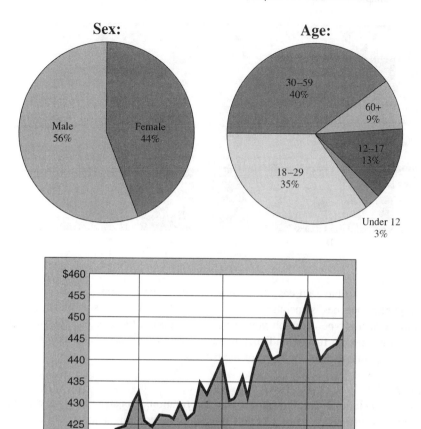

Sex:

Male 56%
Female 44%

Age:

30–59 40%
60+ 9%
12–17 13%
18–29 35%
Under 12 3%

Figure 1

These pie charts show the percentages of male and female shoplifters and the percentages of shoplifters by age group.

Reprinted with permission from *Psychology Today Magazine.* Copyright © 1988 Sussex Publishers, Inc., New York, NY.

Figure 2

This line graph shows the average weekly pay for factory workers between 1988 and 1991.

Reprinted by permission of *The Wall Street Journal,* Copyright © 1991 Dow Jones & Company, Inc. All Rights Reserved Worldwide.

graph will serve you well if everyone can see it, if it is divided into fewer than six slices, and if the parts are clearly labeled. The pie graphs in figure 1 indicate the percentage by sex and age group of the nearly ten thousand shoplifters who were caught in one year. The age graph is interesting, but notice that the population groups are varied with gaps of 12, 5, 11, and 29 years. (In other words, people under 12 years of age represent a 12-year span, people from ages 12–17 represent a 5-year span, people from ages 18–29 represent an 11-year span, and people from ages 30–59 represent a 29-year span.) Why do you think they were arrayed in this way?

The second type of graph is the line graph. The advantage of a line graph is that it can be exact. The disadvantage is that audiences often have difficulty reading and interpreting the vertical and horizontal information. They can see the lines but they do not have the slightest notion of what they mean. The speaker usually has to help an audience interpret a line graph. Even on the line graph in figure 2, the message may not be clear from the data that between 1989 and 1991 average weekly pay for factory workers was on the rise.

The third type of graph is the bar graph. The advantage of the bar graph is that it is easy to read and comprehend; the disadvantage is that it is not a very exact measure.

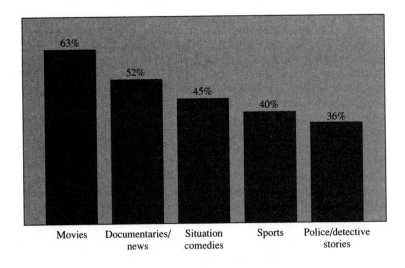

Audiences do seem to have an easy time understanding the meaning of bar graphs, so their use in public speeches is encouraged. For a traditional bar graph, see figure 3.

Regardless of the type of graph you use in your speech, the pie, line, or bar graph needs to be large enough for the audience to see everything on the visual aid, including any print that explains the pie, the lines, or the bars.

Charts and Tables

A **chart** is a presentational aid that summarizes information, lists steps, or otherwise displays information difficult to convey orally. For example, you might want your audience to know the emergency numbers to call in your area for police, fire, rape crisis, or abuse. A chart is an easier way to display that information than to announce it. Similarly a chart showing the names and prices of personal computers is easier to comprehend in print.

A **table** usually consists of columns of numbers. A table is particularly useful because columns of numbers are nearly impossible to communicate orally.

When composing a chart or table, be careful not to overload it with too much information. Table 1 is an example of a chart that overwhelms the audience with information. Table 2 is a simplified version of some of the same information, written in a more digestible form.

Instead of explaining every number to audience members, you should help them interpret the data. For example, with table 2 you could point out that most college presidents were vice-presidents or presidents of other colleges when they assumed the presidency. Actually, the most interesting information is not on the chart: 90 percent of male presidents are married; only slightly more than one-third of all women presidents are married. Said the author: ". . . the overwhelming majority of college presidents are white, male, married, and in their early fifties."[7]

If you use charts and tables, you will want to insure that the audience can read them. What size print should you use? Michael and Suzanne Osborn suggest that the speaker should use three-inch-high letters for titles, two-inch-high letters for subtitles, and one-and-one-half-inch-high letters for other text.[8] Their advice seems highly appropriate in most normal-sized classrooms. If you are speaking in a larger room, you may wish to create presentational aids with larger print. Letter heights are always dependent on distance.

Drawings

Public speakers can use illustrations prepared by themselves or others. A talented artist presented her speech on the various species of ducks. Each species was illustrated by a

Table 1
University Presidents' Prior Positions by Type of Institution

	President		V.P.[1]		Dean/director[2]		Faculty/chair		K–12		Outside academe		Other		No response	
Prior Position	No.	%	No.	%	No.	%	No.	%	No.	%	No.	%	No.	%	No.	%
All presidents (n = 2,105)	361	17.2	880	41.8	390	18.5	169	8.0	48	2.3	136	6.5	110	5.2	11	.5
Doctorate-granting (n = 164)	51	31.1	60	36.6	26	15.9	7	4.3	—	—	8	4.9	11	6.7	1	.6
Comprehensive (n = 359)	67	18.7	166	46.2	51	14.2	23	6.4	7	2.0	22	6.1	21	5.9	2	.6
Baccalaureate (n = 553)	77	13.9	233	42.1	99	17.9	60	10.8	8	1.5	41	7.4	34	6.1	1	.2
Specialized (n = 228)	30	13.2	56	24.5	55	24.1	38	16.7	—	—	37	16.2	9	3.9	3	1.3
Two-year (n = 801)	136	17.0	365	45.6	159	19.9	41	5.1	33	4.1	28	3.4	35	4.4	4	.5

[1]Includes Senior or Executive Vice-President, Vice-President for Academic Affairs, other Vice-President, Assistant or Associate Vice-President
[2]Includes Dean, Director, Assistant/Associate Dean, Director of Student Services
Courtesy of American Council on Education, Washington, D.C. Reprinted with permission.

Table 2
Table of Numbers Simplified from Table 1 for Easier Audience Understanding: What Job Did University Presidents Have Before?

Type of school	Presidents before	Vice-presidents before	Deans before
All colleges	17%	42%	19%
4-year college	14%	42%	11%
2-year college	17%	46%	20%

large colored drawing. She did not say that she had drawn them herself until the question-and-answer session. Nonetheless, her classmates were suitably impressed with her speech and her artistry.

The main things to remember about drawings and illustrations are that they must be relevant to the message, they must add something to the speech that cannot be provided by language alone, and they must be large enough for all to see. (See figure 4.)

Maps
Some informative speeches tell an audience about locations that are difficult to specify without a map. Some informative speeches encourage students to write to legislators, but the audience does not know who the legislator is without the name and a legislative map. As long as your map is large and the lines are clear, it can be useful in your public speech. (See figures 5 and 6.)

You have now seen the appropriate use of photographs; pie, line, and bar graphs; charts and tables; drawings; and maps. In order to review all that you have learned about the kinds of presentational aids and the types of graphics, you are invited to use the checklist at the end of this chapter.

Figure 4

This drawing made the speaker's poster more attractive to the audience.

Figure 5

This map shows a distant view of Sterling Heights, Michigan, and a close-up view.

Copyright © 1991 *USA TODAY.* Reprinted with permission.

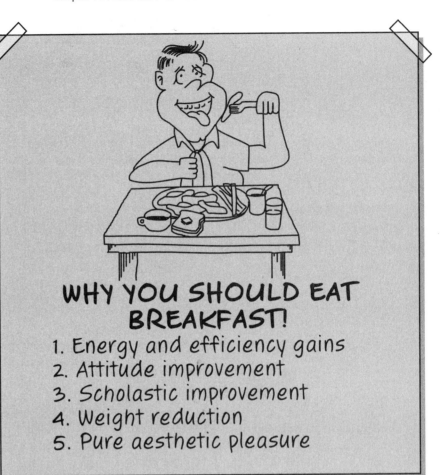

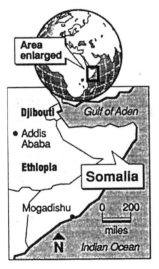

Figure 6

This map shows a distant view and a close-up of the country of Somalia in East Africa.

Copyright © 1991 *USA TODAY.* Reprinted with permission.

Display Boards

Three kinds of **display boards** are commonly used by public speakers: chalk- or slick-boards, posters, and flip charts. Let us examine them systematically and consider the possibilities of each.

Chalkboards or Slickboards

In most classrooms, the chalkboard is the most available presentational aid. It is good for stating your name and the title of your speech, for keeping the audience's attention on the main points of your speech, for spelling out difficult words, and for showing simple drawings. The advantage is that you can use a chalkboard or slickboard spontaneously if you wish; the disadvantage is that, to use them effectively, it is necessary to turn your back on your audience.

The main difficulty faced by speakers who try to write on the board is that their writing cannot be read. If you expect your audience to be able to read what you write, you have to write legibly:

1. Use print instead of cursive writing.
2. Use bold block letters.
3. Use chalk that shows up well on the board (white or yellow on green- or blackboards).
4. Use lettering that is 2 inches high and 1/4 inch wide for every 25 feet of viewing distance.

Display boards on an easel allow for a series of visuals while the speaker faces the audience.

Use the chalkboard to help your audience understand the message.

Another useful suggestion is to use a pointer when talking about items on the board so you do not have to turn your back on the audience.

A slickboard is uncommon in the classroom but relatively common in conference rooms. It is like a blackboard except that is has a slick white or light-colored surface that accepts water markers of many colors.

Both slickboards and chalkboards are good for diagrams, definitions, outlines of main points, brief reviews, a line or two of poetry, and mathematical problems or formulas. Both can make your speech seem too much like a classroom lecture instead of an extemporaneous speech.

Figure 7

A poster showing calories burned in different activities.

Item	CAL./HR.
Skiing downhill	530
Skiing x/country	625
Tennis-singles	380
Tennis-doubles	270
Ice skating	390
Mountain climbing	650
Raquetball	600
Bicycle riding	500
Walking	260
Jogging	450
Horse riding	360
Dancing (continuous)	225
Sitting	75

Avoid writing on the board during your speech by writing your message before class. If you do not want your classmates to see your written message until you speak, then cover it with a sheet of newspaper. If you have any doubts about your teacher's attitude concerning the use of the board, check with the teacher.

Posters

Posters overcome many of the disadvantages of the presentational aids listed so far. Because they must be prepared ahead of time, they can be designed for easy viewing. Because they are made of heavy, high-grade paper, a black magic marker can produce a highly visible message. Because they are prewritten, you need not turn your back on the audience when the poster is being discussed.

A student giving a speech on child abuse used posters to highlight his message. He had five main points and five posters, each displaying a true-or-false question. He placed all five posters on the chalk tray and introduced the speech by asking his audience to answer the questions.

Most abused children come from poor families.	True	False
Most children are abused by their own mothers.	True	False
Most people now in prison were abused as children.	True	False

And so on. The listeners were uncertain of the correct answers, but their curiosity was aroused. The speaker used each of the questions as a main point in the speech. The posters eliminated the speaker's need for notes—they were on the posters.

The following suggestions for using posters might help you use them effectively:

1. Keep your message simple. The audience should be able to quickly grasp what you are illustrating. Consider using only key words and a relatively small number of points.

2. Make sure the poster and the print are large enough and positioned for everyone to see (remember, the teacher usually sits in the back of the room).

3. Use clips or masking tape to keep the poster up while you are referring to it, or ask a classmate to hold it for you. Avoid the embarrassment of having to pick up your poster off the floor, of having it curl off the wall.

Look at the poster in figure 7 for an idea.

Whether you choose to use chalkboards, slickboards, or posters, remember that their purpose is to reinforce your message, not to be used for their own sake.

Flip Charts

A **flip chart** is a large pad of paper, usually on a stand, that allows the speaker to flip the sheets over or tear them off as they are used. Colored pens may be used on this medium as long as the ink does not soak through to the next sheet.

Flip charts are frequently used in business presentations to give structure to, define, explain, or gather ideas. In a brainstorming situation, for example, the ideas can be listed on the page, torn off, and stuck to the wall or board with masking tape for later review or evaluation.

A flip chart can have some material already printed on the pages, but the advantage of the flip chart is that it allows spontaneity. The flip chart shares some of the disadvantages of the chalk- or slickboard in that the speaker usually has to turn his or her back to the audience in order to write, and the speaker must write legibly in block print large enough for all in the room to see. Lettering must be at least 3 inches high and the width of the broad edge of a marker.

Another advantage of the flip chart is that it is portable and relatively inexpensive. Like a board, it can be used for definitions, difficult words, and simple drawings to illustrate or reinforce your message.

Next we will look at some presentational aids that demand specialized equipment.

Computer-Generated Graphics

Many students today have their own personal computers or they have access to computers. If this is true for you, you may want to consider the possible presentational aids that you can make on a computer. Consider, too, some of the sophisticated new software packages that have been especially designed to create graphs, charts, and other presentational aids. You may wish to make handouts, illustrations, transparencies, and slides from materials created on the video screen. While others may use the computer for "desktop publishing," you can use it for "desktop presentations."

Even if you do not have strong artistic talent, you will be able to make professional-looking presentational aids. In general, computer-generated materials are more accurate and may be neater than those you can create by hand. In addition, some computer programs can create dramatic or eye-catching graphics that are more impressive than those drawn by hand.

An example is Microsoft. Powerpoint®*, a software program used on a Macintosh® computer and a laser printer. This program created the graph in figure 8, an illustration used in a speech about where a public radio and television station received its revenue in the 1980s and 1990s. The graphic was used as a handout in the speech. Meanwhile, the speaker used the graph and the four-part explanation in figure 9. The audience did not see the material in figure 9, but the computer program printed a reduced version of the graphic and a boldfaced list of explanations for the speaker. Other software programs that will generate graphics include Aldus Persuasion and Claris Impact.

For a very important presentation, you can convert computer-generated graphics into acetate transparencies for an overhead projector, slides for a slide presentation, or 35-millimeter color strips for use with a projector. The Macintosh Plus with PowerPoint can be used by itself as a "slide show" operated either on a timed sequence or manually. The computer can show your visual creations just as a slide projector does, except the audience sees the graphics on the video screen.[9]

*Microsoft. PowerPoint is a registered trademark of Microsoft Corporation. Macintosh is a registered trademark of Apple Computer, Inc.

Figure 8

This graph was created on a computer as a handout for a speech about public radio and TV revenue in the 1980s and 1990s.

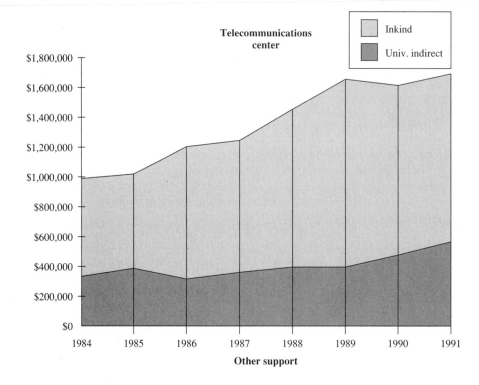

Figure 9

This graph with explanations was used by the speaker to help him remember the handout and to remind him of the explanations. The entire page was computer-generated and laser-printed.

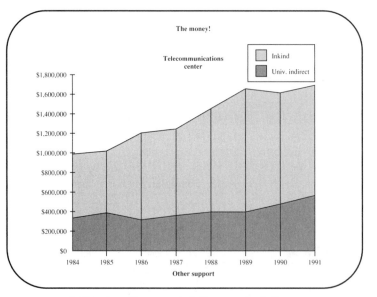

1. This shows the support of other agencies both within the University and without.

2. The *indirect support* from the University includes things like physical plant activities and administrative support. Its total value in 1991 was $584,558—up 21 percent from 1990.

3. The *inkind support* of Center activities by other agencies includes services from OEB, ETS, the State Department of Education, etc. That support had a value of $1,113,961 in 1991—down 2 percent from the prior year.

4. Together these support items added $1,698,519 to the strength of the Center.

10 point

12 point

14 point

18 point

24 point

36 point

Figure 10

Different computer printer font sizes.

If you use a computer to generate your presentational aids, you may want to consider how large your print should be. Printers generally have a wide array of font sizes. Some of the more common sizes are ten point, twelve point, fourteen point, eighteen point, twenty-four point, and thirty-six point. Each of these are successively larger. These different sizes of print are illustrated in figure 10.

The Osborns provide precise suggestions for you if you create your presentational aids on the computer using these font sizes. Their recommendations follow.

	Transparencies	Slides	Handouts
Title	36 pt	24 pt	18 pt
Subtitle	24 pt	18 pt	14 pt
Other text	18 pt	14 pt	12 pt[10]

Display Equipment

This section on display equipment begins with a warning. Do not use display equipment unless you know what you are doing. The types of equipment we are referring to are movies, slides, videotapes, audio amplification and recording equipment, and opaque and overhead projectors. Let us look at each in turn for their possibilities in your public speaking.

Films and Videotapes

Films and videotapes can be great for demonstrating, illustrating, and clarifying. One student used a film very persuasively in a speech on violence in football. A varsity football player, the speaker showed three minutes of punt returns using his own voice to explain the action. He showed how football players can disable an opponent who does not call for a safe catch. He said the coaches taught the players to hurt opponents with fists, face masks, and helmets. The brief film supported his topic on violence in football.

Slides can help the audience understand your information.

Videotape is easier to edit and simpler for the amateur to produce, but it should be used sparingly for support. Your class is about public speaking, not video editing and production. Both video and film have disadvantages. One is that, in inexperienced hands, the content and the aesthetics may be poor. A second is that both film and video presentations require a darkened room, which takes all the attention away from the speaker. Gestures, attire, and facial expressions are lost in the darkness. Film and video presentations also require equipment—which may or may not work—so the speaker has to be ready to deliver the speech in another mode in case of failure.

Videos are becoming increasingly popular with speakers. The equipment necessary to use videos includes a videotape and a VCR with a large monitor. The mechanics of effective use include the following:

1. Show your video in below normal light, but not in complete darkness.
2. Adjust the volume, contrast, and position before the presentation.
3. Center the monitor in the front of the room for optimal viewing (maximum viewing distance is twelve times the diagonal width of the monitor, or 19 feet for a 19-inch diagonally measured screen).
4. Practice with your equipment before your presentation.
5. Cue your videotape to where you wish it to begin. Be careful—some machines begin playing the tape when they are inserted, which could throw you off. Other machines begin rewinding if the pause button is depressed for more than a couple of seconds.

Try to make your videotaped presentation as natural as possible by treating it as an integral part of your speech. Avoid a big buildup on the one hand or making excuses for your video on the other. Also, be prepared to substitute your own material in case of mechanical failure. When machines fail, you will still be expected to succeed.

You may wish to consult your instructor before you decide to investigate the possibility of using film or videotape. Your speech will probably be relatively short, which will lessen the likelihood of being able to use such presentational aids. Generally, films or

Use a video to illustrate your idea.

videotapes provide examples of your main points. If your speech is only five to seven minutes long, for example, an appropriate length for an example may only be thirty seconds or less. Few films or videos can be shown in such a short period of time. In addition, equipment may not be available for you, or it may malfunction during your presentation. You should be able to present your speech even if the equipment becomes unavailable or malfunctions. A presentational aid is an aid and not a substitute for information. Finally, some instructors prefer that students do not take on the additional burdens associated with such presentational aids in their first speech class.

Slides

Slides are another valuable presentational aid. A rather tough-looking fellow who always wore a black leather jacket, jack boots, and lots of studs did an impressive speech using slides. A biker who was always surly toward his classmates, the speaker surprised them by giving a speech on motorcycle safety. His classmates thought this guy probably never wore a helmet, but that is what he encouraged in his talk. He showed six slides, each of a badly battered, vividly colored helmet. They were the helmets of friends who had survived serious accidents because they wore them. Another surprise was that this rough-and-tumble guy taught motorcycle safety to teenagers on his own time.

Slides are much easier to produce than video and film. As long as they do not become the speech—as long as they supplement, illustrate, and reinforce—they are an asset in a presentation. The disadvantages are the same as those cited for film and videotape when it comes to equipment and darkness. A burnt-out projector bulb or an upside-down slide can ruin an otherwise effective presentation.

Some suggestions for the effective use of slides follow:

1. Limit yourself to one basic idea per slide and keep the message or picture short and simple.
2. Arrange your information with more width than height. A slide is one-third wider than it is high.

3. Check for visibility of the screen and slides in the room where the audience will do the viewing.

4. Check your slides to see if they work in the projector—before you use it in class.

5. If possible, use a remote slide changer, so you do not have to stay by the machine.

6. Practice with your visual aids in the same place where your speech will be delivered. You can avoid the problem faced by the student who practiced at home only to find out that the only electrical outlet in the classroom was out of order.

Slides and film can add dramatic impact and involvement to your speech, but think twice before using them if you are inexperienced. Also, whenever you use mechanical devices in your presentation, you should have a backup plan in case your devices fail. The best public speakers are ready for anything—including a fast change of plans.

Audio

Audio aids are presentational aids that you can hear. Audio refers to what you hear. It can include both the projection of the natural voice with a microphone or the use of audiotape to play voice or music.

A microphone is rarely used in classroom speeches, but it is often used in speeches where the audience is larger than twenty-five, when the speech is delivered outside, or where the room is too large for unaided speaking.

Microphones are of two basic types. One type is attached to the lectern or podium. Another type can be carried with or without a cord so the speaker has freedom of movement. Both require that the speaker stay relatively close to the microphone itself to be heard.

If you have never used a microphone before, practice with one before you give your speech. One reason for rehearsal is that you are likely to be startled by the sound of your own voice. Just as your voice does not sound the same to you when you hear it recorded on tape, it will not sound like your own when it is amplified. Being startled by the sound of your own voice can be distracting when you are trying to concentrate on your speech.

Another reason to practice before delivering a speech is to learn the appropriate distance to stay from the microphone. Broadcasters call it "popping the mike" when a speaker stands so close that plosive sounds, such as words beginning with *k, p,* and *t,* blow too much air into the instrument. If you stay a distance of 12 inches away, you are unlikely to "pop" the microphone. On the other hand, you have to speak toward it because averting your head will cause your voice to fade or disappear.

Audio recorders are another form of audio equipment that is a useful presentational aid. In a speech about types of music, a few short excerpts can best illustrate what you mean in an informative speech differentiating among AOR (album-oriented radio), CHR (contemporary hits radio), and easy listening radio formats. One of the effective uses of audio occurred when a student secured the tape of a sheriff questioning a suspected drug pusher. The part of the tape used began at the point where the young pusher's story fell apart, and he started to implicate himself and others. The ninety-second tape was a dramatic illustration of what happens to drug pushers when they are caught. The confession was enough to make the audience members glad they were not suspects.

The mechanical aspects of using tape recorders in a public speech include the following:

1. Set the volume before the presentation so that all can hear.

2. Cue your tape so it will start exactly where you wish.

3. Have the machine turned on and warmed up before you speak.

4. Practice several times with the tape to ensure that you can use it smoothly.

You might want to have someone else take care of turning the machine off and on, but if you exercise this option, practice the speech and the use of the recorder with that person until you establish complete trust in each other.

Some practical suggestions concerning the recorder's use during your speech include the following:

1. Avoid saying anything while the tape is playing: a "voice-over" is inappropriate in this case.

2. Integrate the taped portion into your speech so that it becomes a natural extension of your talk.

3. Avoid any big buildup or excuses for the content of the tape or the quality of the recording.

If you observe these mechanical and delivery suggestions, you can make an audio recording an important supplement to your speech.

Overhead and Opaque Projectors

An **overhead projector** is a machine that shines light through an acetate (clear plastic) sheet. Any images or letters drawn on the acetate with magic marker or grease pencil will be projected and enlarged on a wall or movie screen.

The advantage of this device is that you can face the audience while you speak. The lights immediately over the screen should be dim, but otherwise the room can be bathed in normal light so the audience can see the speaker. The lettering or images can be prepared ahead of time (an excellent idea) or drawn spontaneously during the speech (less desirable).

For the cost of a poster, you can produce your own transparencies for an overhead projector. Use an enlarging copy machine to bring printed material up to a minimum of 3/16 of an inch letter height and then run the master and heat-sensitive film through a Thermofax machine to produce the transparency. These transparencies can be produced even more easily with a laser printer using 18 point type or a larger font. You can even incorporate line drawings or photocopied materials into the master.

Some suggestions for using the overhead projector include the following:

1. Express one idea on each transparency. Otherwise, the screen becomes too crowded with verbiage and too complex for easy understanding.

2. Compose letters at least 3/16 of an inch tall; these letters will be considerably larger when projected.

3. Place most of your message toward the top and center of the transparency. Information close to the bottom or sides of the transparency tends to get cut off of the screen.

4. Place your transparencies in hard paper frames and number them for ease of handling, or the sheets may not separate for you during your speech.

5. Be sure that you know how to place the transparencies on the projector correctly. A transparency that looks correct from your vantage point might be upside-down or backwards from the audience's viewpoint.

6. Practice using the overhead projector while you rehearse your speech until use of the transparencies becomes natural.

At first you may find that your projected light on the screen looks like the images in figures 11 and 12. In figure 11, the projector needs to be aligned horizontally until the keystone image becomes a rectangle; in figure 12, the projector needs to be aligned

Figure 11

Keystone effect, when projector is too far to the side.

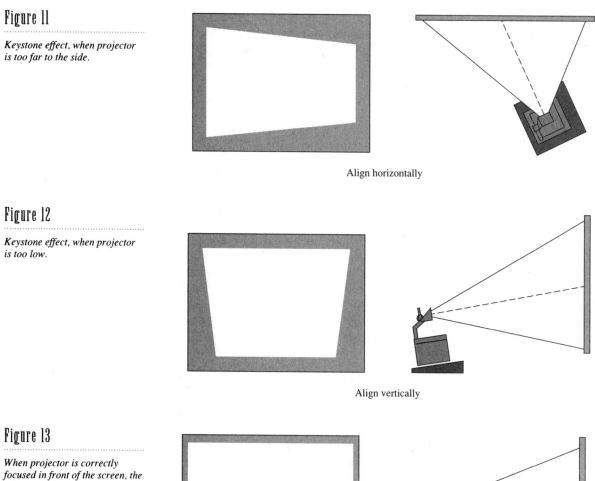

Align horizontally

Figure 12

Keystone effect, when projector is too low.

Align vertically

Figure 13

When projector is correctly focused in front of the screen, the alignment is correct.

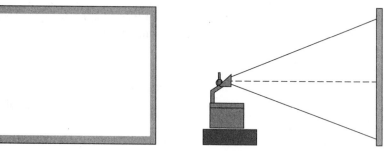

vertically. To completely avoid any keystone effect, the projector needs to be centered perpendicular to the screen, like the arrangement in figure 13. Another preventive measure for keystoning is to tilt the screen slightly to align it with the projector head.

A disadvantage of the overhead projector is that lights must be dimmed for better viewing. When changing materials, you must either turn on the lights or subject yourself to blinding light when the projector bay is opened.

Some helpful hints about delivery when using an overhead projector include the following:

1. You might have to talk a bit louder to compensate for the sound of the machine's fan. Older machines tend to be noisier than newer models.
2. Point with a pencil instead of your finger to eliminate any unwanted shadows.
3. Make sure you have your transparencies numbered on your working outline and on the transparency frames so that you use them in correct order during the speech.

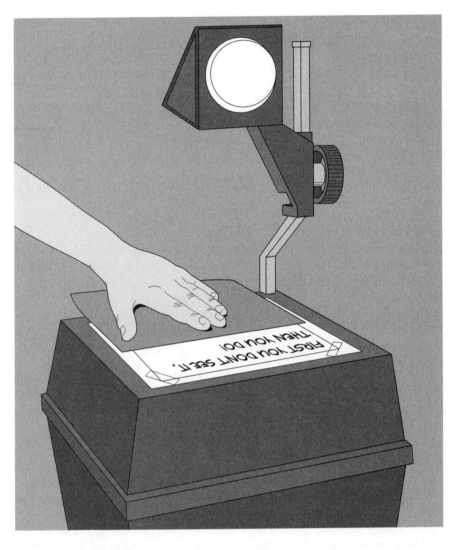

Figure 14

The reveal method of using a transparency.

Finally, you would be well advised to bring an extra bulb and more than one marker. Follow these suggestions and your use of the overhead projector can be an asset to your speech.

Two creative ways to use transparencies are the reveal method and the overlay method. The reveal method blocks out parts of the information on the transparency and is then revealed as the speaker proceeds (figure 14).

The overlay method allows you to use one transparency to make one point and a second transparency placed over the first to make another point. In figure 15, the speaker first shows a line drawing in one color and then places the second over the first to illustrate the different aspects of a van.

The **opaque projector** is an instrument that can project the image of small objects or the top surface of thick items, such as a magazine. Many of the suggestions for use of the overhead projector apply to the opaque projector as well. Older models of both have noisy fans requiring voice projection. They both use screens and lights that can result in the keystone effect. Finally, both require a practice session or two to ensure smooth and uninterrupted use. In addition, opaque projectors often generate considerable heat, which can melt the finish on some photographs.

Figure 15

The overlay method uses multiple transparencies to show layers or levels.

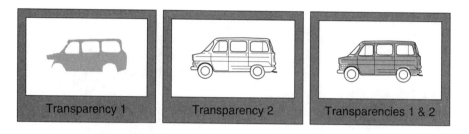

Transparency 1   Transparency 2   Transparencies 1 & 2

Display Persons and Things

Another type of presentational aid used in public speaking is displays—using living models, objects, handouts, and even yourself.

Living Models

W. C. Fields once warned about performing on the same stage with a small child or an animal: they tend to steal the show from the performer. Speakers should be aware of the same danger when they consider using persons or things as presentational aids: human "helpers" can catch the smell of grease paint and steal the show from you.

Charles Roberts, a communication professor, tells of a gentleman who gave a demonstration speech on body painting. When he completed his speech, few could remember his main points, but they certainly remembered the man in the demonstration, who stood there for ten minutes in his bikini briefs.

A living model is a person used in your speech to illustrate an important point. A woman explaining the fine points of ballet found it impossible to deliver her speech and illustrate the moves herself, so she asked another ballet artist to show the audience what she was talking about as she described the moves. A person speaking about pumping iron, playing an instrument, or practicing first aid or lifesaving might similarly find a living model useful in a public speech.

Some suggestions for the use of living models include the following:

1. Selecting a person whom you know to assist you in the speech usually works better than asking for a volunteer from an unsuspecting audience.
2. Except when the living model is demonstrating something, the person should sit down or otherwise move out of the audience's line of vision so the focus shifts to the speaker.
3. The model who performs should be introduced, since the individual's credibility will affect your own in the speech that you share.
4. Living models should be dressed appropriately for the topic, audience, and situation.

One student speech included a thirty-second display of a living model. The speaker was a Big Eight varsity football player. The class thought he was a pretty large specimen at 6 feet 2 inches and 220 pounds. The speech discussed how football was changing and that giants were being recruited into the game. At that point, in walked a first-year football player who was 6 feet 11 inches and over 300 pounds. He stood there for thirty seconds while he was introduced and then went back into the hall. The speaker had made his point with a living model.

Physical Objects

Another presentational aid is the use of physical objects in a public speech. An architecture student who is talking about house design might use miniature models large enough for the audience to see. An art student might show a few pieces of wood sculpture to

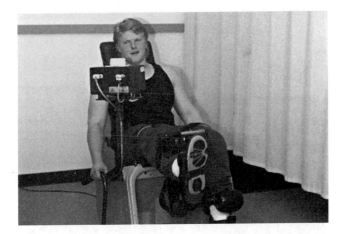

You can use yourself and other objects as a presentational aid.

show how wood can be hewn into marvelous shapes. A physics student might demonstrate some laws of gravity and momentum by showing an audience how a pendulum swings.

Some suggestions about the use of physical objects include the following:

1. Select an object that can be seen by everyone.
2. Avoid passing an object, since that is a distraction from yourself and your speech.
3. Make the object an integral and natural part of your speech through your own practiced familiarity with it.
4. Address the audience instead of talking at or to the object being discussed.
5. Do not use too many objects like all of the parts of a camera. Too many parts can be distracting, time-consuming, and can make you anxious.

When you consider using an object in your speech, be aware that the most common problems with physical objects is that they could be too small, too complicated, or too dangerous for classroom use. A student who tried to give a speech on contact lenses found, to his dismay, that no one past the second row could see what he was showing. A student who tried to show all the parts of a small engine became hopelessly confusing to her audience as she came to her fiftieth small part. Similarly students who come to class with fireworks, handguns, or even a bottle of liquor will find that they are either breaking a community or college ordinance or are so disturbing the audience that the speech is ineffective.

Handouts

Before using any handouts, inquire about your professor's attitude toward them. Some speech communication teachers have a very negative attitude about handouts because they see them as a constant distraction, not only during the speaker's presentation but also for the speakers who follow.

Handouts, if allowed, can be a useful supplement and can reinforce or show what the speaker means. Perhaps a person speaking about the danger signs of diabetes could depend on the audience to take notes, but a way to ensure that the audience has a record of the danger signs is to distribute them on a handout at the end of the speech. Maybe an audience could remember all of the radio stations, their call letters, and their positions on the FM band, but a more definite way is to distribute a chart for future reference.

The distribution of handouts creates problems that you can cleverly avoid. What you want to avoid is wasting your speaking time by passing out papers; having long rows of

Physical objects can help the audience understand your message.

people passing, dropping, and rattling papers; having audience members fight over too few copies; and producing the equivalent of "The Wave" as the papers ripple across the room. Some of the ways to avoid these problems include the following: (1) count out the handouts by row ahead of time, (2) enlist in advance the help of others so handouts can be distributed quickly, (3) have the audience pick up the handouts after class, and (4) make sure everyone has a handout.

Some suggestions for the effective use of handouts include the following:

1. Make your handouts simple so they do not have to be studied for understanding.
2. Type or print your handouts so they are readable.
3. Try to keep your handout to a single page so it is easy and quick to distribute.
4. Be certain that having your information in print is the most effective way to communicate that information to your audience.
5. Provide the handouts just before you are going to refer to them, if you hand them out during the speech. If you plan on distributing them after the speech, have them ready as people leave the room.

By following these suggestions, you can make sure that a handout is an effective means of communication.

Yourself

Whether you realize it or not, you are a presentational aid. They way you look, the way you dress, and the way you behave in front of the audience are part of your presentation. You are an important part of your message.

You do not have to dress up for every presentation unless that is an expectation in your class. Instead, dress in a manner appropriate to the topic and the audience. A person delivering a speech on how to interview for a job can reinforce the point by dressing the way a person should dress for an interview. A speaker demonstrating how to dissect a frog ought to wear lab clothes. A speaker talking about fashion should look like an authority on that subject.

A slovenly appearance is telling the audience how you feel about yourself and about the audience. People who give public speeches often dress in a way that shows respect for the audience. Consider carefully how you fare as a presentational aid in your own public speech.

As a final step in critically evaluating your own use of visual aids and their use by others, ask yourself the following questions:

Summary: A Checklist for Presentational Aids

1. Have I used presentational aids to supplement and reinforce important points in my speech? Presentational aids should not be used for their own sake; instead, they should always be used for clarity, illustration, or explanation.

2. Have I been careful not to let my presentational aids dominate my speech so much that they have become the speech? Do not be so infatuated with your living model, your charts and graphs, and your objects that they become your speech.

3. Have I prepared my presentational aids as much as possible in advance of the speech so I do not have to be absorbed in their use when I give my speech? Most presentational aids, especially the printed, taped, and projected ones should be ready before you give the speech.

4. Have I made my presentational aids big, loud, and central enough for everyone to see or hear? A presentational aid can detract from your speech if it becomes a deterrent to effective communication.

5. Have I displayed my presentational aids where the audience can see them? Most presentational aids cannot be simply set on a desk or lectern. You may need tape or tacks to display poster boards and other presentational aids. Also, do not block the audience's view of your presentational aids by standing in front of them.

6. Have I explained my presentational aid so the audience knows its message and its purpose? Presentational aids rarely explain themselves, so the speaker is expected to reveal their role in the speech.

7. Have I avoided passing my presentational aid? Passing handouts may be permissible, but objects and pictures will detract from your speech if distributed during the presentation.

8. Have I displayed my presentational aids only when I am discussing them? Presentational aids that are on display before they are mentioned or after they are needed may distract the audience. You do not want to compete with an interesting visual or an unusual object.

9. Have I practiced with my equipment, my living model, and my other presentational aids so that they are smoothly integrated into my speech?

10. During my speech, have I avoided talking to my presentational aid, and focused instead on the audience? Sometimes when speakers are nervous, they tend to look at their presentational aids rather than at their audience.

11. Have I spent a reasonable amount of time preparing my presentational aids? Too little preparation can result in chaos; too much can keep you from other important aspects of your public speech.

12. Have I spent enough time practicing with my presentational aids? If you spend too little time practicing with your presentational aids, you may be awkward in your presentation.

Armed with the information in this chapter, you are ready to use presentational aids in an intelligent and effective manner. You will find, as others have, that practice in using presentational aids will help you speak with confidence.

Vocabulary

audio aids Presentational aids that you can hear

chart A presentational aid that summarizes information, lists steps, or otherwise displays information difficult to convey orally

display boards Presentational aids such as chalk- or slickboards, posters, and flip charts

flip chart A presentational aid consisting of a large pad of paper, usually on a stand, that allows the speaker to flip the sheets over or tear them off as they are used

graphics Presentational aids including photographs; pie, line, and bar graphs; charts and tables; drawings; and maps

opaque projector An instrument that can project the image of small objects or the top surface of thick items

overhead projector A machine that shines light through an acetate (clear plastic) sheet, projecting an image onto a wall or movie screen

table A presentational aid that consists of columns of numbers

 **Applications**

Application Exercises

Proper Topics for Presentational Aids

1. Either individually or in a small group, compose a list of ten topics that require audio or visual presentational aids. For example, a speech on the topic of "Comparative Shopping for Certificates of Deposit" demands interest rate figures, time periods, and figures from various banking or lending institutions.

Proper Presentational Aids for Topics

2. After completing Application Exercise 1, you will have a list of ten topics. Examine the topics carefully and list for each the presentational aids that would be most appropriate for that topic. For example, on the topic of comparing certificates of deposit, you could list a chart showing local rates from five banks, a slide showing how the yields change depending on how often interest is compounded, and so on.

Application Assignment

The Presentational Aids Speech

In a five-minute speech, demonstrate how to do something by using presentational aids. Choose a topic (perhaps from the list you generated in Application Exercise 1) that invites the use of presentational aids.

Endnotes

1. Elena P. Zayas-Baya, "Instructional Media in the Total Language Picture," *International Journal of Instructional Media* 5 (1977–78): 145–50.
2. Joe Ayres, "Using Visual Aids to Reduce Speech Anxiety," *Communication Research Reports* 8 (June/December 1991): 73–79.
3. Bernadette M. Gadzella and Deborah A. Whitehead, "Effects of Auditory and Visual Modalities in Recall of Words," *Perceptual and Motor Skills* 40 (February 1975): 255–60.
4. Delores A. Bogard, "Visual Perception of Static and Dynamic Two-Dimensional Objects," *Perceptual and Motor Skills* 38 (April 1974): 395–98.

5. Bella M. De Paulo et al., "Decoding Discrepant Nonverbal Cues," *Journal of Personality and Social Psychology* 36 (March 1978): 313–23.
6. Some of the material and illustrations in this chapter on visual aids comes from an uncopyrighted classroom handout by K. Kealey entitled "Presentational Aids."
7. Madeline F. Green, "A Profile of the American College President," *Educational Record* (Spring 1988): 47.
8. Michael Osborn and Suzanne Osborn, *Public Speaking,* 3rd ed. (Boston: Houghton Mifflin Company, 1994), 250.
9. The authors thank N. Joseph Welling, Director of the Telecommunications Center at Ohio University, for the two graphic creations in figures 8 and 9 and for a quick course in computer-generated graphics.
10. Osborn and Osborn, 1994.

INFORMATIVE SPEAKING

QUESTION OUTLINE

I.   What are four purposes of informative speaking?

II. What are two rhetorical principles of informative speaking?

III. What are some principles of learning that can be applied to the informative speech?

IV. How can you organize your informative speech?

V.   What are four types of informative speeches?

VI. What are some ethical choices to make in informative speaking?

Unless one is a genius, it is best to aim at being intelligible.

Anthony Hope Hawkins

Introduction

Angelique Valdez is a single mother of three young children. A sophomore, she is older than many of the other students, and her day at school can best be described as hectic.

On this particular morning, she has an 8:00 class, which means she must be up at 6:00 A.M. to bathe, dress, and prepare breakfast for the kids. At 7:30 she is at the day-care center, where she has to tell the teacher that her youngest daughter will be picked up at 1:30 so she can keep an appointment with the doctor.

She gets to class just five minutes before the bell. She is lucky to be a little early because she has to ask the professor how long the term paper is supposed to be and whether or not it is supposed to be double-spaced.

On her way to the next class, she sees her friend Diane, another busy student-mother, and arranges to meet her for lunch at the Oasis, a gathering place for nontraditional students. At noon Diane asks her what she should do about her two-year-old, who cried much of the night. If it is an ear infection, she asks, does she have to go to the doctor or will an over-the-counter drug do the trick? Angelique recommends the free clinic and in turn asks Diane about where she can get information for her speech, which is due next week.

We will not continue to follow Angelique throughout her day because the point is already well made: Angelique, like the rest of us, asks for and gives information many times each day. The only difference between our everyday conversations and the informative speech, which we learn about in this chapter, is that the speech is longer, better researched, and given to more people. The similarities between the preceding conversations and the informative speech are more numerous: you tell people about things they want to know, need to know, or can use; you adapt your knowledge to increase their understanding; and you define, explain, and give examples that help them apply your knowledge to their situation.

How do you know what you know? How do you know how to play football, make a dress, drive a car, read a book, or write an essay? For many years, parents, teachers, coaches, employers, and friends have helped you increase your knowledge. In many cases, the vehicle for learning probably has been the informative speech. A physical education instructor may have taught you how to bowl, dance, and participate in team sports. Other teachers taught you how to read, write, and take examinations. Employers may have taught you how to serve a customer, type a letter, or sell a product.

After completing your formal education, you may find yourself conveying what you know to your children, employees, or fellow workers. The purpose of this chapter is to examine the primary means of communicating information to other people: the informative speech. You will discover the purposes of informative speaking, the rhetorical principles for communicating information, and the principles of learning that are especially important for communicating information to an audience. At the end of this chapter, you will find a checklist for the informative speech and assignments that apply what you learn in this chapter. Once you have completed them, you will know enough about informative speaking to increase your confidence as a public speaker.

Four Purposes of Informative Speaking

An *informative speech* can be defined as one that increases an audience's knowledge about a subject, one that helps the audience learn more about an issue or idea. The four purposes of informative speaking are to create a desire for information and to help the audience understand, remember, and apply that information.

Create a Desire for Information

The first purpose of informative speaking is to generate a desire for information. Audiences, like students, are not always receptive to new information. You have observed

Four Purposes of Informative Speaking

1. Create a desire for information
2. Help the audience understand
3. Help the audience remember
4. Invite the audience to apply information

Learn how to generate a desire for information in your audience.

teachers who were skilled at inspiring your interest in poetry, advanced algebra, chemistry, or physical education. You will have an opportunity to demonstrate whether you are skilled at communicating information to an audience of classmates. If you read this chapter carefully, you should become an effective informative speaker. The first step is to arouse the audience's interest in your topic.

To create a **desire for information** in your listeners, you must arouse their need for, or interest in, the information. Can you show how your information will improve their everyday lives? Can you demonstrate to audience members that they can gain the respect and admiration of their peers by knowing what you have to tell? Can you raise questions in the speech for which the audience will seek answers? One way you can learn to generate this hunger for information is to become a systematic observer of your own instructors. How do they arouse your interest? How do they get you to learn information, even in courses that you are required to take? You can adopt others' methods to improve your own ability to generate a desire for information.

How does a person create a desire for information in a speech? One student began like this:

My speech today is on the subject of hydroponics. [The class looked slightly mystified.] How many of you know what hydroponics is? [Two students out of twenty-two raised their hands.] I see that only a few of you know what hydroponics is. Our technology is ahead of our ability to absorb it. Educated people should know what it is. Today you will find out.

289

After this introduction, the audience members were convinced that most of them did not know the topic of the speech, and, as educated people, they began to feel they *ought* to know. The speaker had successfully aroused their interest for information.

Another student created a desire for information by posing questions to which the members of the audience would seek answers in the speech. She began, "Do you know what your chances are of getting skin cancer? Do you know when you are likely to get it? Do you know if anything can be done to cure it?" The questions aroused the audience's curiosity about the answers, which were given later in the speech. Other student speakers have asked: "Do you know how to save money on food?" "Can you repair your own stereo?" "Can you tell a poor used car from a good one?" A student who has carefully analyzed an audience can find ways to instill a desire for information that will make the audience want to hear the informative speech.

Help the Audience Understand

The second general purpose of informative speaking is to increase the ways in which the audience can respond to the world. The more we know, the greater our repertoire of responses. A poet can look at a boulevard full of trees and write about it in a way that conveys its beauty to others. A botanist can determine the species of the trees, whether their leaves are pinnate or palmate, and whether they are healthy, rare, or unusual. A chemist can note that the sulphur dioxide in the air is affecting the trees and know how long they can withstand the ravages of pollution. A knowledgeable person may be able to respond to the trees in all of these ways. Acquiring more information provides us with a wider variety of ways to respond to the world around us.

The informative speaker's goal is to increase the audience's understanding of the topic. Whether the audience is interested in the topic before you speak about it is less important than the interest you arouse during your speech.[1] The effective informative speaker analyzes an audience to find out how much it already knows about a subject, so she does not bore the informed or overwhelm the uninformed. The effective speaker narrows the topic so that she can discuss an appropriate amount of material in the allotted time. Finally, the effective speaker applies her own knowledge to the task to simplify and clarify the topic.

How can you encourage the audience to understand your topic? You can apply the following ideas to your own informative speeches:

1. Remember that audiences understand main ideas and generalizations better than specific facts and details.[2] Make certain that you state explicitly, or even repeat, the main ideas and generalizations in your own informative speech. Limit your speech to two to five main points.
2. Remember that audiences are more likely to understand simple words and concrete ideas than complex words and abstract ideas.[3] Review the content of your informative speech to determine if there are simpler, more concrete ways of stating the same ideas.
3. Remember that early remarks about how the speech will meet the audience's needs can create anticipation and increase the chances that the audience will listen and understand.[4] In your introduction, be very explicit about how the topic is related to the audience members. Unless your speech is related to their needs, they may choose not to listen.
4. Remember that audience members' overt participation increases their understanding. You can learn by listening and you can learn by doing, but you learn the most—and so will your audience—by both listening *and* doing.[5] Determine how to encourage your listeners' involvement in your speech by having them raise hands, stand up, answer a question, comment in a critique, or state an opinion.

Methods of Encouraging Retention

1. Tell audience members what you want them to remember.
2. Indicate to the audience which ideas are most important.
3. Repeat main ideas.
4. Pause to indicate important points.
5. Gesture to indicate important points.

If you will remember and apply these four suggestions in your informative speech, you will probably increase the audience's understanding of your topic.

Help the Audience Remember

The third general purpose of informative speaking is to help the audience remember important points in your speech. How can you get listeners to retain important information? One method is to reveal to the audience members specifically what you want them to learn from your speech. A speaker can tell you about World War I and let you guess what is important until you flounder and eventually forget everything you heard. However, the audience will retain information better if the speaker announces at the outset, "I want you to remember the main causes of World War I, the terms of the armistice, and the immediate results of those terms." Similarly a student speaker may say, "After this speech, I will ask several of you to tell me two of the many causes for blindness that I will discuss in my speech." Audiences tend to remember more about an informative speech if the speaker tells them specifically at the outset what they should remember from the speech.

A second method of encouraging an audience to remember (and one also closely tied to arousing audience interest) is to indicate clearly in the informative speech which ideas are main ones and which are **subordinate,** which statements are generalizations to be remembered and which are details to support the generalizations. Careful examination of students' textbooks and notebooks shows that in preparing for examinations students highlight important points with a highlighter pen. You can use the same method in preparing your informative speech. Highlight the important parts and convey their importance by telling the audience, "You will want to remember this point . . . ," "My second main point is . . . ," or "The critical thing to remember in doing this is. . . ."

Other methods that encourage an audience to retain important information include repeating an idea two or three times during the speech and pausing or using a physical gesture to indicate the importance of the information.[6] At least one experiment showed that speaking in a loud voice does not help the audience to remember your information. The same study also showed that if you repeat important matters either infrequently (only one time) or too often (four repetitions or more), your audience will be less likely to recall your information.[7] You will probably want to repeat your main points two or three times, but no more.

Most of the research on retention has been conducted with middle class European American audiences. If you are speaking to an audience that is more diverse, you may want to accept these conclusions cautiously. Some audiences appear to appreciate and learn more from several repetitions. Others may expect a great deal of vocal volume.

How can you ensure that your audience will retain the information that you provide them? In the classroom, listen to your instructors' and classmates' informative speeches and try to determine what these speakers do to inspire you to remember the information.

Invite the audience to apply the information you provide in the informative speech.

In other settings where you are likely to speak, similarly observe the successful informative speakers you encounter. Then see if you can apply the same techniques in your own informative speeches.

Invite the Audience to Apply Information

The fourth general purpose of informative speaking is to encourage the audience to use or apply the information during the speech or as soon afterward as possible. An effective speaker determines methods of encouraging the audience to use information quickly. Sometimes the speaker can even think of ways that the audience can use the information during the speech. One student, who was delivering an informative speech on the Japanese art of origami, for example, had everyone in class fold paper in the form of a bird with moveable wings. Another student speaker had each classmate taste synthetic foods made with chemicals. Still another student invited everyone to try one dance step to music. These speakers were encouraging the audience to apply the information from their speeches to ensure that they retained the information.

Why should the informative speaker encourage the audience to use the information as quickly as possible? One reason is that information applied immediately is remembered longer. Another reason is that something tried once under supervision is more likely to be tried again. An important purpose of informative speaking is to evoke behavioral change in the audience. It is easy to think of informative speeches as simply putting an idea into people's heads, of increasing the amount they know about a topic. However, there is no concrete indication that increased information has been imparted except by observing the audience's behavior. Therefore, the informative speaker seeks a **behavioral response** from the audience.

What behavioral response should the informative speaker seek? Many kinds are possible. You can provoke behavioral response by inviting the audience to talk to others about the topic, to actually apply the information (for example, trying a dance step), or to answer questions orally or in writing. If the audience cannot answer a question on the topic before your speech but can do so afterward, you have effected a behavioral response in your audience.

The four general purposes of informative speaking, then, are to create a desire for information in the audience, to increase audience understanding of the topic, to encourage the audience to remember the information, and to invite the audience to apply the information as quickly as possible. Next we will examine two rhetorical principles and five learning principles that relate to informative speaking.

Two **rhetorical principles** are related to any public speech, but they need special emphasis in informative speaking because they are so often overlooked. These two principles focus on the relationship between the speaker and the topic and the audience and the topic.

Two Rhetorical Principles of Informative Speaking

Relate the Speaker to the Topic

The first rhetorical principle states that you, the informative speaker, must show the audience the relationship between yourself and the topic. What are your qualifications for speaking on it? How did you happen to choose this topic? Why should the audience pay particular attention to you on this subject? Audiences tend to respond favorably to high-credibility sources because of their dynamism, expertise, trustworthiness, and common ground. This credibility is unrelated to understanding: an audience apparently learns as much from a low-credibility source as from a high-credibility source. However, audience members are more likely to apply what they comprehend if they respect the speaker as a source.

Consider this hypothetical example. Suppose a husky male athlete gives an informative speech to your class on macramé, an activity that helps him relax. Would the men in the class comprehend the information as well if a female art major were to deliver the same information? Research says that the comprehension would be the same: they would learn about macramé equally well from a high- or low-credibility source.[8] However, would the men in the class be more likely to actually try macramé themselves if the male athlete suggested it? The athlete and art major would be equally successful at teaching macramé, but the athlete would be more likely to secure a behavioral response from the men in the audience. Here is an example of how one student related the topic to himself:

> *You heard the teacher call my name: Gary Klineschmidt. This is a German name. My grandparents came from Germany and the small community in which I live is still predominantly German with a full allotment of Klopsteins, Kindermanns, Koenigs, and Klineschmidts. Many German customs are still practiced today in my home and in my hometown. Today I want to tell you about one German custom that has been adopted by many Americans and two German customs that are practiced primarily by people of German descent.*

The speaker established a relationship between himself and his topic by stating explicitly the origins of his authority to speak on German customs.

The point is that you must relate the topic to yourself, so that the audience will respect and apply the information you communicate. Are you giving a speech on street gangs? Let the audience know if you once belonged to one. Are you giving a speech on skydiving? Tell the audience how many times you have dropped. Are you giving a speech on hospital costs? Tell the audience the cost of your last hospital stay.

Relate the Topic to the Audience

A second rhetorical principle of informative speaking is to relate the topic to the audience early in the speech. This tactic is a wise one for ensuring audience interest and understanding. Again, you must be explicit. It may not be enough to assume that the audience members understand the connection between themselves and the topic. Instead, it is best to be direct: specifically tell listeners how the topic relates to them. Remember, too, that many topics may be very difficult to justify to an audience. An informative speech on taxes is lost on an audience that pays none. An informative speech on raising thoroughbred horses is lost on an audience that has very little money. Therefore, the informative speaker is encouraged to scrutinize audience analysis information to discover indications of audience interest in a topic.

Principles of Learning

1. Build on the known.
2. Use humor and wit.
3. Use presentational aids.
4. Organize your information.
5. Reward your listeners.

This example demonstrates the rhetorical principle of relating the topic to the audience:

> Over half of you indicated on the audience analysis form that you participate in team sports. We have two football players, two varsity tennis players, one gymnast, three hockey players, and four persons in men's and women's basketball. Because you already possess the necessary dexterity and coordination for this sport, you are going to find out today about curling.

This speaker carefully detailed the many ways in which the topic was appropriate for the particular audience. When you deliver your informative speech, remember to relate the topic to yourself and your audience.

Five Principles of Learning

Informative speaking is a type of teaching. Listening to informative speeches is a type of learning. If you expect an audience to understand your informative speech and apply the knowledge learned, you must treat the speech as a phenomenon in which teaching and learning occur. Because you, as an informative speaker, are inviting the audience to learn, you can apply these five **principles of learning** to your speech.

Build on the Known

One principle of learning is that people tend to build on what they already know, and they accept ideas that are consistent with what they already know. An informative speech, by definition, is an attempt to "add to" what the audience already knows. If the audience is to accept the new information, it must be related to information and ideas that they already hold.

Suppose you are going to inform your audience about how to kill cockroaches. If many people in your audience live in old apartments, homes, or dormitories, they may have a need for this information. You have to consider what the audience already knows. They probably know that they can turn on the lights quickly and step on the roaches as they flee for the cracks, but they probably do not know the best chemical ingredients to wipe out roaches, so, you tell them about chlorphyrifos. You do not have to tell them that chlorphyrifos is actually the simple name for O, O-diethyl O-3,5,6-trichloro-2-pyridyl

---

Building on the Known Helps an Audience Learn

Gasohol is unleaded gasoline with 10 percent alcohol added.

Modern day care institutionalizes the old practice of having aunts, uncles, and grandparents care for a child when the parents are at work.

Working with electrical wiring is like working with water pipes; you can shut off the supply; you should always have something to contain it; and it is very destructive if it gets loose.

A speaker can use humor to communicate a message.

phosphorothioate. Tell them what they do not know: that chlorphyrifos is an excellent cockroach killer that remains effective for weeks and is available in only three insecticides— Real-Kill Extra Strength in aerosol spray, Rid-A-Bug, and Real-Kill Liquid Extra in liquid spray.[9] In short, you can build on the audience's probable previous knowledge—manual means of killing insects and the general use of aerosols, sprays, liquids, powders, baits, and fumigant cakes—by adding to their knowledge the specific ingredient that they should look for and by giving them the names of the only three insecticides that contain the ingredient. You could elaborate by pointing out that Propoxur is also a good roach killer, but it has an offensive smell and stains. Build on what the audience knows.

Use Humor and Wit

A second principle of learning to observe in informative speaking is to use humor and wit. **Humor** is the ability to perceive and express that which is amusing or comical, while **wit** is the ability to perceive and express humorously the relationship or similarity between seemingly incongruous or disparate things. Any of us can find topics about which we know more than our classmates. They may be our religion, hobbies, travels, political position, eating habits, or major in college. However, the aim in informative speaking is to make the information palatable to the audience and to present it in such a way that the audience finds the information attractive. Notice that the principle does not dictate that you must be funny. The principle says "use humor and wit." Wisdom is the information that you know about the topic. Wit and humor are the clever ways you make the information attractive to the audience.

One premed student, for example, decided to give a speech on chiropractors, even though he was clearly prejudiced against them. He decided to handle his prejudice with wit rather than anger or bitterness. He entitled his speech "Chiropractors: About Quacks and Backs." Another student used wit in her speech about parenting. She was unmarried and well known by her classmates. The audience could hardly hide its shock when she stated in the introduction to her speech, "I did not think anything of parenting until I had my son," Her "son" turned out to be an uncooked hen's egg. She was taking a course on the family, in which she was required to care for her "son," the egg, for one week. When she went out on a date, she had to find a "baby-sitter" to care for the egg. She had to protect it from breaking as she went from class to class, take it to meals, and tuck it in at night. The introduction of her "son," the egg, added wit to the wisdom of her informative speech on parenting.

Often language choices help add vigor to your presentation. A student who was delivering a potentially boring speech on "TV and Your Child" enlivened his speech with witty language. He began this way:

> *Within six years almost everybody in this room will be married with a young one in the crib and another on the way. Do you want your youngster to start babbling with the words* sex, violence, *and* crime *or do you want him to say* Mommy, Daddy, *and* pepperoni, *like most normal kids?*

The speaker hit the audience with the unexpected. It was witty, and it made his speech more interesting to the audience.

Use Presentational Aids

A third principle of learning is to communicate your message in more than one way. Some people learn best by listening. Other people learn best by reading. Some people learn best when they do what the speaker is explaining. Still others learn best by seeing. Effective informative speakers recognize that different people learn best through different channels. Therefore, such speakers try to communicate their messages in a number of ways.

A student giving an informative speech about life insurance used a chart to explain to his audience the main differences among whole life, universal life, and term insurance. Because much of his explanation depended on the use of statistics to indicate costs, savings, and loan value, he and the audience found the chart necessary for the informative speech.

You, too, can find a variety of methods of communicating your message to an audience that learns in diverse ways. Some material in an informative speech is simply too detailed and complex to present orally. You might be able to get more of the message across by presenting these complex materials to the audience at the conclusion of your speech. Other complex data may be easier to understand through a graph, a picture, an object, a model, or a person. Consider using every means necessary to get your informative message to the audience.

Organize Your Information

A fourth principle of learning is to organize your information for easier understanding. Organization of a speech is more than outlining. Outlining is simply creating the skeleton of a speech. In an informative speech, consider other organizational possibilities. How often should you repeat your main point? Where is the best place to repeat it? Where do you try to create a proper setting for learning to take place? Where in the speech should you reveal what you expect the audience to remember? Do you place your most important information early or late in the speech?

Although there probably are no solid answers to these questions, research does hint at some answers:[10]

1. *How often should you repeat main points?* The evidence indicates that two repetitions have little impact and that positive effects fade with four or more, so the best answer seems to be that repeating main ideas three times works best.

2. *Where do you create a setting for learning?* The earlier you create an atmosphere for learning, the better. Make clear to audience members early in the speech exactly what you want them to learn from your presentation.

3. *Where should important information be placed?* The evidence indicates that audiences remember information placed early and late in the speech, so avoid placing your most important material in the middle of your presentation.

A final point about relating your information to your organization: learn how to indicate orally which parts of your speech are main points and which are subordinate or supporting. In writing, subordination is easy to indicate by levels of headings, but people listening to a speech cannot necessarily visualize the structure of your speech, which is why the effective informative speaker indicates early in the speech what is going to be covered. This forecast sets up the audience's expectations; they will know what you are going to talk about and for approximately how long. Similarly, as you proceed through your speech, you may wish to signal your progress by indicating where you are in your organization through transitions. Among organizational indicators are the following:

"My second point is . . ."

"Now that I have carefully explained the problem, I will turn to my solution."

"This story about what happened to me in the service will illustrate my point about obeying orders."

In each case, the speaker is signaling whether the next item is a main or subordinate point in the informative speech.

Reward Your Listeners

A fifth principle of learning is that audiences are more likely to respond to information if it is a **reward** for them. One of the audience's concerns about an informative speech is "What's in it for me?" The effective informative speaker answers this question not only in the introduction, where the need for the information is formally explained, but also throughout the speech. By the time a speaker is in the middle of the presentation, the audience may have forgotten much of the earlier motivating information presented, so the speaker continually needs to remind the audience how the information meets its needs.

A student speaker, talking to his audience about major first-aid methods, made this statement in his informative speech:

Imagine being home from school for the weekend, having a nice, relaxing visit with your family. Suddenly your father clutches his chest and crumples to the floor. What would you do to help him?

The student reminded the audience throughout the speech how each first-aid technique could be applied to victims with heart attacks, serious bleeding, and poisoning. The benefit for the audience was in knowing what to do in each case. Another student began her speech by saying the following:

Did you realize that, at this very moment, each and every one of you could be and probably is suffering from America's most widespread ailment? It is not V.D., cancer, or heart disease, but a problem that is commonly ignored by most Americans—the problem of being overweight.

As the speaker proceeded through her information on low-calorie and low-carbohydrate diets, she kept reassuring the audience members that they could overcome the problem in part by knowing which foods to eat and which to avoid. The audience benefited by learning the names of foods that could help or hinder health.

Explain to your audience how the information you provide is useful to them.

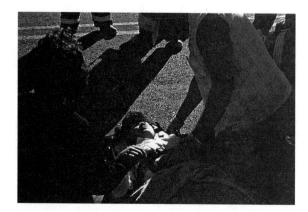

Rewards come in many forms. In the preceding examples, the reinforcement was in the form of readily usable information that the audience could apply. A speaker can use other, more psychological forms of reward. "Do you want to be among the ignorant who do not know what a 'value added tax' is?" The speaker who confidentially tells you about it is doing you a service because you will no longer be ignorant. A student from Chicago found that most of her classmates thought first of muggings when someone mentioned Chicago in conversation. She devoted her informative speech to the positive aspects of living in that city. The result was that the students in the audience had many more positive associations with Chicago, including the fact that one of their fellow students, who looked not at all like a mugger, was from Chicago, and *she* thought it was a good place to live.

Structure of the Speech to Inform

We have considered the purposes of informative speaking, the rhetorical principles of informative speaking, and principles of learning. We are now prepared to examine the structure of an informative speech. We will look at a sample introduction, body, and conclusion.

Introduction

The introduction for a speech to inform is particularly important because you must do the following:

1. Establish your credibility by relating yourself to the topic.
2. Establish relevance by relating the topic to the audience.
3. Gain the audience's attention and interest in the topic by stating it in such a way that you arouse audience curiosity.
4. Preview the message by stating the purpose and forecasting the development of the speech.

An overall objective in the introduction is to create an atmosphere for learning in which the audience will be stimulated to comprehend and remember the important parts of your speech. Figure 1 shows a student introduction to an informative speech.[11] The side notes indicate the functions being fulfilled.

Body

The body of an informative speech should consist of two to five main points supported by illustrations and examples. In the speech outline shown in figure 2, the speaker included only two main points in his outline, but each included a great deal of information. The outline presented suggests that the speech was somewhat dry and uninteresting. When the speaker delivered the speech, he added humorous stories and anecdotal material. He related himself to

Our Prison System

Speaker gains audience attention with questions

Did you know that only 2 percent of the people in prison today will stay there? Did you know that prisoners who are sentenced to life plus 100 years still get out on parole? And did you know that one of the main reasons that prisoners are released is that our prison system simply is not large enough to hold all of the people who are convicted of crimes? Leonard Larsen of the Scripps Howard News service addressed all of these questions in *The Athens Messenger* on the opinion page this week.

Speaker relates topic to audience

You should have an interest in our prison system because as taxpayers you pay for it, you walk the streets with people on parole, and you vote for the legislators who make our prison policies. Learning about the prisons will make you an informed citizen whose knowledge can help you make wise decisions.

Speaker relates self to topic

I may not appear to be an appropriate person to talk about prisons, but I am a sociology major with a special interest in criminology and our penal system. The course work on the subject has provided me with facts and figures, but my visit to our state penitentiary and the talks with the prisoners, the warden, and one of our state legislators has provided the passion on the subject that inspired me to tell you about it.

Speaker reveals purpose, organization, and development

I am going to inform you today about our state's prison system, its strengths and its weaknesses. Especially I am going to focus on our state's policy on parole, rehabilitation, and early release. On another day, in my persuasive speech, I will be taking a position on how I believe this state can solve some of the weaknesses in the system, but today you will learn the facts.

Figure 1

An example of an introduction to an informative speech.

Is Your Blood Killing You?

Introduction:
I. Your cholesterol level can be a silent killer.
   A. You need to know your cholesterol level because levels over 260 increase by four times your risk of heart disease.
   B. I have high cholesterol, which has inspired me to learn more about the subject.
   C. About one-fourth of all American adults are at risk because of elevated levels.

Body:
II. As a victim myself, I wanted to share with you information about reducing cholesterol levels.
   A. Often the foods you eat cause the problem.
      1. Red meat has the most cholesterol.
      2. Fruits and vegetables have none.
      3. Oat bran is said to reduce the level.
   B. Your own system may overproduce cholesterol, making dietary control difficult.
   C. Considerable exercise can reduce levels.
   D. Medicine may be the only answer for some.

Conclusion:
III. A laboratory blood test is the only certain way to detect cholesterol problems.

Figure 2

An example of an outline for an informative speech.

Patterns of Organization for the Informative Speech

1. Time-sequence
2. Spatial relations
3. Cause-effect
4. Topical sequence

the topic because of his own high cholesterol and related the topic to the audience members by asking them questions about their dietary practices and exercise programs. His speech could have been improved by generating more desire for information in the audience.

What kind of plan should you use to organize the body of an informative speech? Many topics can be organized in a variety of ways. You may be able to use all of the patterns discussed below for your particular topic. However, there is usually one best way to organize your speech. The information provided below on the four most common plans— the time-sequence, the spatial relations, the cause-effect, and the topical sequence patterns—should help you choose the best organizational pattern for your talk.

Time-Sequence

The **time-sequence pattern** is chronological; that is, it states in what order events occur over time. This pattern, obviously, is most appropriate for time-oriented topics. If your audience would best understand your message or learn about your topic from a chronological point of view—as it develops or occurs through time—you should choose this pattern. You can use this pattern in speeches that consider the past, present, and future of some idea, issue, plan, or project. It is most useful on such topics as the following:

How the Salvation Army began

The "Today" Show: A brief history

The naming of a stadium

The future for space exploration

How to grow a blue spruce to maturity from seed

The history of our university

The development of the Democratic Party

The formula for foolproof gravy

The building of the Hearst Castle

The development of drugs for treating AIDS

The past, present, and possible future of the U.S. Military

The role of bread in our diet

One person organized her comments about the history of the study of communication and gender by following this time-sequence pattern.

> **I.** The relationship between gender and communication has been of interest to researchers since the beginning of this century.
> **II.** Within the past two decades, the research has increased at a geometric rate.
> **III.** Perhaps of greater importance, issues of *how* gender and communication should be studied have arisen in recent times.[12]

The historical nature of the topic encouraged a time-sequence approach. At the same time, the organization allowed listeners to understand what had preceded their work and directions for future research.

In the example that follows, the speaker did not use a time-sequence for his overall speech, but he did make good use of this pattern of organization within his speech. Kazuo Inamori, Chair of the Kyocera Corporation, gave this speech entitled "U.S.-Japan Relations from the Viewpoint of Japanese Multinational Corporations," on February 3, 1993. We join Mr. Inamori at three different points in his talk.

> *Twice in our history, Japan had to carry out changes in its major policies with respect to foreign affairs.*
>
> *The first of these was 120 years ago at the time of our Meiji Restoration. The second was at the conclusion of World War II. Both occasions called for drastic changes in our government policies. Now Japan is carrying out a fundamental reform and liberalization of its domestic market. It will be the third such historical change.*[13]

Later in the speech, he added,

> *Traditionally, the majority of Japanese corporate managers have been firmly convinced that the best course of action is to manufacture quality products at low cost and export them. They, therefore, deeply believe that "free trade" must be advocated.*
>
> *However, until about fifteen years ago, the Japanese government was laying down various regulations restricting the activities of foreign corporations within Japan. These restrictions on "free trade" helped the growth of domestic industries. Japanese companies grew very strong thanks in part to these protective regulations. Now that Japanese industries have grown to be globally competitive, we are removing our protective regulations, and demanding that other countries do the same.*[14]

Toward the end of his speech, he stated,

> *Our company, Kyocera, began its first manufacturing activities in the United States over twenty-two years ago. We were a pioneer among Japanese companies. Today, we are joined by Elco, AVX, McKenzie and other subsidiaries. Under Kyocera International Inc., we have twelve plants, and over 5,500 American employees.*
>
> *Let us take a few minutes to talk about Elco. We acquired Elco three and a half years ago, when its previous owner decided to offer it for sale to the highest bidder. We decided to make our offer, because we saw a win-win opportunity both for Elco and Kyocera. As a result, Kyocera gained Elco's loyal employees, and Elco Huntingdon gained the opportunity to regain its global strength.*
>
> *Since the acquisition, Kyocera has invested almost $6 million in Huntingdon and has developed new products, such as 50 mil center-line Torson connectors and memory card connectors which are being made in Huntingdon and exported all over the world . . . to Japan, to Southeast Asia, and to Europe.*[15]

Although Inamori did not stick to an overall organizational plan of time-sequence, he made good use of it within the body of his speech. In the first instance, he talked about changes in Japan's major policies with respect to foreign affairs from a past, present, and future perspective. In the second example, he compared traditional and current thinking about trade regulations. Finally, he used an historical perspective to describe the development of his company.

You should be wary of presenting a time-sequence speech that is nothing more than a demonstration of how to do something. For example, if you gave a speech on the steps in making bread, you could simply demonstrate the process without truly informing your audience. You would be better advised to place the demonstration within a context of information. You might discuss, for example, how bread was discovered or created, the different types of breads that exist today, the grains from which it can be made, the statistics about the number of people who eat bread today as opposed to those in the past, the number of loaves that are commercially produced, or facts about bread's nutritional value.

Spatial Relations

The **spatial relations pattern** indicates how things are related in space, position, and visual orientation. When should you use a spatial relations pattern? This approach is appropriate if it is important for your audience to understand your material in a visual or spatial way. You will want to exercise caution that you do not simply provide a visual illustration to your audience, however, without a sufficient informative context. If you talk about landscaping, for example, you may want to talk about the origin of particular plants, the use of plants for different aesthetic and practical purposes, and how the plants might affect each other's growth or development. If you simply visualize a particular garden or yard, you are not providing enough information. Some examples of speeches that would best be organized using the spatial relations pattern follow.

How to Arrange Furniture on a Stage Set

Where to Place Plants When Landscaping

Designing a Home

Planning a Flower Garden

How Electricity Goes from the Power Plant to Your Home

An Explanation of an Audio Board

How to Design a Lighting Board

How to Follow a Road Map

Arranging Your Bedroom for Study and Sleep

How to Best Set Up Your Speakers

The following is a more detailed example of the spatial relations pattern describing the parts of the human heart.

The Human Heart: Form and Function

Immediate purpose: After listening to my speech, the audience will be able to recognize the form and function of the human heart.

Introduction

I. The human heart is the part of the body that fails or falters in more than a million people per year.
II. Learning about how your heart is structured and how it functions can help you keep it healthy.

Body

III. As shown on the visual aid, the heart consists of four chambers, the right and left atrium and the left and right ventricle.
IV. The atria and the ventricles have different functions.
   A. The right atrium and left atrium are thin-walled receiving chambers for blood.
   B. The right and left ventricles are thick-walled pumping chambers that pump eighteen million gallons of blood in seventy years.

Conclusion

V. The heart's structure and functions are simple, but heart failure ends life.
VI. Name the parts and the functions of the heart as a first step in guarding your own health.

Cause-Effect

With the **cause-effect pattern,** the speaker explains the cause or causes and the consequences, results, or effects. The speech may also be effect-cause, or even effect-effect, but cause-effect is the most common construction. When should you choose this pattern? When your audience needs to understand the relationship between phenomena, the connection between events, or the tie between occurrences, this is your best choice. Some examples of speeches best-suited to the cause-effect pattern follow.

How Do Flu Shots Help to Eliminate Influenza?

How Do Chemicals Prevent Weeds?

Does Cohabitation Inhibit Marriage?

What Causes a Coma?

Why Do Leaves Fall from the Trees in Autumn?

What Are the Effects of Sexual Harassment Policies?

How Does an Engine Make a Car Move?

How Does Aid to Dependent Children Contribute to Social Problems?

How Do Hurricanes Cause Damage?

Why Are College Students not Gaining Lucrative Jobs?

What Causes a Wind Shear?

A speech on inflation that uses the cause-effect pattern might review causes of inflation, such as low productivity and high waves, and review effects of inflation, such as high unemployment and high interest. The cause-effect pattern is often used in informative speeches that seek to explain an issue, but does not necessarily reveal what to do about a problem; instead it allows for full explanation of an issue. An example of the cause-effect pattern follows.

Purpose: To inform my audience of the causes for the new student activism on campus.

   I. Student activism has increased in the last five years.

  II. One cause of the new student activism is that students face economic uncertainty after they graduate from college.

 III. Another reason that students are more vocal is that college students have not had a strong voice in the decisions made by university administrators since the Vietnam era.

 IV. Finally, the students may have romantic ideas or idealistic values since many of their parents were involved in student activism twenty to thirty years ago.

Topical Sequence Pattern

The **topical sequence pattern** addresses the advantages, disadvantages, qualities, and types of persons, places, or things. The topical sequence pattern can be used to explain to audience members why you want them to adopt a certain point of view.

When might you use this pattern? When you have a small number of basic points or a few logical, interrelated sub-divisions of your material to present, this approach will work best. It is appropriate when you have three to five points to make: three reasons why people should buy used cars, four of the main benefits of studying speech, or five characteristics of a good football player. This pattern of organization is among the most versatile.

Dr. June E. Osborn, who was Chair of the United States National Commission on AIDS, served as the keynote speaker at the 104th session of the Iowa Academy of Science in Cedar Falls, Iowa, on April 24, 1992. Part of her speech was organized using the topical sequence pattern. She discussed, in part, the facts about AIDS. She made four main points:

   I. The human immunodeficiency virus is a necessary—and sometimes a sufficient—condition to cause AIDS.

  II. The virus is transmitted through blood, sex, or birth to an infected mother.

 III. People know more about the virus and its pathogenesis than about any other infectious agent of people.

 IV. AIDS will not be the last novel microorganism to beset humankind.[16]

In a speech informing audience members about tarantulas, a portion of the topical sequence outline would look like the following.

I. The name *tarantula* has an interesting history.
  A. The word *tarantula* is derived from the name of a small town in Italy.
    1. Taranto was a town in Italy where the people experienced a large number of spider bites.
    2. The people of Taranto were bitten so frequently they developed a dance to sweat the spider poison out of their blood.
  B. The name *tarantula* was applied originally to the European wolf spider, the one encountered in Taranto.
  C. The name was transferred to the tropical spider, which is now known as the tarantula.
II. The tarantula is characterized by five unusual characteristics.
  A. One unusual feature of the tarantula is its size.
    1. Tropical tarantulas are as large as three inches in body length and ten inches in leg span.
    2. Species in the United States range from one to three inches in body length and up to five inches in leg span.
  B. A second unusual feature of the tarantula is that it is nocturnal; that is, it hunts at night.
  C. A third interesting feature of the tarantula is that it can see only two inches and relies on leg hairs to sense the presence of other things.
  D. A fourth characteristic of the tranantula is that the species is cannibalistic.
  E. A fifth characteristic of the tarantula is that it moults.
    1. Moulting decreases with age.
    2. Moulting can be accompanied by regeneration of lost parts, such as legs.[17]

The outline could continue to develop main points on why tarantulas make interesting and economical pets and on the myths about their poison. However, the portion of the outline shown here illustrates the main advantage of the topical sequence outline—it can be used to organize diverse ideas into a commonsense sequence that appeals to an audience.

Conclusion

The conclusion of an informative speech should restate the main points of the speech, give the audience some incentive for understanding and remembering the content of the speech, and if possible reveal how the audience can apply or extend the newly learned information. Figure 3 demonstrates how all three—restatement, incentive, and application—can be included in the conclusion of an informative speech. In addition, you should determine a way, through words or action, to signal that you are approaching the end of your speech.

An informative speech typically includes an introduction, a body, and a conclusion. The introduction establishes your credibility, relates the topic to the audience, gains an audience's attention and interest, forecasts the content of the speech, and states specifically what the audience should learn from the speech. The body of the informative speech communicates from two to five main points, with such supporting materials as illustrations, examples, and presentational aids. The organizational patterns most often used in the informative speech are the time-sequence, the spatial relations, the cause-effect, and the topical sequence patterns. The conclusion restates the main points, provides an incentive for retention, and suggests ways to extend or improve the base of knowledge even further.

Next we will turn to some specific types of informative speeches.

	After seeing the graphs and charts on investments, you know as
Words signal end	much about investments as I do. You know that, when the
	economy goes wild with inflation, the dollar loses its value and
	precious metals gain in value. You know that, when the stock
Restatement	market goes up and up, the value of bonds tends to go down.
	And, finally, you know that all investments are a gamble because
	they change with the economic winds.
Words signal end	My last advice to you, now that you know something about
	investments, is that you protect them by purchasing a variety of
	investments to balance the gains and losses of economic times.
Application	Finally, I would encourage you to add to your knowledge of
	investments by taking courses, participating in seminars, and
	learning by investing. You listened well today, and you learned
	some information that you did not know before you heard my
Incentive for	talk. I think you will find—as I have—that knowledge is a
remembering	necessary prerequisite for the wise investor.

Figure 3

An example of a conclusion for an informative speech.

Types of Informative Speeches

The category of informative speeches includes a wide variety of speeches. In this section, we will explain four of them: the speech of definition, the speech of description, the speech of explanation, and the speech of demonstration. As you will observe, these speeches all fall under the general heading of informative speeches, but each has unique characteristics.

Speech of Definition

The **speech of definition** sounds fairly simple and straightforward. You may even be wondering how an entire speech can be based on definition. After all, defining a word is simply the process of supplying a few other words that explain what the word means. However, if you have reflected on the number of "communication breakdowns" you have had because of differences in definition, you know that defining words and concepts is far more complex than it appears. Supplying definitions for terms may in fact be the basis of all other types of informative speeches, and definition may be the most important of the lines of argument used by speakers.

A number of methods can be used to clarify terms for the audience. You can define a term that is unfamiliar to the audience by using comparisons to show how it is similar to something the audience is already familiar with, or contrasts to show how it is different. Synonyms and antonyms—words that have either the same or opposite meaning of the term you wish to define—are also helpful in communicating the meaning of a word to the audience. Explaining a word's etymology, or origin, is another way to clarify its meaning. You could also supply the audience with an operational definition, or an explanation of how something works.

A number of speech topics lend themselves to the speech of definition. Listed here are some titles of successful speeches of definition:

What Is "Spouse Abuse"?	What Is Bouillabaisse?
What Does "Prolife" Mean?	Defining "Illegal Drugs"
What Are Chemical Weapons?	What Is the Fat in Your Diet?
Understanding the "Greenhouse Effect"	Defining "Cognitive Therapy"
What Is an Antilock Brake System?	What Is "Touring Suspension"?
Defining Recession	Dial-a-Porn: The Limits of Privacy
What Is Postmodernism?	What Does "Prochoice" Mean?
What Is an *Oxymoron?*	

These titles should help you think of other topics appropriate for the speech of definition. Following is a speech of definition without a formal introduction or conclusion. The student was instructed to deliver the body of a speech of definition using at least three means of defining.

The Turkey[18]
Lynette Crawford

Denotation

Has anyone ever called you a "Turkey"? Well, a careful examination of this word indicates that you might have a right to be confused. Most people just think of the turkey as a large bird that we eat on holidays, especially Christmas and Thanksgiving. But the turkey is more complex than that.

Connotation

On one hand the turkey is seen as an ugly bird. Its waddled neck has given the name "turkey neck" to people whose necks are wrinkled. And while condors and vultures are not exactly beautiful, why is the turkey blesssed with that red worm that hangs next to its beak? I guess no one would like to look like a turkey.

Definition from experience

On the other hand, one of America's most brilliant inventors and diplomats thought highly of the turkey. Said Benjamin Franklin in a June 26, 1784, letter: "I wish the bald eagle had not been chosen as the representative of our country. He is a bird of bad moral character, and like those among men who live by sharpening and robbing, he is generally poor and often lousy. The turkey is a much more respectable bird and withal a true original native of America." Very positive testimony from an American genius.

Contrast

But the turkey has a reputation for stupidity. In a thunderstorm, they say, turkeys will sometimes smother themselves in a panic by smashing themselves in a corner. Outside, they have been known to drown while looking up in a rainstorm with their mouths open. Admittedly, their propensity for panic and suicide do not make them sound intelligent.

Comparison

Hunters, however, will tell you a different story. They say the turkey is a wily fowl in the woods. Difficult to call, tough to stalk, and impossible to fool, the wild turkey is anything but dumb. Hunters respect the turkey.

How can we reconcile the apparent discrepancy regarding the turkey? Well, Benjamin Franklin and the hunters are thinking of the wild turkey, that native of the American forest. The dumb and ugly turkey is the domestic turkey raised on a farm for human consumption. So next time someone calls you a turkey, you had better inquire whether they mean the wild variety or the tame one. Then you will know whether you have received a compliment or an insult.

Speech of Description

The **speech of description** is an informative speech in which you describe a person, a place, an object, or an experience by telling about its size, weight, color, texture, smell, and/or your feelings about it. The speech of description relies on your abilities to use precise, accurate, specific, and concrete language; to demonstrate a diverse vocabulary; to use words that have appropriate connotative and denotative meanings; and to offer necessary definitions.

A variety of topics lend themselves to the speech of description. Listed here are some titles of speeches that seem to work particularly well for this type of informative speech:

Portrait of a Los Angeles Bag Lady

How Hormones Affect Human Behavior

What Is a Crack House?

The World's Fastest Cars

Cincinnati: The City's Past

Life in a Street Gang

Airport Security: What's Next?

Trials of the Single Parent

Working in a Crisis Center

Understanding Sculpture

The Smell of Perfume

What to Look for in a Computer

Why Live in a Desert?

Evaluating a Diamond

Training for the Big Fight

This list of topics should be suggestive, but it is certainly not exhaustive of all of the possible kinds of topics that are appropriate for the speech of description.

The speaker who gave the following speech describes a person, a place, an object, or an experience using specific, concrete language, a diverse vocabulary, connotative and denotative meanings, comparisons, and a familiar item described in an unfamiliar way. The student who delivered the speech told about his hometown of Phoenix, Arizona, describing the transition from daytime desert heat to nighttime desert chill. This application assignment is a brief demonstration of the student's powers of description and, therefore, has no formal introduction or conclusion. The marginal notes indicate the means he used in his description.

Transition[19]

Mark Dupont

The heat cannot be escaped. As the sun beats mercilessly on the endless lines of automobiles, waves of shimmering heat drift from the blistering pavement, creating an atmosphere of an oven and making the minutes drag into eternity. The wide avenues only increase the sense of oppression and crowding as lane after lane clogs with rumbling cars and trucks. Drivers who have escaped the heat of the sun in their air-conditioned cars fall prey to the heat of frustration as they do battle with stoplights and autos which have expired in the August sun. Valiant pedestrians wade through the heat, pausing only to wipe from their foreheads the sweat that stings their eyes and blurs their vision. It is the afternoon rush hour at its peak, Phoenix, Arizona, at its fiercest. The crawl of automobiles seems without end as thousands of people seek out their homes in the sweltering desert city.

Comparison with oven

Comparison with war
Comparison with death
Unfamiliar description

Gradually, almost imperceptibly, the river of traffic begins its descent past the 100-degree mark; the streets become quieter and more spacious. The mountains enveloping the city begin to glow as their grays and browns awaken into brilliant reds and oranges. The haze which has blanketed the valley throughout the day begins to clear. The lines of buildings become sharper, their colors newer and brighter. The shadows of peaceful palm trees lengthen, inviting the city to rest. The fiery reds and oranges of the mountains give way to serene blues and purples. The water of hundreds of backyard swimming pools, which have been turbulent with the afternoon frolicking of overheated children and adults alike, calms and mirrors the pink and lavender dusk sky. The fading sunlight yields to the lights of homes and streets as the Valley of the Sun becomes a lake of twinkling lanterns reflecting the sea of stars above. The inferno is gone, forgotten. The rising swell of crickets and cicadas lulls the desert inhabitants into relaxation and contentment. The desert floor gives up its heat, cooling the feet of those who walk on it. The heat of anger and hatred for the valley dissipates, and in the hearts of the people who have braved another summer day in Arizona, there is only the warmth of love for their desert home.

Comparison with river

Comparison with sky and sea and hell

Speech of Explanation

The **speech of explanation** is an informative speech in which you tell how something works, why something occurred, or how something should be evaluated. You may explain a social, political, or economic issue; you may describe a historical event; you may discuss a variety of theories, principles, or laws; or you may offer a critical appraisal of art, literature, music, drama, film, or speeches. A wide collection of topics may be included in this category. Some possible speech titles for the speech of explanation follow:

How to Buy a Good Used Car   What Investments Are Best?
Understanding Electrical Repair   Why Advertising Works
How to Earn Money by Sewing   Yasser Arafat and the PLO

Why Drugs Are Dangerous
Why Art Is Mysterious
Understanding the National Debt
How to Write Poetry
Background on the Battle in Northern
    Ireland

Hispanics and the Public Schools
Why the Pentagon Needs Less
Where to Find Inexpensive Food
Why the World Fears Chemical Warfare

In the speech of explanation "A Sweet Killing," the student speaker explains diabetes and reveals what it is, how it affects a person, and what one can do about it.

A Sweet Killing[20]
Laura Kaval

Topic introduced

Everyone with a brother or sister is an expert on sibling warfare. My little brother and I are no different. We have our share of fights. One of us always ended up crying—usually him. My mother prayed that we would both outgrow it, but my brother and I are still fighting. Only now what we are fighting is my brother's disease—juvenile diabetes.

Facts and figures

According to the American Diabetic Association, another diabetic is diagnosed every sixty seconds.[1] Diabetes with all of its complications is regarded as the third leading cause of death in the United States. It claims over 300,000 lives annually. Diabetes can strike at any age: my brother is sixteen. Although incurable, diabetes can be controlled with early diagnosis.[2] Diabetes is a major health problem, but you can protect yourself with some precautionary measures such as regular visits to your physician.

Definition

Vocabulary

Diabetes is an inability of the body to turn food into glucose, a simple sugar solution, which is responsible for producing energy. The hormone insulin is what makes this process possible. Insulin is produced in the pancreas. When the pancreas fails to produce the proper amount of insulin, the body is unable to process the food. The unprocessed sugar-energy is then released from the body through urination, for it can't be used.[3] Donnell Elizweter of the University of Minnesota and president of the American Diabetic Association states: "Early diagnosis and proper control under the supervision of a qualified medical team generally means a diabetic will be able to live an active and productive life. The trouble is that two out of five diabetics either don't know they have it or choose to ignore it and don't receive proper medical attention."[4]

Testimonial evidence

One type defined

Symptoms listed

There are two different types of diabetes. If a person has juvenile diabetes, as my brother has, where the body creates no insulin supply, there are seven warning signs or symptoms. They include: (1) constant urination; (2) abnormal thirst; (3) unusual hunger; (4) rapid weight loss; (5) weakness/fatigue; (6) nausea/vomiting; and (7) craving for sweets. Juvenile diabetes is treated with direct insulin shots, a planned diet, proper exercise, and regular medical examinations.[5]

Second type defined

The second type of diabetes is maturity-onset diabetes. This is where the pancreas produces insulin, but (a) doesn't create enough insulin or (b) the body doesn't use what is made properly. The warning signals are: (1) slow to heal skin; (2) cramps in the legs and feet; (3) blurred vision; (4) genital rash; (5) men's impotence; (6) drowsiness; and (7) excessive weight. Maturity-onset is treated by proper diet, exercise, and occasionally, by oral medication. Many diabetics never have any warning signs or symptoms and are diagnosed during an annual medical examination.[6]

Fact

First test explained

There are several different kinds of tests that you can perform in your own home to help you monitor yours and your family's blood sugar. The first is a urine test. This test is performed by placing two drops of urine in ten drops of water and one Clentest tablet into a container and then shake. By matching the color of the solution to the colors on the side of the package, the amount of blood sugar can be determined. The normal reading is 120. There are also other test tapes, which just need to be dipped in a urine sample and then read.

Second test explained

The second test is a blood test, which is taken by placing a small drop of blood on the end of a test tape. The reading can be taken after the tape dries.[7] These tests are easy and safe and only take a minimal amount of time. These tests are rather inexpensive and are available at most drug stores. It is a small price when it comes to your family's well-being.

These steps to monitor diabetes should be taken by every family to protect their loved ones. If these early detection measures aren't taken, someone you love could become another statistic before you know it. Half of juvenile diabetics face the possibility of death due to kidney failure. Diabetics are two to three times more likely to develop hardening of the arteries, stroke, and heart attack than are non-diabetics; and diabetics are fifty times as likely to develop blood vessel problems.[8]

Facts and figures

Actress Mary Tyler Moore, comedian Dan Rowan, baseball player Jackie Robinson, and inventor Thomas Edison were diagnosed as diabetic[9]—and so was my little brother. But because we watch his diet, regulate his insulin, make sure he gets enough exercise and sees his doctor regularly, we are winning our fight. I encourage and strongly urge you to become aware of the warning signs of diabetes and to purchase and use the urine or blood tests regularly to monitor your family's blood sugar. It is also important that your family see a doctor regularly because some symptoms of diabetes can only be detected through a medical examination.

Names of famous diabetics

Precautions cited

Diabetes causes too many deaths a year and robs too many people of the sight and the touch of their loved ones for you not to take these simple early detection measures. If more people took these precautions, we might not only win the fight but the battle too.

Conclusion

While this speech is an excellent example of the speech of explanation, it is not a perfect speech. The speaker was encouraged to preview her message in the introduction by stating the purpose of her speech and by forecasting the development of her speech. She could have also related the topic to the audience more clearly. The speaker did not forewarn her audience of the end of the speech, either. Finally, she should have reminded the audience of her main points in the conclusion, which she failed to do.

Speech of Demonstration

The next kind of informative speech, the **speech of demonstration,** is an informative speech in which you show the audience an object, a person, or a place; in which you show the audience how something works; in which you show the audience how to do something; or in which you show the audience why something occurs. In other words, the speech of demonstration may be similar to the speech of explanation or the speech of description, but the focus in the speech of demonstration is on the visualization of your topic. For instance, one of the suggested topics for the speech of description provided here is a speech about Washington, DC. If you were to provide overheads with maps of the city, posters with depictions of major attractions, and photographs of points of interest, the speech would be one of demonstration. Similarly a speech on horror movies, as suggested, may be a speech of explanation. If, however, you add short excerpts from various movies illustrating the four reasons people pay to be frightened, the speech becomes one of demonstration. The key to a speech of demonstration is that you are actually showing the audience something about your topic.

As you consider topics that are appropriate for the speech of demonstration, do not simply recall a speech of explanation or description and add a few pictures, a poster, or an overhead to it and believe that you have an appropriate speech of demonstration. As you attempt to decide on a topic, you should consider those ideas, concepts, or processes that are too complex to be understood through words alone. Similarly consider the wide variety of items and materials that can be used to demonstrate your topic. You may wish to learn more about presentational aids, such as the chalkboard, posters, movies, slides, opaque and overhead projections, living models and physical objects, handouts, and you (as a visual aid). Which items will be most useful for your topic? Do not rely on those aids that are the simplest to construct or the most obvious; instead, use those items that best illustrate your topic. The following list has some titles of speeches that were highly effective speeches of demonstration:

The Latest in Fall Fashions	Selecting Shoes for Serious Walking
How to Fillet a Fish	Learning the Martial Arts
Using Mnemonic Devices to Aid Memory	Comparative Architecture: New Theatres and Old
Trimming the Thighs with Exercise	
Making Electricity	How to Care for Your Compact Discs
Building Big Biceps	Making Vietnamese Food
Uses for Computer Graphics	Where to Visit in Washington, DC
Comparing Luxury Cars	The Best Ads for the Year

Speeches of demonstration are generally quite fun for an audience, and are often engaging. However, just like other informative speeches, they need a sufficient body of information to fill them out and to add interest to them. You will need to rely on your library research skills and your interviewing skills to provide enough information for a speech of demonstration. You do not want to rely simply on your own experience.

Following is a speech of demonstration. Notice in the speech that the speaker has to spend less time and effort describing the origins of her credibility because she shows the audience her credibility throughout the speech. The photos are provided to help you visualize what Donna was doing as the speech progressed.

Back Walkovers in Gymnastics[21]
Donna Griffith

How many of you have heard of Nadia Comaneci? How many of you have heard of Kurt Thomas? How many of you have seen gymnastics on television? How many of you have been to a gymnastics meet or exhibition? What you see in elite-level gymnastics are usually very different moves such as double-back somersaults or back-layout somersaults on the balance beam, among other things. Well, it takes a gymnast a long time to learn moves such as those. A gymnast has to learn strength, flexibility, coordination, and courage before she could even attempt a move such as a back-layout on the balance beam. I would like to show you some of the work that goes into learning gymnastics. It looks easy, but even the simplest skills require a lot of work. For example, I will use a back walkover, which is a basic skill, and show you how it is learned. I will show you what muscles need to be stretched, what flexibility is required, the preliminary moves, the back walkover itself, related moves, and then I will tell you how these skills are used in gymnastics.

Before you attempt anything in gymnastics, you must warm up. Make sure your clothes don't inhibit movement; leotards, shorts, tee shirts, and sweats are some of the best things to wear. In gymnastics, you use almost every set of muscles in your body, so it's important to stretch all of them. I always begin by stretching my arms and shoulders. Try arm circles backward and forward, up and down, and side to side. Then swing your arms around, pivoting at the waist; these are called windmills. To stretch your shoulders, grasp your hands behind you, turn your wrists out, and pull up. As you pull upward, lean forward and let the weight of your arms stretch your shoulders while you begin stretching your legs. Toe touches are really important, but it's also important that you pull gently to each leg; don't bounce because that isn't stretching at all. Next are butterflies. Sit on the floor with your feet together

and your knees apart. Grab your ankles, push your knees down with your elbows, and pull down to the ground. Straddle stretches are important for flexibility. Straddle as far as you can, but make sure your knees and toes are pointing up and out. Pull down to each leg, then to the center, making sure to pull slowly. This next stretch is what I call hamstring stretches. Keep one leg straight on the floor while lying down and pull the other leg straight up and toward your head as far as you can. Do this for both legs. You can stretch your back by walking your hands down a wall or by lying on the floor and pushing up into a bridge.

There are some preliminary moves that you must be able to do before you even attempt a back walkover. You should be able to do the splits in at least one direction: right, left, or center. Flexibility is important to this move. Bridges are important. When you "bridge up," be sure to push simultaneously with your hands and feet. Some people don't, and they can't get up. You should try lifting one leg at a time, and then one hand at a time, off the ground.

After a bridge, you should be able to do a backbend. A lot of people say they can do a backbend, and they'll go down, but they can't come up. Well, it's not a backbend unless you can begin and end standing. So begin standing with your arms overhead. Keep your weight on your feet while you're arching backwards and gradually shift some weight to your hands. Push off the floor with your hands and come back to a stand.

Cartwheels are important because they teach you what it feels like to be upside down and supporting yourself on your hands. After cartwheels and backbends, you should master the front limber. It's a lot like a backbend, but it also involves a handstand. Begin standing, arms overhead, and kick into a handstand. Arch over, but don't throw your weight over, or you'll fall. Push up and end standing.

Now we're ready to do back walkovers. I consider form very important. Arms and legs should be straight, toes pointed whenever they're not on the floor, and legs split as much as possible. Begin standing, arms overhead. Keep your head up and look for the floor as you arch backwards. Extend one leg out (I'm left handed, so I use my left leg) with the toe pointed. Arch over, keeping your weight on your supporting leg while your lead leg moves higher. Look for the floor. As your hands touch the floor and your lead leg rises, kick off the floor with your supporting leg. Keep your arms straight so you don't smash your face. Step out and end standing. A more difficult back walkover begins with the lead leg off the floor.

There are other moves you can learn that are similar to back walkovers. A front walkover is a lot like a limber, except you step out of it. A front tensica combines a cartwheel with a front walkover, and it goes hand-hand-foot-foot. A back limber begins like a back walkover, but you bring your legs together in the air and down on the floor together. There are also back tensicas, which are back walkovers with one hand going down at a time, and back handsprings, which involve an arching jump backwards to your hands and a spring off to your feet.

Back walkovers are used in lower-level gymnastics as a part of a tumbling pass. You can see them in high school and lower-level meets. In higher levels, back walkovers are used as an artistic element in floor exercise and as connecting elements in beam routines. While a back walkover on the beam may be a major element in a high school routine, many elite gymnasts use it to begin a tumbling pass on the beam. A gymnast such as Nadia may begin with a back walkover, do two back handsprings, then dismount with a double twist from the beam.

I hope you now understand some of the work that goes into gymnastics. I showed you some of the flexibility required, some different moves and how they are done, and what back walkovers are used for in gymnastics. Gymnastics is meant to look easy, but it, in many ways, requires more strength and coordination than sports such as basketball and football. The gymnasts you see on television are probably stronger in proportion to their weight and size than any other athlete. So, the next time you watch gymnastics, instead of just being amazed, you hopefully can appreciate the work it takes to be a gymnast, and you may also recognize some of the moves I've shown you.

Can you identify how the introduction or conclusion might have been improved in this speech? Donna did a good job of gaining audience attention and relating the topic to herself and to her audience. She also previewed her message by stating the purpose, but she did not forecast the development of the speech. Her conclusion was generally well done. She reminded the audience of the main points of her speech and she specified what she wanted the audience to do. She did a less than perfect job of forewarning the audience that she was about to end her speech by simply stating, "I hope you now understand. . . ."

Ethics and Informative Speaking

Can you make inappropriate ethical choices when you present information to others? Yes, tainted information is a common problem with people who are less than honest. A bilk artist feeds people incorrect information, bald-face lies: your home is infested with termites, your roof won't last another year, and your paint has lead in it.

What are some guidelines for positive ethical choices in an informative speech?

1. Be sure of the quality of your information. Is it accurate, verifiable, consistent, and placed in context? Have you avoided implying that you have information that you lack? Have you avoided making up facts or distorting information?

2. Exercise caution when using the words of others. Have you accurately quoted the sources you have cited? Have you paraphrased accurately if you have summarized the words of others? Did you cite the sources who are responsible for your material? Have you avoided plagiarism? Have you kept all quotations in proper context?

3. Be careful not to mislead your audience. Have you told the audience of your association with groups whose work or purpose may be relevant to the topic? Have you been honest? Did you present all of the relevant information? Did you tell your audience that your examples were hypothetical or real? Have you used appropriate language so the audience has not been confused by words or concepts that they do not understand?

4. Be sure the information is needed by the audience. Are you providing the audience with new information? You do not want to waste their time by telling them what they already know. Are you allowing the audience free choice? Can they make reasoned choices about the importance and accuracy of the information you are providing?

5. Be sure that the information you are providing is in the best interests of the audience members. You can inform them about how to make a pipe bomb and poison their neighbor, but those would be negative moral choices. Speeches that present new information on how to improve self and society are positive moral choices.

Consider your own character as you make these choices. Are you being honest, trustworthy, and credible?

If you provide accurate information placed in an appropriate context, you are making ethical choices. Cite the sources you are using to avoid plagiarism. Be accurate in direct quotations and in the intent of the writer if you have summarized someone's words. Do not mislead your audience by omission or commission. Consider the audience's need for the information you are providing—do not give them information they already have nor provide them with information about which they cannot exercise free choice. Finally, be sure that the information that you are providing encourages the improvement of self and society.

Summary

In this chapter, you learned that the purposes of informative speeches are to generate a desire for information to help the audience understand the information, to help the audience remember the information, and to invite the audience to apply the information from the speech. Among the important points concerning the purposes of informative speaking, you learned that audiences comprehend generalizations and main ideas better than details; audiences comprehend simple words and concrete ideas better than big words and abstractions; a sense of anticipation can encourage listening and understanding; and audience participation increases comprehension.

Two rhetorical principles function in informative speaking. The first is that the speaker should explicitly state the relationship between himself or herself and the topic. The second is that the audience needs to know its relationship to the topic. These principles can be observed by describing your qualifications to discuss the topic and by demonstrating how the audience will find this information useful.

You learned five principles of learning related to the informative speech. They are (1) build on the known, (2) use humor and wit, (3) use presentational aids, (4) organize your information, and (5) reward your listeners.

Four methods of organizing the informative speech seem to be especially useful. They are the time-sequence, the spatial relations, the cause-effect, and the topical sequence patterns.

Finally, you learned about four types of informative speeches: the speech of definition, the speech of description, the speech of explanation, and the speech of demonstration. The speech of definition is based on explaining the meaning of a word or a few words. The speech of description relies on your ability to offer precise, accurate, and concrete language; to demonstrate a sufficient vocabulary; to use appropriate words; and to offer definitions. The speech of explanation is one in which you tell how something works, why it occurred, or how it should be evaluated. The speech of demonstration includes an object that is actually seen by the audience. Following is a checklist that you can use to assess your own informal speech and the speeches delivered by others.

A Checklist for the Informative Speech

Checklist

_____ 1. Have you created a desire for information?

_____ 2. Have you helped your audience understand your information?

_____ 3. Have you helped your audience remember information?

_____ 4. Can the audience apply the information?

_____ 5. Have you revealed your relationship to the topic?

_____ 6. Have you related the topic to your audience?

_____ 7. Have you used wit and humor when appropriate?

_____ 8. Have you built new information on old information?

_____ 9. Have you used presentational aids when necessary?

_____10. Have you organized your message effectively?

_____11. Have you included rewards for the audience?

Vocabulary

behavioral response One objective of a speech to inform; the audience shows an overt reaction to the speech

cause-effect pattern The pattern of organizing a speech through a cause-effect, cause-cause, effect-effect, or effect-cause method

desire for information A need the speaker creates in an audience so it is motivated to learn from the speech

humor The ability to perceive and express that which is amusing or comical

principles of learning Principles governing audience understanding by building on the known, using humor or wit, using presentational aids, organizing information, and rewarding listeners

reward A psychological or physical reinforcement to increase an audience's response to information given in a speech

rhetorical principles Two principles of public speaking that focus on the relationship between the speaker and the topic, and on the relationship between the audience and the topic

313

spatial relations pattern The pattern of organizing a speech in the order of how things are related in space, position, or visual orientation

speech of definition An informative speech in which you expand upon the meaning or meanings of a word

speech of demonstration An informative speech in which you show the audience an object, a person, or a place; how something works; how to do something; or why something occurs

speech of description An informative speech in which you describe a person, place, object, or experience by telling about its size, weight, color, texture, smell, and/or your feelings about it

speech of explanation An informative speech in which you tell how something works, why something occurred, or how something should be evaluated

subordinate Showing that one piece of information is less important than or merely supports another

time-sequence pattern The pattern of organizing a speech in chronological order

topical sequence pattern The pattern of organizing a speech by addressing the advantages, disadvantages, qualities, and types of persons, places, or things

wit The ability to perceive and express humorously the relationship or similarity between seemingly incongruous or disparate things

 # Applications

Application Exercises

Applying a Rhetorical Principle: The Speaker

1. Think of three topics about which you could give a three-minute speech to inform. List the topics in the blanks at the left. In the blanks at the right, explain how you relate to the topic in ways that might increase your credibility with the audience.

Topics

1. _____

2. _____

3. _____

Your Relationship to Topic

_____

_____

_____

_____

_____

_____

Applying a Rhetorical Principle: The Audience

2. In the topic blank below, name one topic that you did not use in the previous exercise and explain in the blanks following how you would relate that topic to your own class in an informative speech.

Topic: _____

The audience's relationship to topic:

_____

_____

_____

_____

_____

_____

Applying Principles of Learning

3. Write down a topic for an informative speech that you have not used in previous application exercises. Explain in the spaces provided how you could apply each of the principles of learning to that topic.

Topic: _____

One way that I could relate this topic to what the audience already knows is by _____

_____ .

One way that I could relate wit to wisdom in an informative speech on this topic is by

_____ .

One what that I could use several channels to get my message across on this topic is by

_____ .

One way that I could organize my speech to help the audience learn my information is by

_____ .

One way that I could provide reinforcement to my audience for listening to my informative speech on this topic is by _____

_____ .

The Speech of Explanation

Application Assignments

1. Deliver a four-to-six-minute speech in which you explain how something works, why something occurred, or how something should be evaluated. You are encouraged to rely on sources of information, such as encyclopedias, textbooks, newspapers, magazines, and professional journals. You will be evaluated on how well your audience understands what you are explaining. Consider information with which your audience is already familiar and demonstrate relationships between the known and the new information that you are offering. Consider how you can translate unfamiliar terms into known quantities. Try to determine how you can motivate your audience to be interested in what you are attempting to explain.

The Speech of Demonstration

2. Write an outline for a speech of demonstration that is to be about four to six minutes in length. Include in your outline a title, a purpose statement, an introduction, a body, and a conclusion. On the left-hand side of the sheet, specify the presentational aids that will be used and the purpose of each aid. Examine your outline to determine if the presentational aids are really necessary for understanding or if they are merely "props"; try to ensure that no additional aids are necessary for the audience to understand your message. You will be evaluated on your ability to identify creative and appropriate presentational aids for your topic and on your ability to use presentational aids when they are necessary and useful for understanding.

Endnotes

1. Charles R. Petrie, Jr., "Informative Speaking: A Summary and Bibliography of Related Research, *Speech Monographs* 30 (1963): 79–91.
2. Petrie, 1963.
3. Carole Ernest, "Listening Comprehension as a Function of Type of Material and Rate of Presentation," *Speech Monographs* 35 (1968): 154–58. See also John A. Baird, "The Effects of Speech Summaries upon Audience Comprehension of Expository Speeches of Varying Quality and Complexity," *Central States Speech Journal* 25 (1974): 119–27.
4. Petrie, 1963.
5. Elena P. Zayas-Baya, "Instructional Media in the Total Language Picture," *International Journal of Instructional Media* 5 (1977–78): 145–50.
6. R. Ehrensberger, "An Experimental Study of the Relative Effectiveness of Certain Forms of Emphasis in Public Speaking," *Speech Monographs* 12 (1945): 94–111.
7. Ehrensberger, 1945.
8. Kenneth Andersen and Theodore Clevenger, Jr., "A Summary of Experimental Research in Ethos," *Speech Monographs* 30 (1963): 59–78.
9. "Household Insecticides," *Consumer Reports* 44 (1979): 362–67.
10. Ehrensberger, 1945.
11. The information in paragraph one is from Leonard Larsen, "America's Willie Hortons Now George Bush's Problem," *The Athens Messenger,* January 5, 1989, 4.
12. Judy C. Pearson and Leda Cooks, "Gender and Power," in *Gender, Power and Communication in Human Relationships,* Pamela J. Kalbfleisch and Michael J. Cody, eds. (Hillsdale, NJ: Lawrence Erlbaum Associates, Inc. Publishers, 1995.)
13. Kazuo Inamori, "U.S.-Japan Relations from the Viewpoint of Japanese Multinational Corporations: Doing Business in the U.S.," Delivered at the Annual Business Meeting of the Huntingdon County Business and Industry, Incorporated, Huntingdon, Pennsylvania, February 3, 1993. Courtesy of Kazuo Inamori, Copyright © 1993. Reprinted with permission.
14. Inamori, 1993.
15. Inamori, 1993.
16. June E. Osborn, "The Second Decade of AIDS," presented at the 104th session of the Iowa Academy of Science in Cedar Falls, Iowa, on April 24, 1992. Reprinted in *Women's Voices in Our Time: Statements by American Leaders,* Victoria L. De Francisco and Marvin D. Jensen, eds. (Prospect Heights, IL: Waveland Press, Inc., 1994), 205–19. These statements appeared on pp. 213–14 and are slightly modified.
17. This speech was presented by Terry Hermiston at Iowa State University. The outline is reprinted with permission from the student.
18. The authors credit Lynette Crawford, a student in the English and Communications Division of Seneca College, Toronto, Canada, for the idea and some of the content of this example. Courtesy of Lynette Crawford.
19. From a speech of description delivered in Fundamentals of Public Speaking, Iowa State University. Courtesy of Mark Dupont.
20. From a speech of explanation in Communication and Persuasion, School of Interpersonal Communication, Ohio University. The speech contained the following endnotes:
    1. Wentworth and Hoover, "Students with Diabetes," *Today's Education* (March 1981), 42; 2. Wentworth and Hoover, 42; 3. Covelli, Peter J. "New Hope for Diabetics," *Time* (March 8, 1981), 63; 4. Wentworth and Hoover, 43; 5. Wentworth and Hoover, 43; 6. Wentworth and Hoover, 44; 7. Wilkins and Odayle, "Sugar Sensor, Measuring Glucose Concentrations in the Body," *Science News* (September 5, 1981), 154; 8. Covelli, 62; 9. Covelli, 64.
21. From a speech delivered in Public Speaking, School of Interpersonal Communication, Ohio University.

Chapter § THE PRINCIPLES AND TYPES OF PERSUASIVE SPEECHES

. . . .I am convinced that intelligence, patience, and eloquence can, sooner or later, lead the human race out of its self-imposed tortures provided it does not exterminate itself in the meantime.

Bertrand Russell

QUESTION OUTLINE

I. What is persuasive speaking?

II. How does persuasive speaking compare with informative speaking?

III. Why is persuasive speaking important?

IV. What are three purposes of persuasive speaking?

V. How does persuasive speaking affect beliefs, attitudes, and values?

VI. What are three types of persuasive speeches?

VII. What are four ways to organize a persuasive speech?

Introduction

Gabriella Rajna had a big day ahead. Her boss, the CEO of Tidewater Supplies, Inc., had asked her to make a presentation to the company's most profitable customer. That customer, Modern Motels of America, brought in over 30 percent of Tidewater Supplies' annual earnings. Gabriella's job was to convince the CEO and six vice-presidents from Modern Motels to continue using Tidewater Supplies for their linens, soap, shampoo, and cleaning supplies. The presentation would take place in their new high-rise office building in Atlanta.

Gabriella knew that at least three competitors had approached Modern Motels of America about changing accounts. She knew also that Modern Motels was not dissatisfied with Tidewater Supplies. However, like any business, Modern Motels was interested in securing the same service and supplies at a lower price if possible. She had no way of knowing the competition's bids, but her boss had given her the authority to bargain down to a certain point. If Gabriella bargained higher than that figure and still gained the bid, she would receive a healthy bonus. If she had to drop to the minimum, she would receive no bonus and no cheers from her boss or her colleagues, because Tidewater would make little profit at that bottom line figure. Gabriella Rajna knew that she had to give the most important persuasive speech of her life.

This chapter will reveal what Gabriella Rajna needed to know for her persuasive presentation. You will learn to distinguish informative speaking from persuasive speaking, why persuasive speaking is important, three purposes of persuasive speaking, some principles of persuasion, three types of persuasive speeches, and four patterns of organization used most often in persuasive speaking. When you have completed this chapter, you will understand better what persuasive speaking is, how to organize a persuasive message, and what effects to aim for in persuasive speaking.

What Is Persuasive Speaking?

Persuasive speaking is a message delivered to an audience by a speaker who intends to influence audience members' choices by shaping, reinforcing, or changing their responses toward an idea, issue, concept, or product.

Let us compare informative and persuasive speaking. Perhaps no speech is completely informative or completely persuasive, but the following chart might help highlight the characteristics of the two kinds of speeches.

Why Is Persuasive Speaking an Important Topic?

You are a consumer of persuasive messages each day. Persuasive messages bombard you. As often as not, when the telephone rings or the door bell chimes, you are confronted with someone who wants something of you. Television and radio programs are punctuated every few minutes by advertisements. Magazines and newspapers are filled with flashy ads designed to sell. The mall, the town square, and even the grocery store, are designed to sell products and services to you.

Today, more than ever, the media and other people compete for your attention, your money, your time, your vote, or your membership. Small, family-owned businesses have been consumed by large mega-corporations. These large entities war with each other for popularity and profit. As a consumer and citizen, you have become the target of their persuasive campaigns.

You also serve as the producer of persuasive messages. Whether you are selling a product, soliciting votes, marketing services, canvassing for donations, seeking a job, or simply attempting to convince someone that they should believe as you do, you are engaged in persuasive speaking. Whether you have had training in persuasive speaking or not, you are familiar with it.

	Informative speech	Persuasive speech
Speaker's intent	To increase knowledge	To change mind or action
Message's purpose	To define, describe, explain, compare, etc.	To shape, reinforce, or change audience responses
Listener's effect	To know more than before, to advance what is known	To feel or think differently, to behave or act differently than before
Audience's choice	To willingly learn new knowledge	To change behavior by choice

You serve as a producer of persuasive messages.

At the same time, your happiness and success may largely depend on your persuasive skills. If you cannot sell the product you have been given, you may lose important income. If you cannot successfully gain employment, you may live in a manner to which you do not wish to become accustomed. Your inability to encourage others to vote for the party of your choice or to hold particular political views may lead you into disappointment and discouragement.

Your satisfaction in both private and public spheres is dependent, in great part, on your ability to be both a competent consumer and producer of persuasive messages. You do not want to be deceived by fallacious reasoning or unwarranted arguments. You want to be able to understand why you feel compelled to respond to certain messages while you disregard others.

You also want to learn to be an effective and ethical persuader. The success of your personal life and the achievements in your professional life rely not on luck, but on your developed ability to convince others that you are a credible individual who understands how to influence others. Persuasive appeals are expected in a democracy and in commerce. This chapter helps you to understand and to practice persuasive speaking.

Three Purposes of Persuasive Speaking

Central to the definition of persuasive speaking are the three **purposes:** to shape, reinforce, and change responses in an audience.[1]

Shaping Audience Responses

Shaping responses means that the persuasive speaker tries to move the audience toward a predetermined goal. A parent shapes a child's behavior to encourage the child to walk: sitting up draws cheers, standing up brings encouragement, and the first step is picture-taking time. Similarly the persuasive speaker shapes responses in the audience by moving the audience toward a predetermined goal.

For instance, let us say a speaker wants the audience to have a more positive attitude toward the disposal of nuclear waste from power plants. Most people do not want a nuclear waste dump in their state much less in their backyard, so the persuasive speaker must shape the audience's responses by first demonstrating the marvelous potential of nuclear energy to generate the power necessary for our life-style. Next the speaker might shape the audience by asking them to explore alternatives to nuclear power, most of which are even more expensive or too dirty to contemplate. Shaping, then, is moving an audience closer and closer to the speaker's solution by presenting ideas in palatable doses.

Reinforcing Audience Responses

Reinforcing responses is a second purpose of persuasive speaking. Reinforcing means rewarding the audience for sustaining present beliefs, attitudes, and values. This idea is known as "continuance,"[2] and simply means that you want to keep an audience doing what it already does.

Political speakers try to keep audiences loyal to a certain party and a particular candidate. Religious speakers try to encourage faithfulness to a certain doctrine and to a particular organized group. Educators try to persuade a sometimes reluctant clientele that knowing how to read, write, and speak, as well as having a wide knowledge about many disciplines, is the mark of an educated person. All politicians are trying to persuade people to continue voting, believing, and gaining education as in the past.

Changing Audience Responses

A third purpose of persuasive speaking is **changing responses,** altering an audience's behavior toward a product, a concept, or an idea. Often the persuasive speaker pursuing this purpose asks the audience to start or stop a behavior: start exercising, stop smoking, start studying, stop eating unhealthy foods, or start drinking fruit juice instead of alcohol.

Changing audience responses is a tough assignment. People tend to behave the way they have in the past, but the persuasive speaker who adopts this purpose is asking the audience to behave differently. Changes that alter well-established habits are difficult to achieve for most people.

Historically, shaping has been associated with learning; reinforcing has been largely ignored as a persuasive purpose; and changing has been the main focus of persuasive speaking for at least 2,000 years.

A public speaker needs to keep in mind the goal of persuasion. What is it that you are trying to shape, reinforce, or change in an audience? Usually what you are trying to influence are the audience's feelings, attitudes, beliefs, and values for the purpose of securing behavioral change.

What Is Being Influenced?

Feelings

Feelings are our affective states or dispositions, our emotional responses. When you cry at a romantic movie, laugh at a comedian, or become angry at a call at the wrestling match, you are expressing your emotions and showing your feelings. Sometimes you may change your feelings about a particular topic even though you do not express yourself quite so obviously.

Persuasive speakers are sometimes interested in changing the feelings of others. When newly-elected United States Presidents give Inaugural speeches, they are hoping to create hopefulness and optimism in the audience. When a motivational speaker talks about the positive attributes of successful people, she is attempting to engender feelings of excitement and enthusiasm in the audience. The religious leader, the poet, the storyteller, and the entertainer all attempt to change their audience's feelings.

Attitudes

Attitudes, according to psychologist Daryl Bem, are your likes or dislikes toward people, ideas, policies, or situations.[3] Your attitudes predispose you to respond in a favorable or unfavorable way.[4] If you dislike studying, you may indicate that negative attitude by avoiding study, by talking with friends, playing video games, watching TV, or taking long showers. You learn your attitudes about study, work, relatives, and other people. They lead you to dislike smokers, like people with dimples, despise the Internal Revenue Service, or like flying.

In persuasive speaking, your goal might be to alter audience attitudes. You might want them to favor assisted suicide, embrace supply-side economics, enjoy mathematics or support big business. Some attitudes—your attitude toward organized religion, toward other ethnic groups, or toward a step-parent—are difficult to change. Others—liking foreign cars, disliking aspirin, or favoring a certain politician—might be relatively simple to change.

Beliefs

Beliefs are things you believe to be true even though there is no certainty or proof that they are true. You may have once believed in Santa Claus; you believed in him though you couldn't prove his existence. Some religions believe in predestination, other religions believe in reincarnation, and still other religions believe in miracles. None of these beliefs are subject to the usual kinds of proof or evidence that works, for example, in a court of law.

In persuasive speaking, beliefs can be problematical because claims about your beliefs are unverifiable, unprovable. The Roman Catholic can no more prove the existence of Purgatory than the Calvinist can prove predestination. You can tell an audience about your beliefs. You can even say what your beliefs do for you. Ethically you have to accept the personal nature of beliefs and accept the idea that other people's beliefs are equally important to them. Beliefs are not true or false, nor are they facts that can be verified. They exist, they influence our behavior, and they can be changed through persuasion, but not by proving that one set of beliefs is true or false. Be cautious about attacking the beliefs of others because they are often deeply felt and resistant to change.

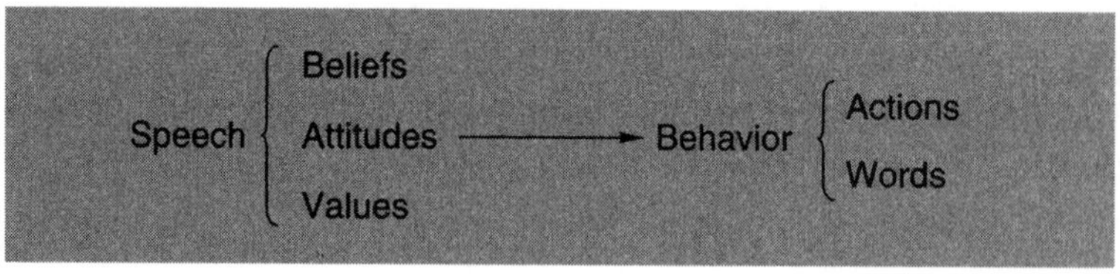

Figure 1

A persuasive speech affects audience values, attitudes, and beliefs in order to elicit certain words or actions (behavior).

Values

Values are learned social principles, goals, or standards found acceptable or even desirable by the people we live with, the groups to which we belong, and the institutions we respect. Values include the abstractions we embrace: honesty, courage, loyalty, friendship, freedom, trustworthiness, and patriotism, to name a few. Values tend to be the basis from which beliefs and attitudes spring. For example, our value of freedom may inspire a belief that government should never interfere with our right of expression or an attitude against rules like not talking in a movie theatre.

In persuasive speaking, values might be the stated or unstated basis of many issues. Prolife advocates have a belief in the sanctity of life, which is based on a value that says life is so precious that no human should tamper with procreation, the survival of the species. Values rarely change abruptly, and often they are held for a lifetime. The persuasive speaker is more likely to chip away at the edges of audience attitudes than to alter the fundamental principles by which the audience lives.

Behavior

Behavior is our observable action. The persuasive speaker sometimes wants to change unobservable feelings, attitudes, values, and beliefs. At other times you will want to change the actual behavior of your audience. The behavioral change may be obvious: vote for a certain candidate, buy a certain product, go to a certain place, or try a certain exercise. Sometimes the behavioral change is less obvious: read more about modern warfare, listen to a talk about taxation, or tell people about socialized medicine. Sometimes the behavioral change is almost imperceptible: an audience member becomes slightly less Republican and votes for a bond issue in the secrecy of the voting booth; an audience member answers questions from a pollster just a little differently than she would have before she heard your speech; or an audience member earns somewhat better grades because of your motivational speech about study habits. In all of these cases, behavioral change took place as a result of a speech. (See figure 1.)

The public speaker often meddles in the cognitive domain, in the minds of the audience, tinkering with this belief, that attitude, or this value. However, we never know if that tinkering had any effect except through the audience's behavior. It is what audience members say and do, their behavior, that tells us what they must think.

Principles of Persuasion

How can the successful public speaker be persuasive? A number of principles are instructive. In this section we identify five principles of persuasion. We will learn that consistency, small changes, benefits, fulfilling needs, and gradual approaches all are effective ways to persuade others.

Consistency Persuades

The first principle of persuasion is that *audiences are more likely to change their behavior if the suggested change is consistent with their present beliefs, attitudes, and values.*

Principles of Persuasion

1. Consistency persuades.
2. Small changes persuade.
3. Benefits persuade.
4. Fulfilling needs persuades.
5. Gradual approaches persuade.

People who have given money for a cause (a behavior) are the likely contributors to that and other related causes in the future. People who like competition (a value) are the most likely candidates to enter into another competition. People who want to segregate old people in communities of their own (a belief) are the most likely to promote bond issues that provide separate housing for the aged. Finally, people who dislike immigrants (an attitude) are likely to discourage immigrants from moving into their neighborhood.

Fortunately for public speakers, people tend to be relatively consistent. They will do in the future what they did in the past. The public speaker uses this notion of **consistency** by linking persuasive proposals to those old consistencies. Following are some examples of appeals based on consistency:

> *The members of this audience were among the first in their neighborhoods to buy home computers, VCRs, and centralized home security systems. Now you can be among the first to own a laser disk sound system. I know that you are basically conservative folks who do not spend money without deep thought and careful scrutiny. That is why you will find this new sound system so appealing: it is expensive but will outlast every appliance in your house; it is small but more powerful than any previous system; and it is new but designed to bring to your ears with great clarity all the songs that you like to hear.*

The public speaker shapes, reinforces, and changes by showing how the promoted activity is consistent with the audience's past behavior.

Small Changes Persuade

The second principle of persuasion is that *audiences are more likely to alter their behavior if the suggested change will require small rather than large changes in their behavior*. A common error of beginning speakers is that they ask for too much change too soon for too little reason. Audiences are reluctant to change, and any changes they do make are likely to be small ones. Nonetheless, the successful persuasive speaker determines what small changes consistent with the persuasive purpose an audience would be willing to accept.

What if you, as a persuader, are faced with an audience of overweight Americans who are loath to exercise and resistant to reduced eating? Your temptation might be to ask for too much too soon: quit eating so much and start losing weight. The message would likely fall on unreceptive ears, because it is both inconsistent with present behavior and asking for too much change too soon. You could limit your persuasive message by encouraging the audience to give up specific foods, or a specific food that is part of their problem. However, an even better example of a small change consistent with the audience's present behavior would be to have listeners switch from ice cream to low-fat frozen yogurt. An audience that would reject a weight-loss program might be more willing simply to switch from one form of food to another, because that change would be minimally upsetting to its present life patterns.

Are there any qualifications or limitations on this second principle of persuasion? One factor that needs to be considered in deciding how much to ask of an audience is **commitment level.** Studies in social judgment show that highly committed persons, people who believe most intensely or strongly about an issue, are highly resistant to any positions on the issue except their own or ones very close to it. To such an audience, reinforcement would be welcome, shaping would be a challenge, and change would be very difficult. On the other hand, audience members who do not feel strongly about an issue are susceptible to larger changes than are those who already have established positions to which they are committed.

To state the principle more concretely: a speaker addressing a religious rally of persons who abhor drinking, dancing, and smoking can get warm acceptance for a persuasive message that reinforces or rewards those ideas; would be greeted with cautious skepticism with a speech attempting to shape any responses different from those already established; and would be met with outright rejection when requesting changes in behavior that run counter to those already embraced. On the other hand, a heterogeneous audience of persons uncommitted on the issue of regular exercise would be susceptible to considerable response shaping, and an audience of the already committed would receive reinforcement and would at least consider adopting some small changes in behavior. The successful persuader is skilled at discerning which small changes, consistent with the persuasive purpose, can be asked of an audience.

Benefits Persuade

The third principle of persuasion is that *audiences are more likely to change their behavior if the suggested change will benefit them more than it will cost them.* **Cost-benefit analysis,** for example, is considered every time we buy something: "Do I want this new jacket even though it means I must spend $150 plus tax? The benefits are that I will be warm and will look nice. The cost is that I will not be able to get my shoes resoled or buy a new watch." The persuader frequently demonstrates to the audience that the benefits are worth the cost.

A student who sold vacuum cleaners told of a fellow sales representative who donned white gloves and a surgical mask when he looked at the customers' old vacuum cleaner. By the time he had inspected the brush and changed the bag, he was filthy. He would then demonstrate that the old vacuum threw dust all over the house as it dragged across the carpet. By the end of his sales pitch, the sales representative was convincing the customer that the old vacuum was not only ineffective but also increased the amount of dirt flying around the house. The cost of the new vacuum would, according to this

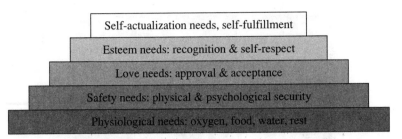

Self-actualization needs, self-fulfillment

Esteem needs: recognition & self-respect

Love needs: approval & acceptance

Safety needs: physical & psychological security

Physiological needs: oxygen, food, water, rest

salesman, be worth the benefit of owning a cleaning machine that picked up dirt instead of spreading it around. Remember that you need to reveal to your audience the benefits that make your proposal worth the cost.

How can you use cost-benefit analysis in your classroom speech? Consider the costs to the audience of doing as you ask. What are the costs in money, time, commitment, energy, skill, or talent? Consider one of the most common requests in student speeches: write to your representative or senator. Many student speakers make that request without considering the probability that nobody in class has ever written to a senator or representative. Even if the speaker includes an address, the letter writing will take commitment, time, and even a little money. Few students are willing to pay those costs. On the other hand, if the speaker comes to class with a letter already composed and simply asks for signatures from the class, then the cost is a few seconds of time, and the speaker is more likely to gain audience cooperation. Whenever you deliver a persuasive speech, consider the costs and how you can reduce them so the audience will feel they are worth your proposed benefits.

Fulfilling Needs Persuades

The fourth principle of persuasion is that *audiences are more likely to change their behavior if the change meets their needs.* Abraham Maslow created an often-quoted **hierarchy of needs.**[5] Maslow's pyramid makes sense. As a human being, you do need all of the items in the hierarchy, though many people never get very far above the second level and few think they have achieved complete self-fulfillment.

You can use Maslow's hierarchy in your public speeches. Are you in a place where the air and water are so bad that they threaten public health? If so, speeches on those issues are about the basic physiological needs. Do the people in your audience have decent places to live? If not, then speeches about space and psychological health are appropriate. Is everyone in your audience happy with his or her relationships? If not, then speeches about approval and acceptance are in order.

You can analyze your audience for specific needs. Do they need money? Jobs? Day care? Do they need help in dealing with government bureaucracies? Do they need better living conditions? Do they need to learn how to study, how to handle children, or how to live with spouses? Check out your own audience and determine what they need because a speech that meets the audience's needs is likely to be successful.

Gradual Approaches Persuade

Gradual approaches work best when the audience is likely to be unreceptive to your message. With friendly audiences, you can ask them to do what you already know they are likely to accept and then simply give them reinforcement and a good rationale for doing so. However, many persuasive speeches ask for audience changes that listeners may not wholeheartedly endorse just because you say they should.

Asking for too much change too quickly can result in a hostile audience.

Do not ask a hostile audience for too much too soon. Persuading a reluctant audience is a kind of seduction in which the audience is more likely to cooperate after courtship than after an abrupt proposition. Start with common ground to show the audience that you share its basic humanity. Move from arguments and evidence that listeners will find quite acceptable to that which they find harder to accept.

A Democratic governor faced a highly Republican audience of radio and television owners and managers. The governor disarmed his potentially hostile audience by beginning with a story about how he sent his young son to school that morning. The story was amusing but, more important, it showed that the governor—like most of the people in the audience—had the same kinds of things going on in his life that they had in their own. This common ground set the stage for the rest of the speech, in which he gently pushed the audience toward his position on the issues.

Similarly in a persuasive speech do not start by saying, "I want you to donate your eyes to the eye bank." Instead, start gently with "safe" information about how many people have been saved from blindness by cornea transplants. Mention that the program is sponsored by the local Lion's Club. Reveal how many other people in the community, students in particular, have signed donor cards to allow their eyes to be used to help another person. Only after this careful courtship do you reveal that you have cards for them to sign if they have compassion for their fellow human beings. The behavioral change—the signing of a donor card—is the end result of a gradual approach.

Remember, as you prepare your persuasive speech, that audiences are more likely to change their behavior if the suggested change is consistent with their present beliefs, attitudes, and values; if it requires small rather than large changes in their lives; if it benefits them more than it costs them; if it meets their needs; and if it is a culmination of acceptable ideas. With these principles to apply in your persuasive speeches, you can move to the matter of content in the persuasive speech.

Three Types of Persuasive Speeches

The three types of persuasive speeches that we will examine in this chapter are the speech to inspire, the speech to convince, and the speech to actuate.

The Speech to Inspire

The **speech to inspire** is a persuasive speech, although we often do not think about inspirational messages as persuasive. The purpose of this speech is to influence listeners' feelings. Speeches of inspiration are often used for ceremonial events. They occur in churches, mosques, synagogues, and temples; at graduations and rallies; and on holidays or special events. An example of a speech to inspire was provided by Patricia Harris, who

Three Types of Persuasive Speeches

1. The speech to inspire
2. The speech to convince
3. The speech to actuate

was the first African American woman to serve in a United States President's cabinet, both as Secretary of Housing and Urban Development and as Secretary of Health, Education, and Welfare. Harris was also the first African American woman to serve her nation as ambassador and to lead an American law school. In a speech to the National Women's Political Caucus Convention, she said, in part,

> I want to hear the Speaker of the House addressed as Madam Speaker and I want to listen as she introduces Madam President to the Congress assembled for the State of the Union. I want Madam President to look down from the podium at the women of the Supreme Court who will be indicative of the significant number of women judges throughout the Federal and State judicial systems.[6]

The Speech to Convince

The **speech to convince** is a persuasive speech given with the intent of influencing listeners' beliefs or attitudes. You may wish to convince the audience that Rush Limbaugh is a reasonable man, that gender equality is beneficial to both women and men, that culturally correct language is a reasonable goal of a multicultural society, that our current health care plan is superior to alternatives that have been suggested, or that our nation's children are at risk.

The speech to convince attempts only to encourage listeners to believe a different position on an issue. They are not required to act. In a speech to convince, you do not ask your audience to do anything, but rather to rethink their beliefs and attitudes. An example of a speech to convince is presented in figure 2.[7] The student speaker, Katherine L. Anderson, assumed that most people would disagree about the ordination of women into the Roman Catholic priesthood, and she attempted to convince them otherwise.

The Speech to Actuate

The **speech to actuate** is a persuasive speech given for the purpose of influencing listeners' behaviors or actions. The foundation of the speech to actuate is the changing of listeners' beliefs and attitudes, but it goes further to request action. You may wish to ask listeners to join an organization, to volunteer their time at local social service agencies, to eat a low-fat diet, to practice safe sex, or to vote for a particular candidate.

In the speech to actuate, the speaker seeks an overt behavioral effect, some evidence of response. In the speech featured in figure 3, notice how the speaker first creates anxieties about being overweight and then allows the audience an escape route through exercise.[8]

Now that we have considered three types of persuasive speeches, let us examine how a persuasive speech may be organized. We will consider the problem-solution pattern, the need-plan pattern, the refutational strategy, and Monroe's Motivated Sequence. In general, these are the most useful methods of organizing a persuasive speech.

Organizing a Persuasive Speech

The Ordination of Women into the Priesthood
Katherine L. Anderson

Gains attention by pointing out current issue

States main idea and previews points

Uses examples to illustrate inconsistency between current attitudes and historical origins

With the problem established, the rest of the speech is devoted to the reasons.

Transition into next point

Uses two modes of proof—examples and testimony

After presenting the facts, the speaker ties the information together by stating the conclusion.

Suggests a response to the speech

Recaps the main ideas

Appeal to idealism

As a woman living in today's sophisticated world, I understand and value the right for equality. My Catholic upbringing in school and at home has taught me that each one of us deserves an equal opportunity to pursue his or her own ambitions. This nation has come a long way in its fight against discrimination, and the teachings of the church have stressed the importance of equality. Catholics have reached out to all people through their charitable programs, their hospitals, and their schools. The Catholic church teaches that all humans have equal rights and worth. However, within the church this principle does not translate to equal opportunity because it denies women the right of ordination into the priesthood. Women feel this denial is unfair because it restricts their participation in the church. In addition, they believe that the church would benefit from having them as priests. Ultimately women could increase the number of priests which would allow the church to influence more people.

Throughout history women have been significant participants in the church. They were active followers of Jesus. They remained with Him even after His disciples fled in fear, and they were the first to whom He appeared after His resurrection. Throughout the Bible, there are many heroines whose models, such as Mary, Sarah, and Mary Magdalene, are the earliest examples of women's participation in the church. Beyond women in scripture, outstanding Christian leadership is recognizable today. One example is Mother Theresa, who dedicates her life to helping others. These heroines inspire women and keep them hopeful that someday they will be permitted to preside over the liturgy and administer the sacraments.

If women were ordained, the number of priests would increase. This increase would benefit the church immensely since there is a tremendous shortage of priests in the world. Each year there are fewer and fewer male vocations to the priesthood. Churches have been forced to cut down on their Mass schedules. The shortage of priests will become even more critical in the next few years. Women can help solve this problem.

Other religions have already recognized the value of female ministers. Women are permitted to be ordained and are heading parishes in the Anglican, Episcopal, and Presbyterian churches. Will the Catholic church be the last to hold on to sexist traditions? Women are not the only ones who support this issue. According to Dr. David L. Coulter of Boston University's Medical Department, "simple faith in the equality of God's love for all people means that women should be able to become priests, bishops, even Pope."[1] How can the church refuse to see the value and need for female priests?

Women are fighting for equality. However, not enough progress has been made. Pope John Paul II expressed his views on the ordination of women in his document *Mulieris Dignitatem (On the Dignity and Vocation of Women)*. He believes that women are acquiring an influence and a power in the world that has never been achieved before. He wrote "the biblical teaching of mutual service between men and women must gradually establish itself in hearts, consciences, behaviors, and customs."[2] Although he believes that the church would benefit from women priests, he feels it is not ready for that kind of change yet. Therefore, he reaffirmed that only men may be included in the ordained ministry. Even though the leaders of the church who deny women this right may sympathize with women's frustration, they continue to tolerate sexist practices within the church.

After hearing this speech, you may think that there is nothing that you can do about this situation, because it does not relate to you. On the contrary, you do not have to be a Catholic woman in order to relate to this topic. A change in the church will probably not occur in the immediate future. But what we can do today is look at the situation, keep an open mind, and remember the hardships women have endured throughout history.

In my opinion, women's involvement in the church has helped make it the institution it is today.[3] Having them as priests would increase their participation and dedication to the church. Also, the church would benefit from their participation. Finally, women would increase the number of priests which could help Catholics influence more people. Women have come so far and have helped create this modern world. They have proven themselves competent in every field. Change may be gradual, but change will come when both men and women realize that out-of-date traditions must be broken. Only then will we be able to accommodate our lives to this changing society.

Figure 2

A speech to convince.

Exercise: A Step to Wellness
Beth Kregenow

Use of striking figures to gain favorable attention

Our society should shock and appall you. Sixty percent of American men and women between forty and forty-nine years old are overweight. In Japan only five percent of the same age group are that fat, and fewer than one-third of Italian men and women—even with all that wine and pasta—are considered overweight.[1]

Those statistics scare me. Most of us have managed to get away with horrible eating and exercise habits. Unfortunately, in the future, maintaining our weight will not be so easy. More children and adolescents are developing weight problems than ever before.[2] Our society turns to alcohol and food as stress relievers. Although we seem to be increasingly fitness-aware, we get less exercise than our great-grandparents did at the turn of the century.

States the main idea

Previews main points

We all need to begin an exercise program and stick with it. Regular exercise can change your life as it has changed mine. Although some people have excuses to remain inactive, their reasons often are unjustified. I will tell you some of the psychological benefits of activity and then explain how exercise will affect your life psychologically. If you do not want to become part of the shocking statistics, learn how to adopt a wellness life-style and begin to exercise.

Clear organization makes the speech easy to follow.

The long-term physical benefits of exercise are lifesaving. Inactive people have a greater risk of cancer, diabetes, stroke, and high blood pressure compared to those who are physically active. You strengthen your cardiovascular system which reduces your chance of heart disease. Since heart disease is the number one killer in the United States today, your heart's condition should be extremely important to you.[3] Exercise strengthens your immune system and enables you to fight disease and infection. Regular exercise today will improve your quality of life in the years to come. It will slow the aging process and help maintain your flexibility, balance, and agility. It will also decrease your memory loss as you age. Not only will exercise improve your quality of life, but it will also lengthen your life span. According to the "University of California, Berkeley Wellness Letter," one study found that active Harvard alumni lived longer than alumni who remained inactive.[4]

A question effectively used as a transition

"What can exercise do for me now?" you might wonder. In addition to the long-term benefits of physical activity, exercise will change your life today. You can lose inches of body fat and improve your appearance dramatically. The immediate changes in appearance brought on by regular exercise have many positive psychological effects. As your looks improve, your self-confidence will grow. Similarly, when you perform well, run farther, or achieve a goal, you boost your self-confidence. As you exercise, you will feel less anxiety and stress.

Thorough coverage of the topic makes this speech difficult to refute.

Use of support material to back claim

Another mental benefit will be an increase in your energy level. One study found that exercise can help alleviate depression. Moderately depressed people were asked to follow a regular exercise program. This form of treatment worked as well as short-term psychotherapy and even better than long-term, unlimited therapy.[5]

Refutes common arguments—another technique that adds to the power of the speech

Although exercise produces these results, people still have excuses for remaining inactive. Some say they do not have time to exercise. Actually, thirty minutes of aerobic exercise three times per week will have an impact on your health.[6] You can accomplish this amount of activity during your lunch hour or between classes. Instead of watching your favorite soap or football game, get some exercise for yourself.

Still other people say that they do not have the energy to exercise. As I mentioned before, physical activity will increase your energy level. The release of norepinephrine and dopamine, neurotransmitters, will make you mentally alert.

Suggests activities that can be accomplished by most listeners

Getting exercise is easy. Start with the basics. Climb stairs instead of taking the elevator. Go for a walk after dinner. Get some friends together and play basketball or go swimming instead of taking an afternoon nap. Anything that makes you physically active is good exercise. Dancing, skiing, cleaning, walking, playing soccer or tennis are all great forms of physical activity. An exercise program should not be a chore. You need to find something that you enjoy and do it. After you have begun to exercise, you will find it easy to continue.

Figure 3
....

A speech to actuate.

Recaps main arguments	Your decision to begin an exercise program is relatively easy. Physically, you will be healthier, look better, and live longer. Mentally, you will feel less stress and more energy. At the same time, you will build self-confidence and feel great about yourself. These are exceptional rewards for doing something that is fun. Set goals for yourself. Find an activity that you enjoy and make a commitment to change your life. Take responsibility for your life and make it better.

Figure 3 (continued)

Problem-Solution Pattern

The **problem-solution pattern** of organizing a persuasive speech occurs when the speaker first discusses a problem that needs resolution and then offers a solution for it. This organizational plan works well, as the problem becomes one main heading in the outline and the solution becomes another main head.

However, the problem-solution method also provides some room for discretion on the part of the speaker. If you are going to use this approach, you must decide whether the problem or the solution merits the bulk of your speaking time. If the audience is relatively unaware of the problem, more time should be granted to explaining the problem. If the audience is well informed on the problem, then the solution should be given emphasis. An example of the problem-solution pattern is provided in figure 4.

Need-Plan Pattern

The **need-plan pattern** is similar to the problem-solution pattern. This design does not simply present a need and a plan, however. It includes four steps. First, the speaker presents the need or inadequacy expressed by the current situation. Second, the speaker recommends a plan that will meet the need. Third, the speaker explains more thoroughly how the plan will answer the problem or need. Finally, the speaker proposes how the plan will be implemented.

If you work in business or sales, you may routinely use the need-plan pattern in your persuasive messages. An automobile dealer may tell a customer why his or her used car should be traded in, why a particular new automobile will solve the customer's needs, how it will be useful to him or her, and finally, explain how a leasing program will allow no money down and minimal payments each month.

Kinko's, which is a well-known name on college campuses, has clever advertisements that show business people with copying and collating needs. The commercials show these demands being easily managed by Kinko's over night. The business people suggest that Kinko's provides an important service in a quick and dependable manner. They intimate that their business is more successful because of Kinko's. These commercials demonstrate an effective use of the need-plan approach.

Refutational Strategy

The **refutational strategy** involves the discrediting of one statement in order to support another statement. Most persuasive messages do not occur in a vacuum. Positions exist on both sides of the issue. Following this organizational pattern, you would first identify the point you are refuting. Second, you would explain how you are going to refute this position. Third, you would state your position. Fourth, you would provide evidence, including examples, testimony, and facts and figures, for your position. You might add emotional proof and personal proof if appropriate. Finally, you would clearly state how your position, with its accompanying evidence, undermines the opposing position.

Figure 4

An example of the problem-solution pattern of organization.

Immediate purpose: To convince my audience to discontinue practices that invite credit card fraud

Introduction:

I. Thousands of credit card holders are bilked each year by thieves.

II. Today, you will find out more about the problem of credit card fraud and some solutions to the problem.

Problem:

III. The problem of credit card fraud is stolen cards, unauthorized copies, and telephone phonies.

    A. When your credit card is taken by a pickpocket or robber, you may be charged for a spending spree by the thief.

    B. When you pay with a credit card, an employee might keep an unauthorized copy of the carbon so your number can be used for phone purchases.

    C. Telephone crooks trick you into revealing your credit card number on the phone to use it themselves for purchases.

Solution:

IV. The solution to credit card fraud is to follow the rules on stolen cards, take carbons, and avoid revealing your number to strangers.

    A. Report stolen cards immediately by keeping phone numbers for your cards in a list off your person.

    B. You should take your customer's copy and any full-length carbons or copies at the time of purchase.

    C. Never tell someone your credit card number on the phone unless you placed the call for a purchase.

Conclusion:

V. You can avoid credit card fraud by being a cautious customer.

    A. Treat your plastic as if it were worth your line of credit because that is what you can lose—and more.

    B. Watch, guard, and protect your credit card with vigilance and maybe even insurance.

VI. Your credit card may be worth a fortune to you and those who would prey on you: use it defensively.

Statement to gain audience's favorable attention

Thesis sentence

Main points

Review

The refutational strategy may be used for controversial topics, or it may be used to show that something commonly believed may be inaccurate. For instance, one student speaker gave a speech about why we should not brush our teeth. The belief that we should brush after every meal is so entrenched in most people's thinking that we suffer guilt when we do not brush our teeth. This student argued that, with people living into their 90s, the practice of brushing three or four times per day is not so smart. She argued that the abrasive elements in toothpaste that remove tartar also wear off enamel. Her pitch was that we would be better off finishing our meals with salads and fruit, such as apples, natural tooth cleaners, instead of relying so heavily on commercial toothpaste and brushing.

The common beliefs that you might choose to refute may not be universal. They could be beliefs common only in the audience you are addressing—as long as that group

Figure 5

A list of possible topics for a speech using the refutational strategy.

> 1. The case for liberal Democrats
> 2. Why fight extinction of rare animals and birds?
> 3. Some major reforms needed in higher education
> 4. Why the government should operate the steel, gas, and oil industries
> 5. Speech anxiety: The case against public speaking
> 6. Negative aspects of organized religion in America
> 7. Eliminating the traditional family
> 8. Why America should ban automobiles
> 9. How to wean yourself from your television
> 10. Why reading and writing are unnecessary today

has a relatively unquestioning perspective on the issue. For instance, bankers rarely see much need for reform in their own practices; neither do educators. Both bankers and educators have their commonly held beliefs. The list in figure 5 might give you some ideas for topics that could be used with the refutational strategy.

If you use the refutational strategy, you will use argument and evidence to oppose another point of view. The speech in figure 6 was provided by David Turnbull, a professor of English and Communication at Seneca College of Applied Arts and Technology in Ontario, Canada. The student who gave the speech opposes an idea that may be viewed as sacred to many.[9]

Monroe's Motivated Sequence

Monroe's Motivated Sequence was developed in the 1930s by Alan Monroe, a speech educator and author, who had previously trained sales personnel. Monroe applied philosopher and educator John Dewey's work on reflective thinking to persuasion. Dewey's method of reflective thinking included seven steps. Individuals or people in small groups were encouraged to recognize, define and analyze a problem under consideration, then they were to establish criteria for evaluating solutions to it, followed by suggesting solutions to the problem, selecting the best solution, and finally, testing the solution.

Alan Monroe used this method to create an organizational pattern for speeches. Indeed, this pattern gains its name partly from Dewey's problem-solution method. In addition to following the reflective thinking approach, the motivated sequence attempts to tie problems and solutions to human motives.

Monroe's Motivated Sequence includes five specific components: attention, need, satisfaction, visualization, and action. Following this sequence, you would first attempt to capture the attention of your audience. You want your audience to decide that it is important to listen to you. If you work in a residence hall, you might speak to a group of first-year students about how to achieve good grades. You might gain your listeners' attention by contrasting the student who flunks out of college in two academic terms with the person who makes the dean's list.

Second, you establish the need for your proposal. You want to describe a problem or show why some need exists. You want your audience to believe that something must be done. In your speech to the new students, you might talk about the waste of human resources that occurs each time a college student fails in his program, and how most students who fail end up living economically and personally dismal lives.

Third, you present the solution to the problem or show how the need can be satisfied. You want your audience to understand how your proposal will satisfy the need. Again, addressing first-year students, you may suggest that they study for a minimum of two hours each day, become familiar with the library, learn computer skills, and know where to go for help. You may advise them to attend classes, to ask questions, and to visit their professors during office hours.

Heaven

Stewart Wallace

Ever since I was a child, I wanted to go to heaven. I studied hard in Sunday School. I learned all the Bible stories and was confirmed in the United Church of Canada. I did not do it because I enjoyed it. Instead, I had a clear goal in mind: when I died, I was going to heaven.

Today, I am delivering a speech of opposition. Our textbook says that the purpose of such a speech is to attack "things so common and widely believed or practiced that we do not even think about why we believe or practice them."[1] Never one to resist a challenge, I am going to attack one of the most sacred cows around, one of the most fundamental concepts of our Judeo-Christian heritage.

Lately I have decided that I really don't want to go to heaven. Don't get me wrong. I don't want to go to that other place either, though I have been advised to do so on several occasions. No, don't take this the wrong way, but heaven just doesn't appeal to me anymore.

In the next couple of minutes, I will talk about what you can expect to find in heaven, a few of the drawbacks, a couple of alternatives, and—finally—I will tell you what I hope to happen to me when I die.

Everyone talks about going to heaven, but when you really ask them about it, few can tell you what it will be like when you arrive. I used to ask my minister about heaven, but he dismissed my inquiries with a string of generalities. So I went to what I consider a reliable source. I looked up heaven in *The New Catholic Encyclopedia*, volume 6: Francis of Assisi to Hiram, King of Tyre. The encyclopedia said: "Heaven is the state of happiness that brings full lasting satisfaction to the whole of our being through our union with the Holy Trinity in Christ, together with all the members of His Mystical Body."[2] Although I liked the bit about lasting satisfaction, I didn't think it gave me much of a clearer idea of what to expect in the great hereafter—or much reason to want to go there.

The encyclopedia went on to talk about adoring God on his throne. The sense of fulfillment, it said, is "heightened by the spectacle of the miseries of the damned." Those views may be interesting for a while, but personally, I don't want to watch either for very long much less an eternity.

I would, of course, have lots of company in heaven. In fact, it is probably getting pretty crowded up there. The Bible says that the poor in spirit, the meek, and the mourners are blessed so they'll all be there. That would be fun.

I also hear we will be reunited with all our loved ones who died before us. That sounds great, too, except it means my Uncle George will be there. Every time I saw him, he slapped me on the back hard enough to make my teeth rattle, and yelled my name so loud I was deaf for close to a minute. I don't think I could stand that for an eternity.

One thing I have always wondered about heaven is whether I would still feel like me, whether I would still remember what it was like to walk around in a body, take in a sporting event, or stretch out with a cold beer on a hot day. My encyclopedia says, "We retain our affection for our background and our contacts. God does not destroy our past but enables it to contribute to our present happiness."[3] If I still had an affection for my background, I would need to check in on the earth from time to time to see how my children and grandchildren were doing. That would be nice.

But I would also want to check in on other important parts of my background. That could mean an eternity of misery as I look down from on high to watch the Blue Jays come so close to a title and the Leafs come so close to last place year after year after year.

Almost every religion has some concept of heaven, a clearing house for souls once we depart this world. They all offer celestial rewards for living a good, devoted life here on earth. As far as I can tell, one of the few religions without a heaven is the Hindu religion which teaches that the soul comes back to earth in another body. That seems like a nice idea, especially in these days of recycling.

But I'll tell you, when I die I want that to be the end of it all, plain and simple. No muss, no fuss, no chorus of Hallelujahs, no angels singing, no eternal life in some hard-to-imagine place: just a tired, fulfilled body returning to the earth after a life well spent—followed by nothing more than an eternity of sleep. That way I can live my life on my terms. I won't have to spend this life preparing for another one. It seems too restrictive to live each moment on some divine incentive plan.

Figure 6

A speech using the refutational strategy.

I want to make the most of this life. I feel uneasy thinking that when I die, some Being will judge all my actions over some eighty years on this small blue planet and then decide my celestial rewards. Would I even have a chance to defend myself in light of the complexity of motives that surround all our actions in this world?

Before I conclude, I want to make it clear that my purpose in this speech was not to offend any of you. I just wanted to make you think about what kind of afterlife you really want. In truth, I hope there really is a heaven. So many people want to go there, and I would hate for so many to be disappointed.

I also hope my family and friends won't miss me too much once they get there because when I die I would rather just be dead. For me, that gives my brief existence on earth more meaning than anything else, and I suspect I am not alone in that thought.

Figure 6 (continued)

Fourth, you go beyond simply presenting the solution by visualizing it for the audience. You want the audience to see themselves enjoying the benefits of your proposal. In your speech to aspiring students you may suggest how proud they, their families, and their friends will be when they learn of their academic success. You may describe a future for them which includes a successful career and a satisfying personal life.

Last, you state the action that you expect of your audience. In this step, you request action or approval. You want your audience to respond by saying that they will do what you have asked. Your speech should have a strong conclusion that asks for specific, but reasonable, action. In your speech in the residence hall, you may ask students to promise to attend all of their classes during the academic term, to visit with their professors outside of classes at least once, and to study for at least two hours each day. You may ask them to sign such a promise and then check in with them periodically to see if they are honoring their pledges.

Summary

This chapter began with a definition of persuasive speaking that indicated the persuader intends to change the audience's behavior through reinforcing, shaping, and changing the audience's responses to an idea, issue, concept, or product. Persuasive speaking is important to you because you provide and consume persuasive messages constantly.

Persuasive speaking has three purposes: (1) shaping audience responses, (2) reinforcing audience responses, and (3) changing audience responses. Typically persuasive speakers are attempting to influence the audience's feelings, beliefs, attitudes, and/or values.

We considered five principles of persuasion. First, we observed that consistency persuades. Second, we noted that small changes persuade. Third, we stated that benefits persuade. Fourth, we asserted that fulfilling needs persuades. Finally, we contended that gradual approaches persuade.

We identified three types of persuasive speeches. The speech to inspire is given to influence listeners' feelings. The speech to convince is intended to influence listeners' beliefs or attitudes. The speech to actuate is given to influence listeners' behaviors or actions.

Four methods of organizing a persuasive speech were provided. They included the problem-solution pattern, which occurs when you first discuss a problem that needs resolution and then you offer a solution for it. The need-plan pattern presents a need, suggests a plan, explains how the plan will meet the need, and proposes how the plan will be implemented. The refutational strategy involves the discrediting of one idea in order to support another idea. Monroe's Motivated Sequence is an organizational pattern developed by Alan Monroe that includes five steps: attention, need, satisfaction, visualization, and action.

The following checklist provides another means of reviewing the main points of this chapter.

A Checklist for the Persuasive Speech

_____ 1. Have you determined if your intent is to shape, reinforce, or change your audience's responses?

_____ 2. Have you shown how the change you are suggesting for the audience is consistent with its past behavior?

_____ 3. Have you kept your requested changes modest so that the audience does not perceive your request as too much to ask?

_____ 4. Have you demonstrated for the audience the benefits received if it does as you request?

_____ 5. Have you shown the audience ways that your request will fulfill its needs?

_____ 6. Have you approached your suggested change gradually so the audience does not perceive that you are asking for change without sufficient preparation?

_____ 7. Did you determine if your purpose is to inspire, convince, or actuate?

_____ 8. Did you identify an appropriate method to organize your speech?

_____ 9. Did you follow the method of organization accurately?

_____ 10. Do you believe your audience will know what you want them to feel, think, or do after you have finished talking?

attitudes Likes or dislikes toward people, ideas, policies, or situations

behavior Observable actions

beliefs Things you believe to be true even though there is no certainty or proof that they are true

changing responses Altering an audience's behavior toward a product, a concept, or an idea

commitment level Intensity of belief that makes one intolerant of opinions that differ

consistency The concept that audiences are more likely to be persuaded by messages that grow out of their current beliefs

cost-benefit analysis The idea that an audience is more likely to be persuaded if costs in time, money, and effort are lower than the expected benefits or advantages

feelings Affective states or dispositions; responses

hierarchy of needs A rank-ordered list of physical and psychological requirements for a healthy mind and body

Monroe's Motivated Sequence An organizational pattern for the persuasive speech which includes five steps: attention, need, satisfaction, visualization, and action

need-plan pattern An organizational pattern for the persuasive speech which includes the statement of a need, a recommendation which will meet that need, an explanation of how the plan will meet the need, and a proposal for how the plan will be implemented

persuasive speaking A message delivered to an audience by a speaker who intends to influence audience members' choices by shaping, reinforcing, or changing their responses toward an idea, issue, concept, or product

problem-solution pattern An organizational pattern for the persuasive speech which includes the statement of a problem and the proposal of a solution

purposes of persuasive speaking The shaping, reinforcing, or changing of an audience's responses toward an idea, an issue, a concept, or a product

refutational strategy An organizational pattern for the persuasive speech which involves the discrediting of one statement in order to support another statement

reinforcing responses Rewarding the audience for sustaining present beliefs, attitudes, and values

shaping responses Moving the audience toward a predetermined goal

speech to actuate A persuasive speech given for the purpose of influencing listeners' behaviors or actions

speech to convince A persuasive speech given for the purpose of influencing listeners' beliefs or attitudes

speech to inspire A persuasive speech given for the purpose of influencing listeners' feelings

values Learned social principles, goals, or standards found acceptable or even desirable by the people we live with, the groups to which we belong, and the institutions we respect

 # Applications

Application Exercises

Student Hierarchy of Needs

1. Persuasive speeches often appeal to an audience's unmet needs. Since needs vary according to the community, college, class, and individual, you can make yourself more sensitive to audience needs by ranking the five unmet needs that you believe are important to your audience.

1. _____
2. _____
3. _____
4. _____
5. _____

Principles of Persuasion

2. After reading the section on principles of persuasion, you should be able to identify cases in which they are correctly used. Examine the following cases and indicate in the blank which of the following principles is being observed:

C = Consistency persuades
S = Small changes persuade
B = Benefits persuade
N = Fulfilling needs persuades
G = Gradual approaches persuade

_____1. To save my audience members considerable time and effort, I am going to provide them with a form letter that they can sign and send to the administration.

_____2. Because I know that most of my classmates are short of cash, I am going to tell them how to make some quick money with on-campus jobs.

_____3. I plan to wait until the end of the speech to tell the audience members that the organization I want them to join will require two hours of driving per week.

_____4. My audience of international students already believes in the values of learning public speaking, so I think the listeners will respond favorably to my recommendation for a course in voice and articulation.

____5. I really want my audience to believe in Jesus Christ the way I do, but I'll try today simply to get them to consider going to church while they are in college.

Answers

1. B, 2. N, 3. G, 4. C, 5. S

The Speech to Inspire

3. Deliver a speech in which you inspire others through emotional and personal proofs. Consider writing your speech for a specific holiday, such as Margin Luther King Day, Memorial Day, Valentine's Day, Benito Juarez Day, Canada Day, Yom Kippur, or Father's Day. Your goal is to create a change in the feelings of the audience.

The Speech to Convince

4. Deliver a speech in which you shape the audience's responses by using arguments and evidence supporting a conclusion that invites the audience to change its mind on an issue. Find facts and evidence. Use reasoning appropriately. Consider emotional, personal, and mythic proof, as well.

The Speech to Actuate

5. Deliver a speech in which you seek to change your listeners' behaviors. Consider the variety of modes of proof available to do so. Use reasoning in an ethical and effective way. Organize your arguments appropriately. Identify a variety of forms of evidence.

1. Gerald R. Miller, "On Being Persuaded: Some Basic Distinctions," in Michael E. Roloff and Gerald R. Miller, *Persuasion: New Directions in Theory and Research* (Beverly Hills, CA: Sage Publications, 1980), 16–26.
2. Wallace Fotheringham, *Perspectives on Persuasion* (Boston: Allyn & Bacon, 1966), 33.
3. Daryl Bem, *Beliefs, Attitudes and Human Affairs* (Belmont, CA: Brooks/Cole, 1970), 14.
4. Martin Fishbein, seminar lecture on attitude change conducted at the University of Illinois, spring 1965, and quoted in Gary Cronkhite, *Persuasion: Speech and Behavioral Change* (Indianapolis: Bobbs-Merrill, 1969), 64.
5. A. H. Maslow, "A Theory of Human Motivation," *Psychological Review* 50 (1943): 370–96.
6. This speech was delivered by Patricia Roberts Harris before the National Women's Political Caucus Convention, Cincinnati, Ohio, June 14, 1979.
7. This speech was composed by Katherine L. Anderson, a telecommunications major at Ohio University. The footnotes for her speech: 1. David L. Coulter, "A Pushed Away Catholic," *Notre Dame Magazine* (Spring 1991); 2. Richard John Neuhaus, "True Christian Feminism," *National Review* (November 25, 1988): 24.
8. This speech was composed by Beth Kregenow from the School of Interpersonal Communication at Ohio University. The footnotes for her speech: 1. Paul M. Insel and Roth T. Walton, *Core Concepts in Health* (Mountain View, CA: Mayfield Publishing Co., 1991), 342; 2. Insel and Walton, p. 343; 3. "Physiology of Aging," *Reebok Instructor News*, 1990, vol. 3 (No. 4), 3; 4. "The Easy Road to Fitness," *University of California, Berkeley, Wellness Letter*, vol. 7 (No. 5), 6; 5. Insel and Walton, p. 39; 6. Insel and Walton, p. 381.
9. This speech was delivered by Stewart Wallace, a student in the English and Communications Division of Seneca College, Toronto, Canada. The endnotes for the speech: 1. Paul E. Nelson and Judy C. Pearson, *Confidence in Public Speaking*, 4th ed. (Dubuque, IA: Wm. C. Brown Publishers, 1990), 316; 2. "Heaven," *The New Catholic Encyclopedia*; 3. "Heaven." Copyright © Stewart Wallace.

Photographs

Chapter A
p. A-3, A-7: © James L. Shaffer; **p. A-12:** The Bettmann Archive; **p. A-13:** © James L. Shaffer; **p. A-15:** © David Wells/The Image Works

Chapter B
p. B-4, B-5, B-8, B-11, B-14: © James L. Shaffer

Chapter C
p. C-3, C-4: © James L. Shaffer; **p. C-8:** © Nancy J. Pierce/Photo Researchers, Inc.; **p. C-11:** © James L. Shaffer

Chapter D
p. D-4: The Bettmann Archive; **p. D-5:** © Stock Montage; **p. D-7, D-8:** UPI/Bettmann; **p. D-9, D-13:** Reuters/Bettmann

Chapter E
p. E-3: Reuters/Bettmann; **p. E-7:** © Richard Hutchings/PhotoEdit; **p. E-11:** © Bob Daemmrich/The Image Works

Chapter F
p. F-3, F-5: © James L. Shaffer; **p. F-7:** © Larry Kolvoord/The Image Works

Chapter G
p. G-3: © James L. Shaffer; **p. G-4:** Reuters/Bettmann; **p. G-8:** © James L, Shaffer; **p. G-13:** © Esaias Baitel/Photo Researchers, Inc.; **p. G-21:** © James L. Shaffer

Chapter H
p. H-3, H-6: © James L. Shaffer; **p. H-7:** © Dan Chidester/The Image Works; **p. H-12:** © Stock Montage

Chapter I
p. I-3: © Margot Granitsas/The Image Works; **p. I-6:** © James L. Shaffer

Chapter J
p. J-4: © James L. Shaffer

Chapter K
p. K-4: The Bettmann Archive

Chapter L
p. L-4: © Bonnie Rauch/Photo Researchers, Inc.

Chapter M
p. M-4, M-6: © James L. Shaffer; **p. M-7:** © Deborah Kahn/Stock Boston; **p. M-14:** © Michael Siluk; **p. M-16:** AP/Wide World Photos

Chapter N
p. N-3: © Elizabeth Crews/The Image Works; **p. N-14:** UPI/Bettmann

Chapter O
p. O-5: © David Weintraub/Photo Researchers, Inc.; **p. O-6, O-8:** © James L. Shaffer; **p. O-12:** © Cecilia Prestamo/The Hartford Courant/The Image Works; **p. O-16, O-19:** © James L. Shaffer

Chapter P
p. P-5: © James L. Shaffer; **p. P-11 top:** © Comstock, Inc.; **bottom:** © Alan Carey/The Image Works; **p. P-16:** © Richard Luria/Photo Researchers, Inc.; **p. P-17, P-23, P-24:** © James L. Shaffer

Chapter Q
p. Q-3, Q-6, Q-9, Q-12, Q-24, Q-25: © James L. Shaffer

Chapter R
p. R-3: © James L. Shaffer; **p. R-5:** Courtesy of the American Indian College Fund © Doug Petty; **p. R-11:** Reuters/Bettmann; **p. R-13:** © Comstock, Inc./Stuart Cohen; **p. R-22:** Reuters/Bettmann

Chapter S
p. S-3: © Erika Stone/Photo Researchers, Inc.; **p. S-10:** © Arthur Grace/Stock Boston

Chapter T
p. T-5: Courtesy of the American Indian College Fund © Doug Petty; **p. T-8:** © Comstock, Inc./Stuart Cohen

Chapter U
p. U-3: © James L. Shaffer; **p. U-4:** The Bettmann Archive; **p. U-7:** © Stock Montage; **p. U-9:** © David Young-Wolff/PhotoEdit; **p. U-10:** Reuters/Bettmann; **p. U-12:** © James L. Shaffer; **p. U-14:** Reuters/Bettmann; **p. U-15:** AP/Wide World Photos

Chapter V
p. V-3: © David Young-Wolff/PhotoEdit; **p. V-9:** © Jeff Greenberg/PhotoEdit

Chapter W
p. W-3: © Ulrike Welsch/Photo Researchers, Inc.; **p. W-8:** © James L. Shaffer

Index

Your instructor has chosen which chapters to include in your text and the order in which those chapters are placed, so that you and your class can learn public speaking as efficiently as possible. Because there are so many possible options for arranging the chapters, each chapter is page numbered separately, starting over with "1" every chapter. To avoid the confusing situation of having several "page 1's," the page numbers in your text are all preceded by a letter. The letters correspond to all the available chapters your instructor *could have* chosen. Your book will not have a chapter for every letter of the alphabet, and you may not find the letters you do have in proper alphabetical order (for example, you may find that your book starts with page B-1, instead of A-1). Use your table of contents to determine which chapters you do have, which letters identify those chapters and the order in which the chapters appear. Then you can easily flip to the appropriate letter-number combination when you need to find a certain page in the book. Use the letter-number combination to access glossary terms and index references.